WOMEN AND RELIGION IN AMERICA

Women and Religion in America

Volume 3: 1900–1968

ROSEMARY RADFORD RUETHER

ROSEMARY SKINNER KELLER

Harper & Row, Publishers, San Francisco

Cambridge, Hagerstown, New York, Philadelphia
London, Mexico City, Saõ Paulo, Singapore, Sydney

1817

FIRST EDITION

Library of Congress Cataloging-in-Publication Data
(Revised for vol. 3)
Main entry under title:

Women and religion in America.

  Includes bibliographical references and index.
  Contents: —v. 3. 1900–1968.
  1. Women in Christianity—United States—History—Addresses, essays, lectures. 2. Women in Judaism—United States—History—Addresses, essays, lectures. 3. United States—Religion—Addresses, essays, lectures. I. Ruether, Rosemary Radford. II. Keller, Rosemary Skinner.
BR515.W648 1981   280″.088042   80-8346
ISBN 0-06-066829-6 (v. 1)

86 87 88 89 90 FG 10 9 8 7 6 5 4 3 2 1

This volume is dedicated to our children, Rebecca, David, and Mimi Ruether, and Jennifer and John Keller, heirs to the heritage of social transformation of the twentieth century.

52940

Contents

Acknowledgments

Grateful acknowledgment is made to the following archives, authors, and publishers for permission to reprint text:

Katherine Tingley, *The Voice of the Soul*, 1928, pp. 82–3, 54, 233–235, 237: permission to reprint from the Theosophical University Press.

Charlotte Perkins Gilman, *His Religion and Hers: A Study of the Faith of our Fathers and the Work of our Mothers.* T. Fisher Unwin, 1924, pp. 37–43, 45–47, 50, 248–249, 251, 270: permission to reprint from Adam and Charles Black, Publishers.

Robert Graves, *The White Goddess,* copyright © 1948, renewed 1975, pp. 24, 386–390, 475–486: reprinted by permission of Farrar, Straus and Giroux, Inc.

From Robert Briffault, *The Mothers,* vol. III: permission to reprint from Macmillan Co.

From *The First Sex,* by Elizabeth Gould David, copyright © 1971 by Elizabeth Gould Davis, permission to reprint from G. P. Putnam's Sons.

Interviews: Myrtle Lincoln to Julia Jordan, December 22, 1969, 1, T-607, 2–4, Mary Poafybitty Neido to David Jones, October 19, 1967, 26, T-173-1, 6–7, Mary Poafybitty Neido to David Jones, June 15, 1967, 27, T-52, 10–15, Richard Manus to B. D. Timmons, February 8, 1969, 16, T-417, 7–8, Leonard Maker by Katherine Maker, December 12, 1968, 47, T-344, 6, Jess Rowlodge by Julia Jordan, December 5, 1967, 5, T-170, 16–18, Alice Apekaum by David Jones, October 7, 1967, 33, T-177-2, 1–4: permission to reprint from the Doris Duke Indian Oral History Collection in the Western History Collections, University of Oklahoma Library.

Sharon Fife, "The Baptist Indian Church: Thewarle Mekko Sapkv Coko," from the *Chronicles of Oklahoma:* permission to reprint from the author, Sharon Fife Mouss.

Interview with Kathryn Kuhlman, "Healing in the Spirit": permission to reprint from *Christianity Today.*

Aimee Semple McPherson, excerpts from *This Is That: Personal Experi-*

ences, Sermons and Writings: permission to reprint from the International Church of the Four Square Gospel.

Katherine Bushnell, excerpts from *God's Word to Women:* permission to reprint from the *God's Word to Women Publishers,* Mossville, Illinois.

John Rice, excerpts from pamphlets "Prayer, Asking and Receiving" and "Men and their Sins": permission to reprint from the Sword of the Lord Publishers, Murfreesboro, Tennessee.

Donald Barnhouse, "The Wife with Two Heads": permission to reprint from *Eternity Magazine,* Philadelphia, Pennsylvania.

Yvonne K. Woods, "The Wife God Uses": permission to reprint from *His* magazine, Downers Grove, Illinois.

Katherine Marshall, excerpts from *To Live Again,* permission to reprint from Chosen Books, Lincoln, Virginia.

Victoria Booth Demarest, excerpts from "I am thy Prophet Still": permission to reprint from the author and her daughter, Evangeline Demarest.

Ethel Mae Baldwin, excerpts from *Henrietta Mears and How She Did It:* permission to reprint from Regal Books, Ventura, California.

Barbara Hudson, excerpts from the *Henrietta Mears Story:* permission from the author, Barbara Hudson Dudley.

Edith Hunter, excerpts from *Sophia Lyon Fahs: A Biography:* permission to reprint from Beacon Press, Boston, Massachusetts.

Aubrey N. Brown, "What DRE's Have Done, Are Doing, for Us": permission to reprint from *The Presbyterian Outlook,* Richmond, Virginia.

Arlo Ayres Brown, excerpts from *A History of Religious Education in Recent Times:* permission to reprint from Abingdon Press, Nashville, Tennessee.

Edna M. Baxter, excerpts from *Ventures in Serving Mankind:* permission to reprint from the author, Edna M. Baxter.

Excerpts from the *Hadassah Newsletter:* reproduced with the permission of the Hadassah Archives, Hadassah, The Woman's Zionist Organization of America, Inc.

Excerpts from the Alice Seligsberg letters, from the Rose Jacob Papers: published with permission of the Central Zionist Archives, Jerusalem.

Marvin Lowenthal, *Henrietta Szold, Life and Letters,* excerpts: permission to reprint from Viking Penguin, Inc.

The Woman's Pulpit, I (1924), p. 3, and XXII (Sept.–Oct., 1944), p. 2, permission to reprint from The Rev. Lavonne Althouse.

"Women as Ministers: The Pros and Cons," by Lyman Richard Hartley, *The New York Times,* (April, 1947), pp. 19, 59, permission to reprint from *The New York Times.*

"Shall Women Be Ordained"? by Hellen C. Woolson, *Outreach,* (Aug.–Sept., 1955), pp. 119–200, permission to reprint from *Concern* Magazine.

"Women Pastors," by Arthur B. Cooper, *Monday Morning*, (Sept. 24, 1956). pp. 3–5, permission to reprint from *Morning Morning*, The United Presbyterian Church, U.S.A.

Women in the Church: A Century of Woman's Place in Building the Kingdom, by Russell C. Prohl, (1957), pp. 79–80, permission to reprint from Wm. B. Eerdmans.

The Office of Woman in the Church: A Study in Practical Theology, by Fritz Zerbst, (1955), pp. 119–121, permission to reprint from Concordia Publishing House.

Women and the Ministry, by Charles E. Raven, (1929), pp. 33–36, permission to reprint from Doubleday and Company.

"Can Women Make Their Way into the Ministry?", by Louise S. Eby, *Christian Education*, IX, (June, 1929), pp. 534–539, permission to reprint from *Soundings: An Interdisciplinary Journal*.

Rabbi Moshe Tendler, excerpts from *Pardes Rimonim: A Marriage Manual for the Jewish Family*, permission to reprint from Judaica Press.

Excerpts from *Henrietta Szold: Life and Letters*, permission to reprint from Viking Press, Inc.

Marie Hall Ets, excerpts from *Rosa: The Life of an Italian Immigrant*, permission to reprint from the University of Minnesota.

Kate Chopin, excerpts from "Madame Celestin," permission to reprint from Macmillan publishing company.

M. Madeleva Wolff, excerpts from *My First Seventy Years*, permission to reprint from Macmillan Publishing Company.

Isaac Metzker, excerpts from *A Bintel Brief*, permission to reprint from Doubleday and Company, Inc.

The authors wish to acknowledge the help of the following persons in research for their chapters:

Kay Parker thanks Jack Haley, assistant curator of the Western History Collections at the University of Oklahoma for help in finding photographs, and William E. Bittle for critical reading of her manuscript. *Ann Braude* thanks Molly Ladd-Taylor, Sally Stein, and George Chauncey for their help in her project; Dr. Lawrence Geller for guidance through the Hadassah Archives and for bringing to her attention the letters of Alice Seligberg; and Judith Sokoloff, editor of *Pioneer Women*, for access to back issues of that magazine, and the staff of the Jewish Room of the New York Public Library for their assistance in research. *Letha Scanzoni* and *Susan Setta* thank Susie Stanley for the loan of her master's thesis on Alma White; Janette Hassey for sharing her research on the Moody Bible Institute; Patricia Gundry for putting them in contact with Janette Hassey; Stanley Gundry, who helped them locate materials on Emma Dryer; and Nancy Hardesty for biographical information on Katherine Bushnell. *Dorothy Furnish* thanks Dorothy Beck, daughter of Sophia Fahs; Cyrus Nelson, chairman of Gospel Light Publications; Ethel Mae Baldwin, secretary to Henrietta Mears; Carl Seaburg, archivist for the Unitarian Universalist Association; Edna Baxter; Mrs. Harry R. Sandefur, secretary for Mary Alice Jones and Tom MacAnally; and Methodist Information, for their help in research. *Barbara Brown Zikmund* thanks Douglas Bracekridge, Trinity University, for his assistance in locating documents.

Introduction

In this volume we seek to document the many roles of women in religion in twentieth century America.[1] The problem of selection of materials and interpretation is both large and complex for this period. The number of available documents is enormous, making it difficult to decide what to include and what to leave out. At the same time, it is hard to gain perspective on the trends in a period so close to our own time. Studies of women's history in America in the twentieth century have lagged behind the stellar work available for the nineteenth century, although there has recently been a spate of significant books on women in this period. But these books focus on secular history and, even less than the work in the ninteenth century, have little to say about religion.[2]

The most basic questions about women in religion in this period are not only unanswered, but have scarcely begun to be asked. Why, for example, did the close identification between progressive feminism and progressive Christianity, so typical of America in the nineteenth century, collapse in the 1920s? When feminism reappeared as a movement in the late 1960s it was generally more secular and more suspicious of the positive character of Christianity. The assumption that the Christian churches are inherently antiwoman is widespread in the new wave of feminism.

In this volume we have not attempted to include French Canadian or Latin American women outside of the United States as we did in the colonial volume, which covered a time period before the colonial revolutions formed the separate nations of North and South America. In addition, we have restricted the time period of this volume to 1900 through 1968. Thus it ends with the rise of the second wave of feminism, when we perceive a new era of women's history to begin. We have chosen to focus on that "middle distance," the era of our mothers or grandmothers, between the peaking of the Victorian women's movement at the end of the First World War and the rise of the new women's movement at the end of the 1960s. We seek to document the changes and the continuities in women's relationship to religion in this poorly analyzed but important period.

The volume opens with a chapter by Rosemary Ruether (Georgia Harkness Professor of Applied Theology at Garrett-Evangelical Theological Seminary and Northwestern University in Evanston, Illinois) on radical Victorians and the quest for an alternative religious culture to Christianity. In this chapter, Ruether shows that Victorian feminists were by no means uniformly convinced that the Christian churches were progressive vehicles for women. An important minority saw Christianity as inherently patriarchal, and linked biblical religion with a religious and social revolution in antiquity that had displaced an earlier era of women's power. These women sought to revive the ancient matriarchal culture and religion, with its female symbols of the divine, as the more appropriate vehicle for female empowerment. Thus the "return of the Goddess" announced by countercultural feminists in the 1970s is not a new idea, but is based on a literature generated in the nineteenth century and eagerly explored by many Victorian feminists.

The second chapter, by Kay Parker, a research anthropologist living in Oklahoma City who specializes in the Indians of the Southern Plains area, is on American Indian women of the southern Plains.

It picks up the story of Indian women and religion begun by Mary Druke and Jacqueline Peterson in the colonial volume.[3] The Druke and Peterson chapter reconstructed the role of Native American women in native religion before Christianization, and then showed the manifold effects on Indian culture created by European conquest. Indians are unique in America in seeking to create an accommodation or syncretism between their own religion and Christianity. This syncretism represents an effort to relate to modern Euro-American culture and yet retain traditional Indian identity.

Kay Parker describes the American Indian of the southern Plains in the impoverished and demoralized state to which they had been reduced by expropriation of their land, forced migration, and cultural colonization. The result is a threefold religion pattern. Native religion continues and is revived despite three centuries of Christian evangelization, which included almost sixty years in which the practice of native religion was illegal. In traditional religion, as practiced today, women appear to concede the more prestigious roles to men, partly to compensate for the demoralization of Indian men caused by deprivation. Women often take the lead in Christian churches and are the more committed Christians, although Christianity generally succeeds among Indians to the extent that it allows syncretism with native religion or provides analogues to it. The most recent development is pan-Indian religions, such as the Peyote Cult or Native American Church, which emerged in large part to compensate for loss of traditional Indian culture. Here again males play the predominant role, supported by women.

The role of black women in religion in America, formulated by Jualyne Dodson of Union Theological Seminary in New York and Cheryl
Gilkes of Boston University's department of sociology, suggests an interesting comparison with that of Indian women. As a conquered people,
brought as slaves to North America, Afro-Americans were more totally
deprived of their traditional culture and Christianized. Separate African
syncretistic cults did not emerge in North America (as is the case with
voodoo in the Caribbean and Brazil), although American blacks did
create a distinct black Christianity which probably contains remnants of
African culture.[4] By breaking with white Christianity to form black
denominations, Afro-Americans forged a black church that could provide a social and cultural base for black identity. Black women have
generally viewed Christianity positively for that reason, despite its heavy
patriarchalism.

As in the Indian case, the secondary and supportive role of black
women in religion is partly a concession to the ego needs of black males,
who they perceive to be demoralized by white oppression. Playing the
prestigious roles in the leadership of the black church, the primary social
institution of black identity, compensates for the status deprivation of the
black male in the dominant culture. However, this patriarchalism of the
black church is somewhat misleading. One has to look beneath the surface to see how black women often wield the real power—although not
the ascribed authority—in local churches through fundraising, education, and other supportive functions. Education became the particular
focus of black women's ministry in local churches, and was defined as the
woman's sphere, as distinct from "preaching" as the male sphere.

Black women also built on the inspiration and experience in local
churches to form many auxiliary denominational institutions, such as
women's missionary societies, as well as training schools and social service
organizations. Through these endeavors they also reached out to social
reform through black women's clubs, antilynching societies, and a variety
of schools and service institutions, such as orphanages. Thus black
women in the twentieth century continue very much the tradition of a
nineteenth-century Christianity, in which women's roles in the church
become a launching pad for women to organize denominational organizations, such as missionary societies, and religiously inspired but non-
denominational philanthropical and social reform movements.

Jews in America, like European Christians, came as voluntary mi-
grants who found this the land of freedom and opportunity. But they
have also clung to their own religion and resisted formal Christianization
as a central expression of their retention of their own identity, having
brought with them a two-thousand-year experience in resisting assimilation by surrounding cultures. In America, Jewish women have experienced crises of class, religious and racial identity, as well as a feminist
struggle. As members of an immigrant people who entered America as

oppressed workers in urban industry, Jewish women became important labor organizers, particularly in the emergence of female unionism. Jewish women also had to cope with the ways that Americanization altered the traditional roles of women in the Jewish family, and many Jewish women found emancipation through secular education, having been traditionally deprived of traditional Jewish religious education. As Americanization and economic upward mobility progressed, it became possible for Jewish women to reembrace their religious identity in a new way and to contend with Jewish men for an enlarged role in the practice of Judaism. Jewish women in the twentieth century have also been a part of the Zionist movement, which expressed the disenchantment of Western Jews with the experience of assimilation into secular nationalism. As Zionists, Jewish women reached out to help shape a new Jewish identity that would be simultaneously ethnic and egalitarian. Ann Braude, a graduate student in religion at Yale University and the author of the chapter on Jewish women in the nineteenth-century volume, also assembled this chapter.

The chapter on Catholic women by Lori Getz, coordinator of the Boston Theological Institute, offers suggestive comparisons with Braude's chapter on Jewish women. Although they were Christians, Catholics also suffered religious discrimination from the Protestant majority when they began to settle in the American colonies. This discrimination intensified in the late nineteenth century, when Catholics from Ireland and eastern and southern Europe came here in large numbers. There was little participation by Catholic women in the nineteenth-century feminist movement, and it was not until the late 1960s that a distinct participation in feminism by Catholic women emerged. We must surmise that, as an embattled cultural group, Catholic women put their energy into affirming their Catholic identity and proving to the Protestant majority its compatibility with American "values." Only when this battle of Americanization was won in the mid-1960s did American Catholic women turn to confrontation with the male hierarchy for enlarged roles in religious leadership.

This suggests that when a religious and cultural subcommunity is oppressed by the dominant community, as has been the case with American Indians, Jews, blacks, and Catholics, women put their ethnic identity first and concede leadership in the distinctive institutions of the subculture to males. Only when a certain cultural and social parity is established between the minority and majority communities do women turn their attention to feminist questions within their own communities. This perhaps explains why feminism was monopolized by middle-class Anglo-Saxon Protestant women in the nineteenth and early twentieth centuries; and only in the late 1960s, as Jews and Catholics emerged into cultural parity and middle-class status, have distinctive Catholic and Jewish feminist movements begun to arise that challenge the patriarchalism of Jewish and Catholic communal institutions, as these are expressed particularly in religion. This has only begun to happen for a smaller group of middle-class black women in this period, while it has scarcely begun at all for Indian women, whose primary battle is still the survival of their people as a distinct cultural community.

Catholic women in the twentieth century were also faced with a militantly antifeminist hierarchy that opposed women's suffrage and reproductive rights and promoted traditional femininity, especially through the cult of Mary. This antifeminism was perceived by the Catholic hierarchy as a key element in its crusade to protect Catholicism from "modernity." The power of the hierarchy was consolidated in the early twentieth century as American Catholicism was organized and accommodated itself to the American situation. In the process the more autonomous roles played in Catholic laity in parishes and by women's religious orders was suppressed (see the chapter on nineteenth-century nuns in America in Volume 1).[5] Only in the 1950s and 1960s did the sister formation movement begin to upgrade the educational skills of American nuns. In the process, it also began to lay the foundation for the full-scale feminist revolt of American religious women in the 1970s.

The chapter on women in the Evangelical, Holiness, and Pentecostal traditions represents those branches of American Christianity that are often stereotyped as "conservative." This comes from the frequent confusion of evangelical and fundamentalist Christianity. Fundamentalism represents a reaction in the late nineteenth and twentieth centuries to liberal religious and secular culture, attempting to preserve themes of classical Christianity in a reactionary, sectarian way. As in Catholic anti-modernism, reaffirming women's "place" in a patriarchal social order is seen as key to reestablishing "true Christianity."

Yet the Evangelical, Holiness, and Pentecostal traditions also represent an opposite tendency, an experiential and charismatic religious tradition that was inclusive of women precisely because it validated the presence of the Spirit. They found signs of the Spirit outside rather than within institutional channels. This inclusive tendency in these traditions did not disappear, but continued well into the first decades of the twentieth century. It was roughly in the 1930s that this inclusive charismatic tradition became more institutionalized and women were shut out of many roles in religious leadershp that they had held in earlier days. This emphasis on the subordination of women was partly generated by a reaction to women's expanding roles in politics and paid employment. In the late 1960s a new evangelical feminism would be reborn, to revive the earlier struggle between a liberatory and a patriarchal evangelical tradition. The chapter was written by coauthors Letha Dawson Scanzoni, a freelance writer on evangelical feminism, and Susan Setta, professor of religion at Northeastern University in Boston, Massachusetts.

The three final chapters of this volume focus on the participation of women in mainline structures of twentieth-century Protestantism—lay-women, professional religious educators, and ordained. Most sections of the book have traced broad movements on cultural identities of women and religions. The approach of Rosemary Keller, associate professor of religion and American culture at Garrett-Evangelical Theological Seminary, diverges from this. In her chapter, "Patterns of Laywomen's Leadership in Twentieth-Century Protestantism," she develops brief case studies of several avowed heroines, the pioneers of major movements and institutions central to the work of the churches and of women's participation even today. These women are important to us for two reasons. First, they are towering figures whose contributions to modern Protestantism were so great that a full picture of modern church history cannot be gained without including these women. The names and stories of these individuals need to be recovered and made a part of our living heritage.

Yet, for each woman that Keller has selected to study, a score of other women who made similar and equally important contributions could have been chosen. Even more significant than their individual prominence are the patterns of their leadership, which bear upon the experience of countless women of their own day and of ours. Keller raises issues of personal lifestyle and team ministry in the case studies. She examines patterns of compromise and confrontation, which one woman employed to gain major rights for women in the church. The bonding of sisterhood and responsibility that women often feel toward each other emerges, as does the characteristic application of theological inquiry to the pressing social justice issues of the day. The cultural significance of these figures to the relationship between women and religion is major; their experience should help latter-day feminists avoid pitfalls and envision new styles of life and leadership in the church today.

Dorothy Jean Furnish, professor of Christian education at Garrett-Evangelical Theological Seminary, has written the chapter on women in religious education. Although stereotyped as a "woman's profession," Furnish shows that the predominance of women as directors of religious education at the local church level did not occur until the depression, when money in churches was short and women were willing to work for a small salary. Religious education as a profession was pioneered by both men and women who were turning from the old model of evangelization as conversion to one modeled on education and lifetime personal growth. Drawing on theories of progressive education, as well as liberal concepts of historical-critical interpretation of the Bible, they sought to make religious education a profession based on sound modern knowledge and methodologies from the fields of history and psychological development.

Although most of the professors of Christian education at the graduate school and seminary level were male, the first women to join theological faculties in the twentieth century were generally professors of

Christian education. Thus women as Christian educators are the pioneers in women's professional ministry in local churches and as theological educators in seminaries, yet today they are being displaced by their very successes. As more and more women become ordained, the director of religious education without ordination loses out to the ordained person with an additional speciality in religious education. Thus the future of religious education both as a profession in its own right and as an avenue of advancement for women in the church has become unclear.

Barbara Brown Zikmund, dean of the faculty and professor of American church history at the Pacific School of Religion in Berkeley, California, has written the chapter on women's struggle for ordination in the twentieth century, as she did in a parallel chapter in the nineteenth-century volume.[6] Zikmund argues that Protestant churches have gone through a pattern in which lay ministry is won first at the local level, and then at the hierarchical level; and only when women have gained full lay rights do these churches turn to the granting of ordained status to women. Here, too, there is a sequential process "up the ladder"—winning first deaconate or local pastor status, next first ordination to the presbyterate, and then perhaps ranks of ordained ministry above that, such as district superintendent. Thus Methodists obtained their first woman bishop in 1981, twenty-five years after granting women full status in the ordained ministry.

Some churches, such as the Congregationalists, Unitarians, Universalists, and Methodist Protestants, progressed through this cycle of winning lay ministry leadership to the ordained ministry in the nineteenth century. But this development was blocked in mainstream Protestantism in the 1880s and was partly diverted into the deaconate for women. Thus this cycle of winning full lay rights and finally full ordained ministry for women began for these Protestant churches at the end of the nineteenth century and progressed to the granting of full ordination in the mid-1950s to 1970s.

For some churches, progress was initially retarded by ecumenism, when the merger of ordaining and nonordaining churches was carried out by conceding to the nonordaining partner and not ordaining women in the new united church. But dissatisfaction with this compromise caused movement within the new denomination, which resulted in the ordaining of women sometime later. This seems to have been what occurred in the Methodist Church, where nonordaining Methodist Episcopals outvoted ordaining Methodist Protestants in the merger of 1939; yet, in 1956, the resultant Methodist Church voted to ordain women. But ecumenical relations could hasten progress, as in the Lutheran churches who were pressed to ordain women because their parent bodies in Scandanavia had voted to do so in the 1950s. The Episcopal Church, which voted to ordain women in 1975, has been caught in a crossfire of opposing ecumenisms—momentum from mainstream Protestantism in ordaining women on the one side, and pressure from the nonordaining Roman Catholic Churches and Orthodox on the other.

The winning of ordained status for most American Protestant women by the mid-1970s has created a new era of women in the churches. Now those remaining fundamentalist Protestants and Roman Catholic and Orthodox churches that don't ordain women feel mounting pressure from within and without to reconsider their historic position. The number of women has increased rapidly in theological schools in the 1970s. They now make up more than 50 percent of many seminaries of liberal Protestantism, and are increasing in smaller numbers even in the most conservative seminaries. This presence of women has, in turn, created a new base for the criticism of the sexism of the theological tradition itself. Feminist studies in the biblical, theological, historical, and practical fields have proliferated in the 1970s. The churches are being challenged to rethink their religious culture from its very roots. This story remains for a future volume. In this chapter we end the story at the point when most of mainstream Protestantism, Methodists, Presbyterians, and Lutherans had voted for the ordination of women, and the Episcopalians were on the verge of joining them.

In conclusion, we might venture a hypothesis on the question with which this introduction began. Why does it appear that Christianity provided a public base of women's progressive movements in nineteenth-century America that seemed to disappear in the twentieth century, when Christianity was perceived more as enemy than friend of women among feminists of the "second wave"? As we have seen, this question is much more complicated than it appears on the surface. Some of the most militant feminists of the nineteenth century also perceived Christianity to be unreformably misogynist. But the most important clue to this apparent change seems to us to lie in shifting boundaries between the religious and the secular in American society.

In the nineteenth century men were beginning to enter a secular public culture and, consequently, religion was being defined as the culture of women and the home. But this meant that religion, although privatized for men, remained a public culture for women. Women used the culture of the home to crusade out into the male "world" to press their issues of women's rights and social reform. For mainstream Protestant women the winning of the vote in 1921 also coincided with a shift in this boundary of religious and secular. Now women who entered into the male public world of business, higher education, and politics accepted the assumption that they should do so on male terms; i.e., with a secular and not a religious cultural platform. The women reformers of the 1920s and 1930s typically spoke the language of sociology and not of theology in their efforts to advance themselves and their concerns. For these women, religion had become a private culture which they did not take with them into the marketplace, if indeed they continued to believe in it at all.

However, for other groups of women, this secularization did not take the same form. Evangelical and Roman Catholic women experienced growing conservatism from their churches on women's issues precisely as these churches battled what they saw as the pernicious influence of secularism. Later in the century both of these churches would repoliticize their religious culture, but primarily as a platform against women's legal, social, and reproductive rights. Jewish women were caught in a culture that had accepted secularism as the way the Jew entered American life, but was also seeking to redefine the relation of religious and ethnic identity. In Zionism, religious and ethnic identity would come together as both a public and a political culture, for American Jews arguing about, American foreign policy toward the state of Israel.

Finally, for American Indians and American blacks, the religious culture became a primary way to affirm the ethnic subculture against white and Christian domination. And so the religious culture remained a base for political organizing for black civil rights and for Indian autonomy. This shifting boundary between public and private, religious and secular, helps us to understand the apparent rapid movement from a left social and political movement for black civil rights, followed rapidly by other concerns, such as peace and women's rights, that was led by progressive clergy in the 1960s; to a right-wing political-religious movement from the traditional religious opponents of secularism and modernity in the late 1970s, which made antifeminism a key part of its ideology. In both cases, the union of political and religious forces were already present in quasi-privatized subcultures, which only needed a spark to call them back into the public arena of contending forces for the American budget and the American soul.

Radical Victorians: The Quest for an Alternative Culture

ROSEMARY RADFORD RUETHER

This chapter, broadly titled "Radical Victorians," encompasses people and movements which seem, at first glance, widely disparate. Some of the writers were political moderates and progressives; some were socialists. Some were apolitical or reactionary. Some were conscious feminists, others were not. What binds this group together is that all were post-Christians. Moreover, their post-Christianity took the form of a revival of some ancient pre-Christian culture, religion, or social order which they saw as the basis for a better society and/or religion of the future. They sought to supplant the religion and social order inherited from the Jewish, Christian, and Western patriarchal traditions by going back to some earlier culture. In so doing they sought to render Western biblical and social history nonnormative, a passing phase of a larger scheme of social development that looked back to earlier origins.

Some of these writers looked to the East, to ancient Egypt, to the Mediterranean world, or to India for inspiration. Others imagined that they were reviving an ancient wisdom from Britain or Europe, before the lamentable conquest by Christianity and patriarchy. For some, this quest for the lost past took the form of speculation about a prepatriarchal matriarchy whose values could be recovered and used to shape a post-Christian and or postpatriarchal society. For others it was the spiritual quest that was primary. They sought a larger wisdom that would be at once more universal and more immanent in one's own psyche and bodily processes than that provided by Christianity. All looked forward to some vastly improved humanity, either personally or collectively, through this process of retrieval and expansion. Some saw it as a process of smooth progress; others as one of cataclysmic collapse of the present social order and the rebuilding of a new society in radical discontinuity with the intermediate past.

This chapter is titled "Radical Victorians" because most of these movements and trends of thought were founded at the end of the nineteenth century and had their heyday in the period between 1900 and 1921. Some of them lingered on into the 1920s, and remnants survive today. But much of the social acceptance of the sort of thinking represented here seemed to fade dramatically after the First World War. One might note, for example, that the category "matriarchy" as a reference to a prepatriarchal state of society appears regularly in the Index of Periodical Literature to 1928. Then it disappears, only to return again in the late 1970s with the revival of feminist interest in this topic. Most of the entries are clustered between 1895 and 1920.

What happened? What we seem to see here is a discrediting of the thesis of a matriarchy as a universal state of civilization before patriarchy among the new anthropologists led by Franz Boas[1] in the early twentieth century, combined with the demise of the sort of female-identified culture that served as the base of late-Victorian feminism. The theory of primitive matriarchy was no longer regarded as scientific by scholars, and this view gradually influenced the general public. But, even more important, the values represented by Victorian culture, with its strong emphasis on the superior moral values of womanhood rooted in maternity, no longer attracted the postsuffrage generation.

What this suggests, then, is the sort of description of superior moral womanhood found in theories of ancient matriarchy were, in fact, closely linked with a Victorian familial subculture. Unconsciously, the description of the better culture of ancient pre-Christian times was modeled on this collection of values of Victorian women. This does not mean that there was no objective historical basis for imagining a prepatriarchal past. Rather, it simply means that these writers had no more ability than we today to separate the objective historicity of such prehistoric times from their own social ideals rooted in their own culture. Because these writers are now three-quarters of a century or more removed from us, it is easier to recognize the extent to which their pictures of ancient matriarchy were ideal projections backward of their own Victorian familialism. We are far enough removed from this Victorian culture that we no longer need feel merely rebellious against it, as did the "new women" of the 1920s and 1930s. We can look with new eyes on the values expressed by this late-Victorian culture.

In the context of a book on women and religion in the twentieth century, the value of the writings lies not with whether or not they said anything accurate about ancient times. Rather, the focus of this chapter is on what such visions of ancient times said about women in America and their values during the years between 1895 and 1928. We wish to show how concepts such as pre-Christian goddesses and matriarchal society functioned for these thinkers as a vehicle for imagining alternative religions and social systems for the future, based on the ideals of a female-identified Victorian subculture.

The concept of primitive matriarchy in nineteenth-century anthropology goes back primarily to the writings of the Swiss classicist, Johann Jakob Bachofen (1815–1887), who published in 1861 a vast tome entitled *Das Mutterrecht* (Motherright).[2] Bachofen represents a Germanic romantic effort to synthesize the ancient Near Eastern and Greek cultures, known to scholars of classical antiquity, with the biblical work in a comprehensive theory of the development of consciousness. Although Bachofen posited a matriarchal stage of culture intermediate between "promiscuity" and "patriarchy," he is far from imagining this to be a better world to which we should return. Rather, he identified mother-rule with the confinement of the human spirit to immanence. He regards its supercession by patriarchy as an expression of progress whereby transcendent Spirit, as the principle of masculinity and fatherhood, triumphs over nature. This use of matriarchy as a primitive stage to be transcended within a progressive scheme of cultural ascent warns us of its ambivalence for feminism. The concept was shaped originally by males to explicate the inevitable transcendence of masculinity over femininity.

However, in the late nineteenth century, radical feminists took up the idea of original matriarchy and began to shape it to their own purposes. One of the earliest to make comprehensive use of this concept for radical feminism was Matilda Joslyn Gage in *Woman, Church and State* (1893). Gage (1826–1893), an American suffragist, was closely associated with Susan B. Anthony and Elizabeth Cady Stanton from the 1860s. A member of Cady's revising committee for the *Woman's Bible,* Gage remained all her life deeply convinced that the Christian Church was the prime source of the oppression of women. She bitterly opposed Susan B. Anthony's maneuveres to merge the American and National Women's Suffrage movements in 1889, which brought Christian suffragists such as Frances Willard into the mainstream of the suffrage movement. Gage lost most of her friends in the suffrage movement as a result, and her name was deleted from the annals of the history of woman's suffrage. She has remained a little-known figure until the rediscovery and reprinting of her book by contemporary feminists.[3] Gage identified the cultures of ancient Egypt and the near East as a time of female ascendency in the family, religion, and the state. The worship of the Mother Goddess gave divine status to the maternal principle. For Gage, this was a golden age of human society that was overthrown by the regressive influence of patriarchy and patriarchal religion, which she identified particularly with the Christian Church. She insisted that women must throw off both Christianity and the patriarchal legal codes shaped by Christianity if they are to be liberated (Document 1).

Twenty years after Gage's book was published, feminists who made use of matriarchy theory were aware of its use in male anthropology as a transitional stage to be transcended by superior father-rule. Freud, in his *Totem and Taboo* (1912), had made passing use of matriarchy as an

intermediate stage between primal father-rule and a more ordered patriarchy, based on a social contract of brothers entered into after the
patricide of the primal father. Catherine Gasquoine Hartley's book, *The
Age of Mother-Power* (1914) (Document 2), represents a feminist reshap-
ing of these androcentric concepts of matriarchy. Like Freud, Hartley
(1869–1928) imagines an original stage of primal father-rule based on
tyrannical rule and suppression of the sons by the all-powerful father.
Women, in conspiracy with their sons, helped to bring an end to this
tyrannical father-rule. The maternal rule which followed represented an
effort by the mothers to create a communal egalitarian society. Hartley
shares the socialist view that this period of matriarchal communism gave
way primarily because of the rise of private property and the desire of
males to pass down property to male heirs. This brought a degradation
to women and a regression in social values, although it also brought an
advance toward a heightened individualism. She then postulates a fourth
stage, which is now dawning, of egalitarian society which will reclaim
women's rights, while at the same time appropriating for women the
individualism won by males under fraternal patriarchy.

Carrie Chapman Catt (1859–1947) represented the second generation of suffrage leaders who carried the struggle for the vote to completion in 1921. A woman of wealth, Catt was a moderate who believed in
the extension of democracy as the key to world peace. She straddled the
conflict between pacifism and participation in patriotic war effort during
the First World War, serving both on the Women's Committee for the
Council of National Defense and joining Jane Addams in founding the
Women's Peace Party in 1915. A world traveler with far-flung international connections, Catt used her travels to network for women's rights.
Her article "A Survival of Matriarchy," published in *Harper's Magazine* in
1914, was based on her recent travels to Malaysia. Here she reports on
a matrilineal tribe, the Menangkabau, which was widely assumed by
anthropologists to represent a living example of ancient matriarchal
society. Catt's description of this group is intended not only to vindicate
the existence of such matriarchal societies, but also to discount the male
view that such societies would be primitive and unable to enter into
modern civilization. Catt portrays this group as enlightened and progressive and able to enter directly into modern democratic (Western)
society, without benefit of having passed through a patriarchal stage
(Document 3).

Socialism has absorbed the theory of matriarchal origins through
Engels's use of Lewis Morgan[4] in *The Origin and History of the Family,
Private Property and the State* (1888). This theory had been stated in a way
more explicitly connected with feminist socialism by the German Socialist, August Bebel, in 1879.[5] The printing of Bebel's book in English in
the turn of the century brought widespread comment from feminist
Socialists in America. Before the First World War, socialism was not yet

split from mainstream American progressive movements. Many feminists at the turn of the century incorporated socialism as part of a comprehensive view of social progress. Some of the major organizers of Christian socialism in the Midwest were the radicals of the Women's Christian Temperance Union leaders who had followed Frances Willard in her famous 1897 speech, in which she had declared that "true Christianity is socialism and true socialism is Christianity."[6]

In the major magazines of feminist Socialists of this period, we find references to a matriarchal stage of civilization as a standard part of Socialist social history. For writers such as Josephine Conger-Kaneko and Theresa Malkiel, writing in the *Progressive Woman* in 1912 and 1913 (Document 4), primitive matriarchy referred to an original stage of communal society where woman existed as a free person whose labor and sexuality was at her own disposal. Patriarchy came about through the rise of private property and resulted in the subjugation of woman to serf or slave status. Thus feminist Socialists focused on the negative character of patriarchy primarily in terms of the exploitation of woman's labor within a patriarchal household where she had lost ownership of her own person. Modern industrial society is freeing women from the cramping conditions of labor within the family, and giving her a broader consciousness and identification with workers as a class. Through this women must advance, along with male workers, to the Socialist revolution.

While feminists in the early twentieth century claimed the theory of matriarchy to write stirring visions of a heritage reclaimed upon which to build a new age of woman's liberation, male writers also took for granted the historicity of this idea. But they generally derided it as an early stage of society fundamentally lacking in higher cultural values. Such a view of matriarchy is reflected in the editorial of *Harper's Magazine* of January 1910. According to the editor, this period of society lacked even the most elementary arts. Men did all the work, and women were pampered as they concentrated on their main occupation, maternity, a view in startling contrast to the feminist Socialist perspective. The ascendency of the male was essential to all social progress and represented the ascendency of civilization over nature. The editor does concede that this process might have involved some passing injustice to women, but all's well that ends well. This ascendency of the male is soon to be completed by a like liberation of woman from nature to take her place in civilization (Document 5).

By the early 1920s, general evolutionary histories of culture had fallen out of favor in anthropology. Westermarck's *History of Human Marriage* had reasserted the patriarchal origin of the family.[7] It was to refute this work that Robert Briffault assembled his three-volume work, *The Mothers* (1927). Briffault, a maverick intellectual, was the son of a Scotch mother and a French father. Educated partly in Europe, he was proficient in languages. He served as a doctor in New Zealand and then returned to England to fight in the First World War. Badly gassed in that war, he turned primarily to literary interests. In *The Mothers* he assembled massive information cross-culturally for a universal matriarchal stage of the family, preceding patriarchy. This matriarchal period he identified with high status of women and with a matrilocal family pattern rather than with female domination. This pattern he saw as going back to animal families where the mother established the household for her children. The family is, for Briffault, essentially a maternal institution.

However, Briffault is far from identifying this matriarchal period with superior values. Rather, like most male matriarchalists, he identifies women with instinct and males with rationality. Women, for him, have an entirely different nature and intelligence than men, and he asserts that women learn nothing after the age of twenty-five.[8] All works of higher culture have been created by males in patriarchal social arrangements. The importance of women, and of matriarchal culture, is that they and it established an instinctual and symbolic base of culture upon which male rationality then "erects its mighty achievements." The reign of women is associated with the magical phase of human religiosity, which Briffault sees as having been created by queens and priestesses. This is then translated by patriarchal religion into intellectual theology (Document 6). When Briffault published his work, this kind of anthropology was out of favor and he was largely ignored, although a revived interest in such ideas brought an abbreviated republication of his work thirty-one years later.

Our third male matriarchalist in this chapter is Robert Graves, the English poet and classicist, who lived for a while in America but spent most of his later years in Spain. More than anyone Graves is responsible for recreating the imagination about an ancient matriarchal stage of culture, linking it both with Goddess worship and nature rites, but also with an alternative form of consciousness which Graves sees as the foundation of poetry. While exalting his female muse, *The White Goddess* (1948), Graves has, however, nothing but contempt for modern feminism and, indeed, also for liberal and emancipatory movements for modern society, which he sees as further uprooting culture from its instinctual base. Women are powerful, for Graves, precisely as the *other*, the embodiment of wildness, irrationality, and compelling instinct. The ancient matriarch was no egalitarian, but an imperious autocrat of a culture bound to the natural rhythms of blood and soil.

Although Graves would have eschewed crude anti-Semitism, he nevertheless espouses the Nazi slogan that "the Jews are the cause of our troubles." For Graves, civilization is in deep trouble because it has departed more and more from this instinctual wisdom. Judaism was the primary creator of a religion of masculine alienation from nature, and this has been further extended in Protestantism and modern technological rationality and liberal ideology. Modern European civilization is on the brink of a breakdown into chaos, and only the return to rootedness in the Goddess can redeem it (Document 7). Thus Graves states in compelling form both the sense of rootlessness and longing for organic community of modern society; but he also veers ominously toward a pattern of thought that has been exploited all too disasterously in fascism.[9]

In contrast to these male matriarchalists, for whom mother-power functions primarily as instinctual base for male achievement, Charlotte Perkins Gilman (1867–1950), the most eminent feminist sociologist of the early twentieth century, constructs a devastating citique of masculinity as a base of Western civilization. In her book, *His Religion and Hers* (1923), Gilman applies her social anthropology to religion. Gilman sees the primal experience of male and female as indicative of two different religious attitudes toward the world. For males, shaped by millennia of the male hunting role, the primal experiences are killing and death. Male religiosity is based on death mysteries and the quest to escape finitude and win immortal life. Since such realms beyond mortal life are outside experience, male religiosity lends itself to dogmatism and the assertion of the will to believe through authority alone.

For the female, the primary experience is birth and the nurturing of children. Female religiosity thus would direct itself in more practical, this-worldly paths. It would focus not on abstract absolutes, but on the day-to-day means of sustaining life and ensuring that future which arises with new each morning and each new season. Women's religion is life-affirming, rather than life-denying. It is also altruistic, giving its life to sustain and assure the future life of the next generation, rather than egoistically bent on its own immortalization. Hers is a religion of service the others, of upbuilding the life of the world, rather than a flight from concrete reality to abstraction. Needless to say, Gilman thought that the masculine religious attitude, which she identified with Christianity particularly, was harmful to the best interests of society. It was essential to develop a new religious spirit, informed by the female perspective (Document 8).

From Gilman we turn to three women who represent that vast subculture of religious experimentation so popular in the first quarter of the twentieth century. New Thought, spiritualism, schools of metaphysical science, the I AM movement, and theosophy were some expressions of that religious restlessness of early twentieth-century Americans who turned to occult knowledge, to oriental wisdom, and to various kinds of mystical disciplines in order to win health of mind and body.[10] Healing was a very important motif in these metaphysical movements. The New Thought movement particularly had direct ties with Christian Science, although rejecting the institutional control of that church. Many of the founders and teachers of New Thought groups were women, such as Myrtle Fillmore, cofounder with her husband of the Unity Church[11];

Emma Curtis Hopkins, New Thought teacher who founded the Illinois Metaphysical College[12]; and Harriette Emilie Cady,[13] foremost writer for New Thought publications.

Ella Wheeler Wilcox (1850–1919) was one of the favorite poets and essayists of New Thought publications. Neither a major intellect nor a major poet, Wilcox was popular precisely because she could put the sentiments of New Thought into popular form. Although New Thought was deliberately eclectic, allowing its adherents to remain members of their Christian churches while also seeking its help, it saw itself as a universal truth that gathered up the best of all religions. Its central message was a metaphysical power of positive thinking which identified the divine Spirit with an immanent power in each person. By affirming the divine self within, linked with the universal divine Spirit, each person could conquer all negativity, ill health, bad fortune, and mental depression. Wilcox affirms this essence of New Thought as the true universal religion over against the gloomy creed she identified with "orthodox Christianity." In another of her essays, Wilcox praises the power of maternity. She suggests that the woman, empowered by New Thought, could not only make over herself anew as healthy and wholesome, but could also guide the gestation of her baby in the womb in these positive directions (Document 9).

While New Thought remained nominally Christian, the theosophical movement turned toward the religions of India for inspiration. Theosophy had been founded by the eccentric Russian mystic, Helena Petrova Blavatsky,[14] and Colonel Henry Steel Olcott in 1875. Blavatsky claimed that she had received her doctrine from secret revelations given to her by hidden masters of mystical knowledge in Tibet. The base of the movement was in New York City until 1879 when Blavatsky and Olcott went to India: In 1895 William Quan Judge broke with the Olcott group, now led by the British theosophist, Anne Besant, to found the Theosophical Society in America. His student, Katherine Tingley, emerged as his successor after his death in 1896. Tingley (1847–1929) had been active in charitable work in New York, having founded a Society of Mercy for hospital and prison visitation and a settlement house called the Do Good Mission. These social concerns remained fundamental to her work after she moved into leadership in the theosophical movement.

Boldly seeking to rival the Indian-based Theosophical Society, Tingley toured the world, and claimed her own direct teaching from the Tibetan mahatmas. A natural organizer and builder, she turned to a vast scheme of building a theosophical college and community that would become the font of theosophical culture and a model of a new way of life. She bought a tract of land in Point Loma, California, where her community flourished for some thirty years. Here she directed experimentation in new kinds of agriculture; sponsored theatre, music, and the arts; and promulgated a holistic philosophy of education, intended to create a higher type of humanity. Always mindful of social concerns, she also tried to make her school a model of interracial and intercultural understanding. A pacifist as well as an antivivisectionist and an opponent of capital punishment, she opposed the American entrance into the First World War, presided over conferences on world peace in Sweden and Holland (1913) and San Diego in 1915, and convened the Theosophical Permanent Peace Conference in Point Loma in 1924.[15] Primarily an activist rather than an intellectual, the excerpts from her book, *The Voice of the Soul* (1928), give a sample of Tingley's high sense of her own authority, as well as her educational program for humanitarian uplift (Document 10).

The theosophical and metaphysical movements spawned a host of eager entrepreneurs of mystical science who plied the lecture circuits and founded their own schools, publishing companies, and religious movements, from which they disseminated lessons in spiritual disciplines. One of these was Aleta Baker (1880–?) who founded the Order of the Portal and published numerous books in the 1920s and 1930s.[16] Another was Harriette Augusta Curtiss (1856?–1932), who together with her husband, Homer Curtiss, founded the Order of Christian Mystics and published numerous books on metaphysical science between 1909 and 1948 through the Curtiss Publishing Company.[17] Baker and the Curtisses were Christian theosophists who proclaimed Christ as the personification of a divine selfhood whose mysteries encompassed all mystical traditions. Like Baker, the Curtisses saw a cosmic union of masculine and feminine powers as central to self-integration, and symbolized the feminine principles as Isis and the Virgin Mary. Curtiss saw the vindication of the female principle as related to a new dignity and power of women. The feminine principle is the higher principle of purity and love, through which one brings to birth in each person the divine self or divine child (Document 11).

These visions of ancient matriarchal society and female divinity, linked with pre-Christian goddesses, seem to have gone underground for some half a century. Discredited by anthropology, the idea of ancient matriarchy nevertheless continued to be carried on in other streams of thought. Classics, particularly classical archaeology, had been deeply shaped by this theory and continued to describe classical Athens as a culture built on the suppression of earlier matriarchal culture, especially from ancient Minoa (Crete).[18] Students of classical mythology, allied with the history of religions school that went back to thinkers such as James Frazer and E. O. James,[19] as well as with Jungian psychology,[20] preserved such ideas for students in the 1940s and 1950s, although their feminist potential lay dormant. Male mythologists had safety relegated such ideas to an ancient past, superseded by higher male civilization, or else interpreted the goddesses as auxiliaries to male psychological development to which women were to be pliant handmaidens. Thus it is only with the birth of the new feminist movement in the late 1960s that such ideas might be reclaimed for radical feminism.

Among the earlier expressions of this revival of matriarchal and Goddess concepts was the German writer, Helen Diner, whose book, *Mothers and Amazons: The First Feminine History of Culture,* was translated into English in 1965. It was followed shortly by Elizabeth Gould Davis's *The First Sex* (Document 12). Through the 1970s, books such as these would gradually penetrate American feminist thinking and lead to a full-scale debate about whether feminism should abandon Christianity as an inherently patriarchal religion and seek an alternative religion from ancient matriarchal times.[21] One of the sources of confusion in that debate springs from the Victorian cultural origins of such ideas. Deriving mostly from the late nineteenth and early twentieth centuries, the sources for such ideas from anthropology, history of religions, classics, and Jungian psychology are deeply penetrated by certain Victorian ideas about the nature of the "feminine" as symbol and essence. Thus feminist ideologists who seek to revive ancient feminist religion, which they imagine to have gone back to the Stone Age before the rise of patriarchy, continue to echo symbols and images of womanhood whose actual cultural ambit lies in the half-forgotten world of their grandmothers.

Matilda Joslyn Gage, suffrage leader and radical critic of patriarchal religions. [Photo courtesy of the Schlesinger Library, Radcliffe College, Cambridge, Massachusetts.]

Carrie Chapman Catt (c. 1897), leader of the women's suffrage movement in the two decades leading to its final victory in 1921. [Photo courtesy of the Schlesinger Library, Radcliffe College, Cambridge, Massachusetts.]

Charlotte Perkins Gilman at her typewriter (c. 1920), leading feminist sociologist. [Photo courtesy of the Schlesinger Library, Radcliffe College, Cambridge, Massachusetts.]

Katherine Tingley (c. 1987), leading theosophist and founder of the Point Loma theosophical community, in Point Loma, California. [Photo courtesy of the Theosophical Society, Pasadena, California.]

Katherine Tingley, seated among the officers of the Theosophical Peace Committee at the Temple of Peace, Point Loma, California. [Photo courtesy of the Theosophical Society, Pasadena, California.]

Documents: Radical Victorians: The Quest for an Alternative Culture

FEMINIST MATRIARCHALISTS

Document 1: Matilda Joslyn Gage

Matilda Joslyn Gage's Woman, Church and State *is a comprehensive effort to write a feminist religious and legal history linking the demise of matriarchal society and the rise of patriarchal society with the influence of patriarchal religion in shaping legal systems of female subordination in Western society. Gage was a leader in the National Women's Suffrage Association in the last half of the nineteenth century.[22]*

A form of society existed at an early age known as the Matriarchate or Mother-rule. Under the Matriarchate, except as son and inferior, man was not recognized in either of these great institutions, family, state or church. A father and husband as such, had no place either in the social, political or religious scheme; woman was ruler in each. The primal priest on earth, she was also supreme as goddess in heaven. The earliest semblance of the family is traceable to the relationship of mother and child alone. Here the primal idea of the family had birth. The child bore its mother's name, tracing its descent from her; her authority over it was regarded as in accord with nature; the father having no part in the family remained a wanderer. Long years elapsed before man, as husband and father, was held in esteem. The son, as child of his mother, ranked the father, the mother taking precedence over both the father and the son. Blood relationship through a common mother preceded that of descent through the father in the development of society. This priority of the mother touched not alone the family, but controlled the state and indicated the form of religion. Thus we see that during the Matriarchate, woman ruled; she was first in the family, the state, religion, the most ancient records showing that man's subjection to woman preceded by long ages that of woman to man. The tribe was united through the mother; social, political, and religious life were all in harmony with the idea of woman as the first and highest power. The earliest phase of life being dependent upon her, she was recognized as the primal factor in every relation, man holding no place but that of dependent.

The Patriarchate under which Biblical history and Judaism commenced, was a rule of men whose lives and religion were based upon passions of the grossest kind, showing but few indications of softness or refinement. . . .

Not until the Patriarchate were wives regarded as property, the sale of daughters as a legitimate means of family income or their destruction at birth looked upon as a justifiable act. Under the Patriarchate, society became morally revolutionized, the family, the state, the form of religion entirely changed. The theory of a male supreme God in the interests of force and authority, wars, family discord, the sacrifice of children to appease the wrath of an offended (male) deity are all due to the Patriarchate. These were practices entirely out of consonance with woman's thought and life. Biblical Abraham binding Isaac for sacrifice to Jehovah, carefully kept his intentions from the mother Sarah. Jephtha offering up his daughter in accordance with his vow, allowing her a month's life for the bewailment of her virginity, are but typical of the low regard of woman under the Patriarchate. During this period the destruction of girl children became a widely extended practice, and infantile girl murder the custom of many nations. During the Matriarchate all life was regarded as holy; even the sacrifice of animals was unknown. The most ancient and purest religions taught sacrifice of the animal passions as the great necessity in self-purification. But the Patriarchate subverted this sublime teaching, materializing spiritual truths, and substituting the sacrifice of animals, whose blood was declared a sweet smelling savor to the Lord of Hosts.

. . . But we have now reached a period in history when investigation is again taking the place of blind belief and the truth, capable of making man free, is once more offered. It is through a recognition of the divine element of motherhood as not alone inhering in the great primal source of life but as extending throughout all creation, that it will become possible for the world, so buried in darkness, folly and superstition, to practice justice toward woman. . . .

The most important struggle in the history of the church is that of woman for liberty of thought and the right to give that thought to the world. As a spiritual force the church appealed to barbaric conceptions when it declared woman to have been made for man, first in sin and commanded to be under obedience. Holding as its chief tenet a belief in the inherent wickedness of woman, the originator of sin, as its sequence the sacrifice of a God becoming necessary, the church has treated her as alone under a "curse" for whose enforcement it declared itself the divine instrument. Woman's degradation under it dating back to its earliest history, the nineteenth century still shows religious despotism to have its stronghold in the theory of woman's inferiority to man. . . .

The whole theory regarding woman, under Christianity, has been based upon the conception that she had no right to live for herself alone. Her duty to others has continuously been placed before her and her training has ever been that of self-sacrifice. Taught from the pulpit and legislative halls that she was created for another, that her position must always be secondary even to her children, her right to life, has been admitted only in so far as its reacting effect upon another could be predicated. That she was first created for herself, as an independent being to whom all the opportunities of the world should be open because of herself, has not entered the thought of the church; has not yet become one of the conceptions of law; is not yet the foundation of the family.

But woman is learning for herself that not self-sacrifice, but self-development, is her first duty in life; and this, not primarily for the sake of others, but that she may become fully herself.

A brighter day is to come for the world, a day when the intuitions of woman's soul shall be accepted as part of humanity's spiritual wealth; when force shall step backward, and love, in reality, rule the teachings of religion; and may woman be strong in the ability and courage necessary to bring about this millennial time. The world is full of signs of the near approach of this period; as never before is there an arousing sense of something deeper, holier in religion than the Christian church has given. The world has seemingly awaited the advent of heroic souls who once again should dare all things for the truth. The woman who possesses love for her sex, for the world, for truth, justice and right, will not hesitate to place herself upon record as opposed to falsehood, no matter under what guise of age or holiness it appears. A generation has passed since the great struggle began, but not until within ten years has woman dared attack upon the veriest stronghold of her oppression, the Church.

Has woman no wrongs to avenge upon the church? As I look backward through history I see the church everywhere stepping upon advancing civilization, hurling woman from the plane of "natural rights" where the fact of her humanity had placed her, and through itself, and its control over the state, in the doctrine of "revealed rights" everywhere teaching an inferiority of sex; a created subordination of woman to man; making her very existence a sin; holding her accountable to a diverse code of morals from man; declaring her possessed of fewer rights in church and in state; her very entrance into heaven made dependent upon some man to come as mediator between her and the Saviour it has preached, thus crushing her personal, intellectual and spiritual freedom. Looking forward, I see evidence of a conflict more severe than any yet fought by reformation or science; a conflict that will shake the foundations of religious belief, tear into fragments and scatter to the winds the old dogmas upon which all forms of Christianity are based. It will not be the conflict of man with man upon rites and systems; it will not be the conflict of science upon church theories regarding creation and eternity; it will not be the light of biology illuminating the hypothesis of the resurrection of the body; but it will be the rebellion of one half of the church against those theological dogmas upon which the very existence of the church is based. In no other country has the conflict between natural and revealed rights been as pronounced as in the United States; and in this country where the conflict first began, we shall see its full and final development. During the ages, no rebellion has been of like importance with that of Woman against the tyranny of Church and State; none has had its far reaching effects. We note its beginning; its progress will overthrow every existing form of these institutions; its end will be a regenerated world.

Document 2: Catherine Gasquoine Hartley

Catherine Hartley, a feminist journalist, lived most of her life in England but was in close touch with American suffragists. She wrote a number of books on the position of women in ancient and modern society. Her book The Age of Mother-Power *is an effort to rework the matriarchal thesis to include a first stage of father-rule, but not in a way that legitimated patriarchy.* [23]

Our most primitive ancestors, half-men, half-brutes, lived in small, solitary and hostile family groups, held together by a common subjection to the strongest male, who was the father and the owner of all the women, and their children. There was no promiscuity for there could be no possible union in peace. Here was the most primitive form of jealous ownership by the male, as he killed or drove off his rivals; his fights were the brutal precursors of all sexual restrictions for women. . . .

From these first solitary families, grouped submissively around one tyrant-ruler, we reach a second stage out of which order and organisation sprang. In this second stage the family expanded into the larger group of the communal clan. The upward direction of this transformation is evident; the change was from the most selfish individualism to a communism more or less complete—from the primordial patriarchate to a free social organisation, all the members of which are bound together by a strict solidarity of interests.

. . . The earliest movements towards peace came through the influence of the women, for it was in their interest to consolidate the family, and, by means of union, to establish their own power. Collective motives were more considered by women, not at all because of any higher standard of feminine moral virtue, but because of the peculiar advantages arising to themselves and to their children—advantages of freedom which could not exist in a society inspired by individual inclination. And for this reason the clan system may be considered as a feminine creation, which had special relation to motherhood. Under this influence, the marital rights of the male members were restricted and confined.

. . . The maternal communal clan was an organisation in which there was a freer community of interest, far more fellowship in labour and partnership in property, with a resulting liberty for woman, than we find in any patriarchal society. For this reason, shall we, then, look back to this maternal stage as to a golden period, wherein was realised a free social organisation, carrying with it privileges for women, which even to-day among ourselves have never been established, and only

of late claimed? It is a question very difficult to answer, and we must
not in any haste rush into mistakes. We found that the mother-age was
a transitional stage in the history of the evolution of society, and we
have indicated the stages of its gradual decline. It is thus proved to
have been a less stable social system than the patriarchate which again
succeeded it, or it would not have perished in the struggle with it.
Must we conclude from this that the one form of the family is higher
than the other—that the superior advantage rests with the patriarchal
system? Not at all: rather it proves how difficult is the struggle to
socialize.

The impulse to dominate by virtue of strength or property possession has manifested itself in every age. It cannot be a matter of
surprise, therefore, that at this period of social development a rebellion arose against the customs of maternal communism. . . . As society
advanced property would increase in value, and the social and political significance of its possession would also increase. Afterwards,
when the personal property was acquired, each man would aim at
gaining a more exclusive right over his wife and children. . . .

This reversal in the form of the marriage brought about a corresponding reversal in the status of women. This is so plain. The women
of the family do not now inherit property, but are themselves property, passing from the hands of their father to that of a husband. As
purchased wives they are compelled to reside in the husband's house
and among his kin, who have no rights or duties in regard to them,
and where they are strangers. . . . The protection of her own kindred
was the source of the woman's power and strength. This was now lost.
In the religious conception of a people we find the true thoughts and
the customs of the period in which they originated. A patriarchal
people could not have given expression to a creation myth in which
the female idea prevailed, and the mother, and not the father, was
dominant. For men have ever fashioned the gods in their own human
image, endowing them with their thoughts and actions. The sharp
change in the view of woman's part in the relationship of the sexes
is clearly symbolised in the creation myths. Yes, they mark the degradation of woman; she has fallen from the maternal conception of the
feminine principle, guiding, directing, and using the male, to that of
the woman made for the man in the patriarchal Bible story.

Another group of legends that I would notice refer to the conflict
between the right of the mother and that of the father in relation to
the children. These stories belong to a period of transition. In ancient
Greece, as we have seen, the paternal family succeeded the maternal
clan. In his *Orestia*, Aeschylus puts in opposition before Pallas Athene
the right of the mother and the right of the father. The chorus of the
Eumenides, representing the people, defends the position of the
mother; Apollo pleads for the father, and ends by declaring, in a fit

of patriarchal delirium, that *the child is not of the blood of the mother*. "It is not the mother who begets what is called her child; she is only the nurse of the germ poured into her womb; he who begets is the father. The woman receives the germ merely as guardian, and when it pleases the gods, she preserves it."

. . . Here we trace a different world of thoughts and conceptions; the mother was so little esteemed as to be degraded into the mere nourisher of the child. These patriarchal theories naturally consecrated the slavery of woman.

With all the evils father-right has brought to women, we have got to remember that the woman owes the individual relation of the man to herself and her children to the patriarchal system. The father's right in his children (which, unlike the right of the mother, was not founded upon kinship, but rested on the quite different and insecure basis of property), had to be re-established. Without this being done, the family in its complete development was impossible. The survival value of the patriarchal age consists in the additional gain to the children of the father's to the mother's care.

The twentieth century is the age of Woman; some day, it may be, that it will be looked back upon as the golden age, the dawn some say of feminine civilisation. We cannot estimate as yet; and no man can tell what forces these new conditions may not release in the soul of woman. The modern change is that the will of woman is asserting itself. Women are looking for a satisfactory life, which is to be determined from within themselves, not from without by others. The result is a discontent that may well prove to be the seed or spring of further changes in a society which has yet to find its normal organisation. . . .

In our contemporary society there is a deep-lying dissatisfaction with existing conditions, a yearning and restless need for change. We stand in the first rush of a great movement.

What is needed at present is that women should be allowed to rediscover for themselves what is their woman's work, rather than that they should continue to accept perforce the the role which men (rightly or wrongly) have at various times allowed to them throughtout the patriarchal ages. This necessity is as much a necessity for men as it is for women.

We, and not men, must fix the standard in sex, for we have to play the chief part in the racial life. Let us, then, reacquire our proud instinctive consciousness, which we are fully justified in having, of being the mothers of humanity; and having that consciousness, once more we shall be invincible.

Document 3: Carrie Chapman Catt

Carrie Chapman Catt, suffragist and peace leader, grew up in the rural Midwest and had brief careers as a schoolteacher and as a newspaper editor before becoming a leader in the National American Woman Suffrage Association, an organisation she was chosen to head when Susan B. Anthony retired in 1900. Catt resigned the post in 1904, but returned to lead it again in 1915 through the war years to final victory. After the war, she became a leader in the international women's peace movement. Her article "A Survival of Matriarchy," about the matriarchal Menangkabau people of Malaysia, reflects both her world travels and her defense of the maternal-dominated family as a positive environment for peaceful and cooperative values.[24]

Now that a closer acquaintance with the Menangkabau is made possible, it is known that their fundamental institutions belong to the Matriarchate, or Age of the Mother's Rights, which many sociologists believe to have been a stage through which all races have passed. They number 1,320,000, and occupy a territory eight times the size of the Netherlands. The women own the land and houses; family names descend in the female line, and mothers are the sole guardians of their children. Some of the customs of the people have been deflected from their normal course of development by two powerful patriarchal influences (the Hindus and the Mohammedans). Since Hindus and Mohammedans alike assign women to seclusion and a position of utter subordination to men, it is evident that there was something tremendously virile in the "Mother's Rights" institutions of the Menangkabau, or something unusual in their environment, to have withstood such all-dominating forces. This conclusion becomes the more apparent when taken in connection with the fact that distinct traces of the Matriarchate are to be found throughout the Malay race, to which these people belong, though nearly all tribes have substituted Patriarchate institutions.

In former times, since the women controlled the land and carried the family pocket-book, the husbands made no contribution toward the family expenses. Instead, the men were supported by their wives and received their pocket-money as a gift from them. Divorce is easy and the children always remain with the wife and keep the name of her family. Children inherit the property of their mother (the *harta poesaka*) and one-half of what the father and mother may earn together (the *harta pentjarian);* the other half of the *harta pentjarian,* and all the father's independent property go to the children of his eldest sister. . . .

Nearly all the land is still owned by the women, and its cultivation is in their hands. The head of the house is called the *Indua,* and as such she controls the family property. At her death her property and authority pass to her eldest daughter, and in the event that there is no daughter, to the daughter of her eldest brother. In case the absence of daughters renders the inheritance too complicated, a girl may be adopted, but she must, in order to continue the family name and property, be a member of the same family. When a girl marries a piece of land is assigned to her, and her husband is expected to aid her in its cultivation. As a matter of fact, men do little agricultural work.

A weekly *pasar*, or market, is held in every village, and for miles around women of remarkably independent and business-like mien may be seen wending their way by every road and mountain-path toward the *pasar*. Hundreds of them carry great baskets on their heads loaded with chickens, ducks, geese, turkeys, rice, and other grains, and an astonishing variety of vegetables and fruits. Sometimes a mother and all her daughters form a group, each loaded with produce for the market. . . . Women money-changers are located at convenient places, where they sit on the ground, Oriental fashion, with their money before them; they make change with quick intelligence . . .

It is evident that the women work much harder than the men, for not only do they produce the food, cook it, care for the house and children, but they make their own utensils of pottery, mats, baskets, and many articles of daily use from braided bamboo rattan or grass. In many families the women still weave the cloth for all the garments of the family, and still find time for skilled embroidery.

The Menangkabau, like most people of similar development, are organized into *soekoes* (clans), the members of each *soekoe* being descended from a common ancestress in the female line. . . .

. . . No decision contrary to the wishes of the women has ever been made. The hereditary chiefs do not derive their authority from their fathers, but are the eldest sons of the chief's eldest sister. Dutch history records communication with the great head of the Menangkabau in the long ago, variously styled emperor, king, sultan, maharajah, but the people themselves say they never had a male head, their chief always having been a queen. One Boendo Kandoung is gloriously remembered for her heroic and victorious leadership of the armies; and another, whose name, Wilhelmina, indicates a European origin, fought side by side with her soldiers, as brave as the bravest. . . .

There are male and female native doctors, who use native herbs as medicine; and skilled massage, practised by the most intelligent of their neighbors, is among their accomplishments. Priests and priestesses, known as *Hadjis*—men and women who have journeyed to Mecca and there become "holy"—administer to spiritual wants. . . .

Their entire country is prosperous, although some sections are more so than others. The people have been well prepared for the impetus which the touch with Western civilization will give them. Upon all the roads leading to the *pasars*, where throngs of women, with baskets upon their heads, and men carrying their little bird-cages, are to be seen, there are also boys and girls—clean, bright, and sturdy, with books and slates under their arms, trudging along to school. . . .

The sons of these Matriarchate mothers are most in demand by Dutch government for positions of trust. . . .

Some ethnologist have claimed that the Matriarchate represents a very primitive condition, in which sex relations are free and the father of the family uncertain. If this be true, the Menangkabau have long outlived that period. Rape is absolutely unknown, and prostitution does not exist.

. . . The people are now taking an intelligent view of their own comparative status among the peoples of the world, and more than one possesses a fair knowledge of ethnology. At present they probably represent the highest civilization existing under this form of social organization.

Document 4: Josephine Conger-Kaneko and Theresa Malkiel

Josephine Conger-Kaneko and Theresa Malkiel were leading feminists, Socialists, and editors of the Progressive Woman, *the organ of the Women's National Committee of the Socialist party of America in the first two decades of the twentieth century. One of the difficulties of the Women's Committee was reconciling within the Socialist movement the cultural gap between the women's auxiliaries of the Socialist party, which came from the more patriarchal German Socialists, and the independent women's Socialist clubs, which sprang from an indigenous American progressivism and feminism.*[25]

Theresa Malkiel (1874–1949) was a Jew who rose to leadership in the party from the predominately Jewish Infant Cloak Maker's Union, while Josephine Conger-Kaneko (active between 1900–1919) came from a Midwest socialism in which reformist Protestantism mingled with theosophy and New Thought. She previously edited the Kansas-based Socialist weekly, Appeal to Reason. *The Women's Committee had made August Bebel's* Women Under Socialism, *in which the matriarchal origins of the family were expounded, a study text, and these ideas were reflected in the pages of the Progressive Woman.*[26]

In a chapter on "The Sex Relations in Germany," Karl Pearson tells very interestingly of the time in ancient Germany when there came a struggle between the men and women of the race, for supremacy. It was the passing from the mother- to the father-age. The "priestess-mother" who had reigned supreme at the hearth stone, and in the tribal councils found herself, under the invasion of new doctrines, the object of distrust, envy and hatred. "The witch-trials of the Middle Ages, wherein thousands of women were condemned to the stake, were the very real traces of the contest between man and woman. For one man burned there were at least fifty women, and when one reads the confessions under torture of these poor wretches, a strange light is thrown over the meaning of all this suffering. It is the last struggle of woman against complete subjection," says Pearson.

But the struggle was ineffectual; woman was completely subjected in the Germanic tribes, and her subjection has been pretty complete over the Aryan world for centuries. Today comes a new struggle. It is not to gain supremacy over man, but to take her old place by his side in civilized society. And today while women are not burned as witches for their efforts toward this place, they have, nevertheless known actual physical torture, and any amount of mental torture has been theirs, and still is. Denunciation, ridicule, vituperation—all of this they have known.

A free being in the beginning of human existence, woman was in time reduced to the position of slave. For in the glory of his conquests, man extended his reign over her. Through his greater physical strength he assumed the role of woman's protector, and then, gradually, as he, with the aid of his stone hatchet, his sword and gun, moved onward toward a higher civilization, he changed it to ruler. While he fought and conquered, he apportioned to woman the detail side of life and compelled her to peform her servile labor in silence. Then, as the human race kept up its climb to the summit, every additional step brought greater power to man, more technical knowledge to woman. In time man conquered land and sea, beast and bird, while woman learned to weave cloth, make cooking utensils, build huts. With every passing age the activities of man and woman became ever more sharply divided, and in time the occupation of each was looked upon as a special characteristic of sex, a law of nature, or the expressed ordinance from above.

The world believed that a God willed it that man should be the warrior, the hero of the battlefield, that he should protect and yet take life; that woman should create life, and in the sweat of her brow provide for the sustenance, of life. Man would not, woman could not, question the justice of this ordinance. Her constant toil left her no time for thought, for doubt; she was taught to believe blindly in the omnipotence of man. She could not do otherwise—she was his ward, her life dependent upon his good-will; he was her nominal supporter, her bodily protector.

"Her status," says Mary Jacobi, "combined both the disabilities of serf and slave. Like the former, she did not own the land or any other property; she was attached to it. And like the slave, she might slave from dawn to dusk, yet have no right to a farthing of the products of her own labor."

Though woman has always worked and produced wealth until the middle of the last century her product as well as herself were considered the property of the man who was her guardian. Her work in the house had no value in the eyes of society. It was never remunerated, but was looked upon as a part of woman's duties. The more the industries developed during the ages of the domestic system of production, the more did woman become enslaved in the performance of her servile labor. And so long as the domestic system of production was the only mode of our economic development, so long was woman destined to remain the appendage of man.

The change of woman's position in society became possible only when the invention and application of machinery in the middle of the eighteenth century changed our economic conditions by transferring the production of wealth from the home to the factory, by supplanting mechanical power for manual labor. With the change in the mode of production the relation of the sexes first underwent a great change.

For the first time since the dawn of civilization woman found a possibility to leave the narrow sphere of her domestic existence, then her work was removed to the factory; economic necessity compelled her to follow it there. The changed mode of production necessitated a changed mode of life. The constant association with other workers was so different from the dull, lonely life led by woman behind the closed doors of her home. Woman's views, so narrow and egoistic during those days, had to change. Conditions taught her to look upon the other inhabitants of the world as something akin to her. Since her life no longer began and ended within the family homestead her conception of life assumed broader proportions. With her entrance into the factory she was relieved from depending upon man for subsistence. Her work had a value, she could live away and independently of her former guardian. Then as the industries developed the former line of demarcaton between the occupations of man and woman became less evident. Woman was called upon to perform tasks heretofore performed by man only, while men were enlisted to tend machinery which produced goods that were considered within woman's sphere and woman's own work since the dawn of history. Man and woman sought work where they could earn a living, and since each found it necessary to support oneself independently of the other, woman, the serf, appropriated tasks belonging to man, the free man, and the latter had to accept employment which was formerly the duty of woman, the serf. Thus has the Industrial Revolution shattered the chains of woman's bondage, thus has it made possible woman's freedom in our future civilization.

What wonder that woman came to realize the change in her position and amidst her new environment sought greater knowledge? As a matter of fact, the widening of her sphere demanded further development. The partial economic independence brought about a greater mental activity, one step of progress led to another.

Document 5: An Editorial on Matriarchy and Social Evolution

This editorial on "The Social Evolution of Woman" from Harper's Magazine, January 1910, is chiefly useful because it shows how much the concept of a primitive matriarchate was taken for granted by American popular culture in the early twentieth century. The unsigned editorial was probably written by the editor, Henry Mills Alden (1836–1919). The male editor naively projects his own assumptions into his account of ancient times, such as his description of the ancient woman as pampered and well nourished, while the males do all the chores. [27]

It was only in the Sacred Mysteries of the popular religion—the survival of a faith so old that it knew no Olympus—that the idea of motherhood was the supreme conception.

This carries us back to a prehistoric society, or rather we should say a primordial humanity too provincial and earthbound to have a social constitution in our sense of the term. It was to this period that the Matriarchate belonged. The essential idea of the Matriarchate was that of motherhood, divine as well as human, for the deity supremely worshipped was the Cybele or Demeter type, the Great Mother. Maternity was the ground of human kinship; paternity counting for nothing. . . . The human *gens* had a communal economy—no marriage, no families, and not much more ethical sense than belongs to a beehive—so little removed was humanity, in this period, above the plane of elemental instinct. Maternity was the glory of woman and, in the masculine regard, worthy of worshipful service. Men, of course, did all the chores. The mothers were well nourished, doubtless in every way pampered. We suspect that the arts, even of the ruder sort like embroidery and pottery, were of later origin. Human faith had not yet lifted its eyes heavenward, but looked only downward to the earth and to the *Mutterseele* of the underworld. It is not permitted us to behold this exceedingly primitive world in its uncorrupted, natural dignity.

We do not know how this order of things was broken up. Possibly it was because of the greater activity of the males, who through long service developed a kind of mastery and came into a more ambitious if not more enviable estate. The pastoral and agricultural habits led to the accumulation of property worth considering, and which, as soon as it became private, made the question of inheritance important, and thus led to the institution of marriage, when polygamy supplanted polyandry.

The change was in the line of human progress, however it may have been away from Nature; it was the beginning of that medley order of things humiliating and triumphant which we call civilization, and which the Rousseau tribe of philosphers say should be repented of. It was not a revolution of masculine contrivance; it was in the course of things, something inevitably incident to a rationally conscious development of the race. Men did not revolt against women. There was in the primitive order no oppression to avenge. Man was all the time physically stronger on the side of action as woman was on the passive side; his service had been a willing one.

In one respect an immense advantage had, in the primitive order, been instinctively and in the fitness of things accorded to woman. As nearer to Nature and, especially by her sex, allied to the mother divinities, she had had a monopoly of communication with the powers of darkness, which she presumably used for benignant purposes. It cannot be denied that the transition from the placid and peaceful state of primitive naturalism to a warlike, intensely competitive, complexly ethical, strenuous civilization involved for ages peculiar hardship, cruelty, and injustice to womankind. As nearer to Nature, woman suffered more than man from the departure. She passed into a new world, shorn of her ancient distinction and of her sacred immunities, and averse by habit and inclination from the prizes sought by men. The mother deities retired before the burning brightness of Apollo and the gods of the open air; and their rites were celebrated in dark places. Motherhood itself came to be associated with servile conditions, exalted only by the birth of sons.

It is evident from the whole history of civilization that man, from the moment of his mastery, had to fulfill his peculiar destiny through an amazing course of errors—follies, vanities, and cruelties innumerable. The course was inevitable, and if women were subjected to tyrannies, so were the vast majority of men. Every successive dominance all along the line—and it has been a line of progression in both the perception and the realization of truth—has been something to be repented of, with the justification of manhood finally in view, which can only come through the full emancipation of the woman and the child.

The consummation of civilization must be the complete justification of its departure from Nature through the creative evolution of a new human nature. Thus only emerge new species in the spiritual world. There is not merely formal progression, which is sterile, but genetic procedure into abundant life. Something of the eternal enters here.

This evolution has been a translation of all that is elemental in man and woman to a higher plane, through psychical inspiration and illumination. There has not really been any departure from Nature, which is always radical in us, but the humanization of every element in it.

The union of men and women in all the essential things of life is a distinctively modern fact; and it is sure to become a union also in

things only relatively important, thus having full organic completeness.

Woman had little to do directly with the shaping of old civilizations; but we cannot help thinking that our modern sense of life and
its more real and human investment are largely and directly due not
only to spiritual qualities distinctively feminine, but to feminine initiative.

In the clarified light of the soul womanhood has been translated.
In its fullest meaning it is the liberation of humanity for finer uses.
She is nearer than man to the new Nature as she was to the old.

The Humanities and, we might also say, the Divinities have been
transformed. A delusive network of sophistication has vanished. The
terms "masculine" and "feminine" have no longer their old elemental
or conventional meanings. There is, or there is becoming, a new
woman and a new man, and the distinction between them is not one
of "spheres." No exaltation of life, here or hereafter, could be humanly interesting or at all human in which woman did not have her proper
share and her peculiar distinction.

Document 6: Robert Briffault

Robert Briffault's The Mothers: A Study of the Origins of Sentiments and Institutions *in three volumes was the most massive effort
to collect the literary and archaeological evidence for a universal state
of matriarchy before patriarchy since J. J. Bachofen's work over sixty
years earlier. Briffault is clear in showing that matriarchy is not to be
understood as a reverse of patriarchy, a system that is based on male
property rights and female economic dependency. Women's high
status in earlier times is based on her role as economic producer and
also center of a matrilocal family system. From this maternal function
there also arose, on a religious level, the magic power of queens and
priestesses.* [28]

Primitive Division of Labour Between the Sexes

The difficulty which many still experience in fully recognizing the
matriarchal character of primitive human societies arises, I believe, in
a great measure from a fundamental misconception which has not
been sufficiently considered. It is assumed that in a matriarchal type
of society the women exercise a domination over the men similar or
equivalent to the domination exercised by the men over the women
in a patriarchal social order, and that the two types of society thus
differ merely in the sex which exercises dominant power in each. But
such as conception is very far from accurate. The characteristics of
societies of a matriarchal type are by no means a simple inversion of
the parts respectively played by the sexes in a patriarchal society. In
the most primitive human societies there is nothing equivalent to the

domination which, in advanced societies, is exercised by individuals, by classes, by one sex over the other. The notion of such a domination is entirely foreign to primitive humanity; the conception of authority is not understood. The ultimate basis of the respective status of the sexes in advanced patriarchal societies is the fact that women, not being economically productive, are economically dependent, whereas the men exercise economic power both as producers and as owners of private property. . . .

The primitive ascendancy of women is not founded on artificial economic control arising from proprietary rights, but on the functional constitution of the social group. The primitive human group is matriarchal in the same way and for the same reasons that the animal group is matriarchal; it is not so by virtue of established domination, but of functional relations. The material biological group subserves the maternal instincts and is governed by those instincts, but that functional fact does not impose a domination over the male any more than the animal male imposes a domination over the animal female. In the primitive group, the motherhood, the functional equilibrium implied, as in the animal group, a preponderance of the female. . . .

In all earlier social phases economic power does not depend upon property, for there exists in such phases no form of durable wealth, nothing of value which is susceptible of being kept and accumulated. The sole form of wealth and of economic power consists, at those primitive social stages, in power to produce. The economic advantage which such power bestows is wholly in favour of the women; for women in primitive society, far from being economically unproductive, and therefore dependent, are, on the contrary, in the highest degree producers of wealth, and are, indeed, the chief producers. The patriarchal theory—that is, the theory that primitive society was from the first patriarchally constituted, and that the social relation between the sexes was essentially similar to that to which we are accustomed—is indeed, apart from any other evidence than that of primitive economic facts, a fantastic unreality. The visionary picture of a primitive patriarchal ruler of dependent women who have no economic value or power except their sex has no basis except in late myth and superficial speculation.

Before the development of private ownership and where productive capacity is the sole source of economic power, the situation is the exact reverse; the advantage is entirely on the side of the women. The productiveness of the hunter can never go beyond hand-to-mouth subsistence; scarcely ever, in fact, can it afford a continuous and reliable means of subsistence. The preservation of meat, all wealth from the soil, all industrial production which is susceptible of accumulation, appertains to the sphere of the sedentary woman. Hence it is that when once private property develops all such property is in her

hands, and even before that development, economic control is collectively in the hands of the women and not of the men.

The Magical Origin of Queens

The mysterious power, which was thus originally an attribute of
the women of the royal family and not of the men, was not in its origin
political or administrative, but was, as Sir James Frazer has shown, of
a magical or magic-wielding nature; and it was that magical power
which was transmitted by the women, or rather was primitively possessed exclusively by the women of the royal family. . . .

The character of primitive and archaic sacred monarchies affords
a strong confirmation of the conclusion to which we were previously
led, that magic and priestly functions were originally exercised by
women. The power of sacred monarchs and of priesthoods, which is
so important an element of established agricultural civilisations, is
founded upon magical attributes which originally belonged prescrip-
tively to women and are regarded as being transmitted through
women. Agricultural religions have developed out of rites and beliefs
that were as much the particular domain of the women as the plying
of their wooden hoe and the watering of the seeds which they planted.
The cults which those primitive priestesses served were addressed to
powers that derived their significance from their association with the
functions of women. Those conclusions take us a long way from the
assumption that women have had little or nothing to do with the
development of religious ideas.

The Great Mothers

In accordance with their primary function as 'the real husband of
all women' and source of all fertility, primitive lunar deities are
predominantly masculine; the moon is a man and the sun is commonly his wife. . . .

In primitive cosmic myths, moreover, the moon, though a male,
is, as has been seen, generally associated with a female deity. In
matriarchal societies it would be an inconceivable incongruity that a
masculine personage have no mother. The metaphysical notion of a
self-begotten god does not enter into the conceptions of primitive
theology. A male god may very well have no father, but it would be
opposed to the most fundamental notions of a primitive society that
he should be without a mother. Generation begins with females, not
with males; women procreate by immaculate conception, men do not;
a mother is indispensable, a father is not. Primitive moon-gods, accordingly, have usually a mother. . . .

She is essentially the Mother of God. And accordingly it is her
enduring, her eternal character, persisting through all vicissitudes,
which is most prominent. . . .

Those characteristics of the Mother of God render her, from the first, a more generalised deity than the moon-god. Although personified abstractions are foreign to primitive thought, the primal Mother partakes from her very nature of an abstract character as the prototype of motherhood in general. She is not only the Mother of God, or as the Algonkin called her, emphasising her primal and timeless character, the 'Grandmother,' she is also generally the Mother of mankind, the primal Mother. The Mother of American or of Melanesian myth is indistinguishable from the First Woman, the Eve of Semitic myth. Often each tribe or clan has its eponymous primal Mother. The Pelew Islanders, for example, have an ancestral goddess for each family, and each tribe amongst them has its eponymous mother. They are the active and important deities of the people, and their cult constitutes the bulk of the religious practices and sentiment in those islands. All good and bad luck comes from the Mothers; as mother of the tribe; she is, above all, the dispenser of food. One of the most common attributes of the Great Mother is accordingly the control of animals and of the food supply.

Document 7: Robert Graves

The White Goddess *by the English poet, Robert Graves (b. 1895) is undoubtedly one of the most influential works of recent times to stimulate the imagination about a female-centered culture in ancient times. A historical novelist as well as poet, Graves also has stimulated a genre of novels, such as Mary Renault's* The King Shall Die,[29] *which seek to recreate matriarchal culture and religion in ancient times, such as in Minoa in the late second millennia B.C. A recent book of the same genre, which shows the conflict between matriarchal and patriarchal culture in the time of the rise of Christianity in early Britain of the age of Arthur, is Marion Z. Bradley's* The Mists of Avalon.[30] *These books, as well as Graves's own account of the Goddess, are primarily influenced by James Frazer's classic study of tribal religion,* The Golden Bough.[31] *Graves ranges across both classical and ancient British myth in his quest for that Goddess who he regards as the muse of poetry.[32]*

The Goddess is a lovely, slender woman with a hooked nose, deathly pale face, lips red as rowan-berries, startlingly blue eyes and long fair hair; she will suddenly transform herself into sow, mare, bitch, vixen, she-ass, weasel, serpent, owl, she-wolf, tigress, mermaid or loathsome hag. Her names and titles are innumerable. In ghost stories she often figures as 'The White Lady', and in ancient religions, from the British Isles to the Caucasus, as the 'White Goddess'. I cannot think of any true poet from Homer onwards who has not independently recorded his experience of her. The test of a poet's vision, one might say, is the accuracy of his portrayal of the White Goddess and of the island over which she rules. The reason why the hairs stand on end, the eyes water, the throat is constricted, the skin crawls and a shiver runs down the spine when one writes or reads a true poem is that a true poem is necessarily an invocation of the White Goddess, or Muse, the Mother of All Living, the ancient power of fright and lust—the female spider or the queen-bee whose embrace is death.

. . . As Goddess of the Underworld she was concerned with Birth, Procreation and Death. As Goddess of the Earth she was concerned wtih the three seasons of Spring, Summer and Winter: she animated trees and plants and ruled all living creatures. As Goddess of the Sky she was the Moon, in her three phases of New Moon, Full Moon, and Waning Moon. This explains why from a triad she was so often enlarged to an ennead. But it must never be forgotten that the Triple Goddess, as worshipped for example at Stymphalus, was a personification of primitive woman—woman the creatress and destructress. As the New Moon or Spring she was girl; as the Full Moon or Summer she was woman; as the Old Moon or Winter she was hag. . . .

In Europe there were at first no male gods contemporary with the Goddess to challenge her prestige or power, but she had a lover who was alternatively the beneficent Serpent of Wisdom, and the beneficent Star of Life, her son. . . . The Son, who was also called Lucifer or Phosphorus ('bringer of light') because as evening-star he led in the light of the Moon, was reborn every year, grew up as the year advanced, destroyed the Serpent, and won the Goddess's love. Her love destroyed him, but from his ashes was born another Serpent which, at Easter, laid the *glain* or red egg which she ate; so that the Son was reborn to her as a child once more. . . .

There are as yet no fathers, for the Serpent is no more the father of the Star-son than the Star-son is of the Serpent. They are twins, and here we are returned to the single poetic theme. The poet identifies himself with the Star-son, his hated rival is the Serpent; only if he is writing as a satrist, does he play the Serpent. The Triple Muse is woman in her divine character: the poet's enchantress, the only theme of his songs. . . . She is the mother of all things; her sons and lovers partake of the sacred essence only by her grace.

The revolutionary institution of fatherhood, imported into Europe from the East, brought with it the institution of individual marriage. Hitherto there has been only group marriages of all female members of a particular totem society with all members of another; every child's maternity was certain, but its paternity debatable and irrelevant. Once this revolution had occurred, the social status of woman altered: man took over many of the sacred practices from which sex had debarred him, and finally declared himself head of the household, though much property still passed from mother to daughter.

... This second stage, the Olympian stage, necessitated a change in mythology. It was not enough to introduce the concept of father-hood into the ordinary myth, ... A new child was needed who should supersede both the Star-son and the Serpent....

Then he became the Father-god, or Thunder-god, married his mother and begot his divine sons and daughters on her. The daugh-ters were really limited versions of herself—herself in various young-moon was full-moon aspects. In her old-moon aspect she became her own mother, or grandmother, or sister, and the sons were limited revivals of the destroyed Star-son and Serpent. Among these sons was a God of poetry, music, the arts and the sciences: he was eventually recognized as the Sun-god and acted in many countries as active regent for his senescent father, the Thunder-god. In some cases he even displaced him. The Greeks and the Romans had reached this religious stage by the time that Christianity began.

The third stage of cultural development—the purely patriarchal, in which there are no Goddesses at all—is that of later Judaism, Judaic Christianity, Mohammedanism and Protestant Christianity. This stage was not reached in England until the Commonwealth, since in mediaeval Catholicism the Virgin and Son—who took over the rites and honours of the Moon-woman and her Star-son—were of greater religious importance than God the Father.... This stage is unfavou-rable to poetry; ... though the Thunder-god has been a jurist, logi-cian, declamator and prose-stylist, he has never been a poet or had the least understanding of true poems since he escaped from his Mother's tutelage.

The Return of the Goddess

While rejecting, in a literal sense, Hitler's claim that "The Jews are the cause of our troubles," Graves nevertheless asserts that this is true in a larger sense.

Yet neither Frazer nor Hitler were far from the truth, which was that the early Gentile Christian borrowed for the Hebrew prophets the two religious concepts, hitherto unknown in the West, which have become the prime cause of our unrest: that of a patriarchal God, who refuses to have any truck with Goddesses and claims to be self-suffi-cient and all-wise; and that of a theocratic society, disdainful of the pomps and glories of the world, in which everyone who rightly per-forms his civic duties is a 'son of God' and entitled to salvation, whatever his rank or fortune, by virtue of direct communion with the Father.

Protestantism was a vigorous reassertion of these two concepts, which the Jews themselves had never abandoned, and to which the Mohammedans had been almost equally faithful. The Civil Wars in

England were won by the fighting qualities of the Virgin-hating Puritan Independents, who envisaged an ideal theocratic society in which all priestly and episcopal pomp should be abolished, and every man should be entitled to read and interpret the Scriptures as he pleased, with direct access to God the Father. Puritanism took root and flourished in America, and the doctrine of religious eqalitarianism, which carried with it the right to independent thinking, turned into social egalitarianism, or democracy, a theory which has since dominated Western civilization. We are now at the stage where the common people of Christendom, spurred on by their demogogues, have grown so proud that they are no longer content to be the hands and feet and trunk of the body politic, but demand to be the intellect as well—or, as much intellect as is needed to satisfy their simple appetites.

As a result, all but a very few have discarded their religious idealism, Roman Catholics as well as Protestants, and come to the private conclusion that money, though the root of all evil, is the sole practical means of expressing value or of determining social precedence; that science is the only accurate means of describing phenomena; and that a morality of common honesty is not relevant either to love, war, business or politics. Yet they feel guilty about their backsliding, send their children to Sunday School, maintain the Churches, and look with alarm towards the East, where a younger and more fanatic faith threatens.

What ails Christianity today is that it is not a religion squarely based on a single myth; it is a complex of juridical decisions made under political pressure in an ancient law-suit about religious rights between adherents of the Mother-goddess who was once supreme in the West, and those of the usurping Father-god. . . .

There are two distinct and complementary languages: the ancient, intuitive language of poetry, rejected under Communism, merely misspoken elsewhere, and the more modern, rational language or prose, universally current. Myth and religion are clothed in poetic language; science, ethics, philosophy and statistics in prose. A stage in history has now been reached when it is generally conceded that the two languages should not be combined into a single formula, . . . Christianity has little chance of maintaining its hold on the governing classes unless the historical part of ecclesiastical doctrine can be separated from the mythical: . . .

However, such a religious change is impossible under present conditions: any neo-Arian attempt to degrade Jesus from God to man would be opposed as lessening the authority of his ethical message of love and peace. Also, the Mother-and-Son myth is so closely linked with the natural year and its cycle of ever-recurring observed events in the vegetable and animal queendoms that it makes little emotional appeal to the confirmed townsman, who is informed of the passage of the seasons only by the fluctuations of his gas and electricity bills or by the weight of his underclothes. He is chivalrous to women but thinks only in prose; the one variety of religion acceptable to him is a logical, ethical, highly abstract sort which appeals to his intellectual pride and sense of detachment from wild nature. The Goddess is no townswoman: she is the Lady of the Wild Things, haunting the wooded hill-tops—. . .

The Protestant Churches are divided between liberal theology and fundamentalism, but the Vatican authorities have made up their minds how to face the problems of the day. They encourage two antinomous trends of thought to co-exist within the Church: the authoritarian, or paternal, or logical, as a means of securing the priest's hold on his congregation and keeping them from free-thinking; the mythical, or maternal, or supra-logical, as a concession to the Goddess, without whom the Protestant religion has lost its romantic glow. They recognize her as a lively, various, immemorial obsession, deeply fixed in the racial memory of the European countryman and impossible to exorcize; but are equally aware that this is an essentially urban civilization, therefore authoritarian, and therefore patriarchal. It is true that woman has of late become virtual head of the household in most parts of the Western world, and holds the purse-strings, and can take up almost any career or position she pleases; but she is unlikely to repudiate the present system, despite its patriarchal framework. With all its disadvantages, she enjoys greater liberty of action under it than man has retained for himself; and though she may know, intuitively, that the system is due for a revolutionary change, she does not care to hasten or anticipate this. It is easier for her to play man's game a little while longer, until the situation grows too absurd and uncomforable for complaisance. The Vatican waits watchfully. . . . nor are any other revivals of Father-god worship, whether ascetic or epicurean, autocratic or communist, liberal or fundamentalist, likely to solve our troubles; I foresee no change for the better until everything gets far worse. Only after a period of complete political and religious disorganization can the suppressed desire of the Western races, which is for some practical form of Goddess-worship, with her love not limited to maternal benevolence and her afterworld not deprived of a sea, find satisfaction at last.

A FEMINIST VISION OF WOMEN'S RELIGION

Document 8: Charlotte Perkins Gilman

Charlotte Perkins Gilman was a descendant of eminent American literary families; her great aunt was Harriet Beecher Stowe. A leading feminist and Socialist, Gilman's major book was Women and Economics *(1898). She also wrote an early feminist utopian novel,* Herland, *in which she imagined a society inhabited only by women who reproduce by parthenogenesis.*[33] *In her major work on religion,* His Religion and Hers, *she links male religion with death and other-worldliness and female religion with the promotion of life on earth.*[34]

Two

Man the hunter, Man the warrior,
Slew for gain and slew for safety,
Slew for rage, for sport, for glory—
    Slaughter was his breath;
So the man's mind, searching inward,
Saw in all one red reflection,
Filled the world with dark religions
    Built on Death.

Death, and the Fate of the Soul;—
The Soul, from the body dissevered,
Through the withering failure of age,
Through the horror and pain of disease,
Through raw wounds and destruction and fear;—
In fear, black fear of the dark,
Red fear of terrible gods,
Sent forth on its journey alone,
To eternity, fearful, unknown—
    Death, and the Fate of the Soul.

Woman, bearer; Woman, teacher;
Overflowing love and labor,
Service of the tireless mother
    Filling all the earth;—
Now her mind awakening, searching,
Sees a fair world young and growing,
Sees at last our real religion—
    Built on Birth.

Birth, and the Growth of the Soul;—
The Soul, in the body established;
In the ever-new beauty of childhood,
In the wonder of opening power,
Still learning, improving, achieving,
In hope, new knowledge, and light,
Sure faith in the world's fresh Spring,—
Together we live, we grow,
On the earth that we love and know—
    Birth, and the Growth of the Soul.

What was the principal crisis in the life of primitive men?

Their occupation was in hunting and fighting. They lived mainly by killing other animals, either to eat or to avoid being eaten, and in addition to these indispensable activities they varied the excitement by killing one another. After the slow, patient hours of tracking, of lying in wait, the strenuous pursuit, the fierce combat, came the climax—death.

Death was the event, the purpose of his efforts, the success, the glory. If he was the dead one, we cannot follow further; but if he triumphed and saw his "kill" before him, here was cause for thought. The death-crisis, coming as the crashing climax to the most intense activity, naturally focused his attention on the strange result. Here was something which had been alive and was dead; what had happened to it? The creature which had fled so swiftly or struggled so violently had now stopped. It didn't go any more. The body was there as before, but something had gone from it. What was it? Where had it gone? The mind of the killer pitched forward, as it were, along the road of the spirit which had fled.

Here we have a simple, an obvious explanation of our early interest in death. . . . It is easy to see how deep and strong became the death-complex in the primitive mind. By the time that definite religious ideas could be formulated, their direction was irrevocably determined. No small effort will be required in the mind of to-day to change that direction.

In one religion after another, as they appear and spread over the earth, we find the continuing imprint of that old death-complex. . . . Since the great religions of the world have one and all come down to us through the minds of men, and since the fighting male kept the world confronted with death of old and young, manufacturing widows and orphans with a lavish hand, this constant horror still monopolized the attention of religious thinkers. . . .

Christians are but too ready to admit how far they fall short of the teachings of their Master, fondly attributing their shortcomings to the fact that their standards are so high; whereas the failure is due to the persistence of the same old death-complex, to the focusing of their hope and purpose on "the other life," with the gross neglect of this one.

Pursuing the evidence of dominant masculinity in the evolution of religions, we find another conspicuous proof—the guileless habit of blaming women for the sin and trouble of the world. One religion after another shows scorn of women, making no provision for their pleasure in heaven, sometimes denying that they have souls at all.

What would have been the effect upon religion if it had come to us through the minds of women?

If we are to trace our engrossing interest in death to the constant fighting and killing of early man, to the fact that death was the crisis in his activities, the significant event, rousing him to thought, what other interest are we to look for in the life of woman? What crisis set her mind at work, and what would have been its influence on religion?

The business of primitive woman was to work and to bear children. Her work was regular and repetitive.

Yet her life held one crisis more impressive, more arousing far, than man's; her glory was in giving life, not in taking it. To her the miracle, the stimulus to thought, was birth.

Had the religions of the world developed through her mind, they would have shown one deep, essential difference, the difference between birth and death. The man was interested in one end of life, she in the other. He was moved to faith, fear, and hope for the future; she to love and labor in the present.

To the death-based religion the main question is, "What is going to happen to me after I am dead?"—a posthumous egotism.

To the birth-based religion the main question is, "What must be done for the child who is born?"—an immediate altruism. . . . With birth as the major crisis of life, awakening thought leads inevitably to that love and service, to defense and care and teaching, to all the labors that maintain and improve life.

The death-based religions have led to a limitless individualism, a demand for the eternal extension of personality.

. . . The birth-based religion is necessarily and essentially altruistic, a forgetting oneself for the good of the child, and tends to develop naturally into love and labor for the widening range of family, state, and world. The first leads our thoughts away from this world about which we know something, into another world about which we know nothing. The first is something to be believed. The second is something to be done. . . .

Birth-based religion would steadily hold before our eyes the vision of a splendid race, the duty of upbuilding it. It would tell no story of old sins, of anguish and despair, of passionate pleading for forgiveness for the mischief we have made, but would offer always the sunrise of a fresh hope: "Here is a new baby. Begin again!"

To the mother comes the apprehension of God as something coming; she sees his work, the newborn child, as visibly unfinished and calling for continuous service. The first festival of her religion would be the Birth Day, with gifts and rejoicings, with glad thanksgiving for life. . . .

The peculiarity of all death-based religions is that their subject-matter is entirely outside of facts. Men could think and think, talk and argue, advance, deny, assert, and controvert, and write innumerable books, without being hampered at any time by any fact.

Thus we have almost from the beginning the assertion of authority which it was impossible to disprove, a sin to doubt, an indiscretion even to consider. Then, with this arbitrary basis, the minds of men soared happily in unbridled conjecture, and built up colossal systems of thought, racial "complexes" or states of mind, which were imposed upon the world. . . .

We see even to-day the movement of those quaint reactionaries called "Fundamentalists," who advance as the "fundamentals" of the Christian religion the group of miracles and legends surrounding the origin and death of Jesus, laying no emphasis whatever on what it was he taught. Here is the persistence of the death-based theoretical "faith" as apart from a system of living. Its main appeal is for belief, that the believer may so be "saved" in the "other life." . . .

But thought of God aroused by birth leads along a different road, to a different conclusion. . . . From hers would naturally arise such thoughts as these:

"Here is Life. It comes in installments, not all at once. The old ones die, the new ones come. They do not come ready-made; they are not finished, they have to be taken care of. It is a pleasure to take care of them, to make new people. . . .

What a wonderful thing is Life! Life everlasting, going on continuously, in steps, the ever-coming new ones taking the place of the old worn-out ones—how beautiful! . . .

Life, always coming, through motherhood, always growing, always improving through care and teaching! And this new product of life— not babies but things, useful things, made beautiful—what a joy life is! . . .

"What does it all? What is behind it all? Who is the first Mother, Teacher, Server, Maker? What Power under all this pouring flood of Life? What Love behind this ceaseless mother-love? What Goodness to make Life so good, so full of growing joy?" . . .

Thus would the woman's mind have reached the thought of God. . . .

The whole feminine attitude toward life differs essentially from the masculine, because of her superior adaptation to the service of others, her rich fund of surplus energy for such service. Her philosophy will so differ, her religion must so differ, and her conduct, based on natural impulses, justified by philosophy and ennobled by religion, will change our social economics at the very root.

NEW RELIGIOUS MOVEMENTS

Document 9: Ella Wheeler Wilcox

Ella Wheeler Wilcox was the favorite poet of the New Thought movement. Her poetry was light and sentimental, although she scandalized Victorian sentiments with her volume. Poems of Passion (1883). Her New Thought essays reflect the typical belief in a good human self rooted in the divine Spirit and the power of the mind to shape one's total physical and psychic well-being.[35]

A Worn Out Creed

I have a letter from an "orthodox Christian," who says the only hope for humanity lies in the "old-fashioned religion."

Then he proceeds to tell me how carefully he has studied human nature, "in business, in social life, and in himself," and that he finds it all vile—selfish—sinful.

Of course he does, because he studied it from a false and harmful standpoint, and looks for "the worm of earth" and "the poor, miserable sinner," instead of the *divine man*. . . .

A "Christian" of that order ought to be put under restraint, and not allowed to associate with mankind.

He carries a moral malaria with him, which poisons the air.

He suggests evil to minds which have not thought it.

He is a dangerous hypnotist, while pretending to be a disciple of Christ.

The man who believes that all men are vicious, selfish and immoral is *projecting pernicious mind stuff* into space, which is as dangerous to the peace of the community as dynamite bombs.

The world has been kept back too long by this false, unholy and blasphemous "religion."

It is not the religion of Christ—it is the religion of ignorant translators, ignorant readers.

Thank God, its supremacy is past. A wholesome and holy religion has taken its place with the intelligent progressive minds of the day, a religion which says: "I am all goodness, love, truth, mercy, health. I am a necessary part of God's universe. I am a divine soul, and only good can come through me or to me. God made me, and He could make nothing but goodness and purity and worth. I am the reflection of all His qualities."

This is the "new" religion; yet it is older than the universe. It is God's own thought put into practical form.

Woman's Opportunity

The greatest opportunity to better the world which can come to any woman is through the experience of maternity.

The power of prenatal influence which a mother possess is awe-inspiring to realize. . . .

Women have been strangely ignorant of this vital truth; until recent years it has not been considered a "proper" theme for tongue or pen, and to-day the great majority of young women marry absolutely uninformed upon the subject of prenatal influence. . . .

It is just here that the "New Thought" can perform its greatest miracles of good.

Even the woman who has not been enlightened upon the law of

ante-birth-influence will, if a true disciple of the Religion of Right-living, bring healthy and helpful children into the world, because her normal state of mind will be inclusive of those three qualities; and her continued and repeated assertions of her own divine nature will shape the brain of her child in optimistic and reverential mould. . . .

Continual assertions of a mother that her child will be all that she desires it to be, will wear away the stone of inherited tendencies, and bring into physical being a maleable nature wholly amenable to the after influences and efforts she may bring to bear upon it.

It is a tremenous responsibility which rests upon the woman who knows she is to be a mother of a human being.

A hundred ancestors may have contributed certain qualities to that invisible and formless atom which contains an immortal soul, yet the mother's mind has the power to remake and rebuild all those char-acteristics, and to place over them her own dominating impulse, whether for good or ill. . . .

Every expectant mother should set herself about the important business God has entrusted her with, unafraid, and confident of her divine mission. She should direct her mind into wholesome and opti-mistic channels; she should read inspiring books and think loving and large thoughts. She should pray and aspire! and always should she carry in her mind the ideal of the child she would mother, and command from the great Source of all Opulence the qualities she would desire to perpetuate.

And they will be given.

Document 10: Katherine Tingley

Katherine Tingley led the Theosophical Society of America from 1896 until her death in 1929. Her best known achievement was the theosophical community at Point Loma, California, which, however, did not long survive her demise. A philanthropist, pacifist, and pro-moter of the arts, Tingley made her International Theosophical headquarters both a school and a center for wide-ranging humanistic concerns. Her school promoted what she called the Râja-Yoga (mean-ing Royal Union) theory of education, which stressed the balance of physical, mental, and spiritual faculties.[36]

I discovered even as a child that the essential need of humanity is a deeper expression of love for every human being. I grew up in this thought, living in a little world of my own; but my opportunity to declare myself did not come until I met, under very remarkable circumstances, William Quan Judge, who was H. P. Blavatsky's Successor as Leader and Teacher in the Theosophical Movement.

He told me of H. P. Blavatsky, who had already passed away, and showed me her book called *The Secret Doctrine*. I was then grown to womanhood, and when I read that wonderful book, and later read her other books, that women's life became to me a glorious and sacred memory, that had come out of the past and would stay with me forever. It fired my blood, warmed my heart; and stirred my mind all these years under persecution, in order that I might tell my story to the world. And that is how at last I came to found the Râja-Yoga School at Point Loma.

The secret of the Râja-Yoga system, for those who know how to apply it, is: gentleness, kindness, firmness, never allowing a child to give way to a temper or to have its own way in anything that is wrong, but patiently helping it to see what is right and directing its energies into useful channels. Cross words on the part of the teachers are not allowed; and never are the pupils punished.

Even our little ones of six and seven years of age very soon learn that they have two natures, and they can and do explain in a rather wise way, yet very childishly and beautifully, the difference between these two natures. We strive never to ingrain into them any ideas that will overstrain them. We keep them close to Nature. They grow up just like the flowers grow, under wise supervision.

The Râja-Yoga education, among other things, gives to the child an opportunity *to find itself,* and to find true knowledge within itself.

Let us teach humanity the true story of Nature; that when the body dies—being physical and material and of the earth only,—all that belonged to the body returns to its material elements; but the well-spring of man's being, the enlightener, the invigorator, the great life-giving urge, the spiritual soul, is part of Eternity and cannot die, but goes on and on upon its evolutionary journey. Nature is very gentle and kind and allows us to leave behind us all sad memories.

It is a fact that humanity has been moving along half-asleep ever since the time when Christianity was established. In saying this it should be remembered that true Theosophists find much in Christianity that is very beautiful, and much of this was found also in the Pagan religions; but many of the forms are not accepted. The forms of the Christian religion were fashioned by the minds of men. Let us not question their motives; let us assume that they did it for the benefit of humanity. But a religion that constantly reminds one of his sins, of his mistakes, and of his weaknesses, appeals principally to the negative side of man's nature, especially when the effort is forever repeated to have him realize that the only way by which he can be 'redeemed' is by resting all hope of spiritual advancement upon faith alone or on a power outside himself.

Let it be remembered that true Theosophists are never disposed to belittle Jesus. We look upon him as a great Initiate; we bow to the divinity of his nature; we have learned that he was one of the few great men who, at different epochs, have arisen to a position where they have consciously known their essential divinity and have lived in it and have rejoiced in it, smiling with complete trust in it. . . . the saving power of the divine that was in him is in all of us, if we could only reach it, if we could only be aroused and awakened, as Jesus was, if we would look forward and accept the spiritual heritage that belongs to all humanity.

With this conception, and with a conviction of the truth of the sacred doctrine of Reincarnation, which gives man opportunity after opportunity in his different lives, at the various stages of his progress, we can face the inmost weaknesses of our own natures with the bright picture ever before us of the godlike qualities lying hid in man. But these must be aroused, developed, accentuated, if man is to advance in self-directed evolution.

Man cannot face the universe with that quality of trust that is the working of the spark of divinity within him, until he is generous enough to see that some of this same spiritual life is in all humanity.

What Theosophists are trying to do is to arouse humanity as a whole; to awaken it, so that it may not waste so much time in despair, so many incarnations in its long turns and twists off the path, while living without the knowledge of Theosophy.

Today, *now*, this very moment, is an appropriate time for man to invoke something new and better within himself. He cannot help others until he believes in himself. He must know the inner quality of his divine nature; he must feel its presence constantly—its support, its inspiration. Verily, he must feel that inner urge which accentuates the fact that all men are immortal; that inner urge which makes humanity like unto a host of young gods traveling along the path to perfection.

Document 11: Harriette Curtiss

Harriette Curtiss was cofounder with her husband of the Order of Christian Mystics and the Curtiss Publishing Company in Washington, D.C., which published most of her books. A Christian theosophist, Curtiss uses the figure of Isis in her book, The Voice of Isis, *to symbolize the divine female principle which has been suppressed and distorted through the ages of male domination and which must now reemerge in the emancipated woman to "uplift the race."*[37]

The Egyptians recognized and adored the Productive Principle, both in Nature and in man, under the symbol of Isis, the Universal Mother, the power of bringing forth in humanity the Divine Child or The Christ. The title of this volume indicates that its teachings are designed to bring forth in humanity a new conception of the spiritual life through the development of the Mother-love, that divine feminine-principle of the Soul which brings forth in the daily life.

Isis was also called "Mother of God," the "Celestial Virgin" and the "Queen of Heaven," just as her counterpart, the Virgin Mary, is among Christian peoples, and was usually represented carrying in her hand the *crux ansata*. It was none other than Cyril, Bishop of Alexandria, who openly embraced the cause of Isis and anthropomorphized her into Mary, Mother of God. While we do not worship Isis or Mary as a personality, yet we recognize that which they symbolize. For it is only by a recognition of the Mother-principle of Love and Compassion that we can bring forth The Christ-child individually in our hearts and lives, and collectively in humanity. . . .

The time has come when woman must take her place as the Priestess of the Most High, the Revealer of Purity and Truth to man. She it is who must lift the corner of the veil that hides the face of the Divine Mother, Isis. Isis is called the Divine Mother because hers is the force, both in Nature and humanity, that brings forth. She is spoken of as having seven veils, alluding to the protection thrown around the sacred mysteries connected with the bringing into manifestation of the creative force (God-the-Father) sent out through the masculine expression. The seven veils are the mysteries upon the seven planes of consciousness and manifestation. . . .

Since through the ages woman has been made the plaything of man and taught to use her powers to entice and beguile him, as the only method by which she could attain her ends, in this new woman's era she is confronted with the task which her training makes most difficult, *i.e.*, the facing of herself and her real motives. For she must turn her feminine powers of love, intuition and beauty to the upliftment of the Race instead of to the beguilement of man that she may satisfy her vanity, love of conquest and desire for creature comforts. Although man, being the positive pole upon the earth-plane, by his superior physical powers has throughout the ages enslaved woman, still woman, upon the more subtile [sic] plane of desire, has dominated and enslaved man. Hence it is woman who must break the shackles, first of her own desires and then for the Race. . . .

In the *Bible* we read of the stone that was rejected by the builders, but which, through the power of The Christ is to become the chief stone of the corner. But this mystic stone can not be perfected and become the cornerstone of the Temple of the New Humanity until its two halves are united, until the positive letters of one fit into the negative characters of the other and the two are fused into one through the power of The Christ.

. . . Until this cycle in the world's history every system of religion and exoteric philosophy has rejected the feminine stone and either taught the absolute separation of the sexes—generating women in convents and men in monasteries—or has in some way rejected woman and forced the stones to remain separate, even to the extent of denying to woman a Soul and barring her from Paradise except to minister to man's desires. The day of the fulfillment of the prophecy is now dawning, and those who can grasp the significance of the blending of the two tables of the Law have a great work to do, that the coming sixth sub-race may lay this chief cornerstone, upon which alone the Temple of Humanity can be erected by the Sixth and Seventh Great Races.

... And until woman awakens to her responsibility and understands her real mission, *i.e.*, her power to play upon man's heart, stimulate his noble aspirations and thus lead him to the heights of spiritual attainment instead of into mere physical union without love, she will continue to be the slave she is today in spite of any political or social liberties she may obtain.

It is woman who must lift up the world's ideas of the sex-force from the mire and degradation of man's misconceptions and give this great power its proper place in the Temple of the Living God (the body) as the highest expression of the Divine in man. Just as it was woman who gave to man the apple of discord, so must woman pluck the golden apples that grow at the top of the Tree of Life and give them to man to eat.

The natural outgrowth of these karmic conditions is unrest and dissatisfaction in marital relations. The woman-question is a burning one. Many are eager for political freedom, some few as eager to prevent it. But the political side of the question is but a bubble upon the surface of the greater question of the unification of the two tables of stone, ... Then it will be seen that neither man nor woman is superior, nor can either, by any possibility, rightfully usurp the place or perform the duties of the other; in fact, neither one can fulfill the whole Law without the harmonious blending and co-operation of the other.

Man is the positive expression of the Law on the physical-plane, but negative upon the spiritual-plane. Hence, it was necessary that he dominate during those stages of evolution which the conquering of the rude outward conditions of physical life were of prime importance to the welfare of the Race. In the united life of the family to him belongs the conditions of the outer world, the physical labor, the fighting, the providing for the protecting of the home, the execution of that which is planned by the two, in fact, all outward manifestations of the Law.

... True woman is positive upon the spiritual-plane, where man is negative, and negative upon the physical-plane, where man is positive. To her belongs the control of all those questions which deal with the higher life. She must use her intuition in the directing of all activities pertaining to the altruistic side of life, just as man uses his reason in worldly affairs. She should be man's moral and spiritual monitor and should be his source of inspiration and spiritual help. The two should work co-equally in all matters.

... No business or worldly affairs should be carried on without the inspiration and moral sanction of woman, and no feminine plans be carried out without man's active help and co-operation in making them positive and practical on the earth-plane. In other words, woman, while she cultivates her intuition, love, sympathy and spiritual aspiration, should have those qualities balanced by reason, logic, courage and common-sense. Man, while cultivating the positive qualities of courage, reason and executive ability, should balance them with love, sympathy and intuition. ... so should the perfect blending of man and woman make this earth a fertile field for the perfect evolution of the New Humanity. Only thus can the two tables of stone fit into each other and be fused by the power of The Christ into the chief stone of the corner, upon which the fire of Divine Love may act co-equally to transmute it into pure spiritual gold.

MATRIARCHAL RELIGION AND THE REBIRTH OF RADICAL FEMINISM

Document 12: Elizabeth Gould Davis

Elizabeth Gould David was born in 1910 in Kansas and received her B.A. from Randolph-Macon College in Lynchburg, Virginia. As a librarian in Sarasota, Florida, she made a speciality of ready "old and neglected books from past civilizations and lost worlds."[38] She was particularly interested in the higher status of women in ancient civilizations. Her major publication, The First Sex, *synthesized much of the matriarchal tradition of Victorian anthropology, sociology, and history of religion to represent to the woman's movement that was rising in the 1970s a vision of women's original power. Like Graves, she believes that the "return of the Goddess" is essential for the rescue of modern civilization from chaos. Grave's approval of her work is indicated in the jacket quote on the 1971 Penguin edition of her book: "The present intolerable world situation . . . cannot even begin to ease until the basic argument of Elizabeth Gould Davis's* The First Sex *is accepted by all schools and universities."[39]*

In original myth, ... there is an original Great Goddess who creates the universe, the earth, and the heavens, and finally creates the gods and mankind. Eventually she bears, parthenogenetically, a son who later becomes her lover, then her consort, next her surrogate and finally, in patriarchal ages, the usurper of her power. In the measureless eons of her exclusive reign, however, she inaugurates civilization in all its aspects. Under her rule the earth enjoys a long period of peaceful progress during which time cities are built, law and justice are instituted, crops are planted and harvested, cattle are domesticated for their milk and wool, fire is discovered and utilized, the wheel is invented, ships are first constructed, and the arts, from ceramics and weaving to painting and sculpture, are begun.

Then suddenly all is ended. Paradise is lost. A dark age overtakes the world—a dark age brought on by cataclysm accompanied by a patriarchal revolution. Nomads, barbaric and uncivilized, roving bands of ejected, womanless men, destroy the civilized city states, depose the queens, and attempt to rule in their stead. The result is chaos. War and violence make their appearance, justice and law fly out the window, might replaces right, the Great Goddess is replaced by a stern and vengeful God, man becomes carnivorous, property rights become paramount over human rights, woman is degraded and exploited, and civilization starts on the downward path it still pursues.

Such is the theme of all myth—from the Golden Age of the Greeks and Romans to the Garden of Eden of Jew and Christian, the Happy Hunting Ground of the American Indian, and the Avaiki of the Polynesians—all ending in a fall from paradise and in utter failure. . . .

When man first resolved to exalt the peculiarities of his own sex, muscularity and spiritual immaturity, he adopted the policy that reality meant tangibility and that what could not be seen or touched did not exist. . . . By discrediting the mystic power of woman, man cut himself off from the higher things, the "eternal verities" the sense of which had distinguished him from the lower animals. By crushing every manifestation of supersensory or extrasensory truth and worshiping only sensate matter, man made of himself a mere biological organism and denied to himself the divine ray that once upon a time woman had revealed to him. . . .

Her animal body, however, remained a necessary adjunct to the new physical man, and he set about to remold her from his own base material into a mere biological organism like himself—a fit mate, a help "meet" for him—his biological complement. Through the long centuries he succeeded in brainwashing her to the belief that she was indeed made from his rib, that she was formed to be a comfort to him, the receptacle of his seed, and the incubator of *his* heirs, who were the perpetuators of *his* name.

Thus the sacred flame of her primordial and divine authority was banked and dampened and finally smothered almost to extinction. Throughout the Arian and Piscean ages of strife and materialism, man's denser nature held sway while woman's etheric light lay hidden under the bushel of masculine domination.

We are on the threshold of the new Age of Aquarius, whom the Greeks called Hydrochoos, the water-bearer, the renewer, the reviver, the quencher of raging fire and of thirst. . . . Today, as then, women are in the vanguard of the aborning civilization; and it is to the women that we look for salvation in the healing and restorative waters of Aquarius.

It is to such a new age that we look now with hope as the present age of masculism succeeds in destroying itself, as have all its predecessors in the incredibly long history of civilizations. . . .

The rot of masculist materialism has indeed permeated all spheres of twentieth-century life and now attacks its very core. The only remedy for the invading and consuming rot is a return to the values of the matriarchates. . . .

The ages of masculism are now drawing to a close. Their dying days are lit up by a final flare of universal violence and despair such as the world has seldom before seen. Men of goodwill turn in every direction seeking cures for their perishing society, but to no avail. Any and all social reforms superimposed upon our sick civilization can be no more effective than a bandage on a gaping and putrefying wound. Only the complete and total demolition of the social body will cure the fatal sickness. Only the overthrow of the three-thousand-year-old beast of masculist materialism will save the race.

In the new science of the twenty-first century, not physical force but spiritual force will lead the way. Mental and spiritual gifts will be more in demand than gifts of a physical nature. Extrasensory perception will take precedence over sensory perception. And in this sphere woman will again predominate. She who was revered and worshiped by early man because of her power to see the unseen will once again be the pivot—not as sex but as divine woman—about whom the next civilization will, as of old, revolve.

American Indian Women and Religion on the Southern Plains

KAY PARKER

The religious attitudes and beliefs of American Indian women are in large measure an unknown. In the sizable body of recorded material on Indian religion, any significant mention of women is rare because, in general, the religious roles of women have been secondary to those of men. Particularly rare are firsthand accounts of women's religious experiences. This can be explained in part by the relatively late spread of literacy among Indians, and also by the fact that religion is viewed as a private matter to be shared only by one's people.

The language barrier has been quite formidable, especially for the bearers of native religions. More than once I have been told by an individual that it was impossible to express "the right words" in English. Yet, carefully recorded oral history comes closer to revealing the true complexity of Indian religious attitudes and beliefs than any other available documentation. Therefore I have depended heavily on oral history for this chapter.

The material is limited to the geographical region known as the southern Plains,[1] where much of Indian culture remained intact quite late into the century. It is here that the most interesting and unique manifestations of American Indian religion of the past century can be found. This is primarily attributable to an unusually high concentration of Indian population with greatly diversified languages and cultures. Of six Indian linguistic families in North America (north of Mexico) still being spoken as late as 1940, four could be found in this area.[2]

Another important factor is that the tribes that inhabited these lands, for the most part, were here not by choice but as a result of white policy. Their demoralization from loss of freedom was gravely deepened by dispossession, as Indians became virtual prisoners in alien lands. Dejected and broken in spirit, they sought alleviation in traditional, new, and sometimes syncretic forms of spirituality.

The land of the southern Plains was considered to be less desirable than that east of the Mississippi. It began to be populated by a policy of Indian removal in the early 1800s, when tribes in the northern states of Ohio, Illinois, and New York were moved by various methods involving force, threats, cajolery, and treaties.[3] The passage of Andrew Jackson's Indian Removal Act in 1830 legitimized and accelerated removal. The climax of the movement came during 1838 to 1839, with the removal of five southern nations—the Cherokees, Creeks, Choctaws, Chickasaws, and Seminoles—in one of the most poignant tragedies in American history, the "Trail of Tears," a journey during which one-fourth to one-half of the Indians died from starvation, exhaustion, and exposure.[4]

The nomadic Plains and seminomadic Prairie tribes who had freely roamed and hunted in the Plains for more than a century proved to be more elusive. With the advent of the California gold rush in 1849, as whites began to push through the heart of the Plains Indians' buffalo range, conflict became inevitable. Raids, skirmishes, and battles quickly developed into a full-fledged war. One by one these tribes were militarily subdued. By the end of 1875, most of the hostilities had ceased and all tribes were confined to reservations.

Reservation life meant the end of an autonomous existence for Indians. They lost all control of their political, educational, health, and welfare conditions to the United States. Outward manifestations of native religion, which had been important integrating forces for many centuries, were now prohibited. Not until the passage of the Indian Reorganization Act of 1934 was this restriction officially reversed.

Many Indians, however, continued to practice their native religions in secret, and sometimes in open defiance of governmental policy. Their perseverance enabled many elements of aboriginal religion to be preserved through the years of religious oppression.

Christian missionary activity among Indians, which had begun as early as the sixteenth century in the Southwest by the Spanish and in the Northeast by the French, hastened to fill a perceived vacuum. The thrust was dual: to Christianize and to civilize. Against this background of accelerating change and widespread disillusionment, pan-Indian movements emerged that incorporated elements of both native and Christian religions.

The changing mosaic of American Indian religion in the past century has been enormously diverse. While a few pockets of traditional forms have stubbornly resisted outside influences, many religious rituals and beliefs have become variously syncretized. Therefore, in the three categories of documentation that follow (native religions, Christianity, and pan-Indian religions), there is considerable overlapping of material.

NATIVE RELIGIONS

Native religion is so thoroughly integrated into the everyday life of the traditional Indian that it cannot be conceptualized as being separate from other aspects of culture. Religious attitudes and values permeate every important and mundane activity, whether in politics, medicine, subsistence activities, arts and crafts, recreation, or family relations. It is interesting to note that Indian languages do not have a word to denote religion, though many words exist to specify aspects of religion.[5]

The conception of a Supreme Being is generally vague, though it has become more pronounced with the influence of Christianity (Document 1). Instead, the focus is on a supernatural world, populated by gods and spirits present in varying degrees in human beings, animals, plants, and inanimate objects. Spirits and gods are imputed powers that may or may not be aided, abetted, or neutralized by certain practices and rituals (Document 2).

The belief in a personal guardian spirit and the vision quest is fundamental in Indian religion. The guardian spirit may be inherited, but most often is attained during an extended vision quest in which a supplicant fasts, bathes, and meditates to invoke the powers of the supernatural. Through visions or dreams, tutelary spirits bestow their powers and instruct the individual in rituals, songs, or a code for successful living. For the Plains Indians the vision quest did not necessarily involve a guardian spirit, because the transfer of supernatural power could occur without a spirit.[6]

Visions were sought at times of childbirth, disease, death, and young adulthood. Both men and women could receive visions, but men sought them more actively and frequently. If a woman were destined to be a shaman or medicine woman, then a vision experience was necessary.

The shaman, or religious and medical practitioner, held one of the most important roles in Indian society. Distinguished by being more religiously and mystically gifted than other vision seekers, the shaman served as the intermediary between the supernatural world and individuals.

Though shamanism was predominantly regarded as a male activity, there were many illustrious medicine women. But women could use their power only after passing menopause. The menstrual cycle was viewed as a sign of impurity, and menstruating women were therefore restricted in supernatural roles.

Sanapia, a Comancce Eagle Doctor who practiced doctoring until her death in 1968, was chosen and trained to be a shaman while in her youth. After a four-year period of rigorous instruction conducted by her maternal uncle, maternal grandmother, paternal grandfather, and mother, who was also a shaman, she was sent on a vision quest to attain supernatural power. Being successful meant that she was entitled to be a full-fledged medicine woman after menopause (Document 3).[7]

The prime responsibility of the shaman was the curing of illness, which extended to all disorders, whether physiological or psychological. As the medical knowledge of white doctors became increasingly available to Indians, the role of the shaman became primarily that of a psychiatrist. Two frequent ailments that required special powers for curing were "soul loss" and "ghost sickness" (Document 4).

Women were the herbalists. They knew which plants were efficacious, and collected specimens for healing. In most tribes there was a proliferation of women skilled in treating illnesses that were not considered specialized or serious enough to require a shaman (Document 5).

A daily reverence for sacred symbols and the creation of those symbols could be ascribed to many traditional Indians. Before undertaking an artistic endeavor, a ritual of prayers was frequently offered. For special tasks of magnitude, a period of fasting often accompanied the prayers. Though the ritualization considerably faded with time, a reverence is still maintained by many (Document 6).

Elaborate ceremonialism, which had been an important integrating force in prereservation days, was forbidden for more than half a century by the government. In 1934, when the ban was officially lifted, tribes began to revive the different ceremonies but in a more simplified, perhaps more relevant form. In the revivals, women continued to play a subordinate participatory role to Indian men as they had in earlier days. This was particularly true in the annual ceremonies that celebrated the beginning or the climax of the hunting season or the harvest year.

Women who had high ceremonial status usually acquired it by inheritance. Suzy Tallbear and Amanda Tallbear Bates, Arapaho women of the same family, were Keepers of the Sacred Pipe. The pipe, which was used to seal contracts between the various tribes or individuals of those tribes, was very hallowed—as was its keeper. In the annual Sun Dance, the unwrapping of the pipe was one of the most sacred of Arapaho ceremonies (Document 7).

The most significant role that women played in the ceremonials was covert. Every ceremonial required considerable preparation and organization. It was the women who were instrumental in planning the annual dances, making the costumes of the dancers, preparing the food, organizing the bingo games and handgames, monitoring the giveaway,[8] and assuring the financial success of the gathering. The perservation of prestige roles for men in the ceremonies has been particularly important in the Plains area, where many of men's former economic roles have been lost or weakened.

CHRISTIANITY

Upon the confinement of Indians to reservations and the subsequent prohibition of native religions, a proliferation of Protestant and Catholic missions and churches could be found. Their thrust was strongly evangelical. Missionaries believed that conversion of the Indian to Christ and to civilization was a process necessary for living on the same continent with Indians. Though a number of Indians converted to Christianity, many remained indifferent or openly hostile.

In a national survey conducted in 1921, 26 Protestant denominations reported 32,164 communicants and an additional 80,000 adherents in 597 churches and mission stations. Roman Catholics had 61,456 members in 149 missions and 336 churches, chapels, and schools.[9] Proportionately, the number of Christians to the total Indian population was approximately 38 percent. If followers were counted, then that proportion would double.[10] Though this undoubtedly varied by region, degree of success was measured by how one defined a Christian.

The varied successes of the denominations can be explained by four factors. First was the degree to which denominations considered elements in Native American religions complementary to Christian teachings. In a 1950 national sampling of members of different denominations, Episcopalians (81 percent), Congregationalists (75 percent), Catholics (75 percent), and Methodists (53 percent) believed Indian elements and Christianity could be compatible. On the other hand, Southern Baptists (100 percent), Reformed (89 percent), Presbyterians (70 percent), and American Baptists (55 percent) believed that Indian faith and ritual were "almost entirely irreconcilable" with Christianity.[11]

The latter attitude is graphically expressed in the photograph of two Presbyterian missionaries visiting an aged Kiowa-Apache woman in 1898. In predominantly white churches, members were often quite candid about their fears of accepting Indians as church members (Document 8).

The most successful denominations were those that established missions or churches solely for Indians. The Thlewarle Baptist Indian Church established for the Creeks had a Christian service that used the Creek language. The scheduling of services also accommodated itself to the needs of Indians (Document 9).

A second factor that influenced the success of some denominations over others was how closely the Christian services approximated Indian rituals. The Pentecostal religion was particularly appealing to some Indians, because it was reminiscent of the Ghost Dance religion that had swept the Plains area in the late nineteenth century (Document 10).

The third factor related to the level of education and personality of the individual. Indians who were educated had contact with white culture and were more likely to feel comfortable with Christianity.

Reverend Hazel Botone, a retired Kiowa Indian Methodist minister born in 1898, was raised in a home in which both parents were educated. Her mother, an interpreter, frequently came in contact with both cultures. From the time of Reverend Botone's baptism at the age of eight to today, she has never doubted her faith. She also maintains an understanding and acceptance of other Kiowas who have remained true to the Indian religions. She married a Kiowa who was not a Christian; but, as a result of her influence, he converted and became an ordained minister in the Methodist Church. After his death she was ordained, and served as pastor of two churches until her retirement (Document 11).

A fourth factor was the degree to which denominations utilized native leadership. Protestants reported in 1921 that they had 160 white ministers, 268 Indian ministers, and an additional 550 native helpers in Indian missions and churches.[12] In 1972, however, the use of Indian leadership was reported to be only 22 percent among Protestants, but 50 percent among Catholics.[13]

Christianity made a greater impact among Indian women than men, largely because of its social and educational aspects. Even in the missions and churches, where membership was equally divided between men and women, the women were more actively involved. They met several times during the week to participate in sewing bees, to learn food preservation methods, and to read Bible verses, which provided a cohesiveness that was a natural extension of the historical and cultural bonding of Indian women.

As the century has progressed, there have been two important positive changes for Christianity. First, the evangelical emphasis has become less important for many denominations. Instead there has been an increasing focus on social welfare and health needs of Indians. Second, the newly recognized importance of preserving elements of native cultures has considerably subdued Christianity's insistence on total change for Indian followers.

PAN-INDIAN RELIGION

Pan-Indian religion had its beginnings in the late nineteenth century, when Indians' survival and way of life were gravely endangered. Allotment (which in the Dawes Act of 1887, gave Indians individual plots of land on which to pursue agricultural endeavors) met with limited success, particularly among Plains Indians. As hunters they had lived and hunted by cooperation. As agriculturalists, they were expected to live and farm individually. They were neither adequately informed nor technically prepared to manage farms. Not only did they lack the regimentation necessary for farming, they had no desire to be farmers. The Indians who were experienced agriculturalists found that they had be given an amount of land insufficient to make a living. The consequence of the legislation, for the most part, was to continue the impoverishment of Indians.

Dejected, they yearned for and were particularly vulnerable to the promise of supernatural deliverance, which came in the form of a messianic movement. The resurgence of the Ghost Dance religion that swept the Plains during 1889 and 1890 was led by the prophet Wovoka, who promised destruction of the white man, a return of the buffalo and old tribal ways, and a millennium in which the Indian dead would return and all would be free from misery, death, and disease.

The movement became a more hysterical, militant cult among Plains Indians than among other tribes. They began to wear ghost shirts, which were purported to be impervious to bullets. At all-night gatherings the participants would dance until they collapsed into a trancelike state. The end of the movement was assured with the infamous massacre of three hundred Sioux at Wounded Knee in 1890, though it continued sporadically until approximately 1900.[14] However, it could not have succeeded because it was an unrealistic movement of revolt against white culture rather than one of accommodation.

The Ghost Dance fostered close contact between the tribes, a mutual antagonism against whites, and a unanimity of Indians across tribal lines. Within this state of heightened pan-Indianism, a new movement, religious in character, diffused rapidly across the Plains. It was the Peyote Cult which would become the most significant and widespread pan-Indian religion of the twentieth century.[15]

Centered on the southern Plains, the cult grew and disseminated rapidly. Because of the extensive intertribal contacts and activities, Oklahoma held a "special magnetism" for tribes outside the state.[16]

The Peyote Cult was a remarkable blending of Christian and aboriginal religions. Using the Christian church as its model, it adopted the basic tenets of Christian ethics, though the degree varied from tribe to tribe. The religion centered on the use of peyote as a sacrament. Peyote, a genus of *Cactaceae*, has a pharmacologically soporific effect that produces a euphoria and corresponding reduction of pain in the body. In the Peyote Cult it served primarily as a psychological support substance.

As quickly as peyote groups organized, state and federal officials sought to suppress them on legal grounds—first on the basis that peyote was a drug in the same classification as liquor, and later as a narcotic. As a defensive measure, several tribes formed a larger organization in 1918 and invoked their constitutional right to freedom of religion. Though the federal government finally accepted the use of peyote within the framework of a religious ritual, it also hesitated to interfere with state laws. Legal prohibitions and restrictions at the state level continued selectively through the 1970s. Today only one state, Texas, restricts the buying, selling, and possession of peyote.[17]

Peyote rituals in the various tribes were similar. Services were held on Saturday nights in a special tipi or other indigenous structure. Inside a crescent-shaped earthen mound held the sacrament, peyote. The communicants gathered round a sacred fire kept burning by the fireman, a man who had special tasks in the all-night meeting. In some tribes his wife also had duties to perform (Document 12).

Women did not attend peyote meetings in most tribes as frequently as men, if at all, unless they had an illness that might be helped by the peyote. But in other tribes, even though women did not hold leadership positions, they attended regularly and sometimes strongly influenced the ritual procedures (Document 13). Women were frequently known as the ones who best remembered the songs.

In all tribes, the two roles always designated for women were the bringing of water into the ceremony in the morning, which was considered to be an honor, and preparing the special breakfast (Document 14).

In 1955, the Peyote Cult officially became the Native American Church. Membership today, which is concentrated on the northern and southern Plains, numbers anywhere from 15 percent to 40 percent in many tribes. An exact membership is exceedingly difficult to obtain because the churches are loosely confederated and membership is not formalized. Communicants may attend only several meetings in a lifetime and consider themselves adherents, or they may attend regularly.

American Indians, and Indian women particularly, are among the most spiritual of peoples anywhere, though few adhere exclusively to a native religion, Christianity, or a pan-Indian religion. With an all-embracing view of what God and religion should be, their religion tends to be pragmatic. The preference for syncretic manifestations of religion should be interpreted as an important, viable way for Indian women to retain their distinctive cultures while accommodating themselves to an alien, industrialized world.

Two Presbyterian missionary women, Misses Tynesdell and Lincoln, visiting a Kiowa Apache woman (1898), Anadarko, Oklahoma. [Photo courtesy of the Philips Collection, Western History Collections, University of Oklahoma Library.]

The Cheyenne medicine woman, Neomia, with Naomi Wilson and child, (1914). [Photo courtesy of the Walter S. Campbell Collection, Western History Collections, University of Oklahoma Library.]

Myrtle Lincoln (Howling Buffalo), Arapaho Indian (c. 1967), at Concho Agency. [Photo courtesy of the Division of Manuscripts, Western History Collections, University of Oklahoma Library.]

Amanda Tallbear Bates, an Arapaho pipe-keeper (1980). [Photo courtesy of the Rose Birdshead Collection, Western History Collections, University of Oklahoma Library.]

Baptism in pond at the Deyo Mission, Rev. H. F. Gilbert officiating. [Photo courtesy of the Gilbert Collection, Western History Collections, University of Oklahoma Library.]

Indian Women's Altar Society, Fairfax, Oklahoma. [Photo courtesy of the Sooner Catholic Magazine Collection, Photographic Archives, Western History Collections, University of Oklahoma Library.]

Indian women presenting a gift to Bess Smith, wife of Bishop Angie Smith, at the dedication of the Mahsetky Methodist Mission (c. 1940); from right to left: Bess Smith, Mrs. Smith (Ponca Indian), Hazel Botone (Kiowa), Dana Chibitty (Comanche), Mae Jay (Apache). [Photo courtesy of the Hazel Botone Collection, Photographic Archives, Western History Collections, Oklahoma University Library.]

Documents: American Indian Women and Religion on the Southern Plains

NATIVE RELIGION

Document 1: Kiowa Prayers

Prayers were an integral part of all Indians' lives long before they came in contact with Europeans. In this account, Reverend Hazel Botone, a retired Kiowa Indian Methodist minister, describes the aboriginal Kiowas' conceptualization of prayer.[18]

Our people, the stories say, we came from somewhere up north. Our people were named after White Bear, a lot of animals up north. Our people prayed and gave sacrifices, not knowing who the true God was. No one told them. They don't read. They don't speak English.

Our people have always been praying people. That's one thing we had all the time, praying. You see a tree begin to leaf, you pray. You see somethin' comin' up—flowers—whatever it is. They always say, "Whoever makes it, whoever someone is that is making these things to come up—the grass—someone that is makin' the grain to come." They knew there was somebody powerful behind it. So they always prayed, always, but they didn't say, "Our Father in heaven," or "Dear God in heaven, listen to my prayer."

Document 2: The Medicine Bundle

Every tribe had at least one "medicine bundle," which served as the physical locus for the supernatural treatment of disease. The bundle was made up of what appeared to be odds and ends of the medicine reserve. It was to be available to those who needed it.

The following account of Myrtle Lincoln, an eighty-two-year-old Arapaho woman, was given in an interview December 22, 1969. Her story centers on the special care and taboos of the medicine bundle.[19]

I don't know how many they had, but I know my mother-in-law had one. And we couldn't take the ashes out while that thing was in there. And it had a certain person that was blessed . . .to take it out. Nobody else couldn't touch that thing. My mother-in-law used to take it out before we take the ashes out. And we wasn't supposed to make a noise in there. And every morning when she gets up she'd take a hatchet and hit that tipi pole over there, so when those kids make a noise, well, it wouldn't bother that thing . . . She used to hit it . . . about four times and then . . . when these kids make a noise it wouldn't bother that medicine bag. Used to have to hit that pole every morning.

I don't know how she got it . . . at times she would get maybe tongue and then, you know, them shank bones, and put it on top of that medicine bag . . . She used to say she was feeding the spirit and then the next day she'd take it and cook it and we used to eat it.

It was just wrapped up . . . I never did touch it. I had a respect for that. I used to even keep my kids from running in and out from there.

They not supposed to open them unless they were all together and somebody make a pledge. It took lot of things for them to open them. Never did see it opened. When she handled that thing we had to keep the kids quiet. It wasn't just so you could go over there and pick it up and all that. She used to pray before she touch it. Now when she's going to bring it in she prays . . . to the Lord.

When asked what happened to the mother-in-laws's medicine bag, she answered:

I don't know . . . When the old man died and then she died, . . . none of us couldn't handle it. We left it at the house and I don't know who got it. I don't know who it could have went to. But my understanding was that Henry Lincoln and Chase Harrington—and there was a black man that used to stay around here. I guess they went after it and they sold it here in the drugstore. Here in Canton. And just think—all three of them were gone. One had a stroke and one didn't know where he was at. He was just out of his head. And he just talk until he died. And this black man, they had to take him to rest home. I guess he used to just scream and jump. See, that's what got them—because they bothered that medicine bag. And this Chase Harrington, he went to bed one night and he didn't *ever* get up again. He died in his sleep.

When asked if there were any reason why the medicine bundle would be opened, she explained:

If they made a pledge for some sick people—if their folks would get well, and they want this one to be painted with whatever paint was in them—in that bag. And they used to give horses and things and cook big dinner. And maybe inside of this sweat lodge, that's where they open it. Nobody ever had anything to do with it. They had a respect for it. They didn't make fun of it or anything. In a way they had a respect for that and . . . nobody used to talk about that. And now I'm crazy to be talking about it.

There [are] only two I knew something about. You know, I used to see them when they take care of them. And when they take them out—when they walk with them—they didn't walk fast. If you walk fast, well, the storm used to come up. They used to be easy with them.

Document 3: Vision Quest

Mary Poafybitty Neido, or Sanapia, the Comanche Eagle Doctor, tells about her vision quest at age seventeen. The four-day ordeal required fasting and solitary meditation while ghosts attempted to frighten and harass her to the point that she would renounce her medicine. She relates in this account what was expected of her. In spite of her failure to stay in the mountains for the required time, she passed the test and was declared a full-fledged medicine woman.[20]

Just sit around, don't eat. You have to go out there by yourself and pray. And then when you pray and then you come back . . . you have to go down to the creek and wash all your sins away, something bad in you. You have to go down to the creek and take a bath. And then they paint you . . . all your face with red paint, you know, that rock paint that they grind, they put it all over your face and your arms and your feet, from your knees down, they paint you up like that.

They gave all that medicine to me. They showed me and they told me how to run it and everything like that. They told me all about that before I fasted. You supposed to go way up there in the hills and sleep up there by yourself. But me I was afraid to go up there by myself. I was afraid to go up there, but you supposed to go up there in the hills, and pray and cry and talk and . . . somebody come to you. They say,

"Somebody will come to you way in the middle of the night. They going to push you and kick you and they do things like that, but don't get scared. Just lay there and let them do what they want to you—just kick you around and slap you and all that. They fighting you for your medicine. They don't want you to have that. It's ghosts."

That's what they said.

I said, "I don't want to go up there. Them ghosts might catch me."

That's what I told them. I didn't want to go out. I didn't go out there. I was afraid to sleep up there in the mountains by myself. I just go up there and come back.

Document 4: Ghost Sickness

Ghost sickness was not generally prevalent in the Plains area, but ghosts sometimes struck particularly vulnerable Comanche and Kiowa-Apache persons by deforming them. The following account, which was recorded on June 15, 1967, is that of Sanapia, in which she describes the victims of ghost sickness.[21]

[They had a] . . . twisted mouth and twisted eyes. Sometimes their eyes would go up on the left side this way and your mouth would be twisted the other way, and just look like your face get all twisted . . . They would be paralyzed on their arms, or the whole bottom half of their body and be twisted. And do you know what the Indians call that? They call it Ghost-Done-It. Ghost twisted person's face like that. In the night time they come right up on you. If you look at them like that they do that to you. The ghost. The Indians believe that. They believe they're ghosts.

When Sanapia agreed to treat a stricken individual, the person was required to bring a ritual payment consisting of dark green cloth, a commercially obtained bag of Bull Durham tobacco, and four corn-

shuck cigarette "papers." She here describes how the contract with the patient was sealed and then gives a detailed account of the treatment. If this treatment failed, she then offered prayers from the Bible. And if this did not get the desired results, she held a special peyote meeting for the patient.

They would get this leaf or corn shuck and they roll their cigarette with that Bull Durham smoke. They wrap it up and light it and they give it to me and say,

"Here take this smoke. Pity me and get me well. I'm tired of this face all twisted up, tired of my legs paralyzed. I can't walk, can't do nothing. I want you to pity me and get me well."

And so I take it. I get a puff on it four times, just four times, and I say,

"Alright , I'll pity you. I'll see what I could do for you . . . Go in there and wash your face and your hands and you come and I'll doctor you."

Chew that medicine and put in on your hands and rub it like that (between the palms) and rub their face with it and their hands—out of my mouth what I chew this medicine . . . Then I would blow this medicine on their face and I would doctor them. Today I doctor three times, and tomorrow I doctor them three times, that's six. And if it's real bad I go ahead and doctor them till I doctor them eight times.

So, I start—tomorrow morning and noon and supper, and the next morning I'm through with them. Take them out there before daylight, and I do all the Indian ways what my mother and my uncle told me to do . . . And in the morning when they get up they ain't a thing wrong with them. They alright. Their face get alright. Their mouth get alright. They don't slobber no more. And then you bring the coals to the front of the house wherever they are, or go to the fireplace and put that cedar on there, and there's another kind of medicine that we mix together and then we just tell whoever it is that's sick—bend over like that. They inhale all that smoke. Take that feather and put it over the fire like that and smoke that feather—that's eagle feather. And take that and smoke that and we fan them all over from head to feet—all over their body. Four this way and four that way and turn around and eight in the back and on top of their head like that. Just fan that bad stuff away from them. That's what that smoke for. And after they do that, they alright. They get well.

Document 5: Special Doctoring

A grandmother's special powers are described in this account by Richard Manus, a Cherokee, in an interview February 8, 1969.[22]

My grandmother was . . . what they call a witch doctor. And anytime they got an Indian in court, if he was an Indian, . . . they'd call my grandmother and she'd make tobacco and she'd have them smoking it in that courthouse. And she claimed that she mixing up that lawyer, the judge in that way. I know they said, (ninety)-five percent of them came clear anyhow. And they'd drop the cases or something. They'd never stick 'em. And I know that she'd go to every trial they had. They used her. And every trial they had, that's the way she went along. And I can look back now and see what she was doing and I presume I guess it was working. I don't know. It looks that a way to me now.

My grandmother was a mid-wife doctor. And she was a doctor of all trades. And right up there, right up above this spring, it's solid rock bottom and there's a place in there that's got a kind of wash stand like and a dish pan, but it's big. And I've seen her take people with running sores and all kinds. . . . And right yonder what I'm talking about now, she'd take them over there and she'd bathe them in there. And of course she'd take some kind of herb and when she got through bathing them, she'd wash them down with those herbs and she'd cure those people.

Document 6: Praying

Annie Hawk, a seventy-seven-year-old Cheyenne woman, relates the importance of prayer before beading or quilling. It is important to note here that Annie was a Baptist. From my long acquaintance with her, my perception is that her idea of "the man up there" was a fusion of the Christian God and the Great Spirit—which one was not important to her. The following account was given to the author in January 1977.[23]

My grandmother, my mother's grandmother *[sic]*, was a very important woman. She was selected by the Cheyennes. The others selected her to tan hides and make a tipi. That's because she was the oldest woman in camp, and the most respected. She tan a big bull hide and heifer hide, a yearling hide and calf hide—five hides she used to make that tipi. There was a few buffalo left then. That was before I was born—a long time ago—before my mother was born. I think in '77, that is 1877 or 1878. And before she started quilling, that is feather work with porcupine quills, she prayed for four days. And she didn't eat, fasted you know. And then she knew that everything was goin' to be alright. She knew the spirits wouldn't get mad or nothin' bad would happen. Then she spent a whole year quilling it.

That's what I do when I make special moccasins. Pray, that is, to the man up there. Say, some designs only women can wear and if somebody else gets 'em, I don't want nothin' bad happenin' to me. And [chuckle] sometimes I just pray for good luck.

Document 7: Arapaho Pipe Keeper

Rose Birdshead, daughter of Suzy Tallbear and sister of Amanda Tallbear Bates, Keepers of the Sacred Pipe, tells about growing up in a family which held an honored position in the Arapaho tribe. Here she describes the purpose of the pipe and its use.[24]

Amanda Bates was my sister. She was older than I was, about nine years. My mother passed the pipe on to her. She knew she was getting up in years and she knew that she would have to pass it to her daughter because it has to stay in the family. It went to her and then it was coming to me. They always have public acknowledgment of that, you know, like at some Indian gathering. They have dance and they recognize it, and I've never done that. But it is mine now.

They don't have the ceremonies anymore. You just know who the chiefs are. But they do not go through that ceremony about the pipe. They have a pipe, but they don't smoke it. When they made treaties, you know, or made peace with a tribe, that was their way of introducing themselves to the other tribe.

And everybody had one language, and that was the sign language. Everybody knew the sign language. That is how they conversed. That's how they knew about the next person even though they don't talk the same language. So that pipe was used for that. And then it was like anybody going into a real estate office or something or signing a binding contract. Well, this pipe represented the same thing in that order. Why you smoke with them, and that's an agreement and you cannot break it.

You have to handle that pipe like it's something sacred. We're not supposed to drop that pipe. They say it's an ill omen to drop it. It's the last thing down here the Arapaho tribe has. All the rest of the lodges and that is gone. But they held on to the pipe.

They used the pipe at the Sun Dance. There are priests, they call them, who are in charge of all that. They know their duties and the pipe is used more in there than you see it any place else. They use it all through the ceremony.

My mother had it. It was given to her when she was quite a young maiden. They choose them according to their backgrounds, and who they are. See her grandfather, her mother's father was—I don't say he's the greatest priest, but he was the oldest. And his name was No One Knows, because no one knows who he is or where he came from like that. So his name was No One Knows. He was a great priest. I hate to say great, because there is no great priest.

She grew up in, well to me, it must have been something wonderful, because when I was growing up my sister and, well, there were a lot of things we couldn't do. You know how young kids will go do something and think nothing of it. And we couldn't do those things and I used to wonder why.

And on Sunday, I was just a little girl then, I'd want to go swimming. Oh, the kids were just havin' a ball. And here come my mother just ready to give me a lickin'. I'd have to go back and clean up and put on a buckskin dress. I didn't know it was such a great honor to wear a buckskin dress. I hated those things. They were hot, them leggins and the fringes. You parade around them in the Sun Dance. And today I just think what a great honor it is to see these Indians, especially when they're so beautiful in them.

That's the kind of life I had. I rebelled. I was the one that rebelled. I wanted to do what everyone else was doing.

And of course we were brought up in the Christian way. We belonged to the northern Baptist church. My father was a deacon and he more or less helped take care of the services with us.

Amanda got into goin' to this church, active and in the women's club meetings. At that time they were really good. They taught you somethin', you know. Of course we learned all that in school, but you come out and you try to practice it when you get home, and that's what she done. She was teaching how to bead and how to do craft work that young people didn't know but wanted to learn.

I believe it was about '63 or '64 when my mother gave her the pipe, because you know my mother was able to be up and around then. The last two years before her death she wasn't able to go places. So she gave that over to her daughter. That is still a Sacred Pipe that the Arapahos hold.

She sat with the chiefs. When they go have their meetings and discuss something important that they had meetings about, she was with them. She always sat with the chiefs.

And the pipe, it was passed to me. I will pass it on to one of my daughters, not sons because, well, it first was passed to a lady. It couldn't pass to a boy. I've got three daughters, but the one I had in mind is—she just lives a few miles from me. That's who I had in mind. And I've got a younger daughter. You know she would be a fine person, such a nice outgoing person. But she clings more to the, you know, white way. My other daughter understands the Indian culture.

My sister was a beautiful person. And you know after she got that pipe, she never would get mad at anybody. No matter what happened, she would always be so calm. And that's kinda the Indian way, kinda sacred. She always took care of me, you know, took the responsibility. And because she was that way, that's why she was chosen. I was the one who rebelled. I just never could understand why my mother was so strict with us. I wish I had understood.

CHRISTIANITY

Document 8: Fears of Church Members

Mrs. Amos Stovall states the policy of the Presbyterian Church in Anadarko, Oklahoma, toward Indians who wanted to become members of the church. This data was collected for the Works Progress Administration in 1938.[25]

Emma, an Indian woman, wished to unite with the church. The session met with her for examination. She was rejected. She said she would abide by the church in so far as it did not interfere with her gods, for they had created the earth and everything and she could not turn against them.

And Annie Jones was the first Indian who came into the church on confession of faith, that is, on record. Care had to be taken in accepting Indians into the church.

Document 9: Thlewarle Baptist Church

The first Thlewarle Indian Baptist Church was built by the Creek Indians in Indian Territory in 1870. To accommodate families who attended church services that lasted all weekend, camp houses were built surrounding the church. The church, which was rebuilt in 1914, remains in use today. In this article from the The Chronicles of Oklahoma, *Sharon Fife, a Creek Indian, describes the participation of women in the church.*[26]

During the services, it is the custom for the men to sit on the south side of the church and the women to sit on the north side. The explanation given by the members is from the Bible which says that men and women should be divided.

The seating arrangement in the church is as follows. The pastor is seated behind the pulpit. All preachers attending are seated at the front wall of the church and the Christian women on the north. The class leaders sit in the first seven chairs from the pulpit on the women's side. On the fourth and eighth Sundays, the head deacon and the visiting deacon sit in a long chair in front of the pulpit. The head deacon sits in this chair at all meetings. The back rows of the church are for the visitors and members.

The women play a very important part as class leaders in the reinforcement of the stability of the church. There are seven class leaders who are the older and more experienced women of the church. Of these women, the oldest is the head. She sits in the chair nearest the pastor's pulpit. The head class leader is equal to the head deacon. Her permission must be given before many procedures concerning the church are possible. She is called *Hoktuke Emathla*—First Lady of the Church.

The most important job of Hoktuke Emathla is to make the Communion bread. This is made before sunrise, before the birds sing or other creatures stir. All must be still while the bread is being made. While she is making bread, she must be praying. If she does not, the bread will tell on her. If the two preachers presiding over the Communion have not been good, the bread will tell on them. This is the miracle of Communion.

On Saturday night before Communion, the women go into the woods to pray. The class leaders talk to and advise the women who want to join the church. They pray for Hoktuke Emathla before she makes the Communion bread. Four times they sing and pray before they return from the woods. While they are there, no one but the class leaders may talk.

Church services at Thlewarle are held in the Creek language. Creek bibles and song books are used during the services. Usually the preacher's voice can be heard fairly well at a distance. When the congregation sings, they seem to reach an ecstatic stage of being, and their beautiful songs can be heard within a radius of a mile or more. A musical instrument is not used.

The Friday night of the sixth week is Ladies Meeting. This is a day of fasting for the women. They begin from the time they arise until after the evening service. They fast for something that is spiritually desired, and are allowed to appoint the preacher for the day. Since it is their day, they are able to tell the men what to do—and they must do it. During the services the women are called upon to lead songs and pray. Sometimes the women lead songs in couples. This is done until all have participated, and then the men proceed to do the same. Usually, not many men attend.

After the prayers and songs are over, the pastor reads from the scriptures and gives the women words of encouragement and well wishing. The congregation lines up and shakes hands in fellowship, and services are dismissed for supper. The women prepare the food, then the preacher they have appointed for the day asks the blessing.

A typical baptism of a young Creek girl is described by the author.

When a girl expresses her desire to be baptized, the head class leader takes her outside and prays for her. She asks the girl whom she wishes to baptize her, and when she wishes it to be done. The girl is taken back into the church, and the class leader tells the pastor what she has decided. The announcement is made to the congregation.

The two main deacons are designated to look for the water. If the person desires to be baptized that day, the deacons begin looking for the water immediately. If the ceremony is to be the next morning, they will wait until sunrise. The water must be navel deep to the person being baptized. A stick is used to measure the depth, and when water is found of the prescribed depth, the stick is stuck into the creek bed as a marker. A piece of white linen is tied to the top of the stick. At Thlewarle, the people are always baptized in creeks or rivers because still or enclosed water will not cleanse a person's sins. It does not make much difference what season a person may want to be baptized. In 1965 the deacons had to chop through two inches of ice to clear a place to baptize a fifteen year old girl.

The whole congregation goes to the baptism. The creek that is generally used is about one-fourth mile into the woods down a hilly, rocky path. The church members walk four abreast into the woods to the water—two lines of men and two lines of women. The congregation stands on a high bank overlooking the water. The pastor, preachers, deacons, class leaders, and the young girl go to the lower bank.

A short service is held before the baptism. The class leaders then dress the girl. Four of the ladies hold up blankets to improvise a room for her. Three of the ladies help her change her clothes. A piece of white linen is tied around her head and waist as a symbol of purity. The class leaders then pray for the girl and advise her before she is taken to the water.

During the baptism, one of the deacons may assist the pastor. The remaining deacons usually are kneeling in prayer a few feet from the bank in the shallow water. After the baptism the deacons and class leaders usually walk into the water and shake hands with the new Christian. The girl is then brought out of the water, and the class leaders change her clothes. A prayer and a song is again given for her, and the meeting at the water is dismissed.

Upon arrival at the church the girl is seated in the center of the church (in the location of the Communion table). She leads a song and a prayer. The pastor encourages her, and tells her what she can do or cannot do. The class leaders advise her. She is talked to as if she were a new-born baby starting a new life. From this time on she will take her place with the Christian women on their side of the church.

Document 10: A Pentecostal Conversion

Myrtle Lincoln, an Arapaho woman, describes the similarities of the Ghost Dance religion and the Pentecostal religion in this 1970 interview. She vividly details her personal experience of getting the Holy Spirit.[27]

It seem like it's same way with this Pentecostal way. You know, they say they get the spirit and all that—that's the way these Ghost Dances used to do. There would be some jumping around shaking their hands—holding their hands up in the air. It's just like a Pentecostal. We always think it might be the same thing.

I heard these songs ever since I used to sing. I used to sing with my grandpa and my grandma—Sitting Bull . . . There was three men that used to dance with my grandfather—they used to have white sheets, you know—white sheets.

And the longer they dance—somebody over there be shaking, and they say, "She's getting the Spirit." They shake around, you know, just like these Pentecostals always hold their hands when they shake hands. That's the way it was. And they always fall. And when they get up, they always tell the story about heaven.

"I've seen my people . . . It's a good place, over there. Everything is green. Everything shines like gold.'

That's the way they used to tell. They used to, when they fall, when they get up again they used to tell their story, what they seen, but you might as well say their "dream". And it's just like—the way I look at it—it's just like this Pentecostal way. I seen one of these white women, you know, in Pentecostal, holler and just yell and jump around, and then pretty soon they fall to the floor and talk in tongues. And I think it's a wonderful way—the way they talk in tongues.

Now one time, over here, we had a church. and my boy was preaching. There was a man by the name of Reed, Park Reed. They were singing together. They were singing a special song. Boy, here was just like—just like pop corn, these women just pop up. We were way in there, and they just circle around and dance around and praise the Lord and everything. One woman fell. She's living yet. Down south there where she fell, and start talking. Oh, she was hollering, "Glory, Hallelujah!" And then pretty soon she talk Arapaho.

In Arapaho she said, "Father in Heaven, give us a blessing here. Bless our Indians. Show them the way."

That's what she said. I never will forget that.

I used to go to the Mennonite Church. That's where I was baptized. And when he (my son) start preaching over here, I used to go Sunday mornings, and sometimes some service at night. You know on Wednesday they have service and on Saturdays. And I'd go on Saturday night instead of Wednesday night. They used to have good services. And when they start, you know, start praising the Lord and everything, somebody getting the Holy Ghost, it was wonderful the way they used to do.

And when my second oldest boy got killed, I lost my voice. I couldn't talk. I used to just try to make signs for what I want. And I used to try to talk but I couldn't talk. So one Sunday, about a month after that, my son said, "Well, Mama, I'm going to take you Wednesday night. I done asked the people, the group, to pray for you. We're going to pray for you. So you will get your voice."

And I didn't want to go. "No," I shook my head. Then when he got ready, he told me to come on. And without me knowing it, I was already out, going with him. So we all went, my girls and my old man went.

And they start having their service. And then they told me to come to the altar and sit down. They said, "Come sit down."

They prayed for me, and oh, gosh, I tell you, I don't know when I went down, I guess I fell off the bench. They prayed for me, and I breathe and my boy was at the head and they said, "Say, glory, glory."

I try to talk—I couldn't talk. Then the longer I laid there, I said, "Glory, glory."

And they got me up and they told me to get up and tell how it was with me. And I thought I couldn't talk, but I come out of it and talk, and ever since then I can talk. And oh, that foam was just running out of my mouth, and boy had a handerchief, and he used it to wipe it off. And every time he wipe it off he used to say, "Heal, heal, heal, Lord," you know.

And my throat was clear and I could talk and I been talking every since.

Yeah, I did. You know, now a lot of people, they deny this Holy Ghost, but it's real. You can feel the spirit when the Lord is in the church with you. You can just imagine things how it is up in heaven. And when I got that Holy Spirit, I seen things that they preach about . . .

And they were singing a song you know—"there's an unseen eye watching you."

And I try to hold myself, you know, I start shaking. Try to hold on and I ask the Lord,

"I live my life up here, whatever you think it should be for me."

And I kept praising Him you know, and thanking Him, you know, for answering my prayers, so finally I fell. I was laying there. And well, they said I talk in tongues. But I didn't know what I said in tongues. But I seen where I was at—everything was green. Just green. And I look west and it was just like sunset, you know. Just kind of gold color like. I kept on, you know. So finally I guess I come to and I praised the Lord and thanked Him for giving me the Holy Ghost. He's done to me what the world couldn't do. That's what I said when I first got up. And then they told me to testify. I got up and testify. I told them that I was thankful that the Lord seen fit to give me the Holy Ghost, and give me the feelings he has given me.

Document 11: Faith in Methodism

In the following interview with the author, Reverend Hazel Botone, an eighty-five-year-old retired Kiowa Indian Methodist minister, relates important events in her young life which influenced her to become a Methodist. Then she tells how she later influenced her husband to become a Christian.[28]

I would have to say I went to school at Methodist School. There was two of us going. My sister and I both—she was six and I was eight and-a-half. It was a Methodist denominational school, a boarding school.

I don't think we came home til—I think a few days 'fore Christmas and no other time because I remember, they were tellin' us how we could be helpers, sunbeams or little workers for the Lord you know. And we got interested. It was in membership class that Ida Swanson had. She'd take us in her room. She had a little foldin', little small suitcase-style organ. And she taught us how to sing. And getting us ready to be on an Easter program. and what we could do to be a worker for Jesus, how we could do things. We wanted to sing for him. See, that's something that was explained to us.

A lot of times the others didn't speak English too well. She would stop, and she'd call on me and I'd tell them in Indian what she was saying.

"Now do you know it?"

You know, I'd keep asking them until they understood. And there was about my age, a Lucille Ware. She was the other one who was selected to sing. She was the leader, so it would be soprano. And I was the leader of the lower voices. And that's how she (the teacher) got us started. She'd teach us the things we could do when we become a church member. We decide from our own heart to become somebody that Jesus could use. There was certain songs we sang. There was a song about light—how we would be a light.

The songs were in English. That was the first thing I ever heard, I guess about membership class. I didn't know nothing about church membership or anything. And then it was Easter. There was three night meetings. Somebody else would come, and there were a lot of older people who would come and sing Kiowa songs, church songs. And some of them would pray. And then, on Sunday, there was another minister who came in to help. And that's when they baptized us.

And the next thing was at Old Man Gaukey's residence. He was a brother to my dad's own father, to Lone Wolf, to Spotted Bird. What I'm trying to say is, my second taste of Methodism was at his home. My Grandpa Gaukey was converted by the Methodist people when they came there. I imagine they did because he was kinda crippled. He became a Christian. And he'd sing. And he'd pray. Then he'd tell us what somebody had read to him and somebody had interpreted from the Bible. He couldn't read it himself. But there was some interpreter that got the understanding. He preached to us, you know, talked to us.

And we'd be swimming just a little ways from their home. Gaukey Creek. We'd have our swimming dresses on and were barefooted.

We'd be muddy. And then we'd hear the bell. He'd ring the bell. Oh, somewheres around eleven o'clock on Sunday. We'd go in just the way we were with our swimming dresses and our bushy hair.

And his wife was out there in the arbor. It was made with these posts. It was made kinda high and inside was where their cooking thing was and their table. And they got a sitting place. and she's got a fireplace and the kettle was hanging on chains. And on this side she's frying bread. She's got prunes cooking. We knew we was going to get a good dinner when we went to church. She had cow hoofs and what we call squaw corn cooking. Squaw corn is hominy, Indian style hominy. We knew we was going to get good food. So we was real ready.

I went to Rainy Mt. Kiowa Boarding School. That's where I met my husband. We got married in 1914, July. He wasn't a minister then. He came up from the wilds. His aunt became a Christian at Saddle Mt. Baptist Church. She would say,

"You little boys get ready. I'm gonna get everybody packed. We're gonna leave in the morning. I'm already gettin' my stuff ready. We'll get over there and we'll have Sunday School."

She was trying to get them there and my husband would say,

"I don't want to go. I'm a member of the Ghost Dance thing. Of course, I'm that kind of member."

His mother never would force him to go. The younger brother would go, but my husband won't. He was worshippin' in the Indian way. He was a member of the Ghost Dance group or the dance group which performed in the wintertime.

I was the one that always wanted to go to church, and I do. I never did fuss at my husband. He'd go to the peyote meeting every now and then, cause he was raised in that lifestyle when he was farming. If you're going to a peyote meeting you kinda have to take all day or all afternoon Saturday to get ready. And you get over there and you go in and you stay up all night and you sing all night. He always say, "It's too tiresome."

So he don't go unless he's invited to be the engineer or the fireman. He's the one who watches the fire and fixes the ashes against the moon.

So my husband took the car to the peyote meeting and the blizzard sort of thing came. But you know when I make up my mind to go to church or what I'm gonna do, I do it. I had everything covered over with thick canvases. So the next day I just took the canvas off and put the mattress in there. It was a buggy, a hack. So the little ones were in the back and my oldest son and I were in front. We took the seat out to fix it that way for them to lay down. It was cold. I had my cookin' all done and I covered that all up with some canvas and some thick rugs.

We went and it was the time when he was comin' back. I guess he was kinda getting' worried. Snow was still on the ground. He came and he met us. That's what kinda finished his thinking. He was selfish to take the warm car that way. And here she was with the children. She had took them to church where I belong and I should be. And she teaches the children. And a lot of time she has to teach 'em Bible verses. That's when I turned my feelings. Ask the Lord to forgive me. In the future he would try. He was gonna try. He always went with us then. After that pretty soon, he became a full-fledged church member.

Mathew Botone then became a lay speaker, a local preacher, and finally a fully ordained minister in the Methodist Church. For the next thirty-eight years, as a minister's wife, Hazel led the music, helped take care of the congregation's social and spiritual needs, and ministered to the sick. Their church for many years was the largest church in the Oklahoma Indian Methodist Conference. Then Mathew became ill.

I'd help with anything that was assigned for him to do. All of a sudden he had the awfulest headache and dizzy spells. Sometimes he'd fall. We didn't know that he had diabetes. I'd say,
"You'd just better stay. I'll go take care of your special prayer meetings or whatever it was. If there's a report to make, you get the figures out and read it to me."
Sometimes we had a conference at night, so I'd go in his place.

In 1961, after Mathew's death, Hazel became a lay preacher; and five years later she was ordained a minister in the Methodist Church. She outlines here what it was like to be a minister.

The most difficult thing I had to do was physical. It was the wood stoves. There was always no wood and especially when it rains, I had to take everything from here, cardboard boxes, gunny sacks, corn cobs wherever I could find 'em. This church just had a wood stove. Those were kinda hard because they were physical, physical work for me. I had to build the fires. If I'm taking children or somethin', I just kept the motor going and the heater, till I get the church warmed up. I'd get everybody off to help me sweep. I had to do everything.

I had two churches, little more over here than over there. That one was taken care of by John Chaino and some others and well, they just gave up. It just sat there idle.

My sister went with me and she said,
"I think our women workers and our youth, we had both, I think we can really clean it up and help you."

They kept going with me and before we knew it, we had everything cleaned up. And then we had another church.

I visited people, those that was sick and those in the hopsital. I'd take some of my canning or if I had a bunch of biscuits made, then I'd take them. I had quilting or tacking for all the ladies in the church basement.

Everybody respected me, you know. It wasn't any different than my husband. And spiritually, to my way of thinking, it was like one lady said,

"I just love to hear you read the Bible. You tell us some Kiowa and then you sing a song that matches. It just makes me float in the air."

PAN-INDIAN RELIGION

Document 12: Duties of the Fireman's Wife

Leonard Maker, an Osage, specifies the duties of the fireman's wife in the Native American Church ritual in this interview December 12, 1968.[29]

The first fireman was picked from an outstanding family or a prominent family, or to be prominent himself. And along with his duties his wife also had duties to perform. And one of her duties was while he was getting all this fire and drum and all this in place, well, her duties was to pound this peyote. The Osage always pound the peyote. And it would take her several times to pound the peyote. We had it in a wooden, sort of a wooden carved tree trunk that I imagine was made of hickory. It was tough and it was kinda burnt out and had a little hole in the holler of the trunk and they would pound this peyote. She would pound this peyote with a large instrument that sort of resembled a large post. It was kinda carved and had different shape and forms. It was a kind of a thing—you didn't just go out and pick up something—it had its special place in the ritual. And her duty was to do all this and all the time that she first began to handle the peyote, why her duty was to pray all this time for certain reason that they were having the peyote meeting or any other reason, pray for her folks or anybody's folks or the entire Indian race or the Osage people. It was her duty to pray during the time that she was handling the peyote, pounding it until she had it just the way she wanted. It was her duty to pray for people at that time. It was one of the beautiful things, we thought, that went into this peyote which we partake as more or less a sacrament.

Document 13: Women in Peyote Meetings

Arapaho women were more active in peyote meetings than women in many other tribes. Jess Rowlodge, an eighty-two-year-old Arapaho, tells how women participated in Arapaho, Apache, and Kiowa peyote meetings in this interview in 1967.[30]

We had one Arapaho woman that run her own meeting. Her

husband always run the meeting for her, but that was her form—
Arapaho way. Her name was Crooked Foot. She had her own way.
She learned it her ... self ... [from] the early Apaches and Arapahoes. She start her own form. Made her own songs, and all that
ritual inside was her own conduction. She always tell her husband just
how to conduct that meeting by her songs, and what came next, and
how to proceed with that fumigation and breakfast and the eating of
peyote and ... all that stuff. She told her husband just what to do. Of
course, he know it already, but she always kept him informed. And
then I know one time she brought water in and somebody told her,
    "Do this and that ..."
    "Wait, now," she said, "I know what I'm gonna do."
    She was kinda independent.
    But she always let her man run it. She'd sit by him. She had a pad
... This pad was about that square. Black on one side and white on
the other. And it had designs there ... I don't remember what those
designs were ... I think one of them was design of peyote. But
anyhow, before she sat down, when she put her bucket down and she
step back and throw that pad down, and she'd turn every corner over,
made a cross, white cross. She sat on it ... She'd offer prayer and
smoke herself and she'd hold out her cigarette ... and the fireman
would get up and come by and get that cigarette and take it to the
chief. And she, of course, would offer a prayer, and he give it to his
drummer to offer a prayer and his cedarman would offer a prayer.
And he give it back to the chief and he'd get up and put that smoke
in front of—in the ash part of the moon ... She knew all what she
was doing, all the way through.
    They say that [Apache women] had meetings of their own, but not
of any recordings that I've been told ... They always have a man
drummer. But they sing. Women sometimes make fire.
    The only woman I ever saw make repair of the fire during the
meeting, even though a man was fireman, was this Molly Dakone,
Kiowa. She was the wife of James Dakone, a Kiowa from Carnegie.
She was the daughter of Red Otter, a famous peyote man.
    Her husband used to run meetings. James Dakone was a good man
to run meetings. He's part Arapaho and Kiowa and Apache. She was
always there. The boys made fire. She'd volunteer and clean up the
fire during the night. And that woman could handle the fire with her
hands. She raked ashes in and fixed the ashes just all pretty. She
wouldn't get burned or nothing. They just notice it. Boy, but she'd
make pretty fire. She went all through the meetings. She'd be about
eighty-six years old last year.

    *Mr. Rowlodge was asked if in the early days, around 1889, very
many women attended peyote meetings, and if Arapahoes had any
feelings about women attending. He answered:*

Not very many. But there was more Arapaho attended, that is, locally that we know of. There's a lot of Arapaho women that attended. I've seen one woman just take peyote. She lived here. She'd take peyote dry or whatever state the peyote was, green or half-dry, just take it, inhale it and swallow it. Come out just like the rest of us. And offer the best prayers I ever heard. I sat with her lots of times at peyote meetings.

A man and a wife could go in there, but they don't let their children go in there, especially suckling kids. Like kids that aren't big enough to eat ordinary food. Especially those that's nursing. They wouldn't let them in. In fact, a mother, during the nursing child period, even though she's a regular peyote member, she wouldn't go there till the child was weaned. That's a Arapaho practice.

One Cheyenne woman used to sing. Her husband's name was Iron Turtle. I think she was a sister of the wife of Three Fingers—a famous Cheyenne chief that lived in El Reno. She's the only one that I heard singing. I heard she drummed, but I never seen her drum. I only heard her sing. But they all know the songs, and they sing with men, all of 'em. They sing with men. In fact the women preserve those songs better than the men do, I think.

When asked why the women didn't sing more often, he replied:

Well, not alone like men do, shaking the gourds, but they sing. They sing all the time but they weren't allowed to use the gourd or hold the cane. In fact, the Cheyenne custom that I know—that I learned from the old ones—a Cheyenne woman's not supposed to have anything to do with, or handle eagle feathers. That's against their tradition. I know when they're gonna fumigate them feathers . . . these ladies . . . gather all the feathers and fans all around there and then they get them in one pile and then they set them in front there and then the cedar is put in there and the chief gets up and fumigates them. Well, when these feathers come by, when Cheyenne woman comes to the eagle feathers, she just covers herself, and they have to skip her. But now, you take these girls at the pow-wows, young Cheyenne girls, they carry eagle feathers.

Document 14: Carrying Water for the Peyote Meeting

Women traditionally carried the water to the peyote meeting. In this interview, Alice Apekaum, Kiowa, elaborates on her role as water woman and the prayers that were offered for her.[31]

My father, when I was a little girl, put up a tipi. He wants to doctor some of us that been sick, you know, and he learn it from my grandpa. He put up a tipi, and when he put it up they all come in, all get ready for peyote meeting. Go in and made medicine and sing all night and pray.

So my father said,

"I would want my oldest daughter." There was four of us you know, two little ones and two sisters. "I want the oldest one to carry water for me in the morning for the men who sit up all night and drink that water. I want to use my feather on her so she can grow up in good health and she become a young woman and get married."

My mother said,

"In the morning I'll wake her up real daylight and then I'll dress her up, get her ready and get her water ready. At midnight a man could get the water and take it in because I can't wake her up at midnight."

And that's a rule, you know, they have. And the first meeting I knew was in the morning, and they woke me up at daylight and I go up, oh, must be about 8 or 9 years old. I started that way. Just like a church member you know. It's a Christian way like because they pray and sing and pray for me and all of us.

So they woke me up and my mother took me to the tipi. I didn't know what I as doing but they told me to come in and stand at the door toward the sunshine where the sun going to come up. So I did and my mother stood with me. And the head chief, you know was my father inside. He start praying for me. He prayed for me almost two hours. I was standing there holding my water to take it in. So when he got through praying, he said,

"Well, tell her to come in. You could come in with her if you want to."

So my mother carried the water for me and set by the door and they tried to tell me how to go about. He said,

"Go around on this other side and then sit down and make a cross mark."

So I did. They just tell me cause I didn't know. I was little. So I made a cross mark and set the water down. And then he began to pray again. He prayed long time, peyote chief, they call him. He got his feathers and he come over there where I was and he put feather over me and prayed for me a long time. And he said,

"Since she's too young to smoke cigarette, I want the one that's making fire smoke for her, pray for her.'

So they give the smoke to me—they call him the fireman, you know, sit at the door and make fire all night. They gave it to him. It was my cousin, Jack Sankidoti. So he prayed for me for long time and everytime he puff he prayed. He was praying for me, you know, to grow up and have a family and enjoy life and become old age and all that, you know. Prayed for my father and mother and rest of my sisters. There was eight of us. There was four girls and four boys . . . So he prayed and prayed and when he got through, he start passing the water so the first one got a cup and drink out of it, next one got a cup and drink, while they were singing, you know. The drum went around to each one and the one that's singing gets the gourd and sings. So they pass it all around you know. It go around all night like that and they drink and drink and when they get to the head chief, you know, he begin to pray again—pray for me again before he drink. And at the same time, they had a peyote in front.

"That's a medicine I'm taking," he said, "and I want children to grow up healthy."

That's what my father prayed. So they all had their feathers in their hands and when he sang they began to shake all the feathers. And he had a man to beat the drum for him and shake the gourd where we was singing. And he sings four songs. So we pass it to the next one, and the next one sang too with his partner. One hit the drum and sing with his gourd. It keep going and keep going till they get to the end and then he prayed again. The sun was coming up. He said,

"I'm going to pray again and if you want to, you can get your mother to take you to the house. Bring breakfast.'

So I went to the door and I went out and he prayed for me again. I was standing toward the sunlight. He prayed and prayed and when he got through, they start singing, you know. My mother took me in the house and they had breakfast all ready, pound meat, it's mixed with sugar, pound meat in a bowl, and they had prunes and cherries, ten cherries. And they had some candy that some people like to take in the morning. So they helped me and my brother to the door— always have bucket of water first, so I brought the bucket of water, set it in the front by the door. Set it right there, and put the meat there and the fruit and things like that.

So he start praying again. He prayed and prayed and prayed. When he got through he said,

"Alright, bring the food in.'

So they helped me and I took the water in first. And they pass it around again and everyone drink out of it. So he prayed for the water. Then he prayed for the food. So they pass it around. Everyone take a little of it. And they drink that peyote juice all night, I guess, and eat some peyote, you know, for their medicine. And he gets up and he fan him and hit them with the feathers he got. And they got their own feathers. When they sing they shake [them].

So they got through with breakfast, but they still got to sing for long while that morning. I got through, and another man prayed for me when they got through eating. So I went to the house. They got ready for dinner. They were still singing in there. I was free then, you know. I didn't know that it was pretty hard for them to do, to sit up all night and pray and sing.

Something Within: Social Change and Collective Endurance in the Sacred World of Black Christian Women

JUALYNE E. DODSON AND CHERYL
TOWNSEND GILKES

The twentieth century began for the black community, its people, and its churches in 1896, when the Plessey *versus* Ferguson decision capped the growing establishment of jim crow (laws segregating blacks from whites). This tide of post-Reconstruction betrayal choked off many hopes for black independence or political participation. Black women and men had thrust their educated leaders and "representative colored men" into public prominence only to see many of them rejected, murdered, and stripped of their public authority throughout the final two decades of the nineteenth century. The "separate but equal" decree of 1896 sanctified numerous state strategies of racial oppression, effecting economic depression, social separation, and political disenfranchisement.[1] "The problem of the twentieth century," observed W. E. B. DuBois, (leading black American writer) "is the problem of the color line." That color line, he stated, was both international and domestic.[2] It was a complex system of racial oppression composed of economic exploitation, political subordination, social denigration, and segregation that was enforced by legal and extralegal violence. For black Christians, 95 percent of whom resided in the South, jim crow represented some degree of institutional sin and an everyday reality. The majority of these black Christians were women, and their diminished status due to gender was no handicap to the ferocity with which they opposed jim crow.[3]

When Baptist educator, convention musical director, and hymn writer Lucie Campbell penned the words to her classic, "Something Within," she intended a musical representation of the almost indescribable yet pivotal experience that leads to public profession of faith in the majority of black churches.[4] If anything characterizes the role of black women in religion in America, it is the successful extension of their individual sense of regeneration, release, redemption, and spiritual liberation to a collective ethos of struggle for and with the entire black community.

The ties that bind the black community together exist primarily because of the vigilant action of black women. Black women are, in a very profound sense, the "something within" that shaped the "culture of resistance,"[5] the patterns of consciousness and self-expression, and the social organizational framework of the local and national expressions of community. Within movements such as the Sanctified Church, which sought to preserve distinctive aspects of black religious and aesthetic expression, women were the primary movers and shakers.[6] The overwhelming importance and pivotal position of black women in all aspects of community organization—education, civil rights, organized labor, business, politics, religion, the professions, and club work—earned them the greatest accolades and the most pernicious stereotypes. In a racist society, their battle against the color line was heroic; in a sexist society their achievement against so many odds was threatening and deviant. Near the turn of the century, Frances Ella Watkins Harper insisted "slavery made us tough";[7] and that toughness was targeted in a variety of negative ways. Regardless, the black women of the twentieth century were the sources of community endurance—the "something within that holdeth the reins"—enabling black people to resist and to hope.

Campbell's song also etched a concise portrait of the role of black women in mobilizing their communities to see justice and to demand social change. Armed with an Afro-Christian imagination that included a justice-oriented reading of the King James Bible, black women also became the "something within that banishes pain." Acting both as comforters and advocates, black women mobilized to eliminate their own suffering as well as the suffering of their men and their children. More often than not, it was the consciousness conerning their children—sons, daughters, nephews, nieces, or fictive kin—that fueled careers in public activism. In *Lifting as They Climb,* a volume that documented the origins and growth of the National Association of Colored Women (later the National Association of Colored Women's Clubs), club women insisted that "as colored women" who had suffered they were unable to be "blind to the suffering of others."[8] The universalism that characterized black women's understanding of a proper women's movement was reflected in the statement of Josephine St. Pierre Ruffin at the "first National Conference of Negro Women in America" in Boston, Massachusetts, in 1895. She declared, "Our woman's movement is a woman's movement in that it is led and directed by women for the good of women and men, for the benefit of all humanity. ... We want, we ask the active interest of our men; ... we are not alienating or withdrawing, we are only coming to the front, willing to join any others in the same work ... and inviting ... others to join us."[9]

The impact of black women can be seen in such organizations as the YWCA with its current "one imperative" to "eliminate racism ... by any means necessary."[10] Black women's public role emerged as an all-encompassing paradox. The maintenance of community integrity was an inherently conservative role. At the same time, the political struggles to eliminate suffering and to "crusade for justice"[11] at local and national levels were expressions of a radical thrust. Any description of the roles of black women in their communities and, therefore, in their churches must incorporate an understanding of this seeming contradiction. Black women's roles in community struggles are not easily compartmentalized. The pressures on and the burdens of the black community were total and pervasive. Black women were forced by circumstance to be holistic in their approach to religious and community life. Thus all of the work was sacred and required "the best of [their] service."[12]

There are, therefore, two approaches to the interpretation of black women and religion in the twentieth century. First, there are their experiences at several levels—the local church, the denomination, and the total black religious experience. Then there is the women's experience in their culture and community. Since the black church is the organizational and expressive core of black culture and community, the boundaries are not easily fixed. However, these two approaches allow us to emphasize the way in which religion pervades lived experience to the extent that religion is "taken for granted." Irrespective of their prestige, access to authority, or levels of power, black women play a most important role in the maintenance and mobilization of religion in black America.

WITHIN CULTURE AND COMMUNITY

One of the most profound impacts of black women on the aesthetics of the black community has been in the area of music. As a women's activity, it remains the least documented and the least heralded. Regardless of the levels of sexism in specific black churches, black women carried a great responsibility for the distinctiveness of the music and prayer traditions. The area of music, although generally viewed as women's work, is particularly important because black sacred music has had a wide-ranging impact on contemporary music in general. From the isolated music teacher in the rural black community who was also the leader of the local church choir, to women such as Mattie Moss Clark of the Church of God in Christ, Lucie E. Campbell of the National Baptist Convention, and Mother Beatrice Brown of the National Convention of

Gospel Choirs and Choruses, one can observe the hand of black women in the black sacred music tradition.

The music ministries of black women advanced and institutionalized arenas for creative and individual expression. Musical expression also united with political expression in a wide variety of ways, ranging from the secret codes of the spirituals to the revitalizing and mobilizing effects of black sacred music observed during the civil rights movement.[13] Almost every popularly recognized musical style indigenous to the United States had its antecedents in the oral traditions of black church worship services. Although both women and men distilled the moods and the styles derived from African influences into profoundly moving hymns and gosepl songs, as the twentieth century progressed, black men could both preach and sing (the preferred combination of gifts), but black women were increasingly limited to the singing. Women such as Mother Willie Mae Ford Smith learned to do their preaching through their singing (and long introductions to their songs) and gained national reputations as "evangelist."[14]

For more than thirty years, Lucie E. Campbell was one of the guiding powers in musical standards for black Baptists in the United States. A teacher of English and American history in Memphis, Tennessee, and nationally recognized in her profession, Lucie E. Campbell marshalled her considerable musical talents for service in her local and national community. She participated in the compilation of several hymnbooks that remain contemporary classics, and her hymns appear in the books of the African Methodist Episcopal Church and the Church of God in Christ.[15] Lucie E. Campbell was most visible as the founder and leader of the National Baptist Training Union. (Document 1)

Roberta Martin is credited with the stylistic refinement of gospel music and she, along with numerous other women, contributed and refined their musical talents through such organizations as the National Convention of Gospel Choirs and Choruses.[16] Although Thomas A. Dorsey (the author of "Precious Lord") is the founder of the National Convention of Gospel Choirs and Choruses, Miss Sallie Martin did much of the work developing a publishing house, marketing strategies, and the fiscal stability that disseminated the new music and enabled Dorsey's convention to survive and grow. Although Reverend Herbert Brewster wrote the song "God is Able,"[17] it was Clara Ward who transformed it into a classic. This song expanded the psalmist's attribution to God as "father to the fatherless," in Psalm 68, to the popular formula of "he's a mother when you're motherless, a father when you're fatherless, a sister when you're sisterless, and a brother when you're brotherless" that can be heard, not only in other gospel songs, but also in the prayer and preaching tradition of black churches. Because of women's voices and the records of the Ward Singers, Mahalia Jackson, the Caravans, Shirley Caesar, Marian Williams, and Bessie Griffin (to name only a few),[18] the oral tradition of Afro-American religion was much less androcentric than the dominant culture and its biblical foundations demanded.

The missionary zeal with which black women approached the problem of social change and racial uplift had a revitalizing impact on the black community. The women's race consciousness united contending segments of the black community into new organizations. These new organizations were often limited in scope to immediate but widely shared problems. The women were so effective that W. E. B. DuBois, arguing the absolute necessity for black men to support woman suffrage, cited the emerging role of black women as "the intellectual leadership of the race."[19] Black women viewed jim crow as the evil of the age. The combination of Christian zeal and astute political observation enabled them to juggle a wide range of organizational commitments and to engage in a startling variety of tasks (Document 2). Such diversity in their lives, and the resulting organizational matrix of the black community, provided a frontal assault on jim crow and an organizational foundation outside of but related to church congregations.

Denominational differences were no barriers to effective strategies in the fight against racial oppression. Church women crossed denominational lines in order to form the National Association of Colored Women's Clubs. Indeed, the merging of two national organizations to form the National Association of Colored Women occurred after national conventions of each group were held in Washington, D.C. in 1896. The Colored Women's League met at the 15th Street Presbyterian Church and the National Federation of Afro-American Women met at the 19th Street Baptist Church.[20] It was such women who organized the National League for the Protection of Colored Women (1905), which later merged with another organization to form the National Urban League in 1911. Not only was the evil of lynching implicated in the origin of the black women's club movement,[21] but black women also participated in the founding of the National Association for the Advancement of Colored People to trample out this evil.

If any one ministry could be identified as central to the black sacred cosmos of the twentieth century, it would be education. Evangelism represented a taken-for-granted aspect of church life; it was assumed that the calling, recruitment, and care of new members in churches was basic to Christian life. However, black people also defined education of the oppressed and the oppressors as central tasks of Christian mission. Education, included political, economic, social, moral, and religious education. This definition of education also defined the black perspective on leadership. Black men and women who were perceived by the community as agents of this sacred vision were described as "educators."[22] Myrtle Foster (Document 2) was just one of thousands of women and men— more often women"[23]—who went to the South as teachers during the late nineteenth and early twentieth centuries.

It is significant that the lives of nearly all of the most famous black women educators spanned both the nineteenth and twentieth centuries. Anna Julia Cooper (1858–1964), Juliette Derricotte (1897–1931), Lucy Craft Laney (1854–1933), Mary Church Terrell (1863–1954), Hallie Q. Brown (1845?–1949), Charlotte Hawkins Brown (1882–1961), Nannie Helen Burroughs (1883–1961), Ida B. Wells (1864–1931), and Mary McLeod Bethune (1875–1955)[24] all lived far enough into the twentieth century to witness the urban migration of black people and the limited choices for black women and black men in the face of urban racism. For many of these women—all of whom were active churchwomen and nationally visible to their own and other denominations—education was the wellspring of lives of service whose length and breadth have become legendary.

A few such women, like Lucy Craft Laney, were explicitly recognized by their denominations as ministers. An uncompromising foe of segregation who refused to patronize segregated institutions, admonishing "don't pay to be kicked," Lucey Craft Laney founded the Haines Normal and Industrial School from a school she had begun in the lecture room of Christ Presybterian Church in Augusta, Georgia. Like many "educators" of her day, she managed to synthesize the approaches of Booker T. Washington and W. E. B. DuBois "regarding the kind of education essential to the full participation of Negroes in all aspects of American life." From the perspective of the United Presbyterian Church, she was engaged "in ministry." "Though not beatified by any ecclesiastical authorization, her ministry of love, enlightenment and kindly discipline is enshrined the lives . . . touched by her compassion and her strength of character."[25]

Being a teacher in the black community meant the kind of visibility that emerged as community leadership. Black women used their leverage as educators to encourage denominational bodies to approach education from an enlightened point of view. For those who became national leaders, such as Mary McLeod Bethune (Document 3), this was an easier task since they had access to newspapers and to pulpits as Woman's Day speakers (Document 13), missionaries, and educators. For educators such as Nannie Helen Burroughs (Documents 12, 14), the founding of a school grew out of activities within a denomination. Since education was one of the largest mission enterprises of black churches, black women wielded quite a bit of influence in spite of their structural subordination.[26] As hostility to women's leadership grew within some black churches, a rigid distinction came to be drawn between "preaching" and "speaking." Sometimes, especially if women's speaking addressed issues of the gospel directly, as in a sermon, that activity would be called "teaching."

WITHIN THE CHURCHES

Regardless of the strength of their club movement, black women never relinquished the voices they had in their denominations. Although visible national leadership was achieved in organizations outside of local congregations and denominational bodies, black women developed a wide variety of strategies to remain effective forces for social change and progressive thinking. In spite of their prominence at national church meetings and in spite of the growth of black women's public speaking abilities, the distinction between speaking and teaching as female tasks and preaching as male tasks continued to grow. Such a sexual division of labor was an accommodation to the dominant culture's reading of the biblical texts on women's roles. Although the women did not share the men's conclusions in such matters,[27] they refused to abandon their increasingly limited opportunities if it meant abandoning the other tasks of their ministries. In spite of their attacks and black women's responses (Document 4), black men were reluctant to exclude women from their deliberations in light of their own experiences of oppression, the militant persistence of the women, and the community's unwillingness to waste one iota of skill. Congregations sent skilled, educated, and erudite women as delegates to conventions.

Not all women agreed with the structural subordination, which decreased their opportunities to exercise their gifts in the field of gospel labor. Sara Duncan's defense of women's missionary efforts (Document 4) provides hints of the gathering storm in the "mainstream" churches. During the late nineteenth and early twentieth centuries the Holiness movement swept the South. A number of women participated in that movement, which produced denominations that ordained women to preaching and pastoral offices. During the twentieth century, that movement was intensified by the Azuza Street Revival in Los Angeles, California. That revival is acknowledged to be the seminal event in the history of the Pentecostal movement.[28]

Depending upon the source one uses, this revival and the cultural origins of the movement can be seen as based within the black community.[29] William Seymour, a one-eyed black preacher, who believed that the baptism of the Holy Ghost should be evidenced in speaking tongues, had preached this doctrine to the Holiness congregation pastored by Reverend Neely Terry, a black woman. When she ejected him, he moved elsewhere; and after a time a revival began that was reported internationally.[30] The revival ran for three years and a number of black churches claim their descent from this revival. The largest of these churches is the Church of God in Christ. Originally founded as a Holiness denomination, disagreement among church leaders concerning the doctrine of Pentecost split the denomination, leaving the pro-Pentecost faction in control of the original church charter and the legal right to use the name Church of God in Christ. It was, then, the first legally organized Pentecostal denomination and its founder, Bishop C. H. Mason, ordained a number of white preachers who later formed newer (and segregated!) works.

Within the black community, Holiness and Pentecostal churches are referred to collectively as "the Sanctified Church." These new denominations never lost their connectedness to the larger black religious experience. In spite of the controversies they engendered within the community, the continuity of the Sanctified Church with the overall religious experience has been of vital importance. These churches maintained the ecstatic Afro-Christian worship tradition and its linkages to slave religion at a time when the Baptists and the Methodists were attempting to eliminate those traditions from their churches.[31] The Sanctified Church, whose denominations disagreed vigorously over the proper role of women in the churches, attracted large numbers of "talented, Spirit-filled women" who felt called to labor in the gospel ministry.

The Church of God in Christ actually recruited educated women to work in the building of the denomination and the educational ministries (Document 6). These women developed a "women's work" that came to be known as the "women's department." Strong women's departments came to be a typical feature in the overall organization of the Sanctified Church; as long as women were subordinate and cooperative to their bishops, the organizations functioned with near autonomy.[32] In some cases, subordination was not an issue, since the church also ordained women to preaching and pastoral office (Document 9). Although the Sanctified Church became stereotyped as a "pie in the sky" church, when the lives and work of the women in these churches are examined, one finds that they participated in the movement for racial uplift with their Baptist and Methodist sisters (Document 7). A number of Baptist and Methodist women came over into these churches in order to exercise their gifts. It was the women who were migrating to the cities who carried the movement to urban areas, preaching revivals, "digging out" new works, and then writing "home" for a pastor.[33] Although the black churches are heavily female—by some estimates 75 percent female[34]— the Sanctified Church is the most female of these churches, with some congregations having 90 percent female memberships.[35]

Among those churches that refuse to ordain women, there are offices and conditions under which women may perform the same roles as men. Additionally, within Baptist associations there are enlightened councils and congregations who will ordain women. For black Protestant women, there is always the opportunity to find a preaching situation among churches of similar practices and styles of spirituality. Among black Catholic women, the National Black Sisters Conference has been the most prominent organization. Black sisters and nuns participate in all aspects of the Catholic Church's ministry in the United States and have been, along with the National Office of Black Catholics and other organizations, an important force in making the Catholic Church in the United States responsive to the needs of black Catholics.[36] Black Catholics have pioneered a practical ecumenism in their overall social relationships with other black Christians before such an approach became popular among Christians generally.[37] Such relationships bore fruit at the first national meeting of the National Black Sisters Conference, when approximately three hundred sisters and nuns sang together the Thomas A. Dorsey hymn, "Precious Lord."[38] The committed criticism of these women is an important model of faith for all Christians (Document 10).

The largest number of black people who express a religious preference are Baptist (60 percent).[39] The roots of the "Afro-Baptist faith" run deep into the heart of slave religion.[40] The impact of the faith has been cultural as well as organizational—there are Methodist congregations in the South who will practice only believers' baptism (Baptism of those who have experienced personal conversion.).[41] Within the black community, Baptists were well organized by the end of the Civil War, and their organizational growth continued well into the twentieth century. Their prominence was aided by the participation of Booker T. Washington in the leadership of the National Baptist Convention.[42] Unfortunately, Washington's male supremacist beliefs created a twentieth-century atmosphere that was more regressive than the period between 1880 and 1900.[43] During the last twenty years of the nineteenth century, black women participated fully in the deliberations of the American National Baptist Convention.[44]

Black Baptist women did not stand by idly during the mounting assault on their position. In 1900, they formed the Women's Auxiliary of the National Baptist Convention. The motion was introduced by Miss Nannie Helen Burroughs, the bookkeeper of the parent body.[45] An outspoken feminist, advocate of racial uplift, and uncompromising foe of jim crow, she became the corresponding secretary of that body and produced a large body of written materials to enable Baptist women to hold on to their positions within the churches and to become effective leaders in their churches and communities (Documents 12, 13, 14, 15). The first president of the auxiliary was Mrs. S. Willie Layten. The tensions that existed among black people concerning women leaders were evident in the responses to her initial leadership. But by the time of her death, nothing but uncompromising admiration existed among Baptist women. She remains a heroine in the telling of National Baptist history. (Document 11).[46]

Baptist women and their organization became models for other women in the churches of the twentieth century. Founders of the Sanctified Church denominations were often themselves Baptists and they recruited Baptist women as educators.[47] Perhaps the most profound and lasting impact of Baptist women was their institution of Woman's Day in the National Baptist Convention of 1907 (Document 13). Not only is

Woman's Day celebrated in nearly every predominantly black denomination, it is practiced by the black congregations within predominantly
white denominations such as the United Methodist Church, the United
Church of Christ, the United Presbyterian Church, and the Disciples of
Christ-Christian. Although it is, much to the sorrow of Nannie Helen
Burroughs, still the biggest fund-raising day within black churches, it is
also the single most important source of role models for black girls and
women in the areas of the professions, political activism, Christian ministry, and overall Christian service. In one way, the institution of Women's
Day brings together, for black women, all of the elements of their sacred
world and emphasizes the inseparability of the political, professional,
social, and economic from the spiritual. They often quote the song, "Only
what you do for Christ will last," to emphasize their holistic approach.

Black women worked within their communities, and applied their
autonomous approaches, within and without their churches, to the problems of changing a racist society, at the same time that they were admonished by the institutions within their community to "step aside and let a
man take over . . . it looks bad for the race."[48] In spite of the increased
pressures to make black women conform to dominant culture expectations in their leadership styles and their public responsibilities, black
women discovered within their clubs and their missionary societies the
secret to maintaining their position as that necessary vital force for
church survival and growth. While black women have transformed their
leadership styles to cope with the problems and dilemmas of sexism, they
quietly persisted with their message—"If it wasn't for the women, you
wouldn't have a church." Finally, they are being heard.

Sue Bailey Thurman, national leader of the YWCA, lecturer and writer, life-long partner in ministry with husband, Howard Thurman. [Photo courtesy of Howard Thurman Consultation, Garrett-Evangelical Theological Seminary, Evanston, Illinois.]

Mary McLeod Bethune, leading black educator, church woman and social reformer. [Photo courtesy of the Bethune Museum Archives, Washington, D.C.]

Bishop Mary E. Jackson, one of the charter members of Mount Sinai Holy Churches, in 1969 at the age of 88 became the fourth bishop to preside over the organization. (1974 photo). [Photo courtesy of Mount Sinai Holy Churches of America, Inc.]

Bishop Leontyne Kelly, bishop of San Francisco, second woman and first black woman to be ordained to the episcopacy of the United Methodist Church, at the time of her consecration in 1984. [Photo courtesy of Bishop Kelly.]

The Rev. Pauli Murray, long-time civil rights activist, lawyer, historian, and episcopal priest. [Photo by Janet Charles, New York City, used by permission of the photographer.]

Nannie Helen Burroughs, pioneer black educator and church woman. [Photo courtesy of the Nannie Helen Burroughs School, Washington, D.C.]

Bishop Ida Robinson, founder of Mt. Sinai Holy Churches of America. [Photo from Mt. Sinai Holy Churches of America, Inc.]

Documents: "Something Within": Social Change and Collective Endurance in the Sacred World of Black Christian Women

WITHIN CULTURE AND COMMUNITY

WITHIN THE CHURCHES

WITHIN CULTURE AND COMMUNITY

Document 1: Hymns by Lucie E. Campbell

"Something Within" and "He Understands, He'll Say 'Well Done!'" are two of more than eighty hymns and anthems written by Lucie E. Campbell.[49] "He Understands" is not only entrenched in the black oral tradition, but it is also well known in white churches and performed by white recording stars. Both "He Understands" and "Something Within" capture the abilities of innumerable black women to persist in serving their churches and communities and to endure in the myriad of struggles against racism and jim crow in the face of the multiple burdens that weighted their lives—burdens often exacerbated by nonrecognition and a lack of appreciation.

"Be not dismayed when men don't believe you" has served as a powerful admonition to persist in the face of the forces of human evil and injustice that often overwhelm black people's lives. It was also an indication that Lucie E. Campbell recognized the profound contradiction that existed in the question of gender. Similarly, the opening lines from "Something Within"—"Preachers and teachers would make their appeal/Fighting as soldiers on great battlefields"—recognized that the gospel labor that men performed was called "preaching" while that same gospel labor, when done by women, was called "teaching."

Regardless of the way in which Lucie E. Campbell's hymns spoke to very subtle dilemmas and paradoxes among black women and men, the hymns became classics because they spoke to the larger and, to the minds of the most militant Christian black feminists, the most important concern—conversion and commitment to the cause of Jesus Christ. Twenty years after her death, it should be noted that one of the first acts of the new administration of the National Baptist Convention, USA, Inc., was to place a headstone on the grave of Mrs. Lucie E. Campbell.[50]

He Understands, He'll Say "Well Done!"

If when you give the best of your service,
Telling the world that the Savior is come;
Be not dismayed when men don't believe you;
He understands; He'll say, "Well Done."

Misunderstood, the Savior of sinners,
Hung on the cross; He was God's only Son;
Oh! hear Him calling His Father in Heav'n,
"Not my will, but Thine be done."

If when this life of labor is ended,
And the reward of the race you have run;
Oh! the sweet rest prepared for the faithful,
Will be His blest and final "well done."

But if you try and fail in your trying,
Hand sore and scarred from the work you've begun;
Take up your cross, run quickly to meet Him;
He'll understand; He'll say, "Well Done."

CHORUS

Oh, when I come to the end of my journey,
Weary of life and the battle is won;
Carrying the staff and cross of Redemption,
He'll understand, and say, "Well Done."

Something Within

Preachers and teachers would make their appeal,
Fighting as soldiers on great battlefields;
When to their pleadings my poor heart did yield,
All I could say, there is something within.

Have you that something—that burning desire?
Have you that something, that never doth tire?
Oh if you have it—that Heavenly Fire!
Then let the world know, there is something within.

I met God one mornin', my soul feeling bad,
Heart heavy laden with a bowed down head.
He lifted my burden and made me so glad,
All that I know there is something within.

CHORUS

Something within me that holdeth the reins,
Something within me that banishes pain;
Something within me I cannot explain,
All that I know there is something within.

Document 2: Biographical Sketch of Myrtle Foster, National Association of Colored Women

Black women became conscious of their political impact as they responded to their communities' needs and received encouragement from them. So great was their impact that Drake and Cayton's research on the Chicago black community demonstrates that "Race women" were better trusted than "Race men."[51] The religious commitment of black clubwomen was so taken for granted that it is rarely mentioned in the histories that detail their community service. For instance, it is seldom noted that Mary McLeod Bethune had obtained a complete theological education and had prepared to become a foreign missionary. She was denied a post in Africa because she was Negro.[52]

*In 1933, the National Association of Colored Women's Clubs pub-
lished a history of the organization entitled Lifting As They Climb.
Not only did this history detail the events and the projects, but it also
included biographical sketches provided by the women themselves or
their admirers. One such sketch, that of Myrtle Foster Cook, was
representative of the kind of lived experience that was woven from
the strands of club work, religious commitment, and professional
achievement. To very religious women, this woman's life was remarkable because she "invaded the pulpit as leader of various programs
and services."*[53]

Myrtle Foster was born a British subject at historic old Amherst-
burg, Ontario, Canada, on the chain of the Great Lakes, but at school
age became a citizen of the United States when her parents became
naturalized residents of Monroe, Michigan. There she grew up with
the educational advantages, academic, musical, artistic, of this liberal
commonwealth.

In her own home town she early became an ardent church worker,
filling many positions, as Sunday school teacher, treasurer, church
organist, and even invaded the pulpit as leader of various programs
and services.

A missionary urge led her to Kentucky as principal of a little
normal school supported by a Baptist district association. A very timid
young woman found herself suddenly the educational leader of a
community. A number of amusing situations, such as a buggy ride of
forty miles over country road, up hill and down dale, to plead before
the grizzled elders of the [Baptist] Association for back salary, make
unique reading.

A high school position in Frankfort offered professional advancement and there Myrtle Foster met and married Dr. Louis G. Todd,
scion of old Kentucky stock. They settled in Muskogee, in the new
state of Oklahoma, and at once Mrs. Todd was drafted into school
work, at first in the government school for the Negro children of the
Indian tribes, and then into the high school.

Carrying into the West the club spirit of Michigan and Kentucky,
she organized the Dorcas Club, first club in Muskogee, with the purpose of establishing a hospital to meet the appalling need of hospital-
ization for Negroes. The club meetings were devoted to sewing and
mending for needy school children in the intervals between money
raising events. The hospital was built after she moved from Muskogee.

Impressed by the dearth of cultural entertainment, Myrtle Foster
Todd instituted a series of lectures and recitals, arranging state-wide
tours through friendly help of members of the State Teachers' Association. Thus came to Oklahoma, Richard B. Harrison, dramatic
reader, now renowned as "De Lawd" in "The Green Pastures,"

Madam Azalia Hackley, Dr. Kelly Miller, Madam Patti Brown. She
was a charter member, writing the constitution of the Oklahoma State
Federation which she counts one of the happiest opportunities of her
life because of Oklahoma's splendid advancements.

A few short years of married life, and Myrtle Todd, a widow, was
called to head the English department of the Lincoln High School of
Kansas City, Missouri. Again, bravely facing life alone. Mrs. Todd
entered into the professional and club life of Kansas City and the state
of Missouri, becoming a member of The Women's League, oldest club
in the city, and the Book Lovers Study Club and the City Federation.
The League was then purchasing property for a Working Girls'
Home and welcomed workers; also the City Federation.

After teaching four years, Widow Todd stepped out of the school
room into home life as the wife of Professor Hugh Oliver Cook, then
head of Mathematics Department, later becoming principal of Lincoln High School. . . .

Free of the restrictions of employment, Mrs. Cook threw herself
whole heartedly into every civic and charitable and social welfare
movement giving volunteer service in the organization and set-up of
the K[ansas] C[ity] Branch of the Y.W.C.A., Branch of the
N.A.A.C.P., and the K.C. Federation of Colored Charities. Through
the Woman's League she initiated the movement for the parental
home for colored boys and served as organizer and secretary of the
Colored Children's Association, Inc., working nine years to secure the
erection, equipment, and staff of the Jackson County Home for Negro Boys, one of the finest institutions maintained by Jackson County,
Missouri. She served six years on the State Negro Industrial Commission by appointment of govenors, assisted Miss Hallie Q. Brown, who
was in the 1924 national campaign, Director of Colored Republican
Women under the Republican National Committee, and succeeded to
the directorship of the Western Division, also one of the nine members of the Executive Committee of the Colored Division in the 1928
national campaign.

In the N[ational] A[ssociation of] C[olored] W[omen], Mrs. Cook
has distinguished herself by her generous service as editor-manager
of the National Notes, as program chairman of six of the last eight
national conventions and co-chairman in 1924, and as a member of
the Board of Control of the N.A.C.W. She is vice president of the
Central Regional Association.

In business life Mrs. Cook organized in 1926 the Home Seekers'
Savings and Loan Association of Kansas City, and has served gratis
as secretary-treasurer for seven years to establish for Negroes this
institution for home buying. She is also the largest stockholder and
director of the Peoples' Finance Corporation of Kansas City.

Document 3: "My Last Will and Testament": Mary McLeod Bethune

Mary McLeod Bethune (1875–1955) was one of the most powerful national black leaders. She made an impact on the institutional life of the black community and on the national policies of the United States. Her entire life was a testimony to the rich tapestries of service black women could weave out of their sense of Christian duty and calling. After her training at Moody Bible Institute was completed, she applied for a missionary post in Africa and was informed that she could not be sent on account of her race. After several teaching positions, she found her own Africa in the United States when she founded the Daytona Normal and Industrial School for Negro Girls in Daytona Beach, Florida (1904). The school, which later became Bethune-Cookman College, had a profound impact on the entire Daytona community and on the lives of individuals such as Howard Thurman, who cited the impact of her school and community programs.[54] Mrs. Bethune rose to national prominence through her participation in the National Association of Colored Women (NACW), over which she presided after besting Ida B. Wells in a national election.

In 1935, she founded the National Council of Negro Women (NCNW) as an umbrella organization that encompassed the NACW and most of the national black women's organizations that had been formed since the beginning of the century. With concerns that were national and international in scope, Mrs. Bethune insured the presence of black women in every major forum, including the United Nations.

Mrs. Bethune was a woman of deep faith and that faith was evident in her approach to her role as educator and national leader. One anniversary of the NCNW was built around the theme "Diversities of Gifts and Differences of Administration." The discussion of spiritual gifts (1 Corinthians 14) provided the basis for the NCNW's interprtation of its past and future role in the black community and the importance of the diversity it represented through its affiliated church organizations, fraternal groups, sororities, and independent affiliates.[55]

Mrs. Bethune was truly ecumenical and interfaith in her approach. She was educated by the Presbyterians and was an active and committed Methodist through the Board of Education and General Conference of the Methodist Church. She was also a member of the Executive Board of the Council of Church Women and an honorary member of Hadassah. Toward the end of her life, she wrote a "Last Will and Testament" for her people as a final exhortation and admonition. It remains an important spiritual document and spiritual statement.[56]

Sometimes I ask myself if I have any legacy to leave. My worldly possessions are few. Yet, my experiences have been rich. From them I have distilled principles and policies in which I firmly believe. Perhaps, in them there is something of value. So as my life draws to a close, I will pass them on to Negroes everywhere in the hope that this philosophy may give them inspiration. Here, then, is my legacy:

I LEAVE YOU LOVE. Injuries quickly forgotten quickly pass away. Personally and racially, our enemies must be forgiven. Our aim must be to create a world of fellowship and justice where no man's color or religion is held against him. "Love thy neighbor" is a precept which could transform the world if it were universally practiced. It connotes brotherhood and to me, brotherhood of man is the noblest concept of all human relationships. Loving your neighbor means being interracial, interreligious and international.

I LEAVE YOU HOPE. Yesterday, our ancestors endured the degradation of slavery, yet they retained their dignity. Today, we direct our economic and political strength toward winning a more abundant and secure life. Tomorrow, a new Negro, unhindered by race taboos and shackles, will benefit from this striving and struggling.

I LEAVE YOU A THIRST FOR EDUCATION. More and more, Negroes are taking full advantage of hard-won opportunities for learning, and the educational level of the Negro population is at its highest point in history. We are making greater use of the privileges inherent in living in a democracy. Now that the barriers are crumbling everywhere, the Negro in America must be ever vigilant lest his forces be marshalled behind wrong causes and undemocratic movements . . . He must not lend his support to any group that seeks to subvert democracy.

I LEAVE YOU FAITH. Faith is the first factor in a life devoted to service. Without faith, nothing is possible. With it, nothing is impossible. Faith in God is the greatest power, but great faith too is faith in oneself. The faith of the American Negro in himself has grown immensely, and is still increasing. The measure of our progress as a race is in precise relation to the depth of the faith in our people held by our leaders.

I LEAVE YOU RACIAL DIGNITY. I want Negroes to maintain their human dignity at all costs. We, as Negroes, must recognize that we are the custodians as well as the heirs of a great civilization. As a race we have given something to the world, and for this we are proud and fully conscious of our place in the total picture of mankind's development.

I LEAVE YOU A DESIRE TO LIVE HARMONIOUSLY WITH YOUR FELLOW MEN. The problem of color is world wide, on every continent. I appeal to all to recognize their common problems, and unite to solve them. So often our difficulties have made us supersensitive and truculent. I want to see my people conduct themselves in all relationships, fully conscious of their responsibilities and deeply aware of their heritage. We are a minority of fifteen million living side by side with a white majority of 177 million. We must learn to deal with people positively and on an individual basis.

I LEAVE YOU FINALLY A RESPONSIBILITY TO OUR YOUNG PEOPLE. Our children must never lose their zeal for building a better world. They must not be discouraged from aspiring toward greatness, for they are to be leaders of tomorrow. We have a powerful potential in our youth, and we must have the courage to change old ideas and practices so that we may direct their power toward good ends.

Faith, courage, brotherhood, dignity, ambition, responsibility— these are needed today as never before. We must cultivate them and use them as tools for our task of completing the establishment of equality for the Negro. We must sharpen these tools in the struggle that faces us and find new ways of using them. The Freedom Gates are half a-jar. We must pry them fully open.

If I have a legacy to leave my people, it is my philosophy of living and serving. As I face tomorrow, I am content. I pray now that my philosophy may be helpful to those who share my vision of a world of Peace.

Within the Churches

Document 4: "In Vindication of Vital Questions": Sara Duncan

To "hold the reins" of their battle against jim crow, black women often had to struggle against men and male-dominated authority within their own churches. By 1904, Southern woman of the African Methodist Episcopal (AME) Church had already achieved a missionary society designed to help alleviate the social denegration and economic deprivation brought on by legalized segregation in the South; but many within the denomination did not believe that the women could, or ought be authorized to carry out this additional missionary endeavor.[59]

Sara Duncan chose to correct and challenge the men of her church who did not agree with the creation of a second women's missionary society. As church opponents held the older Women's Parent Mite Missionary Society forward as the ideal place for all AME women's work, Sara challenged opponents and the elder society to observe the work and returns of southern women after a comparable time of existence.[58]

1st. In perusing the different church papers accumulated during my two months' absence, engaged in the missionary field, I find in the issue of the *Christians Recorder* of December 3, an article from a brother on "Vital Questions—Our Missionary Department." And I wish to say a word to the good brother who seems not to have kept up with the correct records of the missionary department, though were it not for and in defense of the dear sisters who have worked so very hard the past seven years to keep alive the department of Home and Foreign Missions, I should keep quiet, but for their dear sakes "can not hold my peace."

As one of the leaders in the missionary work in this section since 1897, I have traveled to some extent in the South and Southwest, with a chance now and then to look in upon the workers in the North and East. We have made a careful study of the same, perhaps more largely than our brother, having done but little else during these seven years. Some of the points made by our brother are well taken and others are not; we feel them an injustice.

In the second clause of his argument, "Parents' Mite Missionaries," he expresses himself, regretting that the General Conference was unable to so adjust matters as to bring them under one head, viz: Women's Mite Missionary Society. And the organization that was doing real work is the W.M. Missionary Society, even though it exists only in the first, second, third, fourth and fifth districts, and the other section which is by far the stronger—yea, five times as strong—being the domain of the southern Woman's Home and Foreign Missionary Society. If the W.M.M. Society was allowed to enter the strongholds of the South and take such well organized shape as it has in the Northern and Western sections of our church, where our memberships are not so large by virtue of the sections of the country, then we would behold an income of $15,000. in the women's department alone, which would make it such an important factor in the missionary work of our church that our department could meet every obligation with which it might be encumbered and plan for broadening its scope of activity, thus carrying the church in undeveloped regions at home and abroad.

We first ask a question, where peace reigns, why will some persist in stirring up strife?

Nothing good can come out of confusion.

Since the General Conference has and did arrange in 1896, to have two missionary societies, why can not we work more, strive harder, leaving the rest with God?

And since there are so many things of vital interest to the church to be brought before the General Conference, why not let the women alone, and let them be in harmony, doing the will of the Master as best they can.

1st. Our brother is quite mistaken when he says all but the district's is operated by the W.H. & F.M. [Women's Home and Foreign Missionary] Society. He must search the records closely.

2nd. We emphatically deny "that it is the W.M.M. Society that is doing the real work," as our report to the coming General Conference will show; we are proud to be able to agree with our brother and say the W.M.M. Society is a grand and noble organization, and we would and will always be an helper rather than a hindrance; yet, at the same time, look out for that placed in our hands by the church that it may be preserved and prosper.

In '96 we started out with hardly a constitution to work by and not an organization of any kind, subject to the general church, only a few Home Mission Societies in a few churches for the benefit of the immediate communities, and when pastored by a few ministers who had the spirit of missions, would send from two to three dollars to the Annual Conference, and thought something had been done.

We feel that we speak for the sisters of both organizations when we say that the General Conference of the A.M.E. Church settled the matter in 1900 once for all, and there is no dissension among them, they are each working with might and main to have good reports at each annual conference, and each General Conference, and have no time to wrangle over what the name of the society is, or shall be.

Document 5: "A Litany for African Women"

Throughout the nineteenth century women of the African Methodist Episcopal (AME) Church had worked in gender-specific organizations toward an overall general goal of improving the conditions of black people. Such organizations as the Daughters of Conference were nineteenth-century expressions of a women's movement for the race. By the close of the century, black women had accelerated their activities in gender-specific groups and carved out national, denominational spheres of power through the AME Woman's Parent Mite Missionary Society and the Women's Home and Foreign Missionary Society (WHFMS). WHFMS had been initiated, organized, and designed specifically for the southern women.

Although one purpose in establishing a second women's missionary society was to address the social and educational needs of southern blacks, support could only be garnered from the AME bishop interested in missionary work in South Africa. Those portions of funds raised by the WHFMS and not retained for domestic, southern work were contributed to expand the cause of the Church in South Africa. Below is a litany written for African women by Charlotte L. Tshabalala.[59]

This is part of a litany, arranged by the Founder-Organizer of the Daughters of Africa Movement in South Africa, Miss C. L. Tshabalala. It was used at the opening of a new branch of the Daughters of Africa, and is printed here in case other women's organizations would like to use it. It is reprinted from *Listen* with acknowledgments to the *Bantu World*.

Leader: "Except the Lord build the house, they labour in vain that build it."

"The wise woman buildeth her house but the foolish woman plucketh it down with her hands."

People: Oh, God, we beseech Thee, make us willing to serve our homes, our communities and our beloved country by working with Thy guidance and Thy love.

Leader: From Thee alone may we learn to be teachers of peace and harmony in our abodes as we daily go about our duties.

People: Fill our hearts with Thy peace.

Leader: Dear Lord, may we abound in grace, that we may be called virtuous women whose price is above rubies, whose candle goeth not out by night, whose husbands are known in the gates when they sit among the elders of the land.

People: As both morning and evening stars may shine brightly in our corners.

Leader: May we open our mouths with wisdom and be kind.

People: "Whose children called them blessed and say many daughters have done virtuously, but ye excel them all." Lord, we dedicate our bodies to be Thy temple.

Leader: May we do away with fault finding and let alone self-seeking, may we become more sincere friends and put away prejudices.

People: Lord, live Thyself in our lives, and make us always generous and slow in judgment.

Leader: Straightforward and unafraid may we put into action our better impulses with nobleness of mind.

People: Help us to work patiently, make us grow calm, serene and gentle.

Leader: May we ever remember it is the little things that create differences but that in the big things of life we are one.

People: Lord, help us to be broad and generous in thought and deed.

Leader: We pray for our sisters who have not as yet had the privilege of knowing the joys of service to others.

People: Lord, keep us from pettiness, help us to be large in thought and encourage our efforts to aid our youth in its fight for high and noble living.

Leader: From many homes with many minds we come together this day, each to each, bound as daughters in Thy service.

People: May the spirit of wisdom and understanding, and that of counsel and right, and the spirit of obedience and fear of the Lord rest upon us now and for ever.

Amen.

Document 6: "A History of Our Women's Department": Church of God in Christ

The beginning of the twentieth century witnessed the growth and development of what black people called the Sanctified Church. New denominations were formed among white and black Christians as part of the late-nineteenth-century Holiness movement and the early-twentieth-century Pentecostal movement. Since the Holiness and Pentecostal movements were interracial in their origins, and remained so in their practice until the First World War,[60] the cultural influence of the black traditions was as powerful in sacred culture as it was in the secular devlopments of blues and jazz.

The development of the Sanctified Church created at least twenty-five nationally organized churches or denominations and an unknown number of independent congregations and regional networks. A large number of these churches developed northern congregations in the only available space of crowded ghettoes—the storefronts—and so were confused with other storefronts that were labeled sects and cults.[61]

These churches provided extraordinary leadership opportunities for women. In some areas, these churches account for the majority of women clergy.[62] One sociologist confessed that during a major urban research project, he noticed a large number of women pastors, but neglected to research the origins of their churches or to interview them precisely because they were women and their churches were in storefronts.[63]

The Church of God in Christ is the largest of the denominations of the Sanctified Church. Officially a Pentecostal Church, it began as a Holiness denomination and has its origins in a dispute among Mississippi Baptists whose history of independent worship stretched back thirty years before slavery. Although the church does not ordain women to be "elder, pastor, or bishop,"[64] it represented a viable alternative to gifted Christian women (Baptist and Methodist) who felt called to preach and found the church's evangelist role attractive. The deradicalization[65] of the black church coincided with a period of militant masculinization and suppression of black women's leadership roles and of bitter resistance to women's preaching and public speaking. While many churches were founded during this period, the ones that thrived seem to have been those with strong women's departments. Even churches such as the Fire Baptized Holiness Church of God of the Americas and the Church of the Living God, Christian Workers for Fellowship, developed strong women's departments at the same time they ordained women to pastoral and preaching offices.

The Church of God in Christ, (COGIC) developed one of the most powerful and creative women's departments. The department was *founded by Mother Lizzie Woods Roberson, who was previously head of a Baptist academy. The following document, represents one of the many accounts that COGIC women have written extolling their proud legacy.[67]*

In the year of 1906 a great revival under the auspices of Elder W. J. Seymour, started in Los Angeles, California, and swept the western portion of the United States.

The news of this revival reached Memphis, Tenn., and Bishop Mason and other ministers heard of this true gospel that led to the baptism of the Holy Ghost.

After receiving this blessing, Bishop Mason then made himself an "Ambassador of Good Will." In his travel he went to Dermont, Arkansas, a place that must have been predestined by our heavenly Father, for there he met one Lizzie Woods, matron of the Baptist Academy. Mrs. Woods, a women of very high standing, had made quite an outstanding record in public service, as a teacher of the word of God. They met her, they explained their mission, she was interested, she listened, so as Bishop opened his mouth and explained the scriptures to her she answered, "I believe that Jesus Christ is the son of God." Then and there she received the Baptism of the Holy Ghost. She visited the Convocation which was in session in Pine Bluff, Arkansas, where Lillian Brooks, now our Mother Coffey, the singing evangelist, gave her the right hand of fellowship and insisted that she should come to the National Convocation in Memphis, Tenn., in the fall.

The work among the women had been started but lacked organization. God gave the right woman, at the right time, Lizzie Woods, who had accepted the Doctrine of Pentecost, and was prepared more than ever to teach the unadulterated word of God. Bishop Mason with his keen sight that God had given him, saw that this woman was an organizer, able to inspire, and direct. So in a short time she was chosen as General Mother of Women, to organize and create just such work as would be beneficial to the development of the church. On her first tour she met a minister, one Elder Roberson, whom she later married.

Finding two groups of women in the church; one group praying, the other group studying and teaching the word, one known as the Prayer Band and the other the Bible Band, she combined the two under the name of the Prayer and Bible Band.

Mother Roberson's consideration began with remembering Jer. 9:17, 18, 19 and 20 verses: "Thus saith the Lord of Hosts, consider ye, and call for the mourning women, that they may come; and send for cunning women, that they may come.

"And let them make haste and take up a wailing for us, that our eyes may run with tears, and our eyelids gush out with waters.

"For a voice of wailing is heard out of Zion, how are we spoiled! We are greatly confounded, because we have forsaken the land, because our dwellings have cast us out.

"Yet we heard the word of the Lord, O ye women and let our ears receive the words of his mouth, and teach your daughters wailing and everyone her neighbor lamentation."

She strengthened a small group of women, whom she found sewing, called the daughters of Zion, and organized them giving them the name of "Sewing Circle."

For she remembered the great women of Acts, 9:36–40. "Now there was at Joppa a certain disciple named Tabitha, which by interpretation is called Dorcas: this woman was full of good work and alms deeds which she did, making coats and garments for the needy, while she was with them."

In the year of 1926, during Mother Roberson's tour through the western states, she met Elder Searcy of Portland, Oregon, who was interested in Foreign Missions. She invited him to attend the Memphis meeting and meet our brethren. This trip resulted in the formation of a Foreign Mission band of which Elder Searcy became Secretary-Treasurer. She went everywhere organizing the women into Home and Foreign Mission bands. Elder Searcy did not remain with the movement very long. Mother Roberson asked Bishop Mason to appoint Elder C. G. Brown as Secretary of the Home and Foreign Mission Board, and we have our Foreign Mission Bands.

During these days of travel, she and her husband, working as evangelists digging out and establishing churches, underwent great suffering. Finances being most limited with very few doors open to receive them, at most times, their way of traveling was either by foot or in wagons, yet they kept moving on.

Her daughter, Ida Baker, moved to Omaha, Neb., and later she and Elder Roberson followed, where they established a church and their own home. This took Elder Roberson from her side as a traveling companion. She would then choose one of her daughters, then another to accompany her; the late Fannie Jackson, Lucinda Bostick, Jessie Strickland, the late Nancy Gamble and Eliza Hollins. The work grew so rapidly that she began a state organization and these women whom she had trained became her first State Mothers. Then her daughter became her traveling companion. Mother taught the word of God in power against Lodges, exposing their rituals. She was imprisoned, rotten-egged, and beaten for this. Her daughter, Ida was a gifted singer and cheered the hearts of the people. In their hours, made weary from hard traveling, Ida would break forth with song: "I'm Climbing the Hills of Light, I'm Singing Along My way, My Path is as Bright as Day, I'm Seeking a Better Home."

Elder Roberson's health began to fail and soon he was called from labor to reward. Mother's grief was great but she said, "I cannot stop; I must work the work for him that sent me while it is day, for the night cometh and no man can work."

No writer could do justice to the life work of this illustrious woman of God, nor of the numerous deeds of kindness done by her, nor the height of esteem in which she was held by thousands of followers.

The day came when hard work and continued traveling took its toll and her weak frame gave way under it. And she was only able to attend the National Convocations. For five years she battled to regain her strength but kept her program going thru her different State Mothers.

She was greatly interested in the building of our National Headquarters and with her very efficient daughter as her secretary, she kept her National Drives functioning until she knew the building was ready for dedication. She journeyed southward to the 1943 Convocation; she felt that her days were numbered and that she would not return home. After reaching Memphis, she took new strength, walked through the building, looked at the work of her hands, sat in the assembly hall, which bears her name, held conference with her state mothers, revised her constitution, examined every phase of it for soundness, sat by her windows, saw the large electrical sign, allocated the balance of the funds needed to make possible its purchase. The sign which reads, "National Headquarters of the Churches of God in Christ." Her daughter had solicited funds, but the amount was not sufficient: thus she completed the sum.

Mother Roberson ably admonished her daughters on the Women's Day of the Convocation to continue in the Faith, to stay out of lodges, and to not engage in politics. She turned to her daughter, Lillian Brooks Coffey, whom she had trained from girlhood and who later became her assistant, to courageously lead the women on in the fear of the Lord, to stick to the Bible, not to depart from the law of the Lord. She went to her room tired and weary and in a few hours she drew the drapery of her couch about her and fell asleep. Thus ended the career of one of the greatest organizers among Christian women.

Our then assistant mother became our General Mother by the appointment of senior Bishop Mason and the unanimous sanction of the board of Bishops, Overseers, and State Supervisors and the hearty applause of the laity.

At the passing of Mother Roberson, some helpful units were in the making: The Lillian Brooks Coffey Rest Home in Detroit, Michigan, and the Volunteer Mission Movement. Mother Coffey has most successfully built on the platform established by her predecessor, Mother Roberson.

Mother Roberson established a great auxiliary program through the local churches and had begun to build the State and National program. This, our Mother Coffey has continued to build most efficiently. Our State and National Women's Days have taken on color. Our Bible band teachers of yesterday have become our outstanding evangelists and supervisors. The State organizations are no more just Women's Days in Convocation, but each supervisor has a thoroughly organized program with officers handling each unit. The women's work has grown so rapidly that our visioned supervisor, under the sanction of the spirit and divine guidance, has substantiated the district missionary program throughout the work. The home and foreign mission work in its three phases, (a) directors of missions, the women who carry on the mission work in the state through the organized home and foreign mission bands; (b) the stewardess board, women who work exclusively for packages of clothing and foodstuffs for foreign fields and distribute tracts, bibles, candy fruits, etc., in Institutions in the homeland; (c) the counselors of volunteer missions are women who carry full-time mission programs through interested volunteers. Our nurses unit, efficient workers who maintain first aid centers and convalescent wards in our churches and the school and foreign centers. We also glean a stipulated amount for our home and foreign mission treasury.

Each state has its "Big Sister of Sunshine Bands." There is a National leader with co-workers.

Hospitality Committees and Executive Hospitality Committees in most of the states.

Wide Awake Bands, or Mother's Aid Board, which are equivalent to the Pastor's Aid Board.

Church Mother's Board, Missionary Circle, Purity Class, Young Women's Christian Council, Deacons' Wives Circle, Prayer Warriors, Usher Board, Women's Chorus, Board of Examiners, Educational Committee, Women's Evangelistic Conference, Retirement Fund Secretaries Committee, News Reporters, Sunshine Band with its Junior Boys League, Big Brothers Committee, Cradle Roll, and Happy Anticipation Group.

The women have become interested in establishing homes throughout the connection and we are no longer the National Women's Department, but The International Department of the Churches of God in Christ. Since we have stretched across the sea.

Mother Lillian Brooks Coffey has most efficiently done the task for which she has been chosen and today she is esteemed as one of the greatest leaders among Christian women.

Document 7: 1941 Annual Convocation Minutes, Church of God in Christ

The national convocation of 1941 was interesting for several reasons. First of all, although the women are subordinate, they are not marginal to the proceedings of the church. Second, the minutes highlight the connection between the women's department and the National Council of Negro Women. Contrary to the stereotype of the

Sanctified Church as oblivious to concerns for social change and racial uplift, "the Saints" were quite proud of the relationships they had developed with the national leadership of "the Race." Excerpts from these minutes also demonstrate the efficiency of the women's department in the raising of money. Insights are provided into the role of the district missionary and the separation of these roles from marital ties. Within the black religious experience, the Sanctified Church went farther than other churches in separating women's leadership roles from their marital relationships. Since the district missionary was charged with the task, among others, to "inform and remind the churches in her district at least two times a year of their responsibilities toward the local church, district, state and national work," the potential for conflict of interest was present. Such conflicts involving spouses were the subject of the National Convocation. Finally, the devotion of the women and the entire church for the national supervisor, Mother Lizzie Woods Roberson, is apparent throughout these minutes.[68] *They were aware that her health and her age might not permit her to attend many more meetings. Indeed, she passed away at the end of the 1943 convocation.*[69]

So gracious is the Lord in extending another privilege to the Saints of God from North, South, East and West ... to come together in another Holy Convocation. Regardless of the truth that many of the Saints have ceased from the walks of this life, hosts are left to lift up their voices in praise and adoration to God, for his goodness and mercy. At the hour of prayer the presence of God was great among us. God graced all who were looking for "surprise packages" from God, to enter into a 3 day fast. Oh!! how the spirit did intercede for the strength of God's people. God with them, leaving them witnesses of his power to heal all manner of diseases and to cure the sin-sick soul. The house was filled with the glory of God as we fell prostrate before him.

We heard words of exhortation from a few of the State Mothers present. Mother M. Payton, N.Y., Mother L. Bostic, St. Louis, Mo., Mother Buchanan, Mississippi. All greeting the convocation, in love, and acknowledging the truth as taught in the word. They spoke of the suffering it takes to walk with God, for it is an Evil day, God is working: so is Satan.

We had greetings from State Mother Hale, Southern California, who came forth singing, "All Things in Jesus Supplied" for God wills his saints to live righteously in this world. She told of God's help as a physician in child-bearing when all other help had failed. Her message was both spiritual discernment and a help to expectant mothers.

Following our Mother was Eld. S. Crouch, Overseer of California, who gave a God-compliment to his State Mother for her beautiful message, "for we come to this convocation for general instruction. When the rudiments of the church have been instilled in the members, all powers of hell cannot move them. The basic principle should not be tampered with. Make a place for the children. The whole world is headed for chaos, unless the saints hold on; this old world will not last long. The world is suffering for spiritual leadership."

From our Assistant General Mother L. Coffey we received greetings and she thanked God for God's blessing on the Senior leaders, Eld. C. H. Mason and Mother Lizzie Roberson. "Many officials of this church have been stricken, yet their lives are tied up in their work. And all their energy is given to the uplift of the work. Promotion does not take one out of service. We should serve for there is plenty of service to render. I am a servant of the most high God. God gave me this appointment and no man can take it from me." Mother Coffey was blessed to have a consideration opened for her through Pres. [of Saints Academy] Arenia Mallory, to attend the National Federation of Negro Women's Clubs, as a representative of the Church of God in Christ; not as an invited guest but as a leader and a guest of the President's honored wife, Mrs. E. Roosevelt; together with Mrs. Bethune, as president of this organization and the many other women of national repute. We know of no one more eligible for such a position, and to embrace such an occasion, to express herself on "Religious Morale." Also, among the noble women present we were happy to hear of the presence in this meeting of Miss Arenia Mallory, Pres., Saints Industrial School, Lexington, Mississippi and Mrs. Alice Mason Amos, daughter of Bishop Mason. Each had a voice in this meeting. God has given them wisdom to come before rulers and magistrates.

Much praise was accorded the Sisters for attending the call of Gen. Mother Roberson. Over $17,000 was sent in to our Gen. Mother and it made the heart of the Senior Bishop glad in receiving. Financial support was promised by all.

God's favor was to us in that he touched the body of our General Mother and brought her as it were from the dead, and let her be at her post of duty. As she appeared in our midst, accompanied by her beautiful and loyal daughter, Sister Ida Baker, our hearts overflowed with joy. Just to see her, comforted hearts that had been in sorrow. Her appearance was made possible by the love extended to her by her executive board of women. Assistant General Mother L. Coffey asked for absolute quietness to reign, and the Saints of God to arise at her coming, in honor of her presence in the room. Great was the demonstration, in God. Tears of joy were shed. She wanted all to know that she was not dead. She is the National Mother exercising all the power

invested in her by Senior Bishop Mason, in the organizing of the
Women's work. Her gratefulness extended to all her Mother's staff
for their love to her; they coming from far and near to be at her
bedside and administer to her comfort and to pray for her deliverance. She taught her daughters a beautiful lesson. Mother said her
success in the work was due to this truth that she had God's word and
did not fail to use it in the regulation of her work. We listened to the
touching testimony of her daughter, Sis. Baker, as to her untiring care
of mother. Questions were asked Mother concerning the power invested in District Missionaries and those exluded from serving. Those
not serving are Minister's wives in the same district with the husband.
They are privileged to work in any other district. All district missionaries are subject to the State Mother. No district Missionaries are to
be called "Supervisors." Her appointments are under the supervision
of her State Mother: both working in cooperation. Many instructions
were given to State Mothers and Workers.

Elder R. F. Williams gave the message. Text—Romans 1:16, "I am
a debtor" "I am not ashamed of the gospel for it is the power of God
unto salvation to every one that believes." . . . Every auxiliary is subordinate to the one cause of saving souls. He said the women of this
church have a place and you do not have to fight for a place. The
brethren cannot get along without the women, neither the women
without the men. Let the tension down, sisters; when the sisters are
referred to in admonishing do not be offended; for the scripture is
to be given in season and out of season—reprove, rebuke, and exhort."

The Saints Industrial School, Lexington, Mississippi, held it annual program. After a prolonged absence, we welcomed Sis. Arenia
Mallory, President. . . . Discussion of the Negro problem by four high
school girls was note-worthy. . . .

We waited in high expectancy for Mothers Day Service. A beautiful program was arranged by our Assistant General Mother L. Coffey,
one whom Mother styles as her "eyes, feet, hands, and ears"; and left
this edict with all her daughters: "Do what she tells you to do because
she speaks my words." At the appointed hour (Tues., Dec. 9) seated
on the platform were 34 State Supervisors. We beheld our General
Mother walking down the aisle in all the dignity of her office. Our
hopes and prayers were realized. . . . Mother gave her daughters
more instructions. Speaking, she said, that it was the part of the State
Mother to defend the Overseer, and should the wife be serving with
him in the capacity of District Missionary (in case of misunderstanding) it would become a husband and wife issue; for wife or husband
will defend one another. People do not want all the church to be
consolidated in one house. Go from this meeting and make the
changes, then come back to a new appointment. [Monetary] assess-

ments [of the women] should not be raised by the Overseer unless in co-operation with the State Mother.... Evening message [was brought] by Mother B. Buffkin [from] Exodus 33:13–14 [Now therefore, I pray thee, if I have found grace in thy sight, show me now thy way, that I may know thee, that I may find grace in thy sight: and consider that this nation is thy people. And he said, My presence shall go with thee, and I will give thee rest."] The Lord blessed the message and hereto were electrified.

Some services were broadcast over the radio, and Sister Smith included highlights from these services in her minutes. In this final portion, it is interesting to note that the only reference to the entrance of the United States into the Second World War, which began during this convocation, was made in the context of concern for the safety of several missionaries.

Broadcast: Sis. Arenia Mallory, mistress of ceremonies. [The] Women's activities were opened to us by Mother L. Coffey and the speaker to radio land was Mrs. Selma Lockett, Michigan. She spoke with authority the words of "the Book." She was beautiful in her presentation and in her aim to reach and send the message of deliverance....

... Bishop C. H. Mason spoke to an over flowing house, even into radio land. The power of God was present in the healing service, with Mother E. J. Dabney standing by the side of Bishop Mason, interceding for the souls of men.

Listened to Mother singing "A Charge to Keep I Have." Love and loyalty were expressed by the State Supervisors and Missionaries by their love offering to General Mother. Not one State Mother came short of her obligation and pledge. Missionaries responded. The Brethren did not forget her. Tributes of love surrounded her chair. She was treated as a "queen" in her own right. Ass't Mother Coffey put forth every effort to make it a day never to be forgotten.

General Mother Roberson, in appearance, looked as if a vital illness had not been her experience. Her eyes were brilliant; her voice resonant; her speech just like Mother of former days. Unswerved in the doctrine of the Church of God in Christ.

"You may think Elder Mason and I are too old to run this church but we have brought you where you are."

Sister Baker said "chain prayer" was heard in heaven, sent up by the saints everywhere; and she now was rewarded for the sleepless nights and the unshed tears watching and waiting for the end; for God had given her Mother to live.

Mother danced. The saints stood up, looked, and shouted for joy.

Our General Mother's desire was that the Auxiliaries organized by her hand and approved of by Senior Bishop C. H. Mason may be carried on even after she be sleeping [dead]; the teaching and the loyalty be so instilled in the hearts of her supervisors and missionaries that they contend for the continuation of the auxiliaries to remain in the church and nothing be changed. Let her work live on. Every State Mother, who has a contrary woman, one who will not obey, the State Mother is authorized by General Mother Roberson to take her license. Mother appointed one State Mother, Sister L. Coffey, to be [her] assistant. "As long as she speaks my words, hear her. You are going to do right, women, or you are going to be set down." (Can't you vision Mother's talking).

Another day in the Convocation was Mother [Lillian Brooks] Coffey's day. . . . God held her in remembrance to the Executive Body and they responded to a love offering for her. Bishops, Overseers, State Supervisors were responsive to the call, for she has rendered a service of love. Presentations were made to her representing all who loved her. She heartily thanked everyone for their thoughtfulness to her. (All recognized in her graciousness and wisdom). Sister L. V. Hearne, National chairlady of Y.P.W.W. [Young People's Willing Workers], presented a token of love from Field Workers.

The calamity that suddenly came on the United States [Pearl Harbor] did not dampen the ardor of the saints in rejoicing. At the beginning of the meeting, we heard the Spirit crying "destruction," "death". The worst is yet to come. . . . Intercessional prayers are made for those in authority. . . .

. . . The meeting is drawing to a close. Hosts are departing not regretting the coming together. State Mothers Council held its session, Mother Roberson's assistant, Sister Coffey, presiding in her stead. A vital issue concerning Women's Work was talked on. On December 11th, Elder Mason called a joint meeting. The Bishops and Ministers Counsel and the Women's Counsel were together to hear things passed on and things requested from each side. It was an open session to the Convocation at large. Mother Coffey, speaking of misunderstanding, said in expressing opinions on any particular issue, "You will find that all do not think alike; there may be differences among them; but disagreements should not make us enemies; we are brethren and sisters. . . .

Document 8: Church of the Living God, Christian Workers for Fellowship

Among the denominations formed and counted among the Sanctified Church is the Church of the Living God, Christian Workers for Fellowship (CWFF). The founder was a Baptist preacher named William Christian, who began the work in April 1889, in Wrightsville, Arkansas.[70] It is interesting to note that Christian's preaching against racial and denominational divisions created quite a bit of controversy

in the pre-First World War South with its racism, jim crow, and
growing Ku Klux Klan. Once, white policemen tried to silence him
when he preached against "white men intermingling with Negro
women . . . and that without being married to them."[71] Reverend
Christian died in 1928, leaving all of his earthly matters in the care
of his wife.

This church ordained women and permitted them to pastor.
These excerpts are from a church history compiled to celebrate its
seventy-fifth anniversay. Much of the history consisted of biograph-
ical and autobiographical sketches of ministers, officers, and their
spouses. Women are prominent in every aspect of denominational
life.[72]

Bishop Marcellus Ross
Evangelist L. B. Ross

... He and his wife teamed together in the Evangelistic Field.
Together they preached throughout the city of Birmingham [Ala.],
Ensley, Ala., [and] Marietta, Ga. They suffered many hardships and
had to have police protection in many mining quarters at Pratt City.

Evangelist Ross organized the first church in Birmingham, Ala.,
and through her Bishop J. B. Mason became a member of the church.

They moved to Cincinnati, Ohio and organized a church there in
1916. She served one time as president of the Women's Work; president of the Evangelist Board and worked side by side with her husband. In 1943, she departed this life. The convention was in session
at the time of her funeral and they observed a period of meditation
in her behalf. . . . Bishop and Evang. Ross leave an adopted daughter,
Evang. Eula Reese, who is pastoring the church (original) they organized at Cincinnati, Temple No. 50.

Evangelist E. J. Tyree Cooper
First President Y.P.P.U.

Elizabeth Jean Cooper is a native of Ohio. Her parents were God-
fearing people, so they raised their children in the fear and admonition of the Lord. She united with the church at an early age and was
baptized by her father. She received the divine call when she was in
the 4th grade in elementary school. Her father, being a minister did
quite a bit of street preaching. The children usually accompanied
them when they were out preaching. She was affectionately known as
"Little Lizzie." So because of the nature of the surroundings and
environments they did not pay any attention to her when one day she
started speaking of the Lord. She finished high school but because of
the fact that they did not believe in women preachers, they did not
encourage her to continue.

After seeing that she was truly endowed with the gift of preaching.

Rev. and Sister Inman along with Evang. Mays of Cincinnati, Ohio handled her; then on to Chicago with Eld. and Sis. Murf where she met Eld. and Sister L. H. Dixon. They had the church at 4008 S. State. They affectionately adopted her and gave her much encouragement to continue in the ministry.

Although she conducted revivals for Eld. Dixon, her first out of state revival was conducted in St. Louis, Mo., under the pastorate of Bishop E. T. Webb following Evang. J. Kathy Edmonia Buckner and Evang. Kathryn Daniels-Vickers. During this revival, 14 were added to the church. She left there and went to Tulsa, afterwards traveling extensively over the Brotherhood serving all, where she has continued.

In 1938, she was appointed first president of the Young People's Progressive Union, a newly created national organization. Her deep affection and knowledge of our youth and understanding of their problems made her the perfect one for the job. She served two terms and then she realized that her ministerial duties interfered with this job. In 1957, she was ordained by Bishop Overton and Bishop Musgrove in Tulsa, Oklahoma. Her first charge was in 1958 at Dayton, Ohio, her hometown. Soon she found out that pastoring was not a job for her, so she returned to the evangelistic field where she still is today, serving all humanity.

Document 9: National Black Sisters' Conference

In 1916, the Handmaids of the Most Pure Heart of Mary was founded as a "Community of Colored Sisters for Colored People [sic]." Mother Mary Theodore was a cofounder of this religious community of black nuns. In 1929, the congregation joined the Franciscan Order and became the Franciscan Handmaids of the Most Pure Heart of Mary. The Handmaids are a canonical institute of diocesan status who serve communities in Harlem, New York; Georgetown, South Carolina; Wilmington, North Carolina; and Kingston, Jamaica, West Indies. The Motherhouse is in the Archdiocese of New York.[73]

The Franciscan Handmaids are only one of several congregations of black religious women. In 1968, women from the several congregations organized the National Black Sisters' Conference. The following is taken from their Statement of Purpose.[74]

The members of the National Black Sisters' Conference pledge to work unceasingly for the liberation of black people. Black religious women see themselves as gifted with the choicest of God's blessings.

The gift of our blackness gives us our mandate for the deliverance of a special people, our own black people. And the gift of our religious vocation makes accessible to us that union with Christ which guides us to the task, strengthens our determination, and sustains our efforts.

Black sistes are fully aware of that great WEALTH OF PERSON which is the rich heritage of black people in America. The National Black Sisters' Conference appreciates most deeply that total black experience, that indefinable yet identifiable "soul" which is our proud possession.

The communal concern of black folk is our greatest asset. It is the cornerstone of our endeavor to deliver a people who will carry on the great work to which Christ has called us, the work of building the Kingdom of God.

The National Black Sisters' Conference is initiating programs that will enable the people to question the reality and validity of what has been presented to them by the Church, formal education, government and by big business: thereby having a greater part in shaping not only our environment but also our future and, most important, the future of our children and we will share this new determination with all who are interested.

Within this context, we believe it is necessary to express ourselves as black religious women.

Document 10: Mrs. S. Willie Layten: Lifetime Champion for Womanhood

The lack of boundaries between the sacred and secular is exemplified in the lives of most notable black women. Denominational work and "race" work were not seen as separate.

Among the heroines presented to Baptist young, and similar to those presented to young women in the Sanctified Churches, were women who were "active in fighting for the rights of womanhood and the race. . . .[75]

W. E. B. DuBois, writing in the Crisis about the source of motivation for black women in club work and race work, wrote an essay in which he described the divine call and commissioning of black women in terms similar to the biblical stories of Moses, Gideon, and Isaiah. When they protested that they could not face the tasks because they were women, "the King answered: 'Go then, Mother of men.' " When they protested that they were single, "the King cried: 'O Maid made Man, thou shall be Bride of God.' "[76] DuBois described the third call of black women thus:

And yet the third time the woman shrank at the thunder in her ears, and whispered: "Dear God, I am black." And the King spake not, but swept the veiling of his face aside and lifted up the light of his countenance upon her and lo! it was black.

So the woman went forth on the hills of God to do battle for the King on that drear day in the land of the Heavy Laden, when the heathen raged and imagined a vain thing.[77]

Such vision and revelation were attributed to the experience of

*Mrs. S. Willie Layten, the first president of the Woman's Auxiliary of
the National Baptist Convention. Not only did the young people's
handbook contain a summary of her life, but a later edition updated
the biography with a description of her funeral and the text of her
eulogy—"She shall be brought unto the King in raiment of needle-
work." Her pastor then suggested that "Mrs. Layten got a glimpse of
the Palace before she left this world, and came back long enough to
tell us about it."[78]*

*She was an educated woman, well-prepared to lead the Woman's
Auxiliary of the National Baptist Convention. The following excerpt
is taken from her biographical sketch in the handbook. This vignette
demonstrates the combination of political activism, faith, and educational achievement that was emphasized during the first part of the
twentieth century in denominational circles.[79]*

Up; for this is the day in which the Lord hath delivered. . . . is
not this Lord gone out before thee? Judges 4:14

Mrs. S. Willie Layten was the daughter of the late Rev. W. H.
Phillips, one of the most outstanding Baptist ministers of our denomination, and Mrs. Mary H. Phillips. From early childhood she was
trained in the service of the Lord, and has always been active in
church and public service work. Rev. Phillips organized and pastored
his first church in Memphis, Tennessee, where her girlhood was
passed, and her early education received. She was a graduate of
LeMoyne College, and has done post-graduate work in California and
Pennsylvania. She earned her degree and had the honorary degree
of M.A. conferred upon her by State University, Louisville, Kentucky.

At the Baptist World Alliance in Atlanta, Georgia, Mrs. Layten
swayed her audience with the facts and truths of her subject—"The
Advance and Achievements of the Negro Woman." The audience
lived with Mrs. Layten through this message. When she came to the
end of the time allotted her, she said, "My friends I have so much
more I can tell you but I must stop here," and turned to take her seat,
but they stayed her and extended her time ten or twenty minutes. You
could hear throughout the audience of all races when she finally did
take her seat; "Isn't she a wonderful speaker."

Now we will listen to Mrs. Layten tell us the why, and prove that
"practice makes perfect."

"My first public speech was made at the age of three years, so my
mother told me. The subject was, "I Had a Little Doll and Her Name
Was Rose." In my childhood I was often gathering groups of children
from the streets or anywhere, taking them on my mother's back porch
and arranging them in a circle and talking to them about Woman's
Rights or the Civil Rights Bill.

I was converted and baptized at the age of 9 years by my own
father. So sorry to admit it, but I was often the leader in school fights.

Being a preacher's daughter, many eyes were upon me, and among the many to watch me was the wife of a well-known deacon of Memphis. She always seemed to know and preceded me home to report these fights. None of the children liked Sister Wiley, as she was called, and we planned many pranks for her.

I do not remember the year, but I was a member of the first cooking, or domestic science class in the South, taught at LeMoyne School. I learned economy in food-stuffs there. The girl who left her bowl the cleanest, or left the least flour sticking to the sides of the bowl, was the receiver of high credits.

My mother made it a habit to entertain my teachers and faculty of LeMoyne School at our home once a year, and father bought bouquets once a year for me to give to each of my teachers.

My familiarity and love for the Bible is perhaps due to my sainted mother who loved to read to me and tell me Bible stories. Sunday schools used to include in their programs the memorizing of Scripture verses, or of the Psalms. My mother delighted to rehearse me in these and generally at the close of the year I would receive the prizes for having committed and recited the greatest number of Bible verses."

Practice does make perfect, but one is amused to read the confession of the culture, refined and soft-speaking S. Willie Layten, when she says, "So sorry to admit that I was often the leader of school fights." And these soap box talks in the childhood gatherings proved how anxious she was, even as a child, for the rights of women and her race.

Mrs. Layten's early married life was spent in California, where she helped to organize the West Baptist Association of California, and was the first president of its Woman's Auxiliary. She organized the first woman's club in the State of California. This club is still working in the Federated Clubs. She was elected president of the Woman's Auxiliary of the National Baptist Convention when it was organized in 1900, and has continued in this progressive service until 1949. She was one of the organizers and promoters, as well as workers, in the Association for the Protection of Colored Women, a social organization which has done so much to improve conditions among the working women of our race. This Association helped to formulate a National Association for the protection of colored women, which later on, merged with the Armstrong Association of New York City, a committee on Industrial Conditions among Negroes, and formed the present Urban League of New York City. She was the first Negro woman to have ever worked for the Travelers' Aid in this country.

As president, she represented the National Baptist Woman's Auxiliary abroad in three countries: Stockholm, Sweden, Canada and the Bahama Islands. Hers was an active life with youth, because she works with her daughter, Mrs. Madeline Tillman, in child-welfare associations. She was one of the first women to enlist and wear the uniform of Volunteer Civilian Service Corps which carries with it working with children, and helping in the protection of women in the home, not only during Defense time, but for the care of the mothers and children in the home in peace time after World War Number Two.

. . . [M]any who knew her through the years spoke of the great and very kind things she had done while she had strength.

. . . Mrs. Layten lived in Philadelphia, Pennsylvania, and was still active in fighting for the rights of womanhood, and the race in the courts of Pennsylvania until her death in January [1950]. Hers was a versatile mind, and she spoke with as much enthusiasm and kept abreast with the times as did little S. Willie Layten on her mother's back porch, or around the circle in those childhood days in Memphis, Tennessee.

Document 11: Nannie Helen Burroughs: "She Knew What She Wanted to Be"

From 1900 until the time of her death in 1961, Nannie Helen Burroughs was the most pivotal, if not the most prominent woman among black Baptists—and, with the exception of Mary McLeod Bethune, among organized black Christians. She wrote newspaper columns and magazine articles that admonished black people to be proud of themselves and their spirituality.[80] She felt, like DuBois, that the spiritual gifts of black people were essential to the humanization of the American political economy.[81] Nannie Helen Burroughs was also a founder of the Association for the Study of Negro Life and History and an ardent supporter of the work of Carter G. Woodson. Her school emphasized industrial arts rather than liberal arts, but proficiency in Afro-American history was a requirement for graduation from the school. Additionally, she encouraged her students to participate in oratorical contests that focused upon black history and black pride.[82] Although she was officially at odds with the National Baptist Convention for a number of years, many preachers continued to give her financial support. Adam Clayton Powell, Sr., pastor of the Abyssinian Baptist Church in New York City (Harlem), even promoted the celebration of a Nannie Helen Burroughs Day (Document 13).

The National Baptist Convention was and remains antagonistic to women as preachers, yet their lives were included in the handbooks and books of stories that presented Baptist heroes and heroines. The following excerpt presents the life of Nannie Helen Burroughs as told to the Young Peoples' Department of the National Baptist Convention through its "Handbook."

I can do all things through Christ which strengtheneth me.
Phillippians 4:13

On a farm at beautiful Orange Springs, Virginia, in the month of May, a girl was born to the family of Mr. and Mrs. John Burroughs.

Her mother's name was Jennie; her father later entered the ministry. They named the baby Nannie Helen.

Little Nannie spent an unusually happy childhood, for aside from her own parents, there were several aunts and uncles to love her. At a very early age her mother moved to Washington where they shared the home of a devoted aunt, Mrs. Cordelia Mercer. When she was old enough, she entered school, and later joined the 19th Street Baptist Church where she had attended Sunday school. During this growing up period Nannie Helen made many friends in the community.

Her resourcefulness developed very early in life. One day, while making doll clothes with the other little girls, Nannie Helen discovered all the scissors of the household had been put out of reach. Undaunted by this fact, she calmly went out to the wood shed, laid her cloth on a chopping block and cut her doll's dress with an axe!

Soon she was ready for high school. Of course, like all other ambitious young people, she knew what she wanted to be—a domestic science teacher. For six years she studied and worked to that end. By this time many of the qualities which have set her apart as a great leader were quite evident. As a member of the popular Literary Society she had many opportunities to speak.

Although in great demand and at the same time very happy to serve on youth programs throughout the city, she never allowed these opportunities or her successes to swerve her from the ambition of becoming a domestic science teacher. Around the home she displayed unusual artistic ability in home making. She was always cleaning up and changing things.

One day while cleaning she decided to change all the furniture in the house. This decision included the room of her uncle, a very stern man whom the children held in awe. That evening her uncle went up to his room and because it was a very hot night did not turn on the light. After undressing he decided to sit on the bed. Miss Burroughs had moved the bed to the other side of the room, so he sat—very hard—on the floor. When she heard the noise and her own name called out with an ominous sound, realizing what had happened, she ran into her aunt's closet where she spent most of the night.

When she was ready for teaching, she faced a disappointment—few teachers were appointed the year Miss Burroughs graduated, she being so very young, the appointment went to the more mature applicant. That year she entered Strayer Business College (at that time open to colored students). She was a good student and upon graduation secured work in a newspaper office in Philadelphia, Pa.... It was while employed in this office that the late Dr. L. G. Jordan saw her and invited her to join his staff of the Foreign Mission Board at Louisville, Kentucky.

About this time the National Baptist Convention was ready to organize the Woman's Auxiliary at the Richmond, Va., meeting. Mrs. S. Willie Layten was elected president of the women; Miss Burroughs' name was offered as corresponding secretary. Many objected because of her youth, but the election finally went through.

The Headquarters of the Woman's Convention was located at Louisville where Miss Burroughs worked jointly for the women and for the Foreign Mission Board. One of the major objectives of the Woman's convention was Africa. Miss Burroughs traveled throughout the country, now recognized as one of the most forceful speakers among women. Supplies and money were sent to Africa by the women of the Convention through her office. It was through her efforts in speaking and writing that the first house built by Negro Baptist women was put up at Chiradzula, British East Central Africa, for the late Emma B. Delaney.

During this period Miss Burroughs co-authored a book on missions, with the late Dr. Jordan. It was called "Up the Ladder in Missions."

Aside from her field work she began to get out literature for missionary societies. Young people will always be grateful to her for the prophetic vision she had in recommending to the Woman's Convention the organization of a Young People's Department. Thousands of junior missionary groups have been organized and inspired as a result of this movement.

When the World Baptist Alliance met in London, England, Miss Burroughs was in great demand as a speaker, appearing before the general assembly at Exeter Hall and in Hyde Park.

Simmons University at Louisville, Ky., honored her with the Master's degree, and more recently Shaw University conferred a Doctorate upon this worthy woman.

The most daring venture of her career was the founding of the National Training School for Woman and Girls at Washington, D.C., on little more than faith. Located on a hill in a very desirable section of the District of Columbia, for more than thirty years she has trained women and girls who have gone forth to serve their God, their church, their country and the world, motivated by an urge instilled into them by this great character that has set them apart in every community. . . .

In 1948, Miss Burroughs was elected President of the National Baptist Woman's Convention. In the meeting in 1949, and the board meetings, all testified to the reorganization, and the new life and enthusiasm of the National Baptist Woman's Convention with the many new features and projects presented by the fertile mind of this great woman.

Document 12: "Who Started Women's Day?"

As the ministry of education was pivotal to the black sacred cosmos of the twentieth century, Nannie Helen Burroughs was undoubtedly one of the seminal black churchwomen "teachers" of the century. A leader of the Women's Auxiliary Convention of the National Baptist Convention from 1906, Burroughs also founded and was first president of the National Training School for Women and Girls located in Washington, D.C.[83] In many ways, the Training School was a logical outgrowth of Nannie Burroughs's idea and plan for a National Woman's Day within the local churches of the denomination.

The following document, issued by the Burroughs School, recounts that the original purpose of Woman's Day was to "raise women," not money.[87]

"Woman's Day Idea Is Now The Principal "Money Raising Day"
In Negro Churches Throughout America"

> "Sow a thought
>   and reap a deed;
> Sow a deed
>   and reap a character;
> Sow a character
>   and reap a destiny."

The Idea, Purpose and Plan

The Idea, Purpose and Plan of WOMAN'S DAY was first presented by Nannie H. Burroughs, the young Corresponding Secretary of the Woman's Convention, Auxiliary to the National Baptist Convention, in her report at the meeting of the Convention, in Memphis, Tennessee, September, 1906.

The work of the Woman's Convention had hardly begun. At that time, Nannie Burroughs was being dubbed an "upstart", and to which unkind thrust she was provoked to answer back, "I might be an 'upstart', but I am also starting up." The new Convention voted to accept the "Woman's Day" suggestion of its Corresponding Secretary.

The position as Corresponding Secretary gave Nannie Burroughs her chance to write "pieces."

Her proposal as to time was that the fourth Sunday in July be known as National WOMAN'S DAY.

The purpose of the day was to interest women of the local churches in raising money for Foreign Missions. The National day was proposed because the chief interest of the Woman's Convention, at its beginning, was to raise money for Foreign Missions. The Woman's Convention then had its office in the Headquarters of the Foreign Mission Board at Louisville, Kentucky.

The Corresponding Secretary suggested that in order to interest and develop the women, that the Secretary be permitted to prepare and send out the program and three special addresses (short but challenging) on Missions or on some kindred phase of that subject and that the speeches be written from research and study of the firsthand current information about the Missionary enterprise. It was pointed out that the material for the addresses furnished would be committed to memory by speakers selected by the Missionary Society and thus the Convention could discover and develop public speakers for church programs, particularly for Woman's Day. This day was not thought up as a scheme for raising money, but primarily for *raising women.*

The idea was given its first trial in July, 1907. In keeping with her plan, the Corresponding Secretary prepared and sent out "speeches." The returns were encouraging. It was evident that the women liked the idea and the speeches.

In the 1908 Report (Pages 249–250–251), here is in part what the Corresponding Secretary had to say about her "Woman's Day" idea. The last Sunday in July was accepted by you, at Memphis, as "Woman's Day"

We want all the women's organizations in the local churches to cooperate with us in making "Woman's Day" a day of awakening consecration for the cause of Missions. It ought to be that every Missionary Society and educational organization in every church would send for programs, make extensive preparation, and rally the people around the national standard, and report whatever is raised for Missions since that day has been set apart for that purpose; and there certainly ought not to be a woman officially connected with our National Organization who would ignore our appeal for help, and not send for programs, nor even mention the work we are trying to do.

We are sure that in our lodges, when orders reach you from headquarters, that a certain day will be set apart, and observed for a certain purpose, every member would be found in line of duty. The same women belong to the missionary organizations that belong to the lodges.

Why is it that we cannot make the last Sunday in July "NATIONAL WOMAN'S DAY" in deed and in truth. We are glad to report to you that this year we have come in touch with more of the societies than ever before. But even the number observing the day in 1908 is nothing compared with the large number of organizations we have in our churches. If the women in the societies who report to us, will awaken others by calling attention to the suggestions, better results will follow.

We can easily raise Five thousand dollars as Five hundred dollars. There are several societies that had successful meetings and reported every penny raised. There were others who went into the dividing business and, of course, we got very little. Some have not reported at all. Yet they used our addresses, programs and music.

May the Lord hasten the day when we shall not turn everything to our own account, and give the crumbs to the ones who have made possible our success.

You must know that the preparation of the addresses, music and programs require time and mental taxation. We are willing to make the sacrifice mentally and physically if it will help our cause; but it is painful thus to suffer while the missionary societies use the money for church expenses. We have appealed to the State Presidents to recommend at their next session that all women's organizations observe "Woman's Day" and contribute the money raised to Foreign Missions.

Surely it is possible through the combined efforts of the State representatives to have one day on which we will all be aiming at talking about the same thing. It will be a glorious day for our missionary organizations when such a program becomes an actuality.

A Million women praying! A million women singing! A million women desiring! A million women laboring for the coming of the kingdom in the hearts of all men, would be a power that would move God on his throne to immediately answer the petitions. It would mean spiritual dynamite that would blast Satan's greatest stronghold and drive sin to its native heath. Can we have such a day? God grant that we may, and thus hasten the coming of His kingdom.

Let us, therefore, make the last Sunday in July NATIONAL WOMAN'S DAY and call on all women's organizations in our local churches to cooperate with us in making this a day of awakening and consecration for the cause of Foreign Missions."

The Convention accepted the challenge.

Both "rhyme and reason" lay in the Corresponding Secretary's plan for developing public speakers through the prepared addresses and at the same time disseminate information about Foreign Missions. At that time, Foreign Missions was the chief interest of the newly formed Woman's Convention and Nannie H. Burroughs was the "upstart" Corresponding Secretary. It was quite obvious that the "gracious ladies" did not want to be bothered with new fantastic ideas.

It is a fact that God puts some great idea in every longing, human soul. At some time in our life—early or late, the earlier the better—we feel a trembling, fearful longing to do some good thing, something different to help some good cause.

It was just such an impulse and urge that led me to think of what a special day—dedicated to a great cause—could do for church women.

Though just an "upstart," as she was called, her reasons for suggesting such a day are as sound today as they were in 1906. In fact, today, we are in desperate need of women learning to become public speakers, and dedicated to a definite cause for which to speak. The fact of the matter is that the need is greater today than it was then.

Why July?

WOMAN'S DAY was set for late July, because by that time most State Convention activities have ended for the year, and workers in local

124

WOMEN AND RELIGION IN AMERICA

churches—under less strain—would be able to give full time and attention to learning speeches and soliciting gifts, preparatory to the "Great Day."

Be it understood that besides raising money for Foreign Missions, "Woman's Day" was intended to raise the women themselves—training them for public speaking and informed leadership through authentic, prepared, challenging speeches—music and techniques on how to get, willingly, larger contributions for Foreign Missions.

In order to help the churches discover talent in their own congregations, the then Corresponding Secretary, Nannie H. Burroughs, worked earnestly and enthusiastically, doing research and setting up detailed pilot programs for WOMAN'S DAY, complete with resource material, including speeches, music and plenty of factual information on missions and missionary personalities—asking only that the women send for these programs, and "make extensive preparation, rally the people around the national standard, and report whatever is raised, for missions, on the last Sunday in July."

Here is an excerpt from the Secretary's report at the meeting held in New Orleans, Louisiana, September, 1910:

The last Sunday was, as usual, observed as National Woman's Day. Material for making the meetings a success was furnished, and a number of societies cooperated with us in our effort to rally the women, all over the country, in behalf of missions.

We had hoped to place One Thousand Dollars into the hands of the Foreign Mission Board, as a result of our Anniversary effort, but the total receipts was $576.13.

Ten years later, the Corresponding Secretary wrote "Woman's Day" has degenerated into some kind of rivalry to "beat" the men raising money for the local churches. Child's play. That is an easy thing to do and the men like it. The reason is quite obvious.

Our high purpose was to help our women KNOW and GROW. Only the recording angel knows how much good our national ideas have meant to our churches.

It has been said that people do not value ideas unless they bring money to them. This is too true. We have three great ideas that were born to live and bless the world forever—Christmas, Easter and Mother's Day.

What are we doing with these three days? We are prostituting them to our own profit and pleasure—in ways that we choose not in ways originally intended by the initiators. Even Christmas and Easter! are prostituted—commercialized with God left out. On those days the majority of us give to ourselves! Eat, drink, dress and be merry. Now, think of "Mother's Day!" History records the fact that Miss Anna Jarvis, the originator of the idea, lived to see and to deeply regret that her idea was being ungloriously commercialized.

Some years ago the late Adam C. Powell, Sr., Pastor of Abyssinian Baptist, New York City, had the following to say to a great Sunday morning audience:

As much as the churches have gained from Nannie Burroughs' idea of WOMAN'S DAY and her famous play "THE SLABTOWN CONVENTION," every church ought to set aside one Sunday in the year to be known as "NANNIE BURROUGHS' DAY," (Thanks to my devoted friend, Dr. Powell, but Nannie Burroughs does not want a day named for her.) and send this woman every dollar they raise on that one day in the year to endow and operate the school which she founded for women and girls at Washington, D.C.

Continuing, Dr. Powell said: "The churches owe it to her because we are all getting more money off of her idea of WOMAN'S DAY and her play "THE SLABTOWN CONVENTION," than we are getting from any other idea given to the churches in this generation."

The same day, Abyssinian Church gave $500.00 as an appreciation gift, and Dr. Powell made a personal contribution of $300.00.

Because of the way the purpose of WOMAN'S DAY has been diverted, our churches are reaping a financial harvest for church buildings, improvements and every conceivable local benefit. The promoters send off each year to get a WOMAN'S DAY speaker. Somebody who can draw a crowd. Had the original plan been followed, the churches would now have well-prepared speakers of their own. WOMAN'S DAY would be a real educational and spiritual achievement, blessing the local churches beyond imagination. Many women thus discovered and given opportunity to develop would be "tops" in Christian service. People would pack the church to see and hear their own discovery.

The day offers a glorious opportunity for women to learn to speak for themselves and thus become sublime symbols of devotions, lofty ideals, courage, fidelity and grace.

"Woman's Day," properly used, would put women's feet in the path of service and lift their heads up to see the field ripe unto harvest. But instead, women prance up and down church aisles, passing envelopes and baskets begging for money to beat the men.

WOMAN'S DAY should mean "Woman's Supreme Opportunity" to do what the woman did who talked with Jesus at the well. That woman "went to town" and brought the town out to "see Jesus."

Document 13: "The Slabtown District Convention"

Nannie Helen Burroughs made a wide variety of contributions to the Women's Auxiliary of the National Baptist Convention. Her legacy continues to live on in the Progressive National Baptist Convention as well. In addition to founding and encouraging the celebration of a national Women's Day within Baptist churches (which spread to every segment of the black religious experience), she wrote a play that *was designed to teach the proper behavior and role of women in their churches and their communities, to criticize behavior she perceived as unbecoming and counterproductive to the race, and to provide a witty and provocative means to raise funds. The play poked fun at every aspect of a typical convention program from the "welcome" to the annual sermon. While Miss Burroughs was willing to make the sermon a witty object lesson, her piety did not permit her to include prayers in her mock convention. The excerpts are taken from the address of welcome, response, president's address, and an "appeal for the redemption of Slabtown."*[85]

Everybody Laughs the Evening Through at Slabtown But Everybody Gets the Point . . . "Ladies and gentlemen, delegates and friends: I have been selected to welcome you to Big Sandy. Amid the blooming of the flowers . . . singing of the birds . . . and rippling of streams, we welcome you. We welcome you to our homes, our schools, our church, our roads and our paths; our kitchens and our parlors; our farms and our horses; our gates are open and our doors are ajar. . . . Times got so hard about a month ago, we started to write you not to come, but our pastor told us to let you come on. People who are used to hard times at home need not expect better things away from home, especially if they ain't payin' for it. Some of the sisters are kinder complaining now. They say that women are big eaters and are more trouble than the men. . . . So you are welcome—thrice welcome—to Big Sandy. . . ."

. . . "Members of the Local Missionary Society, citizens and friends: On behalf of the delegates in attendance upon the Tenth Annual Session of the Slabtown Women's District Convention, I accept your welcome, such as it is. We shall hurry up and get through with our business and go home where we can get something to eat. We are sorry you are having such hard times here. Anybody who lived through the drought and the depression certainly can feed and sleep this handful of folks a few days. Of course, you all invited us . . . But we shall do the best we can and leave as soon as we can. We thank you for your hard-time welcome." . . . "It is now time for our President's address. . . ."

. . . "Fellow officers, delegates, ladies and gentlemen. . . . I have traveled all over Slabtown visiting missionary societies and waking up sleepy leaders. . . . I have gone to a number of missionary societies where there is about as much spiritual life as you would find in a graveyard. . . . Some of you missionary sisters are raising money for missions and paying church debts and making presents to yourselves and your pastors. The Bible asks, 'Will a man rob God?' I answer, yes. A man will not only rob God, but he will get the women to help him. Sisters, it is not right for you to raise money for missions and use it to make presents and pay church debts. . . ."

... "And now, to these brethren who come to these conventions to tell the sisters what to do and how to vote, I want to say to you that you are welcome to our meetings, and if you will appreciate the courtesy extended to you by this association, you will go down from this place without any mark of displeasure upon you. But if you come here to use some of these sisters as tools to carry points that will work to your advantage in the distribution of funds and other, we want you to look to the Lord and be dismissed right now...."

... "It affords me great pleasure to present Mrs. Betsy Lizzard, to make 'An Appeal for the Redemption of Slabtown.'" ...

... "Sister and Friends: ... I come in behalf of the schools in our district. I ain't no educated woman, but I got plenty of mother wit and common sense, and I got plenty of old-fashioned pride. I know the value of education in building up people and in building up communities. We can't get very far in these days without it and I certainly don't want to live in these woods with this raft of children growing up in ignorance. It is dangerous; and, furthermore, it is expensive.... It don't mean nothing but disgrace and workhouses and jails to let children grow up uneducated. We've been talkin' about making decent citizens, and I want to know how in the name of common sense we are going to make them when these people don't give our children but a few months of schooling and pay such no 'count salaries that they can't get teachers with sense enough to teach. Sisters, we just got to get the right kind of moral teachers who is properly educated, for the schools. We done had enough of that kind that thinks they are better than anybody else because they got a little education. That's all they have got. They ain't got no common sense and they ain't got influence enough to change a run-down community. Anybody can put on airs. We want teachers who can lift up a community ...

... "We want people who'll 'sociate with us; show us how to live; how to organize our community work; build up our Sunday schools and missionary societies. Some of them comes to church late, dressed like a lot of peacocks, and sits back and look in pity or scorn on us poor, unlearned critters, and laugh and nudge each other when we make mistakes.... There are just a few real ones. There's dear Miss Georgia ... She ain't got half the 'plomas that some ... got, but she's got more character and more sense.... She's what I call educated. These other folks are just schooled. She's a model.... Look how she speaks to us when she meets us.... Look how the boys and girls who go to her school talk her up, and look how many she's put ambition into to go to higher schools and get more education.... We want teachers with souls, heads and hands dedicated to the redemption of Slabtown. They are in the world and we must find 'um."

Document 14: Roll Call of Bible Women

Black women shared a legacy of struggle for literacy, based particularly on Bible reading.[86] *They entered the twentieth century with a clear understanding that the biblical text included them.*[87] *The introduction of Women's Day also gave black women the opportunity to lift up those passages of Scripture that were exclusively women's. Not only have black women claimed those passages of the Bible with female heroines, naming such women as Deborah and Mary and Phoebe as the models of service and leadership they should emulate; but occasionally they have also named anonymous women, placing them in the oral tradition by name and embellishing on the biblical text in order to maintain the prominence of a particular character. Within the Sanctified Church, the woman with the issue of blood acquired the name "Saphronia."*[88] *Taken together, all of these customs and traditions provide the foundation for a biblical feminism that embraced the entire English biblical text.*

The following excerpt is taken from a little booklet compiled and written by Nannie Helen Burroughs. Her "Roll Call of Bible Women" lists 148 women in alphabetical order. Burroughs insists that "Jesus taught new attitudes towards women—dignified their lives and gave them definite responsibility in Christian service." Finally, she reminds her readers that "women were not with Jesus in Gethsemane but women were last at the Cross and earliest at the grave."[89]

CANDACE, Queen of Ethiopia. Acts 8:27. She reigned over the Country in Africa, which the Greeks called Meroe. Candace, it seems, was the general official title borne by the queens of Ethiopia, as Pharaoh was the monarch of Egypt.

In the reign of Augustus Petonius, of Egypt, he waged war against Candace. Though blind in one eye, she was clear-headed, sagacious and war-like. It is said by Pliny, that Nero sent men to Ethiopia to explore the country, who had to return unsuccessful, and reported that a female called Candace reigned in Meroe, and she was of great power, therefore he could not stand before her.

Thus it seems that the Cushite nation believed in women's right. They knew how to obey, as well as to command; how to rule as well as to be ruled, when it related to their own dominion. Their queens were not embarrassed by their sex in the administration of their government; and their Ambassadors black and comely never failed to meet with due respect in the execution of their missions to Foreign Courts; for the Candace whose reign was contemporary with that of Caesar Augustus, entered into treaty relations with him, and established a friendly intercourse between the great Roman Empire.

Under the Candadean government, though they had no Gospel light, yet the good citizens found better protection to life, liberty, and the pursuit of happiness, than we find in many Christian lands. . . .

88. MARY, THE VIRGIN No. 1 (Hebrew Miriam). The mother of Jesus Christ. Afterward became the wife of Joseph, the carpenter. She was cousin to Elizabeth, mother of John the Baptist. She was a poetess. She wrote the magnificent—"My soul doth magnify the Lord, and my spirit doth rejoice in God my Saviour."

This song of Mary bears a great resemblance to the song of Hannah. Compared with Psalm 34:2; 35:9.

Who is this Poetess soaring in the high region of fancy with her garland and singing robe? Is she the queenly one among her people? A Miriam rousing the women of Israel to shouts of victory? A Deborah sitting under the stately Palm tree as Judge? A Judith returning with the gory head of the Assyrian general, Holofernes? Is she the honored leader of their schools of arts and social life? No! It is the song of a woman who lived in a mean city, nothing good or great was looked for there. Waifs of Royal blood were scattered over the land, but it had become so diluted that from any family as much might be expected. David's line was inglorious; there was no sign that it would ever again be famous.

Every Hebrew matron had the secret hope that her son might prove to be the Messiah.

Whose song is this? It is the song of a maiden who was to be the mother of our Lord. Tradition pictured her as comely in face and figure, with that excellent thing in woman, a voice ever soft and gentle, discreet, charitable, keen in vision, devout, studious of Sacred Books and delighted in prayer. It found in her the perfect type of training and piety, the ideal of humanity, the handmaid of the Lord.

1. She praised God for His condescension, "For He hath regarded the low estate of His handmaiden." Yes, she was poor and lowly in her worldy condition. Yet in the midst of this, all generations should call her blessed. Here is a proof in Luke 11:27: "And it came to pass as He spake these things (if satan be divided among himself) a certain woman of the company lifted up her voice, and said unto Him, blessed is the womb that bare Thee, and the paps which Thou hast sucked."

2. Mary praised God in the exercise of His power. God's hand had been terrible when lifted up against the evildoers—The Philistines, the Israelites, the Assyrians. He hath showed strength in His arms. He hath scattered the proud in the imagination of their hearts. She spoke as is common in prophecy, of God's purposes as tho already fulfilled. He hath put down the mighty from their seats, and the rich He hath sent away empty. The Scribes, Pharisees, the Chief Priests and rulers of the people.

3. She praised God for the equity of His acts. The people had been starving, while the idolatrous people were feasting. "He hath filled the hungry with good things, and the rich He hath sent empty away."

The needy should have enough, as they had begged God for it, and the full should suffer till they remember who gave them power to become rich. No one's foot can insure its hold on fortune's wheel. The Almighty can easily adjust the equations which puzzle us so much. Let me quote Psalm 75:6,7. "For promotion cometh neither from the east nor from the west, nor from the south: But God is the Judge, He putteth down one, and setteth up another."

4. Mary was jubilant over the fact that Jehovah was faithful to His promise. The glory burst upon her vision with the suddenness of a meteor. Out of a swelling heart she published the people's joy, that they have a faithful witness in Heaven. Yes, the Son of God declares: Though Heaven and earth pass away, His word shall not pass away."

Throughout this song we are to hear the voice not only of Mary, celebrating the praises of Him Who had so magnified her, but the whole Church, giving thanks for the mystery of the Incarnation, and the blessing of the Gospel.

Joy and thankfulness do not necessarily lead to pride and self-exaltation; for as we see in this song of Mary, there may be simple joy in God, unsullied by any thought of self. She forgets everything else in the contemplation of God's exceeding goodness. May every reader of this book have the spirit of lowliness and thankful joy.

Jewish Women in the Twentieth Century: Building a Life in America

ANN D. BRAUDE

"There is no more serious charge made against Judaism," wrote Henrietta Szold in 1915, "than the charge that women are neglected."[1] She saw the disparity between the roles of men and women in Judaism as a problem for Judaism as much as a problem for women, and believed that changes in women's role were necessary for the survival of Judaism in the modern world (Document 1). The history of the Jewish people during the twentieth century suggests that she was right. The incorporation of women into the synagogue service and into the Jewish communal structure have been essential elements of the most successful movements in American Judaism.

The discomfort of Jewish women has been a vital creative force in shaping American Jewish identity. Not satisfied with Judaism as it was practiced, they were no better satisfied with assimilationist alternatives. "I am full of faith," wrote Alice Seligsberg in 1919, "that though you and I may never have the comfort of a Jewish religion that will satisfy us, this religion is going to develop . . . " (Document 6). While many American-born Jewish women shared the convictions of Szold and Seligsberg, immigrant women molded Jewish life in response to other sources of discontent. Still dizzy from their flight from violence and oppression in Europe and Russia, Jewish women struggled for their families' material and educational advancement, and to overcome the hardships of life in the ghetto.[2] As soon as they and their families had achieved minimal economic security, they threw their energies into a vast organizational effort aimed at creating a safe world for Jews and a better world for all. As well as increasing their participation in organized Judaism in the Reform and Conservative movements, Jewish women were leaders in the

Labor and Zionist movements, which proclaimed visions of a new society based on justice and equality.

IMMIGRATION

The twentieth century opened in the middle of one of the great mass migrations of Jewish history. Starting in 1881, tens of thousands of Jews each year fled the poverty and persecution of the Old Country to make new lives in the *Goldene Medina* (golden land) of America, which was said to offer a life of freedom and riches. By 1923, when the United States closed its doors to immigrants, three million of the approximately twelve million Jewish population had crossed the Atlantic to America. Among the three million Jews who arrived from eastern Europe were a larger proportion of women than in any other group that arrived during this period. While some immigrant groups consisted mainly of men who hoped to save money and then return to their homelands, Jewish immigrants had no homeland to which to return. They staked all their hopes on the prospect of a new life in America. They came as families and they came to stay.[3]

The majority of Jews who arrived in the United States disembarked at Ellis Island, and made their way to Manhattan's Lower East Side as soon as they had cleared customs. Crowded into an area of a few square blocks, hundreds of thousands of Jews from all over Europe lived, worked, and worshiped in the same tenement buildings. Since 1900, half of the Jews in American have lived in New York City, forming the largest concentration of Jews ever gathered in a single time and place. Suddenly freed from hundreds of years of censorship, residence restrictions, and legal insecurity, the Jews of New York developed a rich culture of *yiddishkeit* (Jewishness). Also freed from traditional European sex roles, Jewish women approached the challenge of forging a new life in America with immeasurable vitality. A character created by the popular immigrant novelist, Anzia Yezierska, expressed the exuberance of Jewish women who went from the repression of Czarist Russia to the freedom of expression promised by America.

> I am a Russian Jewess, a flame—a longing. A soul consumed with hunger for heights beyond reach. I am the ache of unvoiced dreams, the clamor of suppressed desires. I am the unlived lives of generations of stifled Siberian prisons. I am the urge of ages for the free, the beautiful that never was yet on land or sea.[4]

Jewish women poured energy and determination into the maintenance of family life in the ghetto. A typical tenement floor contained four apartments of two or three rooms, each housing a family with several children, and the front room reserved for boarders. Tenements constructed after 1901 were required to have indoor plumbing, fire escapes, and windows that opened at least twelve feet from the next building; but "old law" tenements, lacking even these amenities, continued to supply a large proportion of East Side housing.[5] Unmarried women and girls went into the sweatshops, while married women labored under equally oppressive conditions. In the crowded kitchens of tenement apartments, married women cooked and did laundry for boarders, and fed their families in shifts, whenever this one or that one returned from the shop. Another Yezierska character described how difficult a routine task like serving meals became in tenement conditions.

> It was either to eat on the floor, or for me the job of cleaning off the junk pile three times a day. The school teacher's rule, "A place for everything and everything in its place," was no good for us because there weren't enough places.[6]

Whether women wanted to adopt American ways or maintain traditions, poverty stood in the way (Document 2). Homemakers struggled to keep the beauty of Jewish observance alive in the ghetto. Settlement worker Lillian Wald wrote of one woman she visited on a Friday afternoon who had put two kettles of water on the stove to boil so that her neighbors would not know that she was unable to fulfill her sacred obligation to prepare a special meal for her family on the sabbath.[7]

AMERICANIZATION

Crossing the Atlantic was not simply a geographic transition. Jews packed their bags in the semifeudalism of czarist Russia, and disembarked in the most modern city in the world, New York. The Judaism they brought with them was imbedded in cultural forms which corresponded to economic and social conditions that did not exist in the United States. The customs of early marriage and large families facilitated men's *halachic* (religious law) duty to procreate, but also reflected the different stages of economic and social development in the Old World and the New. Although some Jews moved to cities in Europe before emigrating, Russia continued to restrict Jewish residence in cities into the twentieth century.

To some Jews, America meant freedom to practice their religion unharassed. To others, it meant freedom from Judaism, freedom from religious authority, and from the pressure to conform to the standards of the Jewish community. For all, life in America presented a conflict between a deeply ingrained heritage and the appeal of Americanization (Document 3). For women, subject to men within Judaism, American ways had a special appeal. Mary Antin, in her paean to America, *The Promised Land*, lamented her sister's early marriage, which occurred two years after the family's arrival in the United States.

> Had she been two years younger she might have . . . evaded her Old-World fate. She would have gone to school and imbibed American ideas . . . it has

always seemed to me a pitiful accident that my sister should have come so near and missed by so little the fulfillment of my country's promise to women.[8]

The *sheitel,* the wig worn by married women to hide the attractiveness of their own hair, visibly distinguished recently arrived "greenhorns," still immersed in traditional Jewish culture, from women who had adopted some measure of American values, and dared to show their own hair. For mothers, the conflict between the new world and the old was experienced every day when their children returned from school, the primary vehicle of Americanization.

Jewish families were quick to take advantage of the public schools. In the Old Country, the chief function of education was to provide religious training for boys, so girls received little or no education. In the United States, the public schools brought boys and girls into the same classroom. So anxious were parents and teachers to have their children enjoy the benefits of life in America, that Americanization was often encouraged at the expense of respect for Jewish traditions. Julia Richmond, the German Jewish district superintendent of the Lower East Side schools, forbade the use of Yiddish, the *mama loshen* (mother tongue) spoken in the Jewish home. Children caught speaking Yiddish to each other at recess had their mouths washed out with soap. In the attempt to Americanize immigrant children, the public schools taught them that their heritage was un-American and lower class.[9] Parents who spoke Yiddish to their children were answered in English. It was often repeated that, "In America, children become the teachers of their parents."

Mothers who did not work outside the home had the least contact with American institutions, and often became embarrassments to their acculturated children. Stories with titles like "Embarrassed by Mother" pervaded the Jewish press.[10] Even Laura Hobson, whose classic novel, *Gentleman's Agreement,* exposed the insidious anti-Semitism of American society, was embarrassed by her parents' Jewishness, and especially by her mother's incessant fight for justice.

> As a child I was ashamed of them . . . They were *foreigners,* they had an accent, they did outlandish things, especially my mother, who would talk socialism to the milkman and the iceman, talk votes for women to one and all, and who would hold forth on the dire consequences of pouring ketchup on a frankfurter because the heartless manufacturers used preservatives like benzoate of soda. . . .[11]

Children learned contempt for their families and their heritage in the public schools and from the examples of German Jews and other Americans. Educators used the "oriental conception of woman's status" held by Jews to condemn Jewish tradition. A 1911 newspaper editorial about education claimed that

> A man whose religion requires him every morning to thank God that he was not born a woman is likely to treat women so that they will wish they had been

born men. We must not shut our eyes to the fact that in the future the Christian conception of womanhood is not to be maintained in this country without a struggle.[12]

America offered women opportunities for self-fulfillment clothed in anti-Semitism.

Outside of school and in the home, Jewish traditions were subject to assault from gentile women and uptown Jews who traveled to the Lower East Side as social workers and charity workers. While some provided genuine services, other made humiliation and degradation the price of material aid. Their constant attempts to distinguish the "unworthy poor" from the "truly needy" led to repeated prying and questioning, which was much resented by the recipients of their assistance. In a short story about charity on the Lower East Side, two "friendly visitors" cut off aid to a family when they burst in unexpectedly to find the children sharing a holiday cake a neighbor had received in the mail. The woman had certified in her application for aid that she had no friends to whom she could turn for help. Seeing that a friend had indeed supplied a cake, the chartity workers charged her with fraud and cut off food supplies to her children. "You call yourselves Americans?" raged the mother, "You dare call yourselves Jews? You bosses of the poor!"[13]

Lillian Wald, founder of the famous Henry Street Settlement, was one uptown Jew who tried to approach the Lower East Side with an open mind. By moving into the immigrant neighborhood, she hoped to understand it as a resident rather than as an outsider. The House on Henry Street provided nursing services and facilities for neighborhood events. In contrast to the example above, Wald tried to make services available to her neighbors while treating them with respect. The community appreciated that her efforts were different from those of Christian missions and social workers anxious to impose external values. She described one woman's reaction to a pageant at the settlement based on the Old Testament story of Miriam: "A woman who had suffered bitterly in her Russian home blocked for a moment the outgoing crowd at the door while she stopped to say how beautiful she thought it, adding with deep feeling, 'I thank most [sic] for showing respect for our religion.' "[14]

THE LABOR MOVEMENT

For the unmarried Jewish woman who arrived on America's shores, the next stop after Ellis Island was the sweatshop, after perhaps a few days respite at the tenement apartment of a family member. Young Jewish women and girls were a large proportion of workers in the growing ladies garment industry. The promises of plenty of jobs were true in a good season, but quickly dissolved during the slack season or during slumps in the industry. When work was available, women worked long hours under poor conditions for a fraction of the wage earned by men.

Twenty to twenty-five percent of the workers in the garment industry were "girl helpers" or "learners," who were paid little or nothing. They worked on the promise of a wage in the future—a promise that was not always kept. Under the piecework system, employers continuously cut the amount paid for each finished item as productivity increased, so that even the fastest worker never earned more than a starvation wage. Women had to bear the indignities of sexual harassment added to other sweatshop conditions (Document 2). Polly Adler, an immigrant garment worker who became a famous New York madam, described how her shop foreman beat and raped her. When she rejected his further advances, he threatened to tell her family about the abortion of the pregnancy he had caused, and she was forced to leave home.[15]

Under such exploitive conditions, it is not surprising that women proved to be excellent strikers, for they had little to lose. In 1909, Jewish women and girls shocked the world by walking off their jobs at the instigation of a twenty-year-old shirtwaist worker, Clara Lemlich. At a meeting called by tiny Local 25 of the International Ladies Garment Workers Union, the waistmakers' local, thousands of women listened to a long series of speeches. The labor leaders on the platform hesitated to urge the young workers to strike, knowing the material sacrifice and police brutality they would encounter. Finally, Clara Lemlich rose from the mass of workers and asked for the floor. She spoke in Yiddish.

> I have listened to all the speakers, and I have no further patience for talk. I am one who feels and suffers for the things pictured. I move that we go on general strike.[16]

In response, twenty thousand women took to the streets. Most were in their teens and twenties, and most were Jewish, although some Italian- and American-born women joined them. Wealthy New York women rallied to support the strike, as did the Women's Trade Union League, which included both workers and middle-class "allies." The "Uprising of the Twenty Thousand" was the first successful general strike in the garment industry, giving impetus to the emerging labor movement.[17]

In 1911, the Triangle Fire burned an indelible image in the hearts and minds of Jewish workers. People on New York's East Side watched 147 young women jump to their deaths from the flaming windows of the Triangle Waist Company. The fireproof building with inadequate fire escapes sustained little damage, but the East Side never forgot the sight of crushed bodies lying like bundles of clothing on the sidewalk (Document 2).

The martyred shirtwaist workers of the Triangle Factory added fuel to the labor protests in the garment industry. Although women were effective strikers, they faced great obstacles as union members and leaders. Alice Kessler-Harris has observed that these women "were caught between a trade union movement hostile to women in the work force and a woman's movement whose participants did not work for a wage."[18] They also had to face the ojections of traditional Jews to women assuming roles of public leadership. Their triple-bind was completed by the anxiety of the labor and Socialist movements not to appear foreign, which caused them to discourage Jewish leadership. Characteristically, when the Jewish labor leader Theresa Malkiel wrote her *Diary of a Shirtwaist Striker*, published by the Socialist party, she told the story in the first person through the mouth of a native-born non-Jew.[19] Nevertheless, Jewish women provided important early leadership for the organization of women wage workers.

Although they faced difficulties in the labor movement, Jewish women also benefitted from their participation in the garment industry and the culture to which the labor movement gave rise. Eleanor Learner has shown how the experience of men and women working together in the garment industry won the votes of Jewish men for women suffrage, thus swinging New York City and winning the important 1917 New York State election.[20] Jewish women also supplied important leadership in other political movements. Socialist Rose Pastor Stokes was a product of the Lower East Side who married into riches, but continued her Socialist activities.[21] Emma Goldman started off as a sewing machine operator, and became an internationally known speaker for anarchism, birth control, and free speech.[22]

Although some who became political activists were lost to the Jewish community, for others, radical politics became a way of being Jewish. Vivian Gornick has described how Jewish workers found meaning in the Communist party which reinforced their identification with the Jewish community. As a child she studied Yiddish after school, then came home to the culture of Jewish socialism, which included women's accomplishments in its elevated idea of the life of the worker.

> At the wooden table in our kitchen there were always gathered men named Max and Hymie, and women named Masha and Goldie. Their hands were work-blackened, their eyes intelligent and anxious, their voices loud and insistent. They drank tea, ate black bread and herring, and talked "issues." . . . I would point to one or another at the table and whisper to [my mother]: Who is this one? Who is that one? My mother would reply in Yiddish: "He is a writer. She is a poet. He is a thinker." Oh, I would nod, perfectly satisfied with these identifications . . . *He,* of course, drove a bakery truck. She was a sewing machine operator.[23]

In radical politics many Jewish women found a way of maintaining Jewish identity which promised to acknowledge the equality of men and women.

WOMEN IN THE SYNAGOGUE

"Perhaps the single most disruptive force . . . to American Jewish Orthodoxy," wrote the sociologist Marshall Sklare, "has been the position of woman." He found that failure to adapt to the American norm, in which women supply the bulk of time, energy, and money for the maintenance of religious institutions, would have meant "organizational suicide" for American Judaism.[24] Indeed, once exposed to American freedom, many Jewish women could not accept the restrictions placed on them by Jewish traditions. "Woe to us women who got to live in a Torah-made world that's only for men," exclaimed one fictional immigrant mother.[25] Emily Solis-Cohen, Jr., was shocked by the attitudes she encountered during field work for the Jewish Welfare Board in 1932.

> It was disturbing to encounter, the country over, the notion that in respect to proscribed religious observances, to the conduct of public worship, to education, even to some phases of domestic life, Jewish law discriminates in favor of the sons of Israel, and that such favor springs from its fundamental attitude toward Israel's daughters. Personal experiences of many a girl are cited by her, as warrant for the assertion that apparently "woman does not count in Jewish life."[26]

The traditional rabbinic explanation for the exclusion of women from the *mitzvot* (religious obligations) was that women were exempted from all religious duties that had to be performed at fixed times, because these conflicted with their duties as mothers and homemakers. The rabbis never felt compelled to explain why women had sole responsibility for home and children. Emily Solis-Cohen and Henrietta Szold accepted the view that exemptions from positive commandments "arise from a consideration rather than a disregard for women."[27] Szold extended the logic of this view to argue that the rabbis never intended to disqualify women from the *mitzvot,* but only to excuse them. Having no maternal or household responsibilities with which religious duties would interfere, she did not believe that she was exempt from the ritual obligation of saying *kaddish* for her mother, a responsibility usually limited to sons (Document 1).

Sklare attributed the great success of Conservative Judaism to the increased role allotted to women. The Conservative movement, which attempted to adapt Judaism to American life without departing from the process of historical development, followed exactly the Protestant model of "formal equality coupled with limited participation." Women were seated with men in services, and joined them in liturgical responses. However, the principle of equality was not extended to the most important part of the ritual, the handling and reading of the Torah scrolls, much less to ordination of women as rabbis.[28] Conservativism has become the dominant form of worship for American Jews, accounting for approximately half of those affiliated with synagogues.[29]

The incorporation of women into the synagogue service was also a significant factor in the success of the Reform movement in the nineteenth century, which, by 1880, represented almost all American congregations, until the influx of Jews from Eastern Europe introduced more traditional forms of worship. In the nineteenth century, Reform Jews made women the religious equals of the male laity. In 1923, when Martha Neumark, a student at Hebrew Union College, the Reform rabbinical seminary, petitioned the faculty to lead High Holy Day services, the Central Council of American (Reform) Rabbis had to decide whether to recognize her as a candidate for ordination (Document 4). Although they found that women could not "justly be denied the privilege of ordination," Hebrew Union College refused ordination to Martha Neumark, and to Helen Hadassah Levinthal in 1939, both of whom had completed the course of study for the Reform rabbinate. The Reform movement did not live up to its promise of equality for women until the ordination of Sally Preisand in 1972.[30]

No less than Reform and Conservative Jews, Orthodox Jews were faced with the reality of American sex roles, in which women had freedom and opportunities that were unheard of in the old country. During the 1920s, one Orthodox Rabbi observed that the debate over seating women behind a curtain in the synagogue was so heated that "congregations are formed or dissolved" over it.[31] Another found that "The modern Jewess, more than the modern Jew, is responsible for the disintegration of our faith," because women were not spending enough time at home creating a "Jewish atmosphere."[32] Although the Orthodox have emphasized the benefits of traditional sex roles over the need for change, some Orthodox leaders responded to the American scene with a resolve to offer women increased opportunities within traditional Judaism. Yeshiva University, itself an adaptation to the desire of Orthodox youth for secular education, opened a high school for girls in 1948. In 1954, Yeshiva opened Stern College for Women, at which students could pursue a collegiate program combined with an extensive Jewish curriculum under Orthodox auspices.[33]

The response of Orthodox Judaism to changing expectations of woman's role in America can also be seen in rabbinic opinions on a variety of contemporary issues. Rabbis have attempted to strike a balance between the good intended by such practices as the participation of husbands in natural childbirth and the strict halachic prohibition against a man touching a parturient woman—who, according to Jewish law, is in a state of ritual impurity (Document 5). The current controversy over the extension of the *eruv* is another example of Orthodoxy's responsiveness to women's desire for greater participation in the synagogue. The *eruv* is a rope or cord that creates a symbolic extension of domestic space, thus allowing Jews to do one form of labor—carrying—which is otherwise forbidden on the Sabbath, within its boundaries. Outside the *eruv*, mothers must stay home from services until their youngest child is old enough to walk. Some Orthodox communities would like to extend their *eruv* so that mothers can attend services on the sabbath.[34]

Although Orthodox Judaism has made some concessions to the role

of women in the modern world, women have periodically pressed Orthodox leaders to seek avenues of further change in accordance with Jewish
law. In both 1924 and 1928, the International Council of Jewish women,
with substantial American participation, passed resolutions "for establishment of a World Conference of Rabbis, which was in accordance with
the principles of traditional Judaism, to concern itself with the legal
problems of women with reference to marriage and divorce."[35] This
campaign continued into the 1930s, but was cut short when the incarcera-
tion of the Jews of Europe in Hitler's death camps made an international
assembly of rabbis impossible.

With the destruction of European Jewry, the way of life that had
supplied models of piety for Jews throughout the world ceased to exist,
and American Jewry assumed a new cultural significance. A total of
250,000 Jews arrived in the United States during and after the second
World War. This immigration included some Jews so traditional that they
would not leave their ancestral communities in Europe until death was
the only alternative. Among these were Hasidic Jews, who emphasized
a traditional role for women, including practices such as attending the
mikvah (ritual purification following menstruation). The Hasidic Luba-
vitch Women's Organization encourages nonobservant women to light
Sabbath candles and observe the "women's mitzvah's." It is too early to
judge the full impact of this most recent immigration on women's roles
and religious practice.[36]

ZIONISM AND SOCIAL SERVICE

In 1931, the widely respected civic leader Rebekah Kohut observed
that,

> The exemption of women from the performance of all legal and ceremonial
> obligations imposed by Jewish law on the male has placed her in an anomalous
> position where she appears virtually ignored, whereas morally she is an object
> of exaltation. However, from time immemorial, we see her combatting this
> supposedly inferior social status, and today we see that she has successfully
> assumed a place of leadership in the community.[37]

For Rebekah Kohut, the Jewish women's organizations of the 1930s
represented a victory in women's fight against their subordinate status.
Although we may find her judgement premature, one cannot help but
be impressed by the vast array of associations that came into existence
during a few short decades. Jewish girls who arrived alone at Ellis Island
were greeted by a representative of the National Council of Jewish
Women, organized by women of German descent at the turn of the
century.[38] As Jews worked their way out of the ghetto, the vitality of the
Lower East Side no longer nourished their group identity. Throughout
the boroughs of New York and the suburbs of American cities, women
organized a network of organizations to meet every need of the Jewish

communities. Jewish activist Goldie Stone described how she and other Chicago women organized homes for the Orthodox aged and for Jewish orphans, a Jewish hospital, a Jewish People's Institute for adult education, a home for Jewish working girls, a home for working mothers, and finally a Federation of Jewish Charities, as well as maintaining their synogogue and Hebrew schools.[39]

Participation in Zionist and social service organizations provided Jewish women with a way to maintain contact with each other. In America, a set of voluntary associations replaced the *kehillah,* which had governed Jewish communities according to Jewish law in Europe. Next to the synogogue, women's service organizations became among the most important factors in knitting together the fabric of the Jewish community. National Jewish women's organizations were composed of small local chapters, so that members could join women of the same age and background in monthly meetings. In Chicago, for example, chapters of Pioneer Women have been formed exclusively of survivors of Nazi Germany, who chose to work together to support the women of Israel. Zionism acted as a counterforce to the strong pulls toward assimilation experienced by Jewish women in America (Document 7).

Women have been at the forefront of the modern movement to secure a national homeland for the Jewish people. The early women Zionists were visionary idealists who worked to gain equal rights both for homeless Jews and for men and women. They envisioned a binational state of Arabs and Jews that would be a model to the world of justice and cooperation. Hadassah, the Women's Zionist Organization of America, was founded in 1911 by Henrietta Szold to provide health care for the residents of Palestine. It was America's first national Zionist organization, and has remained the largest.

"The Zionists organization," according to Szold, "since it believes in the equality of men and women, must educate Jewish women not only to Judaism but to a realization of their civic and national responsibilities."[40] Hadassah argued constantly with the male leadership of the Zionist Organization of America (ZOA) over strategy and authority. Hadassah members were eligible to vote in the ZOA, and they outnumbered the male members. Fearing Hadassah's electoral strength within the Zionist movement, the ZOA tried unsuccessfully to disenfranchise Hadassah's members and discredit Hadassah leaders. The ZOA charged that women's organization should stay out of politics, and concentrate on its medical projects. To these accusations, Henrietta Szold replied,

> To be womanly, in twentieth-century America, is to be comrade and partner. To be womanly in Zionism means nothing less; to participate freely and completely in all that concerns the upbuilding of Palestine, to share the responsibility as well as the labor, to be fearless and resolute where the welfare of the land of Israel is concerned.[41]

Perhaps more important than its medical work in Palestine, Hadassah
provided Jewish women with a positive way to express their identity.
Hadassah made American women partners in an exciting mission that
linked them to their ancestral homeland and to dreams of a Jewish future
of self-determination. Like the contemporaneous Protestant women's
missionary movement, Hadassah gave women a sense of meaningful
service and a feeling of solidarity with women of a distant land. Hadassah
members could feel satisfaction both as women and as Jews when they
read the results of their activities in the *Newsletter:*

> The mortality of mothers and infants has been lessened considerably by the
> great work the Hadassah has done through its physicians and nurses on
> Jerusalem. Many and many a life has been saved by their heroic efforts, and
> many a Jewish soul did they rescue from the clutches of the mission where
> the babies of poor Jewish women were baptized.[42]

This was the "Woman's Way" that Alice Seligsberg described (Document
6).

In its early years, Hadassah attracted members from a broad range
of class, religion, and political backgrounds because it emphasized medical work and did not require its members to take a strong Zionist stance.
As American Jews became upwardly mobile, Hadassah became a middle-
class organization. In 1924, another Zionist organization sprung up
among Yiddish-speaking women. Pioneer Women, the Women's Labor
Zionist Organization of America, criticized Hadassah members for not
being true Zionists because they were motivated by mere charitable impulses, and lacked a consistent ideology (Document 7). Having brought
the ideals of European socialism and the Russian revolution with them
to the United States, Pioneer Women believed that a Jewish homeland
had to be built on a cooperative basis. "As Jews, they believed in the
positive expression of Jewish peoplehood; as members of the American
working class, they believed in labor unionism and socialism. They simply
combined in their ideology that which was already combined in their
lives.[43]

Pioneer Women and another Jewish group, the Women's American
ORT (Organization for Rehabilitation Through Training), aimed to insure the equality of Jewish women by training them in agricultural and
industrial skills, which would prepare them to work side by side with male
workers. In response to the anti-Semitic view, prevalent in nineteenth-
century Europe, that Jews were parasites because the petty trade by
which they lived was not a "productive" occupation, Zionists developed
the idea that the redemption of the Jewish people lay in learning to till
the soil of their homeland, and therefore engaging in "productive" labor.
Sexist and anti-Semitic ideology overlapped in the devaluation of
women's work as "non-productive." Jewish women's organizations took
these ideas a step further by insisting that women would be redeemed

from inequality both as women and as Jews by "productive" labor, and training them to do so.[44]

Jewish women's organizations formed part of the international women's movement of the early twentieth century. The early women Zionists saw the Jewish settlement in Palestine as an opportunity to provide an example to the world of a nation governed by the ideals of women's culture. The National Council of Jewish Women joined the Women's Christian Temperance Union and the League of Women Voters in calling national women's peace conferences that included women of all faiths. Jewish women shared with the larger movement the belief that women's participation could inject humanitarian concerns into government and public life.[45]

CONCLUSION

The status of Jewish women continues to prompt some women to leave Judaism, others to press for change within Judaism, and still others to fight against changes in roles which they have found meaningful and fulfilling. Dramatic changes in the lives of American Jewish women have taken place throughout the twentieth century both because of and in spite of all three of these groups. Shortly following the completion of this essay, the faculty of the Jewish Theological Seminary of America voted to ordain women as Conservative rabbis. This is an event of tremendous significance, both because of the numerical importance of Conservative Judaism, and because the Conservative rabbinic body claims to make its decisions in accordance with Jewish law. The occurence of this decision in 1983 suggests that women will continue to take increasing leadership in Judaism and to make significant contributions to the definition of American Jewish identity throughout the twentieth century.

Mother and daughters doing piece work in a crowded tenement. New York City (c. 1912). [Photo by Lewis Hine, courtesy of National Child Labor Committee, New York City.]

"Abolish our Slavery"; young Jewish women garment workers on strike. [Photo courtesy of the George Bain Collection, The Library of Congress.]

Woman reading Tasklikh on the Brooklyn Bridge (c. 1910), a ceremony performed on the first day of Rosh Hashanah, the days of repentance, traditionally at a body of water, in accordance with Micah 7:19: "I will cast their sins into the depths of the sea." [Photo courtesy of the George Bain Collection, The Library of Congress.]

Henrietta Szold, founder of Hadassah, the Woman's Zionist Organization of America. Here she speaks to another group she founded, the Youth Aliyah, which rescued thousands of Jewish children from the Nazis and relocated them in Palestine. [Photo courtesy of American Jewish Archives, Cincinnati, Ohio.]

The Woman's Labor Zionist Organization of America, at their tenth anniversary meeting, Chicago, 1934. [Photo courtesy of American Jewish Archives, Cincinnati, Ohio.]

Documents: Jewish Women in the Twentieth Century: Building a Life in America

Document 1: Henrietta Szold

Henrietta Szold had a literary career as an editor and translator before founding Hadassah, the Women's Zionist Organization of America, and Youth Aliyah, which saved thirty thousand Jewish children from the Nazis and provided homes for them in Palestine. The selections reprinted below reflect her commitment both to equality for women and to traditional Judaism. Her argument for religious education for Jewish girls includes a critique of the Reform movement, which, in her view, offered women an equal role in a religious system that had been emptied of all meaning.[46]

The Education of Jewish Girls

Why, ... does Israel hesitate to endorse the modern view of the education of women? Why does he lag behind in this important matter, and give the lie to his history?

The beginning of the movement to raise the standard of woman's education was practically contemporaneous with two occurrences in Israel's history: with the emergence from the ghettos of West European cities, and with the rise of Jewish reform. Unfortunately, Israel entered into the larger world, continued to hark back to the old cynic of the Talmud[47] though good authority might have been found for abandoning him to well-merited oblivion, by a judicious application of rabbinical dialectics, usually so keen to discern an advantage when one was sought.

The first attack upon the problem, however, was made without resort to dialectics. The opportunist character of Jewish reform never presented so attractive an aspect as when it put the Jewish education of women upon its banner. Israel without a doubt had arrived at the juncture when women should have participated in his public activities. The principle was unexceptionable, but its application was disappointing. The confirmation service for girls, in which the principle embodied itself, and which was to be the flower of female education, fell far short of fulfilling the hopes it had aroused. Like much of the work attempted by the reformers it will have to be done over again by another generation. It was sterile, ineffectual. It failed to stimulate the Jewish development of women, because it was assertion of the principle of female education in theory only. In practice it put up with a minimum of superficial knowledge and an apology for Jewish training. With those outside of the reform party, it had the effect of throwing discredit upon the principle of female education, for to subscribe to a principle that seemed perforce to involve the introduction of a "custom of the Gentiles," looked dangerously like dalliance with reform. . . .

With these notions and this attitude, the Russian Jew arrived in the United States. Before he knew it, his girls had slipped into the public schools, and were being taught pretty much all his boys were learning. To his own amazement he found himself not half as rabid as before in opposing the "custom of the Gentiles." Circumstances, or, in modern parlance, economic and industrial conditions, had not a little to do with his stoicism. They forced his hand, as two generations earlier they had forced the hand of all peoples in the matter of woman's education. From being independent manufacturers in a home which was a miniature workshop for a dozen or more trades, women, with the removal of all industries from the home to the factory, became industrial agents in public life. They no longer worked for the home comforts of their men, but at the side of the men, as rivals. They worked for their own maintenance, and incidentally for the maintenance of the home. Things have come to such a pass that the economic no less than the spiritual survival of the family depends upon the exertions of its women as well as its men. The adequate education of women follows by consequence. This is the history of enlarged educational opportunities for women—this is the iron logic to which the Jew bows as every other nationality bowed to it. If there is another current —that woman with broader education demanded and obtained broader opportunities—it is not the dominant current.

So much for secular education. As for the Jewish education of his girls, that, happily or unhappily, still depends upon the father's initiative. How does he show himself worthy of his privilege? Does he square their Jewish education by the secular standards of public education?

Nothing he sees in America is calculated to weaken the feeling that the conservation of Judaism is safer with the women of the old school than with women of the new. On the other hand, his traditional inertia in the matter of woman's education is reinforced by American conditions, which put an education ready-made at the door of every citizen. He has but to stretch forth his hand and draw it within. Being relieved of responsibility for the character of the one sort of education, he has the less power to shape the other sort. His faculty for feeling responsibility for the education of his household is in a measure atrophied. He shirks the whole question. If things go ill, his daughters grow up untaught heathens. If things go well, they drift into a Sunday School, or that abomination, a Jewish mission school—schools to which, if the worst came to the worst, he would not entrust his sons. His daughters, however, are only women, who would be better off without education, therefore, an inferior education will do for them. So the Jewish girl's Jewish education is no better taken care of in a land of golden opportunities than in a crowded Jewry of the East, where she at least lives an intense Jewish life with its manifold educational inferences.

The remedy, however, lies, not in abandoning it, but in making it more intelligently earnest, more vital. But earnestness is not synonymous with the exercise of parental authority. The time has passed when the argument holds: So your forefathers did, so I do, so you must do. The forefathers did many things which the parents of this generation have been forced to sacrifice on the altar of necessity, and the children are not slow to transfer the same logic to other domains. The parents must argue, not with their children, but with themselves: So my forefathers felt, so I feel, so I must and so I shall, with God's help, teach my children to feel.

In this particular of Jewish defection, as in that of economic readjustment in the family, the relation between parents and daughters suffers a more serious disturbance than the relation between the parents and sons. Girls once brought to the point of rebellion are more radical than boys, or they appear so. A woman's revolt affects the home, a man's the synagogue. There can be no doubt which is the more alarming and offensive. To the Jew, accustomed from time immemorial to regard Jewish women as symbols of loyalty, a daughter's insubordination is nothing short of a catastrophe. The integrity of family life is at stake, the morality of one generation at least, not to speak of the fate of Judaism. Unless the heart of the fathers is turned to the children, and the heart of the children to the fathers, the earth will be smitten with a curse. If parents and children can be prevailed upon to approach the subject of Judaism in the same loving spirit, then, no matter how far apart their conception of Judaism may remain, their other differences will be minimized, and a Jewish *modus vivendi* will be arrived at.

But is it possible for Jewish feeling to be restored or created anew by any system of education? Is the intellect the source of feeling? Can sweetness come forth out of the strong?

In other generations and other countries, the Jewish mother and the Jewish daughter were virtuous and valiant women, whose price is above pearls, though they knew of Judaism only what Jewish life taught them. But if they knew only that, they knew much. Moreover, what they learned from Jewish life, Jewish life afforded them the opportunity to give out again in the form of domestic ceremonial and communal, neighborly responsibilities. Before the days of woman's emancipation, Jewish life offered them a large sphere of activity. That old Jewish life seems not to bear transplanting to the soil of this country. What we need is to reproduce its atmosphere as nearly as can be in a new climate, country, and set of conditions, by interpenetrating ourselves with its fundamental principles. This is no new theory. It is what all nations do in their regenerative periods. They go back to their origins for unused material. It is what Israel did again and again, and all the time, in his wanderings, with their constantly shifting problems. He refreshed himself at the sources from which those drank who had had the shaping of Jewish life in the first place—those, for instance, who held that the ignorant cannot be truly pious, and whose authority was at least as commanding as the authority of the obscurantist who gave woman the choice between ignorance and immorality. The Jewish heart has always starved unless it was fed through the Jewish intellect. This is the point at which the example of the reform movement is a warning. The failure of the confirmation service as the climax of woman's Jewish education was due to its having degenerated into an exclusive appeal to the sentiments.

That the exercise of the Jewish intellect stimulates Jewish self-consciousness and feeling is a commonplace in Jewish history. The new point is whether the excuse of the Jewish intellect is an esoteric privilege reserved for Jewish men; whether, in fact, Jewish women have a Jewish intellect.

During the last decade American communities have been making a bugbear of the feminization of Judaism when they might have been better employed in concerning themselves about its emasculation, which is not synonymous with the other. If the fear of feminization ever becomes a reality, it will be because Jewish women are ignorant, not because they are too learned. . . .

We are concerned about the regeneration of a whole people. If the new movement means anything, it means that it is a movement of the Jewish masses, springing from the masses and determined by the masses, and the Jewish masses, it cannot be denied, have not been alive to their duty in the matter of woman's education.

Yet, it would seem that I have neglected the more important aspect of my subject. If I have been fortunate enough to convince a contrary-minded Jew of the necessity of educating Jewish girls Jewishly, he will complain that I have not supplied him with a plan of education to apply to concrete cases. He is right. But I must leave the new Jewish education commensurate with our modern attitude toward Judaism to be formulated by others, with technical knowledge and varied experience. In general, I may say that whatever system of Jewish education is devised for boys, as uneducated hitherto, if not so neglected as their sisters, should be used almost as it will stand, for girls also.

I would emphasize the religious education of girls as distinguished from the Jewish education. Throughout this paper I have avoided a reference to Judaism as a religious system. I kept before my mind Judaism as a mode of living, the national aspect of Judaism, the whole sum of its spiritual and practical manifestations. There are today hosts of self-declared Jews who look upon the Jewish religion as one of the Jewish nation's outworn habiliments. It was once, they say, the glory of our nation, and it will ever remain a marvelous expression of the Jewish spirit, of the same Jewish spirit that continues to operate in the nation, and still produces valuable manifestations, though different from those of the past. Such Jews, from their point of view, ought to be as circumspect as the most religious in providing a Jewish education for their children. The history, the language, and the literature, the ceremonials, the forms, and the prayers, though primarily religious in character, have their uses for him in communicating the spirit which he cherishes. But the religious Jew, with his belief in the Jew's religious mission, has a larger task. In the education of his boys and of his girls, he must present the history, the language, and the literature of the Jew, his ceremonials, forms, and prayers, not only as material out of which new creations shall be fashioned, or as instruments with which to fashion them, but as the realities themselves, the models for the present, the hopes and ideals that await realization in a glorious future, the eternal verities, the beatitude of this world and of the world to come, the divine warrant for human striving after justice, mercy, and humility. In communicating the religious spirit to Jewish girls, I would have the emphasis laid upon those states of mine, impulses, and vitrues that would make them "rise early and say: Sovereign of all worlds! Not in reliance upon our righteous deeds do we lay our supplications before Thee, but because we trust in Thy abundant mercies. For what are we? What is our life? What is our kindness, our righteousness, our help, our strength, and our power? What shall we say in Thy presence, O Lord our God, and God of our fathers?" I should like the Jewish girl to be imbued with the teachings of the Jewish religion, that, modern though she be, educated, accomplished, self-respecting, self-conscious, and self-reliant, she will daily utter, not with rebellion and scorn in her heart, but with sincerity and with fervor, that much-maligned benediction: "Blessed art Thou who hast made me according to Thy will." If ever she departs from the spirit of humility it conveys, let it be when in repeating that benediction, she thinks herself superior to her brother who negatively boasts of his manhood.

With such proud and humble Jewish women the Hebrew poet of a happy future will find sympathetic understanding in his most exalted flights of fancy and genius.

On Saying Kaddish[48]

[TO HAYM PERETZ]   *New York, September 16, 1916*

It is impossible for me to find words in which to tell you how deeply I was touched by your offer to act as *"Kaddish"* for my dear mother. I cannot even thank you—it is something that goes beyond thanks. It is beautiful, what you have offered to do—I shall never forget it.

You will wonder, then, that I cannot accept your offer. Perhaps it would be best for me not to try to explain to you in writing, but to wait until I see you to tell you why it is so. I know well, and appreciate what you say about, the Jewish custom; and Jewish custom is very dear and sacred to me. And yet I cannot ask you to say *Kaddish* after my mother. The *Kaddish* means to me that the survivor publicly and markedly manifests his wish and intention to assume the relation to the Jewish community which his parent had, and that so the chain of tradition remains unbroken from generation to generation, each adding its own link. You can do that for the generations of your family, I must do that for the generations of my family.

I believe that the elimination of women from such duties was never intended by our law and custom—women were freed from positive duties when they could not perform them, but not when they could. It was never intended that, if they could perform them, their performance of them should not be considered as valuable and valid as when one of the male sex performed them. And of the *Kaddish* I feel sure this is particularly true.

My mother had eight daughters and no son; and yet never did I hear a word of regret pass the lips of either my mother or my father that one of us was not a son. When my father died, my mother would not permit others to take her daughters' place in saying the *Kaddish,* and so I am sure I am acting in her spirit when I am moved to decline your offer. But beautiful your offer remains nevertheless, and, I repeat, I know full well that it is much more in consonance with the generally accepted Jewish tradition than in my or my family's conception. You understand me, don't you?

Henrietta Szold

Document 2: Bintel Brief

The "Bintel Brief" was an advice column that appeared in the Jewish Daily Forward, *the most widely circulated Yiddish newspaper in the United States. The newspaper was aimed at workers and their families, and had a moderate Socialist stance. The* Forward's *editor, Abraham Cahan, gave the immigrant's personal struggles as much significance as political or economic news. The "Bintel Brief" became a popular feature and an arbiter of conflicts in the Yiddish-speaking community.*[49]

Months Passed Without a Word (1906)

Worthy Mr. Editor,

I was married six years ago in Russia. My husband had not yet been called up for military service, and I married him because he was an only son and I knew he would not be taken as a soldier. But that year all the originally exempted men were taken in our village. He had no desire to serve Czar Nikolai and since I didn't want that either, I sold everything I could and sent him to London. From there he went to America.

At first he wrote me that it was hard for him to find work, so he couldn't send me anything to live on. I suffered terribly. I couldn't go to work because I was pregnant. And the harder my struggles became, the sadder were the letters from my husband. I suffered from hunger and cold, but what could I do when he was worse off than I?

Then his letters became fewer. Weeks and months passed without a word.

In time I went to a rabbi of our town and begged him to write to a New York Rabbi to find out what happened to my husband. All kinds of thoughts ran through my mind, because in a big city like New York, anything can happen. I imagined perhaps he was sick, maybe even dead.

A month later an answer came from the Rabbi. They had found out where my husband was, but didn't want to talk with him until I could come to America.

My relatives from several towns collected enough money for my passage, and I came to New York. They tricked my husband into coming too. Till the day I die I'll never forget the look on my husband's face when he unexpectedly saw me and the baby.

I was speechless. The rabbi questioned him for me, sternly, like a judge, and asked him where he worked and how much he earned. My husband answered that he was a carpenter and made twelve dollars a week.

"Do you have a wife, or are you single?" asked the Rabbi. My husband trembled as he answered, "I have committed a crime," and he began to wipe his eyes with a handkerchief. And soon a detective appeared in the rabbi's house and arrested my husband, and the next day the story appeared in the newspapers. Then some good women who had pity on me helped me. They found a job for me, took me to lectures and theaters. I began to read books I had never realized existed.

In time I adjusted to life here. I am not lonely, and life for me and my child is quite good. I want to add here, too, that my husband's wife came to me, fell at my feet and cried, but my own problems were enough for me.

But, in time, my conscience began to bother me. I began to think of my husband suffering behind bars in his dark cell. In dreams I see his present wife, who certainly loves him, living in dire need without their breadwinner. I now feel differently about the whole thing and I have sympathy for my husband. I am even prepared, when he gets out of jail, to wish him luck with his new life partner, but he will probably be embittered toward me. I have terrible pangs of conscience and I don't know what I can do. I hope you will print my letter and answer me.

Cordially,
Z.B.

The Foreman's Vulgar Advances (1907)

Dear Editor,

I am one of those girls thrown by fate into a dark and dismal shop, and I need your counsel.

Along with my parents, sisters and brothers, I came from Russian Poland where I had been well educated. But because of the terrible things going on in Russia, we were forced to emigrate to America. I am seventeen years old, but I look younger and they say I am attractive.

A relative talked us into moving to Vineland, New Jersey, and here in this small town I went to work in a shop. In this shop there is a foreman who is an exploiter, and he sets prices on the work. He figures it out so that wages are very low, he insults and reviles the workers, he fires them and then takes them back. And worse than all this, in spite of the fact that he has a wife and several children, he often allows himself to "have fun" with some of the working girls. It was my bad luck to be one of the girls he tried to make advances to. And woe to any girl who doesn't willingly accept them.

Though my few hard earned dollars mean a lot to my family of eight souls, I didn't want to accept the foreman's vulgar advances. He started to pick on me, said my work was no good, and when I proved to him he was wrong, he started to shout at me in the vilest language. He insulted me in Yiddish and then in English, so the American workers could understand too. Then, as if the Devil were after me, I ran home.

I am left without a job. Can you imagine my circumstances and that of my parents who depend on my earnings? The girls in the shop were very upset over the foreman's vulgarity but they don't want him to throw them out, so they are afraid to be witnesses against him. What can be done about this? I beg you to answer me.

Respectfully,
A Shopgirl

To Save My Children I Have To Give Them Away (1910)

Worthy Editor,

My husband, . . . deserted me and our three small children, leaving us in desperate need. I was left without a bit of bread for the children, with debts in the grocery store and the butcher's and the last month's rent unpaid.

I am not complaining so much about his abandoning me as about the grief and suffering of our little children, who beg for food, which I cannot give them. I am young and healthy, I am able and willing to work in order to support my children, but unfortunately I am tied down because my baby is only six months old. I looked for an institution which would take care of my baby, but my friends advised against it.

The local Jewish Welfare Agencies are allowing me and my children to die of hunger, and this is because my "faithful" husband brought me over from Canada just four months ago and therefore I do not yet deserve to eat their bread.

It breaks my heart but I have come to the conclusion that in order to save my innocent children from hunger and cold I have to give them away.

I will sell my beautiful children to people who will give them a home. I will sell them, not for money but for bread, for a secure home where they will have enough food and warm clothing for the winter.

I, the unhappy young mother, am willing to sign a contract, with my heart's blood, stating that the children belong to the good people who will treat them tenderly. Those who are willing and able to give my children a good home can apply to me.

Respectfully,
Mrs. P.

The Terrible Triangle Fire (1914)

Worthy Editor,

I am a girl of twenty-two years of age, but I've already undergone a great deal in my life. When I was born I already had no father. He died four months before my birth. And when I was three weeks old, my mother died too. Grandmother, my mother's mother, took me in and soon gave me away to a poor tailor's wife to suckle me.

I was brought up by the tailor and his wife and got so used to them that I called them Mother and Father. When I grew up I learned from the tailor how to do hand sewing and machine sewing too. . . .

In time one of the tailor's apprentices fell in love with me, and I didn't reject his love. He was a fine, honest, quiet young man and a good earner. He had a golden character and we became as one body and soul. When I became seventeen my bridegroom came to me with a plan, that we should go to America, and I agreed.

It was hard for me to take leave of the tailor's good family, who had kept me as their own child, and oceans of tears were shed as we parted. . . .

In time I went to work at the "famous" Triangle shop. Later my bridegroom also got a job there. Even at work he wanted to be with me. My bridegroom told me then, "We will both work hard for a while and then we'll get married. We will save every cent so we'll be able to set up a home and then you'll be a housewife and never go to work in the shop again."

Thus my good bridegroom mused about the golden future. Then there was that terrible fire that took one hundred and forty-seven blossoming lives. When the fire broke out, the screaming, the yelling, the panic all bewildered me. I saw the angel of death before me and my voice was choked in my throat. Suddenly someone seized me with extraordinary strength and carried me out of the shop.

When I recovered I heard calming voices and saw my bridegroom near me. I was in the street, rescued, and saw my girl friends jumping out of the windows and falling to the ground. I clung to my bridegroom and rescuer, but he soon tore himself away from me. "I must save other girls," he said, and disappeared. I never saw him alive again. The next day I identified him, in the morgue, by his watch, which had my picture pasted under the cover. I fainted and they could hardly bring me to.

After that I lay in the hospital for five weeks, and came home shattered. This is the fourth year that I am alone and I still see before me the horrible scenes of the fire. I still see the good face of my dear bridegroom, also the black burned face in the morgue. I am weak and nervous, yet there is now a young man who wants to marry me. But I made a vow that I would never get married. Besides that, I'm afraid that I will never be able to love another man. But this young man doesn't want to leave me, and my friends try to pursuade me to marry him and say everything will be all right. I don't believe it, because I think everything can be all right for me only in the grave.

I decided to write to you because I want to hear your opinion.

Respectfully,
A Faithful Reader

The Secret That Weighs On My Heart (1923)

Worthy Mr. Editor

I was born in a small town in Russia and my mother brought me up alone because I lost my father when I was a child. My dear mother used all her energies to give me a proper education.

A pogrom broke out and my mother was the first victim of the blood bath. They spared no one, and no one was left for me. But that wasn't enough for the murderers, they robbed me of my honor. I begged them to kill me instead, but they let me live to suffer and grieve.

After that there were long days and nights of loneliness and grief.

I was alone, despondent and homeless, until relatives in America brought me over. But my wounded heart found no cure here either. Here I am lonely too, and no one cares. I am dejected, without a ray of hope, because all my former dreams for the future are shattered.

A few months ago, however, I met a young man, a refined and decent man. It didn't take long before we fell in love. He already proposed marriage, and he is now waiting for my answer.

I want to marry this man, but I keep putting off giving him an answer because I can't tell him the secret that weighs on my heart and bothers my conscience. I have no rest and am almost going out of my mind. When my friend comes to hear my answer, I want to tell him everything. Let him know all; I've bottled up the pain inside me long enough. Let him hear all and then decide. But I have no words and can tell him nothing. I hope you will answer and advise me what I can do.

I thank you,
A Reader

Document 3: Judaism And The Modern Woman

The "modern woman" of the 1920s threw off the familiar trappings of femininity. Many wondered whether she would also discard religion when she shortened her skirts and bobbed her hair. A. Irma Cohen had just become a "faculty wife" at Hebrew Union College, the Reform rabbinical college, when she wrote this article in 1924 for The Jewish Woman, *the quarterly magazine of the National Council of Jewish Women. She describes the experiences that made Judaism meaningful to Council members, many of whom were financially secure women of German descent and Reform leanings.*[50]

Who is this modern American Jewess with whom our problem lies? She was born, in most instances, during the last quarter of the past century. If, by chance, her birthplace was across the ocean, she was brought here in early childhood. Her father had either had a little Hebrew instruction in the Old World and had forgotten practically all of it, or had received a bare rudimentary schooling in this land— instruction that offered neither knowledge nor spirit. Her mother either could or could not read and write. There were few gradations of her preparation. If reared abroad, the mother had had no schooling and had lived most of her few European years in the preparations for migration. If reared in this land, she had passed through some or most of the public school grammar grades.

Both parents were uprooted beings, trying to send weak tendrils into this new soil. If they had had any acquaintance with the old Jewish life, it had been brief and superficial, and their eyes had already been turned toward the unknown New World. They had no understanding of, no appreciation of, no love for the old associations. They had started out empty-handed and empty-hearted. They were the product of the ruthless struggle for physical self-preservation in an unpropitious transplantation. They had therefore neither the blessings of the past nor the proud pain of the present, neither the spiritually reassuring information of their forebears nor the religiously disconcerting knowledge of their children. Their daughter was an "American." She went to school—either through High School or also through College. She was away from home much; and, insofar as she and her parents had spheres of association, their worlds were divorced. Her parents' crudities disturbed her, and her crudities disturbed her neighbors. With her schooling completed, her real inner struggle began. Her chief inheritances were an awkward, apologetic self-consciousness before the Gentile world, and an empty, hungry heart. She was harassed with all the questions born of human doubts and of Jewish experience. She had heard some myth of the Jewish home, the religious spirit of which brought peace to the soul. She had known no such home. The so-called educated world about her scoffed; and this scoffing became an attitude of mind. To be intelligent, one must doubt—doubt everything ever held sacred, doubt everyone who professed an ideal. Her soul became a question mark. It was popular to attend lectures, but to doubt the educators and the value of their work. It was usual to employ medicine, but to doubt the physician and to belittle his science. Her broad, thin education had banished the humility of simplicity and precluded the humility of learning.

The pose of superficial scientific inquiry sapped her sincerity. "Modernity" was her ideal. She was the "new woman." Her problems were new. And answers to them, if they would satisfy, must be something new. She gave herself to fads labelled "new," to made-over superstitions labelled "science." She was different from all women before her. Was she not a part of the economic world? Were not her associations cosmopolitan? Was not her vision broader? She needed a new God, a new system of ethics, a new philosophy of life. She required a new social doctrine. Everything interested her, but nothing satisfied. Everything was hollow to her. Her soul ached. Day after day through three hundred and sixty-five days of the year, the monotony wore on her. Her pastimes left a sour after-taste, her occupation brought no contentment.

Then, after either a little sentimental flurry or a really serious emotion she married. While she sometimes apologized for the circumstance, she usually married a Jew. She established a home labelled "modern," the modernity of which consisted almost entirely of labor-saving devices, tasty furnishings, a few ultra-modern books on a little shelf in the parlor, and a hollow atmosphere that gnawed at her heart.

In the following few years, she bore a family. She joined organizations: sewing circles, charity societies, collegiate alumnal groups, card clubs. She attended "modern" lectures, discussed "modern" problems, spoke knowingly of the "vital things of life," and came home with an empty heart and a ruffled temper. The prolonged spiritual groping, from which she could not run away, was wearing on her.

She wanted a logical view of life! No, she really desired something of a mystical relation with great Spirit of Life. Then again she felt that her cultured modern nature demanded beauty, symbolism, poetry. With her own questions burning, she was now besieged by those of her children, and by the real or fancied difficulties of her husband's associations in his business life. She sought to maintain her post at the rudder of the family ship. But she was utterly ignorant of the tides and currents of her people's life. She was incapable of sounding the ocean depths of their spirituality. She was unprepared for the adverse winds of open popular antagonism or the lurking shoals and reefs of insidious, pernicious influence. Her ship tossed at the mercy of the sea. She stood at the helm, bewildered by the visionless struggle.

. . . Due partly to external influences and largely to sheer exhaustion, the modern American Jewess finally faced the calm critical question: "For what am I looking? Do I know what I want?" . . . Her want was two-fold: first, a satisfying answer to her own inner questionings; and, secondly, some purpose in life—some thing to do that would count in the future.

But were these demands hers alone; or did others share them? Were these, then, new questions? In the generations of Jewish women, was she the first to feel them? She began to suspect a kinship to those who had lived prior to the dawn of her modernity. There had, after all, always been the same necessity for a sanctifying power to support life. She looked about for a teacher for her questioning spirit. And not without misgivings, did she turn to the Synagogue.

She found an atmosphere to which she was a stranger, and phrases that awoke no vibrations in her heart. She became unpleasantly conscious that, despite her school degrees, she was ignorant of even the outline of the history and of even the simplest customs, that might offer her the key to this ritual that she visited. Not only was there no mental satisfaction here; there was even the postponement of the longed-for help, because of the need of acquainting herself with so much that she did not know. Her impulse was to turn away. But two forces held her: the social bond with the people, and the recollection of so much fruitless impatient searching elsewhere. She remained to learn.

But even her enforced patience and self-imposed optimisms could not prevent her from feeling that there was something empty, something apologetic about this Synagogue. Surely a conviction that had

nurtured generations could not be so spiritless. This house had been
built by a few enthusiasts and by multitudes like her parents.
Suddenly she was confronted with a tremendous purpose: to examine
the supports of this spiritual structure; and, if they were sound, to
breathe new life into the Synagogue. She had not found her task;—
her task had found her! She did not stop to ask if she was fitted. She
threw herself into the work. Slow to replace her ignorance by knowledge; over-eager to act before prepared; repeatedly misdirected in
her instruction; all too often too far removed from her people's
tradition to sympathize with it, her judgment was frequently warped.
She was, simultaneously, destroying by her haste and building by her
persistence. After much devotion and with much effort, she gained
a vantage point from which she could more knowingly analyze the
past, draw faith for herself, and build for her children.

She gazed sympathetically toward the lands of Israel's longer so-
journ, the home of her grandmother. It was not a religion that she
found there, but a religious culture, accumulated and sifted through
full thirty-five centuries, which had at once rested upon and sustained
the unnumbered generations of Jewish women—maidens and
mothers. Its frank dealing with the realities of life, its provision for
every circumstance of daily existence, its prescribed forms of expression, made it the impulse of each woman's heart, the thought of her
mind, the occupation of her hands, the very atmosphere in which she
moved. It took cognizance of her problems, from the minutiae of her
own physical life to the stern ideals for which she reared her sons. It
protected her relation to her husband and family; specified her obligations to the people of Israel; responded to her soul's questionings—
tempering her joy, sustaining her in sorrow, sanctifying every conscious impulse with its sane and abiding truth.

It reached into all the ramifications of her life. The prescribed
regulations for the food of the household and the customary preparation of specified dishes for certain seasons, linked (in a human, home-
like manner) the food and the festival, the kitchen with the Synagogue. The appointed home ceremonials for Sabbath and festivals,
birth, bar-mitzvoh, marriage, and death, busied the Jewish woman
with poetic symbols, bound her family closer, and presented and
preserved profound religious conceptions, by means often, in more
than one sense, palatable to the participants. The tenets concerning
the duties to children, the relations to neighbors, the obligations to the
stranger, defined her position towards others; gave her a place in life
to be filled in accordance with noble conduct. For her imagination also
there was food. For those of a little knowledge, there were tales
recounting simply, the heroic stories of Israel's history and the trea-
sured romances of her heroes. To the unlettered, this lore came by
word of mouth, and indeed so bound up are the tales of Israel with

her daily life and festival observance, that the unschooled woman of the old Jewish home was more familiar with many characters of Jewish history than some school graduates of our day. Through this Jewish atmosphere, vibrated the strains of its own harp. The cradle songs and the home songs, the Zimiroth and the festival tunes, became habits of thought and enriched the woman's life with an appealing melodic content.

Thus in its completeness, this religious culture embraced the mental, the physical, the spiritual. It wove its art and history into the fabric of daily being; it fitted philosophy to life, and fashioned life philosophically; it translated ethics with the faith and prayer and humility of religion. It provided a spiritual bath. It fitted as a garment.

Indeed, it were absurd to imagine that all the generations of women gloried in the beautiful and profound significance of all their practices and principles. But just here lies the sanity of Judaism: that its provision grew out of such genuine comprehension of human life and of the Jewish heart, that the simple soul was occupied and held and led by the practical tasks and the pleasant forms, and directed by the stern precepts, while the thoughtful woman might penetrate into and live by the signifance of these same forms. In other words, Judaism's ceremonies were poetry that was food, that charged by its form, and fed by its substance.

Here was an assurance of the logic that she had demanded, an atmosphere of the devotion that she had craved, a wealth of the poetry for which she had yearned. She began to sense the security of roots that ran deep into the past, and to breathe the healthy joy of buds that promised future flowering. The sound and humble vigor of the Jewish faith was responding to her two needs; it was answering her heart's queries; it was imposing a duty upon her—a duty for the future.

Under this awakened impulse, she drew understanding strength from her Synagogue; and she breathed into it a warmth and an exhilaration. Steadied after her stormy struggle, she became the calm and forward-looking ally of the spiritual leaders in their public work. And then she turned with mature conviction and unpretentious devotion, to the greatest of her tasks—the work in which she is at this moment earnestly engaged—the work that falls to her as the grandchild of her grandmother: the beautifying and consecrating of a Jewish home; for in the end she is the guardian of the future—at the same time providing the men of the morrow and saving for them their noblest treasures.

Document 4: The Woman Rabbi

Martha Neumark, the daughter of a faculty member, entered Hebrew Union College at the age of fourteen. In 1923, when she

approached completion of the Reform rabbinical training program,
the college's board of governors voted to deny her ordination. In this
article she presents her own arguments for women in the rabbinate.[51]

Because of the publicity that had been showered upon me, other
women began to think of entering the Hebrew Union College, with
a view toward the rabbinate. Their application blanks received the
identical replies: they might enter the College, and take all the work,
but under no conditions would they be granted the regular scholarships nor the privilege of being ordained. The faculty had no choice
in the matter—under the present regime, scholarships and ordination
were available only to *male* students, who had signified their desire of
entering the ministry.

The problem had reached its highest stage. What was to be done
with these women applicants; was I to be regarded as a "regular
student," with the prospect of being ordained? The faculty decided
to take official action, with the result that it declared itself in favor of
ordination for any woman rabbinical candidate who had undergone
training under the same rules as those of the men students. I was
particularly grateful for this decision, because a short time previous
I had applied to the faculty for a fall "holiday position," which request
had been refused. (Even though my position had been assigned me,
it is highly problematical whether any congregation would have accepted a woman—and so young—to officiate at the high holiday
services.)

The question was finally referred to the Board of Governors,
which has the final authority in such matters. The Board declared that
it was a problem too weighty to be decided arbitrarily, and transferred
the decision to the Central Conference of American Rabbis, despite
the fact that the Faculty of the College, a representative body of the
foremost Reform Jewish scholars, had decided in favor of ordination.

Two summers before this time I had read services at a certain
summer resort, while my father preached the sermon. I shall never
forget the occasion. The curious, yet sympathetic, interest of the
congregation (the women relished the idea more than the men did),
the unique quality of the event, the generous approval of my father
inspired me to persist in my intention of becoming America's first
woman rabbi. It was as I incanted the Hebrew that the witchery and
charm of the service surged through me. I began to feel the value of
ritual in a religious service. The formal and academic nature of the
Reform service became emphasized. Since then I have come to the
belief that ritual and ceremony are invaluable adjuncts to a religious
communion. The next summer (1921) I read services in conjunction
with one of my college class-mates, which experience, more than the
one with my father, gave rise to an idea which I shall broach later.

In the summer of 1922, the Central Conference, at Cape May,

debated the question of women in the rabbinate. Dr. Jacob Lauterbach, Professor of Talmud at the College, read the first paper, contending that it would be in violation of tradition and prejudicial to the
best interest of modern, Reform Judaism to have women admitted to
the rabbinate. But in what a kindly, tolerant vein he spoke. . . .

But Dr. Lauterbach met with very little approval. As a body the
Conference was overwhelmingly in favor of the ordination of women
as Rabbis. It was interesting to observe some of the rabbis, dignified
impressive men, who regarded the whole affair with an amused smile.
These were the true scholars of the assembly. They scorned this petty
concern with a matter that should have been settled long ago. Women
or men in the rabbinate—their scope was to broaden and advance the
culture of Judaism. It was mostly the younger rabbis who joined in
the combat with zest.

The liberals among them conceived this to be an excellent point
of vantage from which they could demolish some of the hoary, en-
crusted Jewish traditions. To have women admitted as rabbis would
give them an excellent wedge with which to pry further into the
crumbling dogmas of a moribund Judaism. But, probably to the
regret of these latter, there was no struggle involved. Almost unanimously the Conference was in favor.

The Board of Governors, however, decided otherwise. At the
meeting where this decision was arrived at, there were two rabbis
present and six laymen, who voted unanimously and respectively Aye
and Naye. This illustrates, in general, the attitude of rabbis and laymen toward the admission of women to the rabbinate. The rabbis,
who know the duties, functions, and handicaps of their profession
assert that women can enter the ministry; whereas laymen, for the
most part unacquainted with the ministerial technique, aver that the
duties of the office are too burdensome on a woman. The irony of
fate! My father, who from the beginning had advised me against my
purpose, was primarily interested in the principles of the question,
and the tradition's attitude toward it. I repeat verbatim his reply to
the assertions of some of the opposition: ". . . . If woman is to be
debarred from the rabbinate in orthodox Judaism because she cannot
serve as reader, then the only logical consequence would be that
Reform Judaism, which has decided in favor of the woman reader,
should disregard the orthodox attitude, and admit women to the
rabbinate . . . The entire question reduces itself to this: women are
already doing most of the work that the ordained woman rabbi is
expected to do. But they do it without preparation and without authority. I consider it a duty of the authorities to put an end to the
prevailing anarchy by giving women a chance to acquire adequate
education and an authoritative standing in all branches of religious
work. The practical difficulties cannot be denied. But they will work

out the same as in other professions . . . Lydie Rabbinowitz raised a family of three children while being a professor of bacteriology. The woman rabbi who will remain single will not be more, in fact, less of a problem than the bachelor rabbi. If she marries and chooses to remain a rabbi, and God blesses her, she will retire for a few months and provide a substitute, as rabbis generally do when they are sick, or when they have met with an accident. When she comes back, she will be a better rabbi for the experience. The rabbinate may help the woman, and the woman rabbi may help the rabbinate."

The discussion about the admission of women as rabbis is merely another phase of the woman question. Despite the fact that so many women have achieved eminence in their chosen fields, a struggle ensues each time that a woman threatens to break up man's monopoly upon any industrial, political, or social province. The usual feminist recapitulation of the achievements of women from Sappho down to George Sand and George Eliot has become too threadbare for use. We need but look at the noteworthy contributions which our own American Jewesses have made to their people and to the country. Henrietta Szold stands out as the most zealous worker in the cause of the restoration of the Jewish homeland. Indefatigable, ceaselessly energetic, she sacrifices herself and her interests for her people. Mrs. Rebekah Kohut has distinguished herself as a communal worker. Edna Ferber has, acknowledgedly, enriched American Literature.

Surely, a woman rabbi is more adapted to the needs of the Reform synagogue as it exists at present than is a man. Our services have become haunts mostly for women, and no one can doubt that the spiritual struggles which a woman has had will be more vitally interesting to these women parishioners than those of the man. At least, their paths of spiritual storm will coincide more.

But why be restricted to the question: Should a man or a woman be the rabbi? Those who phrase the problem thus, misunderstand or misstate it. Many congregations have two rabbis. In fact, this practice is becoming more general all the time, due to the fact that one man is fitted for a certain type of work, the next for another. One is adapted to pastoral work; one is brilliantly gifted as an orator. One is interested in social service; the other has powers as a religious teacher. Why could there not be a division of labor between the man and woman rabbi? The division of their work would be entirely dependent upon their capacities; the same standards would hold as in the division of labor when there are two men rabbis. There are many, very many problems which members of the community, men and women, have, with which they feel they cannot go to the man rabbi, because of the delicacy of the matter, or their sensitiveness. Men and women compose the congregation; a man and a woman should serve this congregation's needs.

The present attitude of some of the laity is to be regretted, in view of the fact that women rabbis will benefit them incalculably. Women can aid in the solution of the problem by devoting themselves to Jewish study, by fitting themselves for ordination. The general community can help by showing a willingness to accept women as their spiritual leaders.

Document 5: Laws Of Nidah

The Laws of Nidah govern when a woman may have contact with her husband according to the course of her menstrual cycle. Strict observance requires a minimum separation of twelve days beginning with the onset of menstruation. During this separation husband and wife are forbidden to touch each other, or do anything suggesting intimacy. The following rabbinic interpretation of the laws attempts to explain them in terms of modern values.[52]

The nidus laws, in broad outline, establish the following procedure: Marital relations are interrupted at the first onset of menstruation. After the total cessation of any menstrual bleeding, as ascertained by an internal examination, *seven preparatory days* must pass during which time there is no evidence of bleeding. At the end of the seventh day of preparation, the wife immerses herself in a ritually approved pool of water, the *mikveh,* and may then resume marital relations with her husband. . . . Leviticus 15:28—" . . . Then shall she count seven days and then may she immerse herself in a mikveh."

The woman is in full charge of all the halachos governing nidus. The Torah has assigned both responsibility and authority to the woman. Onset of nidus, cessation of menstruation, observance of the seven preparatory days, and immersion in the mikveh are components of her responsibility and authority. Her statement of fact becomes Torah law. If she reports onset of nidus, her husband is bound to conduct himself accordingly. If she reports fulfillment of all requirements for resumption of marital relations, her husband may respond accordingly. This power must not be misused. It is not to serve as a weapon in any interpersonal strife with her husband. If a wife states that she has noticed blood on the bedika,[53] this must be a statement of fact, not of pique or tasteless levity. A later explanation that the report was just to show her annoyance with her husband, and that in fact the bedika did indicate total cessation of menstruation cannot be accepted without the analysis and approval of Rabbinic authority.

During the "seven days of counting," the woman should ascertain by means of bedika morning and evening that indeed menstruation has ended, not just ceased for a day. A "count" presumes a beginning number and an end number; hence the bedika of day one and the bedika of day seven of the preparatory days assume critical significance. If the bedika of one of the intermediate days is omitted, the count is not interrupted. If the bedika of day one is omitted, the entire seven day preparation may be jeopardized.

In the event that no bedika was made (other than the differential bedika) until, for example, day four, then day four must be considered day one of the preparatory days.

During these preparatory days, it is customary for the woman to wear white undergarments and to inspect them daily.

At the end of the seventh day, after nightfall (30–45 minutes after sundown) the woman may perform the tevila (mikveh immersion) and thus end her nida state. Prior to this immersion, her biblical nida state, with its attendant prohibitions and severe penalty for transgression, is in full force. A bedika that confirms cessation of menstrual flow, even when reconfirmed fourteen times on seven consecutive days, does not end the nida state. The differential bedika, the seven day preparation for mikveh, and the tevila, combine to remove the nida status. Omission of any of these components retains the nidus.

Conduct During the Nida Period

The blessing recited under the chupa (marriage canopy) refers to the couple both as "chasan v'kalah" (bride and groom) and as "rayim ahuvim," (loving friends). Praise and petition is offered to God for the sharp peaks of joy, love and happiness ("gila diza chedva, etc.") but also for the peacefulness and friendship ("shalom vrayus") that is to exist between bride and groom. A successful marriage demands both relationships. The "bride and groom" phase must mature to that of "friends in love." There must be contentment in the ebb as well as the flow of emotions.

Prior to tevila in the mikveh the conduct of husband and wife must reflect the relationship of "loving friends," not of bride and groom. This relationship of "peacefulness and friendship" prepares the emotions for the fuller appreciation of the "joy and happiness" of the bride and groom relationship. All contact of sexual import must be avoided. All activities that hint at shared intimacies are to be suspended. Custom has established laws that modify the usual home behavior so as to acknowledge by deed the present temporary status of their marital relationship.

This relationship requires the formality of separate beds, avoidance of all physical contact, even during the day, modesty while preparing for bed or dressing, and a reminder at eating time that they are not at an intimate repast. The latter is accomplished by not sharing food or drink from the same utensil, and by an unobtrusive, private signal such as a candlestick moved from the bureau top to table. Sitting close together should be avoided. The husband should not sit down on his wife's bed even in her absence, as evidence of her need for increased privacy. In case of illness requiring the personal ministrations of the husband, or vice versa, rabbanic advice should be sought for a protocol of conduct acceptable to the halacha.

Halachic Responsum Sent to *Raphael Society* of the Association of Orthodox Jewish Scientists, December 5737.—M.D. Tendler

SUBJECT:
Assistance of Husband During Natural Childbirth

Question:

Is a husband permitted to assist during natural childbirth (as in the Lamaze method)? When is the wife considered a *Nida* or a *yoledeth* (parturient woman)? Is the husband's role during natural childbirth an exemption from the usual *Nida laws* because of his contribution to his wife's physical and psychological welfare?

Answer:

Within certain guidelines (see below) the husband is permitted to be present during natural childbirth and to provide solace and comfort to his wife.

Comment:

The wife is considered a *Nida* or a *yoledeth* immediately upon the appearance of any blood (the "bloody show"; mucus plug tinged with blood) or any active bleeding from the cervical canal. She is also considered to be a *yoledeth* if there is no bleeding at all but labor has progressed to a point of: (a) contractions of such frequency and/or severity to make it very difficult to walk without assistance. (b) the nurse or physicians report that the cervix is fully dilated.

Under the above conditions, the *Nida* state is established with all its halachic restrictions.

Prior to that time (i.e., during labor) if no blood appears, the woman is not a *Nida. and may even have physical contact with her husband. When she becomes Nida,* however, as defined above, no further physical contact is permitted.

Although the hospital environment, the presence of the medical team members, and the preoccupation of both husband and wife with the birth process, minimize the halachic concern lest physical contact lead to forbidden intimacies, it is *not permitted* for the husband to "wipe her face, or rub her back, or support her during contractions." Indeed, proper preparations for natural childbirth should include the husband's supportive role—but without physical contact. His presence, encouragement and reassurances are the sum total of his contributions. Any physical ministrations can be better performed by hospital personnel.

In the delivery room itself, the husband should not view the act

of birth of the child but should stand near the head of the table and
offer encouragement and reassurance to his wife. He should not even
view the birth process through the mirrors present in most delivery
rooms.

Document 6: Alice Seligsberg

*Alice Seligsberg was one of the tight-knit group of early Hadassah
leaders who corresponded incessantly as they devoted their lives to
Palestine and Zionism. She sailed to Palestine with Hadassah's American Zionist Medical Unit in 1918, and remained for two years as its
director. The first letter was written from Palestine.*[54]

"Any Future Religion of the People of Israel Must Connect Up with the Past ..."

There is a man living somewhere further North, a man called
Gordon[55] who,—so I am told,—is idolized by many of the young men
and women of Palestine, because he has made a sort of religion of
work. Now to me, nothing can ever be religion unless it takes eternity
into account, and makes all life continuous, binding the living with
those others, making for the perfection (completion) of each one of
us in time to come, binding generation to generation on earth, too,
by means of an unbroken tradition, a religious system. Any future
religion of the people of Israel must connect up with the past, must
develop out of the old tradition. It need not be, it cannot I am sure
be, according to old tradition, I mean identical with it, any more than
a flower and fruit are identical with the seed, but it will evolve from
the old. It cannot be wholly apart, like a religion of work, or of
socialism, or of nationalism pure and simple. All these may be incorporated in the faith of our people; but they will only be parts of our
religion. . . . I am full of faith that though you and I may never have
the comfort of a Jewish religion that will satisfy us, this religion is
going to develop right here, in time to come, even though there are
no visible signs on the horizon.

"We Jews Still Have a Passion for Rightness ..."

I am more and more certain that the human nature *can* change;
it *cannot* change (except in very rare cases) until the system of society
that conditions it will have changed. It is impossible to be a decent man
free from cruel hardness of heart and indifference to the interests of
those who are in our way, so long as we live in a society in which
inevitably one man's gain is another man's loss, in which we must
struggle for possession and for power-over-other-lives (e.g., employer
over employee, executive over staff, social worker over clients) though
we do not want these, and though we think they are the roots of evil.
It doesn't seem to me that the Russians are solving this fundamental

problem tho' they are [keeping?] the world forward. They too are cruel, they too excel in the use of power, there is no ethical basis—not even a desire for more than an economic reason for all conduct. Can we Jews work out new forms of living that will do away with Possession and Power used against some while they are used on behalf of others? Can we build up a cooperative society, all inclusive[?]. . . . We Jews still have a passion for rightness and for righteousness, we still believe in more than we can understand; therefore I think we could not be satisfied ever, with even universal material well being; we would still be filled with discontent unless we related human life to a power more than human.

On Arab-Jewish Relations

To the 1936 Hadassah Convention, advocating the study of Arab-Jewish relations in each chapter.

I mean an honest study that faces facts. No statement can be that attributes to the Jews all the virtue, all the strength of argument. Please do not think that I weaken in my conviction in the justice of our cause or that I would apologize to the Arabs. Not for an instant. But I admit that the means we have used, our ways of doing things, have not always been conciliatory. And the means we have failed to use to bring about not only Arab friendship, but understanding of our aims by the other peoples of the East—these omissions we must study, and, if it is still possible, rectify. Let us as Zionists accept responsibility for becoming a dynamic force in the solution of the Arab Jewish problem.

In conclusion, let me say that as all men and women who work for a collective purpose that lifts them out of merely personal concerns, are fortunate in acquiring an expanded Self, so each of us has the inward joy and the gain of strength that comes from dynamic Zionism. But our Zionist collective endeavor and the concomitant enlargement of our individual lives through our identification of our own Self with our People, must, if it is to succeed, be seen by us as only a part, only our share, in a still greater endeavor, namely, the creation of a new society in which the interest of every individual, every People, will be in accord with the interests of all. We must try to see life as a whole. Our collective endeavor, *if it is to succeed,* must be [geared?] to the still greater collective endeavor that is evolving out of the history of mankind.

The Woman's Way: A Brief Analysis of Methods

Instead of recording the achievements of women in the Zionist Movement, let me today rather call attention to the distinctive methods used by women in furthering the Jewish national cause. Hardly anyone will deny that there is a difference of method in the Zionist work of organized women and the organized mass. . . .

Where men interested in Palestine have engaged at one and the same time in many different kinds of undertaking, philanthropic, economic, social, educational—women have concentrated upon the preservation of life (by means of the medical aid already referred to and help given to orphans) though this intensive activity has gradually led them to develop on sidelines. For example, in the Training School for Nurses, and in some of the workshops for orphans established through the initiative of women, one can see how "life-saving" has led them into vocational undertakings that will fit the youth of Palestine to live as self-supporting citizens, who will ultimately contribute to the establishment of normal economic conditions in the country.

If women wish to contribute to the Zionist Movement those talents that are peculiar to women, they must unite as women. One of the explanations of Hadassah's persistence may lie in the desire of all human beings to count for the utmost; and the realization by the Zionist women of America that unless well organized, they will not count at all in the formation of opinion and the control of policies in those matters in which, as women, they have the deepest concern; namely, the protection of the weak, the healing of the afflicted, the safeguarding of the present and future generations.

Document 7: Pioneer Women

Pioneer Women, the Women's Labor Zionist Organization of America, was founded in 1924 by Yiddish-speaking women to continue their European Socialist heritage as American Zionists. Since the establishment of the state of Israel in 1948, Pioneer Women has continued to support programs for women and children in Israel.[56]

Action, not Charity

1. Pioneer Women does not give charity. Rather, it exists to aid Palestinian women to become workers on a self supporting basis.
2. Pioneer Women trains newly arrived girls for agriculture and industry.
3. Pioneer Women assists women in employment and educational activities.
4. Pioneer women serves working mothers and children and homemakers.
5. Pioneer women fosters the concept of social and economic opportunity.
6. Pioneer Women's aim for Palestine is a cooperative Jewish Commonwealth.
7. Pioneer Women is an ideological organization based upon ideals of labor.

The Pioneer Women's Organization in the Life of the Individual

Tamar Shultz (d. 1981) was a graduate of the Teacher's Institute of the Jewish Theological Seminary. After working for many years as a Hebrew teacher and raising a family in the United States, she moved to Israel permanently with her husband, Isaac Levitas. She was one of the young English-speaking women who joined Pioneer Women around 1930. Her article describes the appeal of Zionism to American women in the 1930s.[57]

The saying that "Faces grow out of people's lives," is wholly applicable to life in all its aspects; its meaning is descriptive of life's changes and impositions; its truth is the cause of social experimentation which has wrought both havoc and progress.

Surely, the lines in the face of an old ghetto Jew tell clearly the story of a life of endurance, of frustrated hopes, of unjust intolerance, of physical oppression, and spiritual suppression. But the eyes—they tell another story—a story of self-conviction, of faith, of hope, of vision. The Jews of the hemmed-in narrow-laned ghetto, felt superior to the people of the outside world. They were sustained by an inner faith of redemption; they were content by virtue of their Judaism; they were part of a unity; they shared a life that was common to all children of Israel. Their differences were harmonized and integrated by this unitary way of life.

We of the present generation reflect another story. We have grown up under conditions of "emancipation." The destruction of the ghetto and the attainment of liberty enabled the Jew to enter into the common life of his country. New fields were opened for his talents and powers. . . . Emancipation brought not only opportunity to the Jew but also destruction. The Jew no longer sought to preserve his inner life—he lost vision and foresight—he became a man of the present part of the life that responded to influences from the outside. In order to enjoy the fullness of life offered by the emancipated period, it was necessary, according to Jewish thought, to abandon the Jewish differences.

These Jews began to escape from themselves. They attempted to liberate themselves from their Jewish identity in order to freely express their allegiance to particular economic classes. The consequences of this de-Judaizing movement set up by "Emancipation" brought the "Jewish question" before the world. The Jew, instead of losing himself in world movements, instead of finding himself a place in the fraternity of nations, was, by force of the outside world, made more conscious of his Jewish identity.

Any organism that possesses life has the desire to live and create. The Jewish people, as an organism, possess this desire to keep alive and to make its contribution to humanity. How can this be possible under conditions of repression? We in this generation, are experiencing intensely not only the manifestation of Jew-hatred, so characteristic of national endeavor, but also the effects of economic degradation. The very obscurity of our own world outlook, the failure of all previous attempts, of adjustment to world situations, compels us as Jews to recognize our own homogeneity and to render our lives creative by solving our problems from Jewish sources and inspiration.

The situation in Germany concretely proves, as nothing else can, the false illusion of assimilation, the improbability and impossibility of eradicating Jewish consciousness. The Jews of Germany were more German than Germans themselves. For the sake of Germanism, they nullified every Jewish relationship. They served the German spirit with their lives, their property, and their honor.

What is their reward?

Although all Jews in Germany were equally affected by the sudden insecurity of their position, one small group existed that succeeded in overcoming the despair that settled upon the Jews. These were the German Zionists. To them there remained a vestige of hope—the ideal of a rejuvenated life in Palestine enabled them to overcome the disillusions of a frustrated democracy. These many experiences and revelations have given rise to a multitude of organizations that have attempted to answer these problems and reconstruct the Jewish outlook.

The Pioneer Women's Organization recognizes and understands the shattered, restless, conflicting personality of the modern Jew. Its Zionist-Socialist ideology solves the inconsistencies of modern life and answers the fundamental needs of the individual.

Since life has proven that no Jew can possibly lose his Jewish identity—that sooner or later, and probably against his will, it is brought back to him—the organization advocates Jewish unity; it aims to render Judaism helpful to the Jew by emancipating him for himself, and through his group. Not through unfamiliarity with his culture, but through preservation and development of Jewish ideals and Jewish achievement, can Jewish life be enriched. First and foremost, then, we must accept the fact that we are Jews. Next, we must know ourselves through our historic past. . . .

We are parasites as long as we deny ourselves national development. The upbuilding of Palestine as the national homeland of the Jews is the basic element in the program of the P. W. O. The development of Palestine as the national homeland means the creation of new values both in Palestine and in the diaspora. The interaction of Palestine and the diaspora makes us freer to mind ourselves and develop our own life as Jews. But this is not sufficient—we are Socialist-Zionists; and as Socialist-Zionists we aim to secure for the Jewish people a normal political, productive economic and cultural existence. The parasitism that has robbed us of our vitality, of our individuality, and creative capabilities can be rectified and readjusted through a life of labor. It is through work that an individual finds his realization. "Work is a means of self-expression," one of the prime needs of men. If Palestine is to symbolize a functioning organism, it must be founded upon the elements of productive Jewish labor. And because the life of the Galuth with its mental and physical stagnancy, its wounded spirit, must not be transported to Palestine, this idea of work has become the vitalizing note in the philosophy of this organization. It is through Chalutzuith that we are learning to find ourselves. Through Socialist-Zionism there is born an army of Jewish laborers who are courageous to face the hardships of a pioneer life. They are pioneering not only a rock-hardened soil but a deeply welded spirit. Through life and labor, they mean to redeem themselves, to achieve personal fulfillment, and to solve the problem of how best to live one's life. But we are Socialists not only in Palestine. We seek a life of social justice and equality, of creative living not only in Palestine, but in every land where human beings are conscious of society.

Conditions today in America are hardly conducive to purposeful living. Youth can find no outlet for its energy. The concentrated effort spent in years of study result in nothing. Economic degradation has destroyed youth's ideals. There is no outlook for personal fulfillment, for individual contribution. . . .

The P. W. O. with its Socialist-Zionist philosophy provides the answer.

We are socialists. We oppose the oppression of nations and races, especially the oppression of national minorities. We oppose the present capitalistic economic system which is the cause of the economic upheaval that is prevalent today. But as Zionist-Socialists, we differ from other socialist groups. Our recreated life in Palestine has enabled us to live and act while others are still forced to preach. The ideals of Chalutziuth have penetrated our own lives here, and the ideas of productive labor, self-expression and purposeful living, all of which characterize our national ideology find meaning in our individual lives. These are the new values in Jewish life and we must live them at all times wherever we are. . . . Labor Zionism has created a new meaning for manual labor. Through our Palestinian activity, we have come to learn that manual work is redeeming and satisfying, that through this means can our spirit be healed. . . .

Let me conclude with a quotation from A. D. Gordon:

" . . . For a parasitical existence nourished by strange life, the toil of others' hands, the thoughts of a stranger's brain, and the emotions of a heart not our own—this is not life. We need some one territory on the face of the earth that may one day be our own. We need a spot where we may create a new life conceived in our own spirit and

Women Struggle for an American Catholic Identity

LORINE M. GETZ

The shape of the Catholic Church in the United States during the first half of the twentieth century was determined largely by the naturalization and assimilation needs of its immigrant members in dialogue with the traditional teachings of the Roman Catholic hierarchy and its new American Protestant milieu. As early as the 1850s, Roman Catholics comprised the largest single religious body in the country.[1] The chief external problem they faced was the anti-Catholic sentiment that pervaded American society. To stem the tide of defecting members and to maintain the loyalty of the burgeoning Catholic population, the Church developed parochial schools, Catholic hospitals, and religious institutes of charity. Religious sisters staffed these institutions; laywomen were expected to cultivate the faith in their families.

Catholic women found themselves divided in their responses to societal pressure and to the demands of their faith. Many women, both lay and religious, were content to be passive members of the Church and of society. For the most part, they accepted the gender identities and roles defined for them by the male establishment: father, husband, employer, priest, bishop, and pope. They dutifully sought ways to live them out in an environment which was not merely foreign, but indeed hostile to Catholics, and which was in ferment with regard to the proper place of women. Some struggled to inculcate the traditional Catholic values into the American mainstream. Others found it difficult to represent or live out values and positions that ran counter not only to the progressive movement of the times, but also to their newly awakening consciousness. Regardless of their personal stance, all Catholic women were doubly bound at the point of convergence between Church and civil society.

This chapter is divided into four sections: (1) Women as Workers, Wives, and Mothers; (2) Religious Sisters in Education and Nursing; (3) Lay Leaders of Social Action Movements; and (4) After the Wars—Changes in Focus. Much of the emphasis in the chapter will be on lay

Catholic women. In the first half of the twentieth century, they provide a richer resource for our understanding of Catholic women in the United States than do religious sisters. Lay Catholic women began to come into their own in ways that they had not done for several centuries. At the same time, religious sisters experienced the curtailment of their lifestyles under the 1917 Code of Canon Law and an overextension of their energies to meet the needs of immigrant Catholics. The sisters worked at teaching, nursing, and caring for orphans. Many congregations opened overseas missions following the termination by Rome of the missionary status of the Church in the United States in 1908. Several new orders were founded. But most sisters had little involvement with the emerging social concerns of the day. They prospered numerically, provided the backbone for the development of the Catholic school and hospital systems, and one of their number, Mother Frances Cabrini, became the first United States citizen to be declared a saint. Nonetheless, the sisters were in large measure removed from the cutting edge of American society, a position they had occupied during the eighteenth and nineteenth centuries.

Laywomen, whose previous roles were primarily domestic, emerged to lead the Church in its further integration into American economic, political, and social life. They actively participated in efforts to support the two world wars, thus signaling the nation that Catholic immigrants made patriotic citizens. But issues such as divorce, birth control, suffrage, college education for women, child labor laws, settlement houses, and labor unions divided them. A few radical women took up positions on these concerns to the right and to the left of official Church teachings. They led their various causes, often with the explicit approbation of the institutional Church, but also occasionally in opposition to it. By the 1950s, laywomen had firmly established an American identity and had expanded their roles in society.

WOMEN AS WORKERS, WIVES, AND MOTHERS

Between 1860 and 1910, the urban population of the United States multiplied sevenfold, growing from little more than six million to more than forty-four million.[2] Women from southern and eastern Europe arrived in large numbers with the second wave of Catholic immigrants. Like the German, Irish, and Canadian women who had preceded them, they settled primarily in the eastern and midwestern cities. Whereas many women in the earlier group, especially single Irish women, took up work as household domestics, women in the second group, more used to working alongside their husbands and brothers in construction, handicrafts, and even industry, gained employment in American factories and sweatshops. Nearly all of these were poor women whose work both at home and in the labor market was essential to the survival of the working-class family. By the 1920s, the move from single workers, who often lived at home with their parents, toward married female workers, who often also sought employment for their children, had become apparent. A more dramatic increase in the total number of females in the working force was occasioned by the industrial needs of the Second World War. The federal government provided job training for two-and-a-half million women. Thus eight million women were active in the work force during the war.[3]

The conditions of immigrant women's lives (Document 2) and their preponderance in the public workplace caused concern in the Church. Bishops and priests addressed the question of women's vocation (motherhood) amid the changing mores of the times (Documents 1, 6). They reminded women of their divinely created nature, which formed them as mothers, homemakers, nurses, and educators of youth. They called woman the symbol of the human "ideal," as opposed to the "real"—male. Sodalities and other women's groups were formed, which brought women together to perform various works of mercy. These groups also provided a social context for those who were excluded from secular groups because of their religious affiliation and solidified the Catholic identity of their members. In the face of the two world wars, the clergy further called upon women to reach out to save men from their tendency toward violence and destruction.

Women responded to the Church's call and to its teachings in various ways. Some, including members of the National Catholic Women's Council and the president of the Boston League of Catholic Women, took up the Church's challenge to expound upon women's duty and responsibility to protect her home and family from the violent attacks of the secular society. The recognized societal dangers included divorce, birth control, and women's suffrage (Documents 3, 6, 7). On this third issue, Martha Moore Avery took Boston's Cardinal O'Connell to task for allowing pro-suffrage meetings to be announced in the archdiocesan newspaper. This was an instance where a zealous woman convert, believing suffrage to be detrimental to a Catholic understanding of the family, urged an archbishop to take a stand against the women's movement (Document 12). Other Catholic laywomen recognized the injustices against women found in aspects of the Church's teaching and practice (Documents 4, 5). Those who sought to stay in the Church and challenge her moral and ethical teachings in their regard paid a dear price. No doubt some women were lost to the Church over these issues.

RELIGIOUS SISTERS IN EDUCATION AND NURSING

The vigor accurately reflected in the chapter on "The Leadership of Nuns in Immigrant Catholicism" in Volume 1 of *Women and Religion in America*,[4] concerning the important leadership roles played by Roman

Catholic sisters in the nineteenth century does not persist through the first half of the twentieth. This is not to say that the nuns of this era did not continue to flourish in their established works, were less dedicated, or ceased to perform essential services for the struggling immigrant Church. However, the direct involvement of the sisters in the challenge of new quests in the service of the Catholic population diminished as the Church became established. The services rendered by members of religious orders became institutionalized and homogenized for the most part; new strictures, such as the imposition of the cloister, the requirement of solemn vows, and the separation of professed from nonprofessed sisters, all imposed by the 1917 Code of Canon Law, severely curtailed the activities of women religious. They did not become significantly involved in the ethical and moral issues that so concerned laywomen until the 1970s, when, following the Second Vatican Council, American nuns democratized many of their orders.

In Document 8, Archbishop John Ireland accurately described the work of the religious sisters during this period and the Church's urgent need for more dedicated women religious to take up their work in schools, hospitals, and other Catholic service agencies. He noted the extent to which many of the congregation of women had become dependent upon local priests and bishops for such necessities as new vocations. In relation to this, it is interesting to note the rapid development of the parish grade school, usually completely staffed by members of a women's congregation, and under the direct supervision of the pastor and the diocesan supervisor of schools. By 1900, there were 3,811 parish elementary schools serving 854,523 students.[5] Catholic secondary schools and colleges grew more slowly, in proportion to the needs of the immigrant Catholic population.

The sisters had been involved in a major way since the 1800s in the founding, staffing, and administration of Catholic hospitals in cities with a concentration of Catholic families. While these institutions were generally more autonomous in their operations than were the parochial schools, the standards of Catholic ethics were developed and totally determined by the male clergy in conjunction with male doctors.[6] With the development of hierarchical structures in the Church, and especially with the advent of a new breed of bishop more interested in corporate financial affairs, the women who administered these hospitals began to be challenged for control of their institutions. Some successfully withstood this further encroachment of the hierarchy (Document 9).

Few sisters were involved in the development of Catholic colleges and universities. One who does stand in the forefront of college education for Catholic women is Sister Madeleva, teacher, administrator, and published poet, who served as the president of St. Mary's College, Notre Dame, for nearly thirty years (Document 10). Her writings with regard to women in the Church are quite traditional, but her own achievement of the office of president of a major institution of higher education and her actions while in office were real departures from the norm. In 1943, for example, she opened the first school of sacred theology designed for laywomen. Providing women direct access to Scripture and ethics, and historical, systematic, and pastoral theology produced a revolutionary effect on the Church in the United States.

During this period, outreach to new constituencies at home and abroad was begun by some of the established orders and by several new American foundations. For example, Mother M. Katharine Drexel founded the Sisters of the Blessed Sacrament for Indians and Colored People (Document 11). Working extensively with the black and Indian communities, she established Xavier University in 1915 to meet the higher education needs of minority Catholics. Similarly, in 1914, four female secretaries to the recently established male order of Maryknoll Missioners were constituted as the Pious Society of Women for the Foreign Missions. In 1920, under the leadership of Mother Mary Rogers, they begame a diocesan religious order, the Foreign Mission Sisters of St. Dominic. In 1954, the congregation was renamed the Maryknoll Sisters of St. Dominic and placed under the auspices of the Sacred Congregation for the Propagation of the Faith. By that time there were nearly eleven hundred Maryknoll sisters working in approximately seventeen countries. With the close of the United States as a mission field in 1908, many established nursing and teaching congregations sent sisters as missionaries to other countries.[7]

LAY LEADERS OF SOCIAL ACTION MOVEMENTS

Catholic women tended not to get publicly involved with the feminist issues of the day. But several outstanding laywomen did lead militant Catholic social action movements. Among these were Martha Moore Avery, Mother Jones, and Dorothy Day. These three Catholic women shared much in common beyond their citizenship, religious affiliation, dedication to the improvement of human conditions, and status as single laywomen. Each of them had been married or had lived in a common law relationship. The husbands of Martha Moore Avery and Mother Jones died tragically young, leaving them widows; Dorothy Day left her common law husband after her conversion to Catholicism. Both she and Martha Moore Avery were former Socialists. For them, the truth of Catholicism formed the explicit focus of their work and they consistently strove to establish links between their work and the institutional Church. Mother Jones, though honored by the hierarchy at her funeral, maintained an anticlerical stance throughout her life. Though their methods and issues were different, each of these lay leaders founded a movement that had a significant impact on the secular society.

On issues such as suffrage and birth control, these women and others like them upheld the position of the Church against the feminists of the day. Their works focused rather on resisting atheistic socialism through the preaching of the gospel; providing shelter, clothing, food, and community for the poor; and organizing unions to establish and protect the rights of divided and disorganized workers (Documents 12, 13, 14). In many ways they became symbolically the mothers, wives, and housekeepers of society. In an era in which the Catholic working poor were fragmented and dislocated, they provided systems of communication, personal support, and nonviolent resistance for social change.

AFTER THE WARS—CHANGES IN FOCUS

The period immediately following the Second World War, leading up to the Second Vatican Council, was one of reflection on the world and society, and of self-discovery for American Catholic women. The focus of concern moved out of the city with its immigrant poor, beyond the boundaries of the nation, and into the depths of the soul. The inhumanity of raw urban industrialism was recognized, and some religiously inspired back-to-the-land movements began. The Catholic Worker Movement, for example, sought to complement its urban settlement houses with farms where workers could get back in touch with the earth. According to at least one version of the new agrarian ideal, women were specially suited as the primary nurturers to lead this type of societal renewal. A new kind of woman was called for, one who would pioneer in the development of rural Catholic homesteads (Document 15).

In another sphere, the National Catholic Welfare Conference organized existing social action groups to establish an international network to relieve the sufferings of the war victims (Document 16). Largely under the leadership of laywomen, and utilizing various Catholic women's groups, they sought to care for and to assist in the resettling of people orphaned or displaced by the war. From this initial effort, cooperative systems have been established to continue the cooperation of the Church in the United States with that in other countries around the world.

With the new immigrants now settled in their new land, Catholics accepted as fellow citizens, poor workers unionized, and the wars won, women began to experience their own need for the nurturance of their souls (Document 17). Among lay people in general, and women in particular, this focus on personal holiness signaled a new stage of maturity for American Catholics.

CONCLUSION

This brief look at the documentary history of American Catholic women during the first half of the twentieth century gives some hints to the developments of the next period. Along with continued commitments to education, nursing, and social work, the broadened foci on international concerns and personal spiritual development will persist. The problems caused by the distinctions between and parallel development of laywomen and women religious remain to be addressed. Two forces, however, which have caused major changes in the history of American Catholic women since the 1950s, could not have been forecast accurately from the data of the preceding period: the Second Vatican Council and the feminist women's movement.

The Second Vatican Council would be read by American nuns as a mandate to democratize their religious orders and to upgrade the education of their members. It would also be seen by lay women as the impetus for a much more autonomous conscience, no longer dictated by clerical authority, but responsive to lived experience. The feminist movement would draw these newly conscious lay and religious women into its orbit and make them conscious of their oppression as women by the Church hierarchy. Thus the coming together of these two movements in the 1960s would set the stage for a confrontation between Catholic women, both lay and religious, and the Vatican in the 1980s.

Mother Katherine Drexel, founder of the Sisters of the Blessed Sacrament for Indians and Colored People in 1891. [Photo from *Katherine Drexel, A Biography* (Cornwall Heights, Pa.: Mother Katherine Drezel Guild, 1965).]

Dorothy Day, cofounder of the Catholic Worker Movement, shown being arrested during a farm workers' strike, Lamont, California, August 1973. [Photo by Bob Fitch.]

Mary Moore Avery, founder of the Catholic Truth Guild, with the support of Cardinal O'Connell of Boston, shown here with the auto-van from which she conducted street preaching. [Photo courtesy of the Beaton Institute, University College of Cape Breton, Nova Scotia, Canada.]

Sister Medeleva Wolff, leading educator of Catholic women and president of St. Mary's College, Notre Dame, Indiana. [Photo courtesy of the Archives of St. Mary's College, South Bend, Indiana.]

Mother Jones, an Irish immigrant who became a major labor organizer, particularly with the railroad and mine workers, shown here leading a march of mine workers' children. [Photo courtesy of the Illinois Labor History Society, Chicago.]

Documents: Women Struggle for an American Catholic Identity

WOMEN AS WORKERS, WIVES, AND MOTHERS

Document 1: Bishop's Pastoral Letter of 1919

Whereas the Third Plenary Council of Baltimore thirty-five years earlier "prepared the Church in America to meet, on the solid ground of faith and disciplining the changing conditions of our earthly existence," Cardinal James Gibbons, Archbishop of Baltimore, in his pastoral letter of September 26, 1919, set the tone of the U.S. Church for the period following the First World War. He addressed the question of women's "vocation" in life amid the changing social norms of the time, especially in light of the increasing divorce rate, which in another place he called "the national scandal." [8]

In society, as in the home, the influence of woman is potent. She rules with the power of gentleness, and, where men are chivalrous, her will is the social law. To use this power and fashion this law in suchwise that the world may be better because of her presence is a worthy ambition. But it will not be achieved by devices that arouse the coarser instincts and gratify vanity at the expense of decency. There will be less ground to complain of the wrong inflicted on women, when women themselves maintain their true dignity. "Favor is deceitful and beauty is vain; the woman that feareth the Lord, she shall be praised" (Prov. 31:30).

The present tendency in all civilized countries is to give woman a larger share in pursuits and occupations that formerly were reserved to men. The sphere of her activity is no longer confined to the home or to her social environment; it includes the learned professions, the field of industry and the forum of political life. Her ability to meet the hardest of human conditions has been tested by the experience of war; and the world pays tribute, rightfully, to her patriotic spirit, her courage, and her power of restoring what the havoc of war had well-nigh destroyed.

Those same qualities are now to undergo a different sort of trial; for woman, by engaging in public affairs, accepts, with equal rights an equal responsibility. So far as she may purify and elevate our political life, her use of the franchise will prove an advantage; and this will be greater if it involve no loss of the qualities in which woman excels. Such a loss would deprive her of the influence which she wields in the home, and eventually defeat the very purpose for which she has entered the public arena. The evils that result from wrong political practice must surely arouse apprehension, but what we have chiefly to fear is the growth of division that tends to breed hatred. The remedy for this lies not in the struggle of parties, but in the diffusion of good will. To reach the hearts of men and take away their bitterness, that they may live henceforth in fellowship one with another—

this is woman's vocation in respect of public affairs, and the service which she by nature is best fitted to render. . . .

Document 2: The Account of a Italian Immigrant

Rosa, an Italian woman, was one of thousands of European Catholic immigrants who came to the United States in the early part of this century. Here she relates the problems of maintaining her religious ideals, coping with her husband who does not share them, and adapting to conditions in Chicago.[9]

I had never seen houses like these before—nothing but boards. The one where we stopped was larger than the others and had two doors to go in. Me and Santino were going to live in the side we were going in, and Domiana and Masino in the other. There was one large room with a long table and benches and a big cook stove and some shelves with pans and things. Then behind was a little room with an iron-frame bed and straw mattress. Gionin and some of the other men carried in my two chests. Then they came back and put food on the table.

Bread! White bread! Enough for a whole village! And butter to go on it! I ate until I no longer had any pains in my stomach. Then I went back by the stove to watch Gionin. He had built a fire and was making coffee. Never in my life had I made coffee and I would have to learn if I was going to cook for these men in America.

"But it's easy, Rosa," Gionin said, and his eyes smiled into mine. "Just make the water boil and grind the coffee and put it in like this. And always we have plenty of sugar and cream to go in. The German women on the farms taught me that."

When the coffee was on the table Gionin sat down with the others and started telling Francesca the plans he had made for her. Until she and Orlando were married on Sunday she was going to stay with an old Sicilian woman, Angelina, who was like a mother to all the young girls in camp. But after Sunday she and Orlando would live in a shack by themselves and she would do the cooking for another bunch of men. She was going to be married in a little village four miles down the tracks. But before then, on Saturday night, she must go to confession. Enrico, the boss of the iron mine, would go with her and interpret.

"*Santa Maria!* I have to tell my sins to a man not a priest? Better I don't get married!" Francesca was so comical she made everyone die laughing.

Gionin was laughing too and teasing Orlando about choosing a wife with sins so black that only a priest could hear them. But then he explained. He told how Enrico went in the priest's house with the girls and stood one side of the priest and the girl the other. Then the girl put her hand in the priests's hand and the priest asked the questions in English and Enrico said them in Italian. If the girl *did* make the sin—she did not go to mass on Sunday, or she stole something worth more than a penny—she must squeeze the priest's hand. Enrico couldn't see if she did or didn't. And in the end the priest gave her the penance and that was all.

"God is a dog," muttered Santino. "I'd burn in hell before I'd squeeze the hand of one of those black crows!"

"Listen to Santino!" laughed Pep. "Every Saturday night he's pinching the backside of his fat Annie or of some of those other bad women over Freddy's saloon. But he wouldn't squeeze the hand of a man—even to keep out of hell."

"Man, bah! I spit on all those black crows that wear dresses!"

As soon as I could I went into the bedroom and opened up my chests. I had never expected to see them again. And there inside I found the featherbed and sheets Mamma Lena and Zia Teresa had put in. And I found the little Madonna and the crucifix Don Domenic had blessed. I kissed the bleeding feet of Jesus and said a little prayer. With that crucifix over my bed I would not feel so alone—so afraid. God would help me to be meek. I went into the other room to find a nail and Gionin came back and nailed the crucifix up for me. "Tomorrow, Rosa," he said, "I'll make you a shelf for the little Madonna."

Summer was not yet over but it grew dark early. That little boy Giorgio, had fallen asleep with his head on the table. So now Domiana went off her side of the house to open her chests and make her bed. Then some of the men left too. Gionin and Orlando went off to take Francesca to Angelina's. So me, I lighted the lamp in the bedroom and made the bed. Then I sat down on one of my chests and took out my rosary. *"Ave Maria, Mater Dei, ora pro nobis. . . ."*

When everyone else had gone Santino blew out the lamp in the big room and came looking for me. Just inside the door he stopped. It was the crucifix over the bed that stopped him. He started cursing: "God is a dog! God is a pig!' Can't a man sleep with his own wife without God watching him from the wall? Take it down, I tell you! Take it down!"

A wife doesn't have to obey her husband when he wants her to do something against God or the Madonna. I held my rosary tighter, waiting for him to come after me and watching for him to tear the crucifix down himself. But he didn't do either. He stood for a while just staring at it. Then without moving his eyes he backed away to the lamp and blew out the light. He was afraid—I could tell by the way he acted—afraid to have Jesus on the cross looking down at him.

Document 3: A Description of the Ideal Catholic Woman

This radio address by Mrs. Francis E. Slattery, president of the Boston League of Catholic Women from 1919 to 1932, was aired by station WNAC, Boston, during the Catholic Truth Hour. Using the

*relationship between Jesus and Mary as a model for male and female
roles, she challenged Catholic women to stand together against the
new societal ideas that were upsetting years of tradition and threatening to destory faith in God and country.*[10]

In this season of supreme rejoicing our eyes are turned in imagination to the crude crib in the rough stable in Bethlehem where Christ,
the God-man, was born of the Virgin Mary. He became man to
redeem us all, made the supreme sacrifice on the Cross, and Mary was
with Him to the agonizing end.

What a change has come over the civilized world since that awful
event. Not one cross but millions are scattered over the face of the
earth in devotion to Him who saved us, and Mary has become the
model for all Christian women. . . .

Today, after the Church, the greatest single influence for the good
of the people, for the protection of their morals and the preservation
of their spiritual ideas is woman. In all the activities of human endeav-
or her influence is striking and impressive. Under the authority of her
husband, she rules the Christian home, she influences the standards
of the community, she leaves her impress upon the works of the State.
In the arts, in sciences, in politics, in religion, in industry and trade
and community movements, her influence cannot be discounted today. Yes, her influence is great, but is it properly effective? Is it fully
used? Are we women alive to our responsibilities and opportunities?
In other words, are we doing our full duty to our God and our
country? Let us see. . . .

What are we women doing to influence public thought, to build
up a real public conscience, to make a better America, to develop a
higher Christianity? Almost nothing! Let us abandon our negative
attitude and take a positive stand on matters that are vital to our
individual and national well-being.

To be specific, are we content with conditions on the stage and
screen? Are we indifferent to the violent attacks on the family and the
home: divorce, trial and companionate marriage, birth control and
the aims of the Feminist movement? Are we satisfied with our public
educational system that forgets God in its scheme? Have we no concern with a Federal movement that menaces the inherent rights of
parents and the welfare of their children? Have we no interest in the
causes and cures of the appalling crimes that seem to multiply with
the days? Shall we do nothing to wipe out prejudice and bigotry,
apparently so deeply rooted in some sections of the land? Shall we sit
idly by and watch with mere curiosity the growth of these movements,
from without and within, that are calculated eventually to weaken and
destroy our belief in God?

These are largely moral issues and touch the very soul of the
nation. Upon their solution depends the future of our country. If

solved aright, American will continue to hold her high place of leadership among the nations of the earth; if wrongly, she will slide down the chute of grievous error to the lowlands of disgrace and chaos.

Here, then, is our duty and our opportunity. Men, God bless them, are our natural guides and protectors in most things, but in matters of morals, women should be leaders, not merely followers. It is our particular province to stress the moral virtues, to uphold the moral standards, to develop the underlying principles, spread a knowledge of them in the public mind, and insist upon their application to the great political and ethical issues of the present day. . . .

The heart of the nation is in the home, where it beats happily in peace and contentment, however the winds blow outside and the storms beat against it. Our home is a castle, made legally impregnable to intruders, even as the feudal barons of old were protected by the moat and the great gates and walls. Yet, as in those days they were occasionally taken by ruse and deceit and assault, so are our castles in danger from insidious and powerful enemies. The methods and weapons are different. They now seek to enter under cover of present and proposed laws which have a semblance of authority and a guise of assistance. Their aim is to destroy the family and family life. Under their attack the castle weakens and Bolshevism enters.

Are you familiar with the purpose of the so-called Equal Rights Bill which, under the guise of emancipating women, attempts to make her the competitor rather than the companion of man? This proposal, if enacted into law, would wipe off the statute books all those humanitarian safeguards that are now thrown around woman for her physical, mental, and social welfare. It would even separate the identities of husband and wife and, by retention of her unmarried name, encourage the use of separate domiciles; measures calculated to deprive the children of a protecting home influence and sending the family to the four winds.

But an even greater problem confronts the home. If these so-called leaders of thought have their way, the problem of children and their up-bringing will eventually cease to be a problem at all, because there will be no children. Those who preach birth control can hardly appreciate what they are doing. We Catholic women know that the practice they advocate is contrary to the laws of God and nature, and we stand firm and determined against its practice and its sanction in the law. We know also that it is un-American, because no less distinguished an authority than the late President Roosevelt called it race suicide, and race suicide means the destruction of the American people, even as the nations of antiquity were destroyed by its ravages. Thus our castle would become a tomb. . . .

Finally, the attack is on marriage itself, the very basis of the Christian family and the American home. Divorce is rampant. Its numbers are appalling. The consequent effects on the children are beyond the power of description. . . . To us Catholics, marriage is not merely a civil contract with all the obligations that contractual relations imply, but a sacramental state, under Divine sanction, in the words of Christ, "Whom God has joined together, let no man put asunder." Divorce has no place in the life of a practical Catholic, but in the interest of Christianity and the preservation of the State, we hope to see divorce made more difficult under the laws of all the States. Let us safeguard marriage and save civilization itself.

Let us see how they work. Watch their scheming in the capital city of the nation, where their lobbyists seek by cajolery and camouflage to secure the passage of laws, innocent in appearance, but, in reality, tending to take control of education in the States and to interfere in the functions of the home and the family. For examples of this maneuvering I ask you to recall the so-called Child Labor Amendment, the Maternity Act and the Federal Education Bill. Women of all classes and creeds in the Commonwealth of Massachusetts, scenting the perils in the Child Labor Amendment, organized in opposition and, to their everlasting credit, with the aid of the high-minded men of this State, succeeded in defeating this Amendment by the overwhelming vote of three to one, to be followed by the other States of the Union, until its ratification was soundly refused.

The same Patriotic forces in this State and throughout the land have fought the Maternity Act and the Federal Education Bill with conspicuous success, and will continue to fight until their sponsors retire from the battle. These measures touch upon great moral issues which are, or should be, the special concern of women, and will never be settled until they are settled right. They threaten our home, our castle, and they cast a deepening shadow over the eternal life to come. To borrow the words of the indomitable General Nivelle, "They shall not pass."

You all, my dear radio friends, are devoted to Him who gave us His only Begotten Son to save us. So am I. You all, I am certain, love America and will sacrifice freely for her. No different from you am I. You of the North want to see the South prosper and progress. The South, I believe, holds the same sentiments for you. You of the West rejoice in the happiness of the people of the East. Surely, they feel the same about you. There must be no North, no South, no East, no West, no sectionalism, no divisions, but a united America working together for one purpose, the preservation of American ideal and the common good of all. These are my sentiments, they are the sentiments of the women of my Faith. They must be the sentiments of all good men and women, because they were planted in the souls of us all by the Creator of all things, the good God who reigns on high. This season of "Peace

on earth, good will to men" is an approriate time to accept the beautiful message of Christmas in the full richness of its meaning and
resolve to dedicate ourselves to the glorious task of solidifying the
American people into one great brotherhood of man, under the
Fatherhood of God.

These, my dear friends, are some of the things that have engaged
the attention of the League of Catholic Women of Boston. Under the
impulse of our great Churchman and distinguished citizen, Cardinal
O'Connell, we have cooperated with all who have sought to maintain
our national ideals. Out of it has come a better understanding and
mutual respect.

Let us think less of rights and more of our responsibilities. Let us
try to appreciate the full scope of our duties as happy citizens of the
greatest country in the world. Our Declaration of Independence is
one of the great documents of all history, exalting and protecting the
rights of man. Our Federal and State Constitutions, with our practice
of local self-government, have given us the greatest framework of
government in modern times. We have natural resources, and wealth
and citizenship beyond compare. We are happy, peaceful and con-
tented people. To be an American citizen is to be a king. Yet all these
things we owe to God Himself, our Creator and our Redeemer. Let
us not fail in our full duty to Him and in so doing we shall not fail
America. Let us turn our thoughts back once again in adoring reverence to that humble manger in Bethlehem. Let us fashion ourselves
to the model of the Holy Family. Let us bow our heads in deepest
reverence to the Cross of Christ and raise our arm in salute to the flag
of flags—the Stars and Stripes of America.

Document 4: Diocesan Editor's Request for Over-Due Pay

*This letter by an educated Irish-American woman, who published
two novels and a number of poems and received the Laetare Medal
from the University of Notre Dame for services to the catholic cause
in 1907, revealed that economic justice was not easy for women workers to obtain, even from the Church.*

*Katherine E. Conway was the last lay editor of the Boston archdi-
ocesan newspaper,* The Pilot. *With Cardinal O'Connell's reorganization of archdiocesan structures, she was replaced, after a long and
successful editorial career, by a cleric. In this letter, she made reference to her years of sacrifice, often working unpaid, and to the paper's
present prosperity. In addition to having foregone her just pay, Katherine Conway also earlier lent the paper five hundred dollars of her
own money to help it meet expenses. In a later letter she also requested the repayment of that amount, which she wished to recover without interest.*[11]

1 Atherton Place, Egleston Square.
Boston, January 31, 1910.

Most Reverend dear Archbishop,

It has often come to me during the past few months that Your Grace could not know that the late Manager of the Pilot, Mr. James T. Murphy, never did anything towards the settlement of my long-standing account with The Pilot Publishing Company. Mr. Gargan got all of his; Mr. Murphy took care of his own interests, as is well known in Boston business circles; but there was no thought of the poor little editor, who nearly destroyed her life in trying to hold things up until Your Grace came in. Even the wages due me for the year in which I went out, 1908, might be still unpaid, had it not been for Your Grace's merciful intervention.

That is why I am emboldened to write you now. I don't even know who the Business Manager of the Pilot is; but I look at the paper very carefully every week, for old associations' sake, and I am glad to see that the word is of doubled circulation, etc. The increase of advertising patronage was, as I told Your Grace at the outset, a certainty, once your name was associated with the enterprise.

But I have no hope except in you, and in the good words you said to me at my outgoing in 1908. Not a thing done for me yet and much of the money due dates back nine years, and even longer. Then, as the account was closed up on July 1, 1908, I am a steady loser, by not having the money where it would do me a little good. Of course, $1432.00 is a small sum to a journal with the great Archdiocese of Boston behind it; but it means a lot to me. If the management can't, or doesn't want to give it to me all at once, I would be well content to take it in installments of from $50 to $100 per month. Even at that, it would take a good while to pay it off.

Will Your Grace say a good word to the management for me? Otherwise, I will never be remembered. Pardon me for troubling you about this matter, but I don't know to whom else I can appeal. All my hope is in Your Grace, and I beg to remain in continued hope,

Most respectfully and faithfully,
Katherine E. Conway

Document 5: "Madame Celestin": In Pursuit of a Catholic Divorce

Though not all women found it easy to live out the Church's ideals for their lives, few examples survive of women challenging the teachings of the tradition. One who did, though only in her fiction writings, was Kate Chopin (1851-1904). Born Kate O'Flaherty Chopin to a prominent St. Louis family, she lived much of her married life in Louisiana, where she learned the ways of black and Creole women.

After the death of her husband, she left their plantation to return to St. Louis. There she wrote a novel, The Awakening, *and several short stories, which were first hailed as pieces of local color. However, her depictions of the inner lives of her heroines shocked the Catholic public. Chopin was banished from the Catholic Literary Guild and was so hurt by her critics that she ceased writing.*

In the following short story written in 1893 from her collection Bayou Folk, *entitled "Madame Celestin," a Creole woman actively pursues the idea of divorcing her husband.*[12]

Madame Celestin always wore a neat and snugly fitting calico wrapper when she went out in the morning to sweep her small gallery. Lawyer Paxton thought she looked very pretty in the gray one that was made with a graceful Watteau fold at the back: and with which she wore a bow of pink ribbon at the throat. She was always sweeping her gallery when Lawyer Paxton passed by in the morning on his way to his office in St. Danis Street.

Sometimes he stopped and leaned over the fence to say good-morning at his ease; to criticise or admire her rosebushes; or when he had time enough, to hear what she had to say. Madame Celestin usually had a good deal to say. She would gather up the train of her calico wrapper in one hand, and balancing the broom gracefully in the other, would go tripping down to where the lawyer leaned, as comfortably as he could, over her picket fence.

Of course she had talked to him of her troubles. Everyone knew Madame Celestin's troubles.

"Really, madame," he told her once, in his deliberate, calculating, lawyer-tone, "it's more than human nature—woman's nature—should be called upon to endure. Here you are, working your fingers off"—she glanced down at two rosy finger-tips that showed through the rents in her baggy doeskin gloves—"taking in sewing; giving music lessons; doing God knows what in the way of manual labor to support yourself and those two little ones"—Madame Celestin's pretty face beamed with satisfaction at this enumeration of her trials.

"You right, Judge, Not a picayune, not one, not one, have I lay my eyes on in the pas' fo' months that I can say Celestin give it to me or sen' it to me."

"The scoundrel!" muttered lawyer Paxton in his beard.

"An' *pourtant*," she resumed, "they say he's making money down roun' Alexandria w'en he wants to work."

"I dare say you haven't seen him for months?" suggested the lawyer.

"It's a good six month' since I see a sight of Celestin," she admitted.

"That's it, that's what I say; he has practically deserted you; fails to support you. It wouldn't surprise me a bit to learn that he has ill treated you."

"Well, you know, Judge," with an evasive cough, "a man that drinks—w'at can you expec? An' if you would know the promises he has made me! An, if I had as many dolla' as I had promise from Celestin, I would n' have to work, *je vous garantis.*"

"And in my opinion, madame, you would be a foolish woman to endure it longer, when the divorce court is there to offer you redress."

"You spoke about that befor', Judge; I'm goin' think about that divo'ce. I believe your right." Madame Celestin thought about the divorce and talked about it, too; and lawyer Paxton grew deeply interested in the theme.

"You know, about that divo'ce, Judge," Madame Celestin was waiting for him that morning. "I been talking to my family an' my frien's, an it's me that tells you, they all plumb agains' that divo'ce."

"Certainly, to be sure; that's to be expected, madame, in this community of Creoles. I warned you that you would meet with opposition, and would have to face it and brave it."

"Oh, don't fear, I'm going to face it! Maman says it's a disgrace like it's neva been in the family. But it's good for Maman to talk, her. W'at trouble she ever had? She says I mus' go by all means consult with Pere Ducheron—its my confessor, you undastan'—Well, I'll go, Judge, to please Maman. But all the confessor' in the worl' ent goin make me put up with that conduc' of Celestin any longa."

A day or two later, she was there waiting for him again. "You know, Judge, about that divo'ce."

"Yes, yes," responded the lawyer, well pleased to trace a new determination in her brown eyes and in the curves of her pretty mouth.

"I suppose you saw Pere Ducheron and had to brave it out with him, too."

"Oh, fo' that, a perfec' sermon, I assho you. A talk of giving scandal an' bad example that I thought would neva en'! He says, fo' him, he wash' his hands; I mus' go see the bishop."

"You won't let the bishop dissuade you, I trust," stammered the lawyer more anxiously than he could well understand.

"You don't know me yet, Judge," laughed Madame Celestin with a turn of the head and a flirt of the broom which indicated that the interview was at an end.

"Well, Madame Celestin! And the bishop!" Lawyer Paxton was standing there holding to a couple of the shaky pickets. She had not seen him. "Oh, it's you, Judge?" and she hastened towards him with an empressement that could not but have been flattering.

"Yes, I saw Monseigneur," she began. The lawyer had already gathered from her expressive countenance that she had not wavered in her determination. "Ah, he's a eloquent man. It's not a mo' eloquent man in Natchitoches parish. I was fo'ced to cry, the way he talked to me about my troubles; how he undastan's them, an' feels for me. It would move even you, Judge, to hear how he talk' about that step I want to take; its danga, its temptation. How it is the duty of a Catholic to stan' everything till the las' extreme. An' that life of retirement an' self' denial I would have to lead,— he tole me all that."

"But he hasn't turned you from your resolve, I see," laughed the lawyer complacently.

"For that, no," she returned emphatically. "The bishop don't know w'at it is to be married to a man like Celestin, an' have to endu' that conduc' like I have to endu' it. The Pope himse'f can't make me stan' that any longer, if you say I got the right in the law to sen' Celestin sailing."

A noticeable change had come over lawyer Paxton. He discarded his work-day coat and began to wear his Sunday one to the office. He grew solicitous as to the shine of his boots, his collar, and the set of his tie. He brushed and trimmed his whiskers with a care that had not before been apparent. Then he fell into a stupid habit of dreaming as he walked the streets of the old town. It would be very good to take unto himself a wife, he dreamed. And he could dream of no other than pretty Madame Celestin filling that sweet and sacred office as she filled his thoughts, now. Old Natchitoches would not hold them comfortably, perhaps; but the world was surely wide enough to live in, outside of Natchitoches town.

His heart beat in a strangely irregular manner as he neared Madame Celestin's house one morning, and he discovered her behind the rosebushes, as usual plying her broom. She had finished the gallery and steps and was sweeping the little brick along the edge of the violet border.

"Good-morning, Madame Celestin."

"Ah, it's you, Judge? Good-morning." He waited. She seemed to be doing the same. Then she ventured, with some hesitancy, "You know, Judge, about that divo'ce. I been thinking,—I reckon you betta neva mine about that divo'ce." She was making deep rings in the palm of her gloved hand with the end of the broom-handle, and looking at them critically. Her face seemed to the lawyer to be unusually rosy; but maybe it was only the reflection of the pink bow at her throat. "Yes, I reckon you nedd n' mine. You see, Judge, Celestin came home las' night. An' he's promise me on his word an' honor he's going to turn ova a new leaf."

Document 6: National Catholic Women's Council

The emergence of a Catholic middle class brought about the desire to become part of American social life. Many social clubs excluded Catholics from membership. Catholic men and women formed groups such as the Women's League, the Catholic Daughters of America, and the Knights of Columbus. Usually, these were distin-

guished from secular clubs by a spiritual purpose and charitable works.

The National Catholic Women's Council (now known as the NCCW) was a federation of women's organizations formed in 1920 at the request of the Catholic bishops to unify the efforts of various women's groups in the Church, and to extend the range of their charitable services. At this first meeting, the goals and work of the group were defined by clergymen representing the American bishops. The invited women participants assented and took up the challenge presented.[13]

The Conference called at the direction of the Administrative Committee of the National Catholic Welfare Council, for the purpose of forming a National Catholic Women's Council, met at National Catholic Community House, 601 E. Street, Northwest, at 10 o'clock a.m.

The Conference was called to order by Reverend John J. Burke, C.S.P. (Chairman). . . .

The Chairman: There is hardly need for me to give you, in the name of the National Catholic Welfare Council, a word of welcome and also of the sincerest gratitude for your presence at this conference. We are conscious of what it has cost many of you in the matter of time, and also financial expense, and your sacrifices are an indication, surely of the earnestness of your purpose, and of your determination to make the deliberations of the Conference a success.

The work of the Conference is under the National Catholic Welfare Council, and is immediately under the Department of Lay Organizations, the Episcopal chairman of which is Bishop Schrembs. . . .

He has been appointed by the hierarchy of the United States itself as chairman of the Lay Organizations. It is his duty as such chairman to establish a National Council of Catholic Women. Through his direction and under his guidance this call has gone forth. . . . I therefore take extreme pleasure in introducing to you the Bishop of Toledo, Bishop Schrembs. (Applause)

Bishop Schrembs: My dear Catholic women, delegates representing the various dioceses and archdioceses of the country, and the great national organizations:

Of course it goes without saying that my first word to you this morning is a word of very cordial greeting and of welcome to you all, who come here to attend this meeting, which is bound up, if it is fruitful—as we hope it shall be—with wonderful success and wonderful service by the Catholic church of America.

Of course we are all proud of our Catholic women, old and young. We are proud of them for the wonderful work they have accomplished during the trying days of the war. When that great storm period broke over our heads, our Catholic mothers veiled their tears with smiles, and gave cheerfully and self-sacrificingly of their labor and of their love. With deft hands and unflagging energy they labored through all the days of that war, sewing and knitting for the comfort and the welfare of the soldiers, both in action and wounded, or in the hospitals, dying. They never tired. Whole armies of them, in the depots of our cities and the various stations, acted as canteen women for the Red Cross, to bring courage, cheer and comfort, as well as material relief to the thousands of soldiers that were in transit from one camp to another, or in training for "over there". They labored unceasingly through our great national drive for the United war work and for our great Liberty Loans, and it was their action which helped to make these drives such a wonderful success.

Now, the great compensating lesson that the war has taught us is this: We have learned to do things on a big scale and in a national way, and that is the lesson which we must never forget. (Applause) That is the great lesson, and that, ladies, is why we called you here—to do things on a big scale and in a national way. . . .

You may perhaps wonder why I chose the women first. Well, I suppose it is according to the accepted canon which we have all through the church, and which manifests itself especially in time of missions; whenever we have a mission we always have the women's mission first (laughter), and we feel that when the women thoroughly organized, they would be the best missionaries for the men, and they will see to it that the men come into line. . . .

Take, for instance, such questions as the great divorce question— the sanctity of the home. Why, we all know that the Catholic Church, wherever she exists, wherever there is a Catholic heart that beats in unison with the Catholic faith, the sanctity of the home is considered the very foundation piller of our society. We all know that; and yet we know, too, the terrible statistics which are being handed us by the United States Government today, and which tell us that on an average, out of every seven marriages contracted all over this country, one at the present time is sure to land in the divorce courts—one out of every seven. We know that in certain States the proportion is even much larger. . . . My God, when you think of the consequences, the vision is one that may well terrify the stoutest heart!

We have made efforts to do something along, the line of securing for the benefit of the country, some kind of a uniform divorce law. We know that we have had strong men advocating that movement. . . . But the response has not been uniform. . . . Because there was no unified power; there was no concentration of effort in the country to take up this work. . . .

Take the girl problem; take the child welfare problem; take the problem of public health, of public morality—this so-called sexology, which is coming to the fore again and again in the most pernicious way; advocated, I dare say, by well-meaning persons, but having a totally false conception, as we view it, of the relation of the sexes and of the ideals that underlie this whole question.

[The purpose of the National Catholic Women's Council then briefly is this:]

"(1) To give to the Catholic women of the country a common voice and an instrument for united action in all matters affecting Catholic or national welfare.

"(2) To insure proper Catholic representation on, and the proper recognition of Catholic principles in, national committees and national movements affecting the religious, moral and material well-being of the country.

"(3) To stimulate the work of existing Catholic women's organizations to greater service and usefulness in meeting the needs of our time. . . ."

You will ask me, how is this to be accomplished? Why, that is what you are called for. You are to be deliberate. We have no cut and dried scheme to offer you. We have definite ideas, of course. But we know, too, from experience that you have always been responsive to the church in all these matters, and therefore we trust your good sense, we trust your womanly dignity, we trust your womanly zeal to do the right thing and to find the right basis.

That is why you come here to deliberate during these days. You will have full and free scope given to speech. You were not brought here to be mere automatons, and possibly to answer to the question of a vote, and merely assert "yes" or "no". Oh, no. You are going to be granted every liberty to express yourselves honestly and openly for the best interests that we all have at heart. The purpose and the function is merely to establish—if I may use a very homely expression which I used on another occasion similar to this—the idea is to establish a great, supreme, Catholic power-house; a power-house of thought and a power-house of action, from which will go out radiating to every part of our country the divine message of our holy protecting religion, and bring back thunderous response of our millions of Catholic men and Catholic women.

God bless your presence and your deliberations. I thank you. (Great applause.)

Document 7: Why Maternity Guilds?

This address, written by Dorothy Weston, a lay volunteer at the Catholic Worker, and first printed in The Catholic Worker *in June 1935, was delivered before the Catholic Women's Union at the organization of Maternity Guild in New York City.*[14]

. . . It was something of a shock to me to discover last summer that, despite the teachings of the Church on the sanctity of the family and the evil of birth-control, no Catholic hospital in New York City, with the exception of Misericordia will accept free maternity cases . . . that, along with free public maternity care, in our city and in others, goes birth control advice and even compulsory abortions and sterilization.

We all know the manifold burdens of our Catholic hospitals today. Most of them in New York have rates as low as $40 or $50 for complete maternity care—a rate that is certainly far below the actual cost to the hospital. But we have only to look at the ever-growing relief rolls to realize how many thousands of mothers there are in this city to whom $40 is as impossible a sum as $40,000,000. Doctors give unstintingly of their care to the poor in clinics and in private practice —they can do no more. It is up to us, then, the Catholic laity, to remedy the situation. It is a necessary part of the fight upon birth control.

Father McNabb, the English preacher and writer, declared recently that the poor woman in the slums who practices birth-control may be guilty of a lesser evil before God than the well-do-do Catholic who condemns her and does nothing to remedy her situation. We have heard the solution that the Holy Father urges upon us: first, to change the social system which penalizes married couples desirous of bringing up families for the honor and glory of God; and second, as an immediate alleviation of the situation, the formation of guilds such as the maternity guild, to make it easier financially for Christian parents to bring children into the world.

The efforts of meddling and muddled social reformers toward compulsory birth-control, sterilization and the like are condemned in forthright terms by our Holy Father when he says:

"To take away from man the natural and primeval right of marriage, to circumscribe in any way the principle laid down in the beginning by God Himself in the words 'increase and multiply' is beyond the power of any human law."

But even among Catholics who subscribe to the Church's teachings against contraceptives, what I may call the birth-control spirit, a product of today's materialistic sense of values, is rampant. A year or so ago, there was a heated controversy on this subject in the correspondence columns of a well-known Catholic magazine. To one writer who pointed to instances of large families who were thoroughly Catholic and even happy, though living in extreme poverty, a man who called himself a Catholic replied that such people had no right to have children, that God had meant the truly poor either not to marry or to practice self-control, so that their families would not become a burden on the State. If I recall correctly, it was the same writer who said that he hoped and expected to see the day when the Church would require a priest, before marrying a couple, to investigate their financial circumstances, and refuse them Christian marriage if they were, in his opinion, unable to raise a family in decent comfort!

   This, of course, is an extreme example, but we are all familiar with
the attitude among Catholics which frown sternly upon good Catholic
parents who have the misfortune to be poor, instead of trying to
lighten their load—the attitude of "forbid the babies" instead of helping their parents to care for them. A communist friend of mine said
to me not long ago: "I can't understand why you want to have children, when you and your husband have such important work to do.
In the Communist Party, a woman organizer is considered far more
useful than a woman who merely breeds children for the revolution."
I tried to explain to him that the entire Catholic social idea is based
on the family; that we on *The Catholic Worker* are trying to exemplify
the truth that the teachings of Christ in their literal fulness are intended for all, not merely for those living the religious life without
worldly obligations, and that we consider the four family groups who
are part of *The Catholic Worker* community the most important part
of our work of social and religious propaganda. It didn't take, of
course. . . .

   It is this last aspect of the problem of birth-control and its solution
in the Maternity Guild which I would stress. It is a splendid ideal to
remove the occasion of the sin of birth-control; but there is a still
nobler motive for this work, a still higher necessity. Let us not take
an attitude of vexation that the poor should have large families, that
the Church should permit them to and should forbid them to prevent
children; let us not say, in effect: "We can't let them use birth-control
(with the implication 'more's the pity'); but in justice to us, the better
off, such people should refrain from marrying, or from making use
of their marriage rights. If they will have children, of course, we've
got to take care of them, but they should be educated to realize that
they have no right to."

RELIGIOUS SISTERS IN EDUCATION AND NURSING

Document 8: Our Catholic Sisterhoods: An Archbishop's Statement

*During the years following the turn of the century, the Catholic
immigrant population continued to swell in the United States. The
growing congregations of Catholic sisters sought to meet the immigrant needs for schooling, nursing care, and even refuge.*

*In this sermon given by the Right Reverend John Ireland, D.D.,
Archbishop of St. Paul, Minnesota, to the Sisters of St. Joseph at the
opening of their new Novice House On March 26, 1913, two themes,
common to the immigrant Church in these times, emerge: sacrificial
ideals of the religious sisters related to their outstanding work in
education, hospitals, and other charities across the country; and the
great need of the Church, especially in the Northwest, for more*

vocations. He remarks on the parish priest's special responsibility to foster vocations to religious life and congratulates this congregation on its growth in little more than a half a century.[15]

. . . What are our Sisterhoods doing for fellow-creatures? Our Sisterhoods pray and make expiation. Those of us who have the knowledge of the mysteries of divine grace, know the value before God of prayer for others, of expiation of sin for others. This, the gift of the Sisterhoods to their sisters and brothers, tossed hither and thither on the perilous billows of worldliness, exposed to death in fatal shipwreck unless succor from God's throne be invoked upon them. . . .

. . . The land is strewn with their schools, hospitals, orphan asylums, refuges and protectorates. No ill is there that their hand does not soften, no sorrow that they do not appease, no sore that they would not help, no uplift of mind and heart to which their help is not promptly rushed. The deeper the evil and the more repulsive the sore, the more prodigal and the more unremitting their zeal. . . .

The debt of gratitude the Catholic Church owes to its Sisterhoods finds no measure in words. . . . I speak particularly of our own times and of our own country. What were the Church in America without Catholic schools and Catholic charities? Without Catholic schools our little ones were the prey of unbelief and secularism. Without Catholic charities the world of unbelief would ask: To what serves in humanity the Catholic Church? Is it not a voice without interest to us, without touch with the world in which alone we are concerned? Well, as matters are with us in America, our schools and our charities were impossible, if we had not our Catholic Sisterhoods. . . .

I plead for vocations to our Catholic Sisterhoods. In so pleading I plead for an increase in the supernatural life within the Church, for an increase in the outward exhibitions of this life in the works of Christian education and of Christian charity. Speaking more directly of the Northwest, the need of our vocations is urgent. With our rapid growth in population, we must widen our works of charity, we must multiply our Catholic schools if we keep pace with needs and opportunities. To this end we must bend our best energies in giving increase to the membership of our Sisterhoods . . .

To the Catholic maiden, in the silence of prayer and meditation, there comes the vision of ideal service; her heart impels her to higher and better things than the mere observances of the common precept; it is the voice once spoken in Palestine—"Come and follow Me" . . .

The maiden tells father and mother that she has heard the voice of the Master, that her soul burns with ambition to be altogether the daughter of His love. But father and mother, poor themselves in generosity, do not brook generosity in their child. . . . A vocation is lost, because of the lack of strong faith in parents.

Frequently—shall I dare say it—where vocations do not germinate and thrive, blame belongs to the priest, who fails to lend a keen eye to the discovery of vocations; who, when the discovery is made, fails to give them increment and direction. . . . All things said, the work of fostering vocations to the Sisterhoods falls, primarily and preeminently, to the pastor. It is his word that brings to the maiden the consciousness of her vocation; it is his hand that props it up in its subsequent efflorescenses; it is his advice, given in season, that wards off opposition of father and mother. . . . To priests, the official caretakers of the garden of the Lord, the divinely appointed distributors of the enriching dews of Heaven, I address my special appeal on behalf of vocations to our Catholic Sisterhoods . . .

To the Sisterhood of St. Joseph, of St. Paul, I speak my congratulations. It is a meaningful day in the story of your congregation. The completion of this splendid Novice-Home tells the progress made in past years, and gives omen of progress yet more wondrous in future years. Short the journey, if we measure by lapse of time, from the morning of 1851, when the pioneer Sisters first set foot on the soil of Minnesota—not yet sixty-two years. But long, indeed, the journey if milestones be your numerous institutes of service spread abroad, far and wide, through our Northwestern regions, the ever increasing throngs of Christian maidens, vowing themselves to God in obedience to your rule. From the four pioneer Sisters in 1851 to the six hundred and twenty in 1913—from the log-built cabin on Bench Street to St. Joseph's Novice-Home and St. Catherine's College on Randolph—the march is marvelous. The Lord has been gracious to you in past years; be He no less gracious in the years that are coming!

Document 9: Hospital Sister Struggles with Hierarchy

As the new Code of Canon Law, which would place new restrictions on various groups, including religious women, was being prepared, a new breed of men took office as bishops and cardinals. Cardinal William O'Connell of Boston was one of these who was interested in corporate business and management.

This letter of response is one item in a lengthy correspondence between Sister Gonzaga, a Sister of Charity of St. Vincent de Paul, who served as administrator of pontifically erected Carney Hospital in Boston from 1890 to 1910, and the local head of the Archdiocese. Through the director of Catholic Charities, Cardinal O'Connell requested to be named president and treasurer of Sister Gonzaga's hospital; to obtain a complete record of its bequests; and to have control over its solicitation of funds. He has suggested that he would withhold Catholic Charity funds from the hospital if his wishes were not granted. Respectfully, Sister Gonzaga stood her ground that the hospital, since it was under the jurisdiction of the pope and account-

able to the sister superiors of the Order, should not come under the governance of the archidocese. She was willing to provide the requested materials on unrestricted bequests, and to request his permission for the solicitation of funds from local sources, but she held firm against his attempt to take over the hospital's administration.[16]

January 15, 1908

Most Reverend Dear Archbishop,

After consulting my Superiors, permit me to reply to the communications Your Grace sent me through Father Anderson about certain points in the administration of the hospital and I beg, very respectfully, to say to the first that the administration of our houses is under the Jurisdiction of our Superior General, as declared by the Sovereign Pontiff again and again. Hence we could not, without infringing on his authority, elect your Grace President of our Corporation. The Community has, of course, no objections, on the contrary is pleased that you are President of the corporations of the other three houses of our Sisters in the City, but in case of this house, which is the property of the Community, such would not be proper.

To the second request regarding bequests, etc., we have always retained a competent lawyer to look after our interests, and nothing, I think, has been needlessly lost. We shall certainly as you wish it, give our account of all bequests without any obligations attached thereto.

Your third direction to secure written permission, etc., will be faithfully and cheerfully complied with.

I am sending, under separate cover, a copy of our "Privileges and Indulgences" which will explain, better than I can, our dependence on our Superior General.

In conclusion, dear Archbishop, please let me express in the name of My Superior the hope and the assurance that you will always find the children of St. Vincent most obedient and loyal to Your Grace and devoted to the interests of Your diocese.

Most respectfully in X,
Sr. Gonzaga

Document 10: Sister M. Madeleva on Educating Catholic Women

In this century, women religious have been recognized as the primary educators in Catholic elementary and secondary schools. For twenty-seven years president of St. Mary's College, Notre Dame, Sister Madeleva was one of the few women leaders in Catholic higher education. During her administration, she brought in a new curriculum in a deliberate attempt to make St. Mary's a center of Christian humanism. In 1943, she opened the School of Sacred Theology designed for laywomen. The following excerpt is from an address on the values and goals of Catholic college education for women.[17]

At this spring's meeting of our board of lay trustees one report was submitted that is basic to our consideration, that of the president of the college. This report made particular mention of the major and minor fields in which students were qualifying, or had already qualified, particularly in medical technology, in the nursing arts, in teaching. Attention focused rather sharply on specializations. We took a look at the advisability of training mathematicians for certain areas of engineering, of artists and photographers for commercial advertising.

The real objective of the students' education began to be pretty tangential. One blue-ribbon trustee asked the quietly innocent question, "Does anyone think of educating a woman as a woman?". . .

Should college educate a woman as a woman? If so, how? Do all types of colleges educate our daughters equally well in their proper vocation of being women?

Running the gauntlet of semantics we may say that we always educate a woman as a woman. The quantity and quality of her womanhood depend very much, first upon herself, then upon the school that she attends, the school that is her Alma Mater. She will probably resemble her intellectual mother. I think that our trustee had in mind a quintessence of womanliness as a quality to be preserved, if not indeed to be developed in the education of our daughters. We, too, believe in the quintessence of womanliness as the very flower and fruit of the education of women. . . .

Since 1898 Saint Mary's College has been granting Bachelors' degrees to these daughters of hers.

Just how does she educate young women as women? She recognizes the great fields of knowledge, the sciences, the liberal arts, the fine arts. Since Theology is the queen of the sciences she makes it the core, the central and integrating subject in the curriculum. The student's entire experience becomes significant in terms of its relation to God. The student herself grows in the knowledge of her own supernatural stature in consequence, and of the supernatural world itself in which we all live and move. Her womanhood is measured by, and uplifted to the womanhood of Mary. This in itself educates her as a woman.

Around the science of Theology, the profane sciences range themselves in orders and potencies which atomic energies and electronics merely shadow. Women can move among these as freely as men, with the authentic freedom of truth. Such fields as cancer research, the care of premature babies are being successfully investigated by teachers and students in Catholic colleges for women.

The liberal arts are most liberal, most liberating when they rest on complete rather than on partial truth. Here the Catholic college is the authentic exponent for the first sixteen centuries of Christian arts and sciences. One may say the same of the fine arts.

... Girls study, learn, and respond to teaching differently from the way boys do, and differently in classes with boys from in groups of girls only. Whatever the reasons for the delicate psychology governing these facts, they are facts. Girls achieve a type of womanhood when educated with girls which differs from the results of coeducation. We believe that this difference is a more refined, a more perfect womanhood, the quintessential womanliness which our blue-ribbon trustee had in mind.

Perfection is not achieved without costs. The women's colleges in the United States are monuments to the enterprise, the sacrifice, the fortitude of women. They are the most expensive to maintain, the last to benefit by philanthropy. Present educational crises are being met by colossal gifts from corporations, foundations, individuals.

At a recent meeting of the American Council on Education, the question was asked, "Where in the order of these gifts do colleges for women stand?" This is the answer which was given, not without embarrassment: "Gifts for education go, first, to schools with big names; second, to big schools; third, to co-educational schools; fourth, to women's colleges." Considering that half the parents of the world, all the mothers, the wives, the daughters, and the sisters are women this does not reflect gloriously to the generosity, the chivalry, the gratitude, or even the justice of the manhood of our country....

Handfuls of sisters in our teaching communities of women, with or without money, are making this possible. They believe in educating our daughters as women. Years ago, Coventry Patmore wrote in a prelude to *The Angel in the House*:

> Ah, wasteful woman, she who may
>   On her sweet self set her own price,
> Knowing man cannot choose but pay,
>   How has she cheapen'd paradise;
> How given for nought her priceless gift,
>   How spoil'd the bread and spill'd the wine,
> Which, spent with due, respective thrift,
>   Had made brutes men, and men divine.

The Sisters of the Holy Cross believe this. Saint Mary's College is their act of faith.

Document 11: Mission to Indians and Colored People: Mother M. Katharine Drexel

Katharine Drexel, a well-educated and wealthy banker's daughter, felt called to serve neglected blacks and American Indians in a special way. She entered the Novitiate of the Sisters of Mercy in Pittsburgh, Pennsylvania, in 1889, to prepare herself to found a new order dedi-

cated to this mission. In 1891, she took her final vows, and with twelve other young sisters founded the Sisters of the Blessed Sacrament for Indians and Colored People, of which she was the first superior general. In 1913, the new order received final papal approval. By the time of Mother M. Katharine's death in 1955, her order had grown to more than five hundred members. They had spread across the West and South, establishing elementary and high schools for Indians and blacks, and founding Xavier University, the first Catholic college for blacks in this country.

Two documents are included here. The first is a letter written by Mother M. Katharine Drexel in 1905 to a Nashville banker who had sold his homestead to the Sisters of the Blessed Sacrament, not realizing that it would be used as an Industrial Academy for Colored Girls. The issue became a public one when the newspaper, the mayor, and the city council became involved. In the end Mother M. Katharine prevailed, insisting that she wished to fulfill her God-given mission as quietly and perfectly as she could. The second document is a statement by Pope Pius XII on the fiftieth anniversary of the Sisters of the Blessed Sacrament.[18]

St. Elizabeth's, Maud P.O., Pa.

My dear Sir:

I am just in receipt of your letter of February 17th, transmitted to me from Drexel and Company. I hasten to answer it, and to express to you my regret that you and your neighbors should feel as you do concerning the purchase of the property. I think there is some misapprehension on the part of you and your neighbors which I should like to remove. The Sisters of the Blessed Sacrament, who have purchased the property, are religious, of the same race as yourself. We will always endeavor in every way to be neighborly to any white neighbors in the vicinity; we have every reason to hope we may receive from our white neighbors the cordial courtesy for which Southern people are so justly noted.

It is true we intend to open an industrial school and academy for Colored girls, but the girls who will come there will be only day scholars. In coming to the academy and returning to their homes, I am confident they will be orderly and cause no annoyance.

I observed very carefully when in Nashville, that the property which we purchased was within very few blocks of numerous houses occupied by Colored families, and therefore, even were the property to be the residence of Colored teachers, which it is not, I think no just exception could be taken to the locality selected.

I can fully realize, I think, how you feel about your old and revered home, around which so many attachments of the past—the sweet relations of home life—hover. I acknowledge I feel the same with regard to mine, and confess that some time ago, when passing it in the trolley cars, when I saw a bill of sale on it, a whole crowd of fond recollections of father and mother and sisters, etc., came vividly to my imagination. Then I more than ever realized how all things temporal pass away, and that there is but one home, strictly speaking, that eternal home where we all hope to meet our own, and where there will be no separation any more. And so temporal things, after all, are only to be valued, inasmuch as they bring us and many others—as many as possible—to the same eternal joys for which we were all created.

With warmest trust that all misapprehension be removed, believe me,

Very sincerely yours,
M. M. Katharine (Drexel)

Pope Pius XII—Mother M. Katharine's Fiftieth Anniversary

It was with profound joy and heartfelt satisfaction that We learned that you are about to observe the fiftieth anniversary of your religious profession and We hasten to extend to you, beloved daughter, a to all the Sisters of the Most Blessed Sacrament, Our cordial felicitations. With what consolation and spiritual gratification you may now look back over those years! For they have, indeed, been years dedicated to the service of Almighty God; a half century given with self-sacrificing zeal and devotion to the propagation of Christ's Kingdom among the Indians and Negroes of the United States. The history of your work and of the uninterrupted progress made by the Sisters of the Most Blessed Sacrament, who have served as your devoted handmaids in that magnificient mission, bears ample testimony to the fruitfulness of your labors.

With the paternal encouragement of Our predecessor, Leo XIII, of happy memory, and under the guidance of James O'Connor, Bishop of Omaha, and Patrick John Ryan, Archbishop of Philadelphia, you courageously renounced a life of worldly comfort and pleasure in order to insure that, through your missionary efforts, others might share with you the joys and consolations of a higher and nobler life in Christ. With thirteen devoted companions, the first Sisters of the Most Blessed Sacrament, you set forth to bring the Word of God to countless thousands who had until then, through no fault of their own, been deprived of that inestimable privilege. We know that you and your associates have spared neither effort nor expense in extending your apostolate. We realize, too, that the trials were many and the labors difficult; for you were among the pioneers—Christ's pioneers in the North American desert. And yet, from that day, in the year 1894, when a small band of Sisters established the first mission among the Pueblo Indians at Santa Fe, you have persevered with courage and confidence, undaunted by the many obstacles and difficulties which lay in your path. But your beloved apostolate was favored by Almighty God and encouraged by the bishops and priests of your own country; and today, as a result, that inspiring work continues in twenty-one dioceses. From that small beginning at St. Catherine's Mission, you and your eager associates have extended your field of endeavor to include sixty-nine schools, in which each year more than fifteen thousand Indian and Negro children receive the light of Christian teaching and are rescued from pagan darkness. . . .

LAY LEADERS OF SOCIAL ACTION MOVEMENTS

Document 12: Martha Moore Avery: Founder of the Catholic Truth Guild

Martha Moore Avery, a former Socialist who converted to Catholicism, established with David Goldstein, also a former Socialist, the Catholic Truth Guild. The object of the Guild was the widespread dissemination of theological and sociological literature refuting the claims of Socialism. Avery approached Cardinal O'Connell of Boston to provide the necessary funds and to serve as protector of the Guild. Her first letter requested permission to seek financial aid from Catholic sources to build a second "auto-van" from which to conduct street-preaching. It made reference to the recent success of a preaching tour on the Pacific Coast. The second letter, also addressed to the cardinal, requests clarification of the archdiocesan policy on women's suffrage. Notices of woman's suffrage meetings appeared in the archdiocesan newspaper, The Pilot, *seeming to indicate local Church approbation for the movement. Martha Moore Avery herself had been a proponent of women's suffrage while a Socialist, but reversed her view of the matter when she converted to Catholicism.*[19]

To His Emminence William Cardinal O'Connell
Archbishop of Boston,

My dear Lord Cardinal:

If the Catholic Truth Guild had another auto-van we could do twice as much work as we did last summer in Massachusetts. I write to ask if we are privileged to seek financial aid of some Catholics with money to build one?

The first meeting in San Francisco, Dec. 30th, was a marvelous success, so we are assured that the campaign for truth on the Pacific Coast will pay its way. Six hundred thirty-eight books—"Catholic Religion" were sold and one hundred eight dollars collected.

Hoping for a favorable response and ever mindful of God's goodness in the presence of our Cardinal I am

Sincerely
Martha Moore Avery
1-4-1918

The Woman Suffrage Question

My dear Lord Cardinal:

Frequently since notices of woman suffrage meetings have been published in *The Pilot* inviting Catholic women to be present, those opposed have wondered—Has His Eminence given permission for the organization as "they say" he has? Uncritical Catholic women contend that having seen Alice Stone Blackwell listed as a speaker at these meetings in *The Pilot,* that "she must be a Catholic." If woman suffrage is *not* favored by the Cardinal why may not an organization of Catholic women be anti-suffragists? There is not a little resentment regarding the matter.

I have taken this attitude—As the issue has now become political the Church is put in a difficult position. Yet since Woman Suffragists insist that the individual *not the family* is the unit of civil society the Church cannot favor its basic contention any more than it favors the false principle of divorce. Yet divorce is a matter of fact under civil processes and several states have *votes for* women.

However, it is essential that Catholic women learn what in fact the movement is. Yet, since this knowledge cannot be given by those who desire to propagate a philosophy in strict contradiction to Catholic principles and practices I am considering whether or not I should take part in the discussions at the "Margaret Brent Suffrage Guild"? Certainly, if our commonwealth should adopt the measure—God forbid!
—it would be necessary for Catholic women to vote.

I am mindful that some four years ago when as a Committee from the Common Cause Society I wanted to go to the State House to protest the Suffrage bill Your Eminence wrote me to "wait" until I was directed regarding the matter. Hoping that this will seem worthwhile I am

Sincerely in Christ
Martha Moore Avery
5-13-1918

Document 13: Mother Jones: Labor Organizer and Unionist

An immigrant from Cork, Ireland, labor organizer "Mother" Mary H. Jones led nonviolent protests to win strikes for various labor groups, including railway and mine workers. Her remarks were critical of woman's suffrage, because she did not think their vote would

bring about freedom. Rather, she used traditional gender values to
fight industrial despotism. Often she utilized women marching with
mops and brooms to win her point.[20]

I came to New York to raise funds for the miner's families. Although they had gone back beaten to work, their condition was pitiful.
The women and children were in rags and they were hungry. I spoke
to a great mass meeting in Cooper Union. I told the people after they
had cheered me for ten minutes, that cheering was easy. That the side
lines where it was safe, always cheered.

"The miners lost," I told them, "because they had only the constitution. The other side had bayonets. In the end, bayonets always win."

I told them how Lieutenant Howert of Walsenberg had offered
me his arm when he escorted me to jail. "Madam," said he, "will you
take my arm?"

"I am not a Madam," said I. "I am Mother Jones. The Government
can't take my life and you can't take my arm, but you can take my
suitcase."

I told the audience how I had sent a letter to John Rockefeller,
Junior, telling him of conditions in the mines. I had heard he was a
good young man and read the Bible, and I thought I'd take a chance.
The letter came back with "Refused" written across the envelope.
"Well" I said, "how could I expect him to listen to an old woman when
he would not listen to the President of the United States through his
representative, Senator Foster."

Five hundred women got up a dinner and asked me to speak. Most
of the women were crazy about women suffrage. They thought that
Kingdom-come would follow the enfranchisement of women.

"You must stand for free speech in the streets," I told them.

"How can we," piped a woman, "when we haven't a vote?"

"I have never had a vote," said I, "and I have raised hell all over
this country! You don't need a vote to raise hell! You need convictions
and a voice!"

Some one meowed, "You're an anti!"

"I am not an anti to anything which will bring freedom to my
class," said I. "But I am going to be honest with you sincere women
who are working for votes for women. The women of Colorado have
had the vote for two generations and the working men and women
are in slavery. The state is in slavery, vassal to the Colorado Iron and
Fuel Company and its subsidiary interests. A man who was present
at a meeting of mine owners told me that when the trouble started in
the mines, one operator proposed that women be disfranchised because here and there some woman had raised her voice in behalf of
the miners. Another operator jumped to his feet and shouted, 'For
God's sake! What are you talking about! If it had not been for the
women's vote the miners would have beaten us long ago!' "

Some of the women gasped with horror. One or two left the room.

I told the women I did not believe in women's rights nor in men's rights but in human rights. "No matter what your fight," I said, "don't be ladylike! God Almighty made women and the Rockefeller gang of thieves made the ladies. I have just fought through sixteen months of bitter warfare in Colorado. I have been up against armed mercenaries but this old woman, without a vote, and with nothing but a hatpin has scared them.

"Organized labor should organize its women along industrial lines. Politics is only the servant of industry. The plutocrats have organized their women. They keep them busy with suffrage and prohibition and charity."

Document 14: Dorothy Day and the Catholic Worker Movement

Perhaps the most significant modern lay Catholic action movement in the United States is the Catholic Worker Movement founded by Dorothy Day and Peter Marin in 1933. Shaped by their collaborative vision, and largely under Day's leadership, the movement grew to have more than fifty houses of hospitality and farming communes where the hungry and homeless poor were welcomed, fed, housed, and indoctrinated with Catholic teachings. For more than fifty years, Dorothy Day also published The Catholic Worker, *a newspaper in which she applied her prophetic understanding of the gospel to economic, political, and social issues of the times.*

Born in 1897, Dorothy Day was the third of five children of a lower-middle-class family. Though she was a baptized Episcopalian, she joined the Socialist party at eighteen and spent the next eleven years in journalism covering various Socialist and Communist activities. Her conversion to Catholicism and her insistance on the baptism of their daughter led to her permanent separation from the Communist common law husband whom she loved. After years of searching for meaning, she met Marin, the French Catholic social activist twenty years her senior with whom she established the Catholic Worker Movement.

Included here are several selections from her writings. The first excerpt is taken from an early autobiographical sketch; the second describes the goals and objectives of the Catholic Worker Movement; and the third contains her statement on pacificism as the gospel value at the time of America's entrance into the Second World War.[21]

Autobiographical Account

. . . It is strange that at the time my novel was published and before the motion picture rights were sold, I was living in New Orleans on St. Peter Street, just around the corner from the cathedral. My work on *The Item* was pleasant, and things were going smoothly for me, and

I had the leisure every night to attend Benediction of the Blessed Sacrament at the cathedral. I bought a rosary and I began to pray. I did not attend Mass in the morning because I had to be at work by seven-thirty or eight, my newspaper being an afternoon one. But this slow and sweet return to God made me resolve to see a priest and receive instruction.

But the excitement of my sudden prosperity was too much for me and for two years more I delayed. I felt that "having Him, I could have naught beside" and I was avid for experience, for enjoyment.

However, God works in His own ways. I bought a little house in the country with my money and settled there to write and to enjoy myself. And life in the country, seeing the miracle of growth each spring, started again in me the love of God. Having a child completed my conversion. It did not matter to me that I lost a husband then in my desire for God. My husband was a Communist in sympathy and his hatred for the Church was so great that I could not do other than separate myself from him and go on alone. I had not even suspected this hatred until I had the child baptized; then it flared forth in an intense bitterness.

I lived with this bitterness and sickened under it for a year. I was sick with the struggle to keep human love and the love for God. I can say truthfully that I gave up human love when it was at its strongest and tenderest, because I had experienced the overwhelming conviction that I could not live longer without God. There was no compromise possible.

And now I am very much alone. My friends—the people with whom I come into daily contact—are Spaniards, Russians, Jews, Americans, artists, writers and revolutionaries. I know them intimately. They are old friends, or they have married into my family, which is a large one. We know one another intimately, yet there is a tremendous barrier between them and me. I have the Faith. They have not. As much as in me lies, I practise "the presence of God."

I am among people and yet I am in a desert place and, since God wills it, I shall love Him there. Only in the morning when I hasten to the church do I feel myself in a green and fertile place, and I hasten, so anxious I am to leave my desert for a time. During the day when I think of that early hour, it is as though the sound of fountains was in my ears, and the taste of fresh cool water on my lips. And I look forward to the evening to the Benediction which I can no longer do without.

St. Francis de Sales speaks of spiritual friendships, but I have never known these. He says too, "You must not forsake or disregard the friendship which nature and former obligations constrain you to cultivate with relations, with connections, with benefactors, with neighbors and with others." Though I no longer seek out those friends and have become estranged from many of them, still there are those with whom I come in close daily contact who are so hostile to the Church that they consider it an ideal to be obtained to banish religion from Russia, Mexico or Spain, and who think it a crime to teach a child to pray.

Duty and bonds of relationship and affection tie me to these people, but I am lonely in their presence. It is a pleasure in this writing to communicate with the faithful, those friends of God who know how sweet it is to love Him.

Catholic Worker Aims and Purposes

For the sake of new readers, for the sake of men on our breadlines, for the sake of the employed and unemployed, the organized and unorganized workers, and also for the sake of ourselves, we must reiterate again and again our aims and purposes.

Together with the Works of Mercy, feeding, clothing, and sheltering our brothers, we must indoctrinate. We must "give reason for the faith that is in us." Otherwise we are scattered members of the Body of Christ, we are not "all members one of another." Otherwise our religion is an opiate, for ourselves alone, for our comfort or for our individual safety or indifferent custom.

We cannot live alone. We cannot go to heaven alone. Otherwise, as Peguy said, God will say to you, "Where are the others?"

If we do not keep indoctrinating, we lose the vision. And if we lose the vision, we become merely philanthropists, doling our palliatives.

The vision is this. We are working for "a new heaven and a new *earth* wherein justice dwelleth." We are trying to say with action, "Thy will be done on *earth* as it is in heaven. We are working for a Christian social order.

We believe in the brotherhood of man and the Fatherhood of God. This teaching, the doctrine of the Mystical Body of Christ, involves today the issue of unions (where men call each other brothers); it involves the racial question; it involves cooperatives, credit unions; crafts; it involves Houses of Hospitality and farming communes. It is with all these means that we can live as though we believe indeed that we are all members one of another, knowing that when "the health of one member suffers, the health of the whole body is lowered."

Christian Pacifist Stance against the War

Dear Fellow Workers in Christ:

Lord God, merciful God, our Father, shall we keep silent, or shall we speak? And if we speak, what shall we say?

I am sitting here in the church on Mott Street writing this in Your presence. Out on the street it is quiet, but you are there, too, in the

Chinese, in the Italians, these neighbors we love. We love them because they are our brothers, as Christ is our Brother, and God our Father.

But we have forgotten so much. We have all forgotten. And how can we know unless You tell us? " 'For whoever calls upon the name of the Lord shall be saved.' But how are they to believe Him whom they have not heard? And how are they to hear, if no one preaches? And how are men to preach unless they be sent? As it is written, 'How beautiful are the feet of those who preach the gospel of peace.' " (Romans X)

Seventy-five thousand copies of *The Catholic Worker* go out every month. What shall we print? We can still print what the Holy Father is saying, when he speaks of total war, of mitigating the horrors of war, when he speaks of cities of refuge; of feeding Europe . . .

We will print the words of Christ, who is with us always, even to the end of the world. "Love your enemies, do good to those who hate you, and pray for those who persecute and calumniate you, so that you may be children of your Father in heaven, who makes His sun to rise on the good and the evil, and sends rain on the just and the unjust."

We are at war, a declared war, with Japan, Germany, and Italy. But still we can repeat Christ's words, each day, holding them close in our hearts, each month printing them in the paper. In times past Europe has been a battlefield. But let us remember St. Francis, who spoke of peace, and we will remind our readers of him, too, so they will not forget.

In *The Catholic Worker* we will quote our Pope, our saints, our priests. We will go on printing articles of Father Hugo, who reminds us today that we are all "called to be saints," that we are other Christs, reminding us of the priesthood of the laity.

We are still pacifists. Our manifesto is the Sermon on the Mount, which means that we will try to be peacemakers. Speaking for many of our conscientious objectors, we will not participate in armed warfare or in making munitions, or by buying government bonds to prosecute the war, or in urging others to these efforts.

But neither will we be carping in our criticism. We love our country and we love our President. We have been the only country in the world where men and women of all nations have taken refuge from oppression. We recognize that while in the order of intention we have tried to stand for peace, for love of our brothers and sisters in the order of execution we have failed as Americans in living up to our principles. . . .

Our Works of Mercy may take us into the midst of war. As editor of *The Catholic Worker*, I would urge our friends and associates to care for the sick and the wounded, to the growing of food for the hungry, to the continuance of all our Works of Mercy in our houses and on our farms. We understand, of course, that there is and that there will be great differences of opinion even among our own groups as to how much collaboration we can have with the government in times like these. There are differences more profound and there will be many continuing to work with us from necessity, or from choice, who do not agree with us as to our position on war, conscientious objection, etc. But we beg that there will be mutual charity and forbearance among us all. Because of our refusal to assist in the prosecution of war and our insistence that our collaboration be one for peace, we may find ourselves in difficulties. But we trust in the generosity and understanding of our government and our friends, to permit us to continue to use our paper to "preach Christ crucified."

And may the Blessed Mary, Mother of beautiful love, and of fear, and of knowledge, and of holy hope, pray for us.

January 1942

AFTER THE WARS: CHANGES IN FOCUS

Document 15: The Postwar Agrarian Ideal

This address, given at the National Catholic Rural Life Convention in Cincinnati, Ohio, on November 13, 1944, was delivered by Janet Kalven, a member of the staff of the Grailville Agricultural School for Women in Loveland, Ohio. In it she ties women's nature as nurturers to the vision of the Church for economic and social renewal.[22]

... No healthy, balanced, sane pattern of rural living is possible without the wholehearted interest and cooperation of the woman. Agriculture needs the influence and the unique contribution of woman to achieve a human and satisfying way of life on the land. America needs a new type of woman to accept the challenge of our times and to pioneer in working out a full, rich pattern of rural life.

Every woman is made to be a mother, to find her center outside herself in other human beings who are dependent on her loving care. Her motherhood need not be realized physically, but it must be realized spiritually if she is to achieve her fulfillment and her true happiness. Woman is most truly herself when she is utterly forgetful of self, absorbed in the service of those around her, alert to their needs, and spending herself without stint for them. She is made to be the heart of the home, the center of light and warmth, of physical and spiritual well-being in the family....

An intimate experience of life on the land is an essential part of education for motherhood, even for girls who live in the cities. Women's nature demands close contact with the beauties of creation and with growing plants and animals for her fullest physical and spiritual development. She needs the simple, rhythmic life on the land, with its fresh foods and outdoor work, to build abundant health and vitality. She needs contact with young plants and animals to help develop her motherly qualities. Women have always been great agriculturists, mothers of the earth. The mystery of the seed is very close to her, for she bears the seed of new life in her womb and nurtures it with her blood. A rich experience of the cycle of birth and death in plants and animals is in harmony with the deepest tendencies of her nature and develops her womanly talents. . . .

Woman learns best through concrete experience, and the practical work of sewing, cooking, canning, weaving, releases her intellectual energies and develops sound judgement.

The new pattern of life on the land must meet the fundamental requirements of woman's nature if it is to win her enthusiastic interest and active support. It must provide the conditions under which she can be at her best, and give her fullest contribution to family and community. Only then can we have a really healthy and well-balanced rural life.

First of all, the woman needs the small, diversified family farm. The homestead, producing primarily for family use and only incidentally for sale, should become the basic unit of the new agricultural pattern. The ideal of practical self-sufficiency can be realized on much smaller farms than are customary today, although the exact acreage will vary with local conditions.

Because it is family-centered, organized first of all to supply all that the family requires for a full life, the homestead is deeply satisfying to the mother of the family. Because it is diversified, it is admirably suited to woman's nature, for she is a universalist and a personalist. Woman is made to be everything to somebody, some person. That is why the large commercial farm with its hundred cows or thousand acres of wheat has little interest for her. . . . She enjoys the homestead, with its few cows to furnish butter, milk and cheese for her family; its few pigs for meat; its few sheep for lambs and wool; its small flock of chickens for really fresh eggs; a few bee hives for honey; perhaps a flock of ducks to add a note of color and humor to the farm yard. She wants to plant an orchard, a vineyard, a berry patch, an herb and flower garden, as well as a plot of vegetables.

Another fundamental requirement of woman's nature, and one which the rural pattern in this country has not met, is the need for a strong community life. . . . The fact that women connect farming with loneliness constitutes one of the most formidable psychological barriers to the rural movement, a barrier which can only be broken down by the development of flourishing, closely knit, rural communities.

It is a task for the rural apostolate to demonstrate the fulness of Catholic community life on the land by establishing homestead communities which will exemplify concretely the doctrine of the Mystical Body of Christ.

Under the influence of a stable and well-integrated community, inspired by the Catholic vision of life, women will blossom forth and be stimulated to contribute the best of their qualities and talents to the creation of a new social order.

Like Anteus, the mythological hero, modern society must renew its strength by contact with the earth. Women have an essential role to play in that renewal. If they only glimpse the vision of the rich, full Catholic life on the land, they will turn enthusiastically toward the creation of a new pattern of rural living. Like the valiant woman of scripture, they will "put out their hands to strong things," and throw themselves wholeheartedly into the fundamental work of reconstruction, the work of building Christian families and Christian communities on the land.

Document 16: International Cooperation in Catholic Social Welfare

After the conclusion of the Second World War, Catholics turned their attention to questions concerning the establishment of a lasting peace and to developing international networks for social action, especially to relieve immediate needs of war victims. Catholic schools of social work were developed in the United States and across Europe. The National Catholic Welfare Conference—War Relief Services, established in 1943, flourished. Women who had previously focused attention on survival as Catholics in America finally felt accepted there. This excerpt indicates their surprise in being welcomed as Catholics and Americans in postwar Europe, and their sense of responsibility to provide for the welfare of the world's poor and disenfranchised.[23]

Twice within the past year I had the privilege of visiting Europe. In August 1946, as a representative of the Social Action Department of the National Catholic Welfare Conference and of the Catholic Association for International Peace, I attended a preparatory meeting of the International Conference of Social Work in Brussels, and subsequently the Twenty-fifth Anniversary Congress of PAX ROMANA in Fribourg, Switzerland. On the second occasion, in the Spring of 1947, I went on a special mission to Germany, under the War Department, as Consultant to the Welfare Branch of the Military Government. During these six months, I traveled through ten countries—Holland, Belgium, Czechoslovakia, Switzerland, Italy, France, Germany, Austria, England, and Ireland. I witnessed the terrible destruction and the acute suffering of millions of people—the aftermath of the most devastating war in history.

I visited camps for displaced persons, where mothers and children, young girls and old people crowded together in the most forlorn and depressing surroundings, await plans for their resettlement. I visited hospitals, shelters for unwed mothers and their babies, institutions for children, day-care centers and homes for working girls. . . .

I met the leaders of Catholic thought and action groups in these countries—men and women of strong character, zealous in the service on their fellow-men. To a world plunged in hatred, misery and destruction, they believe that Catholics have a message to give: "Christian Charity—this universal love which is the resume and the most elevated end of the Christian ideal" (Pius XII). Everywhere I was welcomed as an American and as a Catholic. They are most eager for closer relationship with American Catholic Organizations.

Europeans are more internationally minded than we in the United States. Even before the first World War they had taken the initiative in the development of international organizations. . . .

In the past, Catholics in the United States have been so occupied in the development of their own national organizations, the National Conference of Catholic Charities founded in 1910, and the National Catholic Welfare Conference in 1919, that participation in these international movements has been very limited. But now, after the terrible tragedies of a second World War, we have become increasingly aware of our responsibility in international affairs. More than 10 million of our young men fought in foreign lands for our ideals of liberty, security, peace and justice. These countries are no longer to them just names in the geography and history books. These peoples are now very real to them. Our men have brought back a deeper understanding of their sufferings and needs, and with that generosity of spirit which is typical of true Americans, they desire to work for the common welfare of all the peoples of the world.

The establishment of the headquarters of the United Nations in New York has also served to bring us into more intimate contact with the cultures, customs and problems of the nations of the world. . . .

In September, 1946, Miss Catherine Schaefer was appointed as an Assistant to the General Secretary of the National Catholic Welfare Conference on United Nations Affairs, and serves as an observer for the NCWC at the United Nations. Through the courtesy of the Cardinal Archbishop of New York, offices have been made available at the N.C.C.S., 17 East 51st Street, New York, N.Y. During the year informal gatherings have been held with discussions on current problems at the United Nations, and frequently foreign guests have participated in these meetings. One of the most important of these affairs was the recent Institute on the United Nations, sponsored by the Committee on International Relations of the National Council of Catholic Women (October 30–November 2, 1947). Consideration was given to such vital problems as European relief and reconstruction, the care, maintenance and resettlement of Displaced Persons, numbering nearly a million persons, the Marshall Plan, the achievement of human rights, the status of women, women's responsibility in international affairs, and a report on the International Congress of Catholic Women in Rome in September 1947. . . .

The times are very crucial. The economic, political, social and moral problems in the world today are of such enormous complexity that they require the joint planning and cooperation of all organizations. Catholics could contribute most effectively to laying the foundation of a world social order through a Catholic international program based upon the acceptance of and obedience to supernatural ideals and spiritual principles. Such a program would provide central machinery through which international planning and coordination of efforts in promoting human welfare could be carried on. It would serve to strengthen the cooperation among organizations in various countries which has been developed through joint participation in war-relief services. . . .

Document 17: Laywomen's Spirituality

This article points the way toward a movement that continues in the Church today, that of laywomen's spirituality and spiritual direction. Once basic survival and American identity were achieved, many Catholic women broadened their focus to include more than the material needs of the family, the nation, and the world. Finally, realizing their own need for nurturance, especially for their souls, Catholic women began to seek actively guided ways to holiness. In this article, Catholic writer Dorothy Dohen defined this hunger and suggested some guidelines for its satisfaction. She outlined particular problem areas in the new attempt by the clergy to integrate modern psychology into the ancient science of spiritual life and to apply these principles to laypersons.[24]

In October 1954, *Integrity* magazine published an article on spiritual direction. It was the result of a questionnaire answered by about fifty laymen and laywomen who told of their aspirations and needs in regard to Confession and spiritual direction. The article was received with a great deal of interest, for it is one of the acknowledged phenomena of our day that lay people are showing an avid desire to advance in holiness. The life of prayer and all that it entails is no longer considered foreign to a life in the world; engagement in temporal interests need not keep one from contemplation of eternal verities. It is also pretty much agreed that the way to holiness for lay people today is unchartered. True, they have the Gospel counsels, the traditional masters of the spiritual life, and the directives of the recent Popes, to give broad general outline of their journey, but the exact way they will follow can be termed *experimental*. Theirs is the surety of the guidance of the Holy Spirit, but it presents itself in the sacrament of the moment which too often seems haphazard and unpredictable. Without rule, habit, cloister, or superior, the lay person is on his own in a way unknown to the religious.

It is not surprising then that an earnest desire for holiness has often caused him (and especially *her*) to bend over backward in dependence upon a director to give him the desired spiritual security. This over-dependence on spiritual directors, particularly on the part of women, was mentioned repeatedly in the answers to the *Integrity* questionnaire. It was seen not only as a stumbling block to the persons involved who mistakenly sought in spiritual direction the emotional support they failed to find in other areas in their lives, but it was viewed also as a deterrent to more mature, independent personalities who misinterpreted the real role of spiritual direction because of what they saw of it in actual practice.

It is not the purpose of this present article to attempt to solve any of the very real difficulties involved in spiritual direction for lay people, but the writer, who had the privilege of compiling the answers to the *Integrity* questionnaire, would like simply to point out three general problems that lay people see in spiritual direction. This article is written not in a spirit of carping criticism, nor to provoke controversy, but in the hope that the presentation of the problems *as they appear to a lay person* may be of help to confessors and directors who are generously striving to guide souls to union with God.

The First Problem—Direction and Psychotherapy

The first problem arises from the present great interest in the connection between religion and psychiatry, between Confession and psychotherapy. There are priests—very few—who have been competently trained in some sort of psychotherapy and make use of it in their pastoral dealings; there are priests who feel that any form of psychiatry is diabolic and that any neurosis should give way to absolution; there are priests—an increasing number—who try to make use of psychotherapy while knowing very little about it. This categorization is obviously a gross over-simplification, but there is enough truth in it to hint at the difficulties of lay people who seek spiritual guidance from priests who approach psychiatry from varying points of view. The poor person, burdened with neurotic guilt, who hears a Sunday sermon to the effect that psychiatric treatment is not only wrong but unnecessary and that Confession is the only remedy for guilt feelings, suffers an increase in anxiety, for wasn't he to Confession the night before? Does this persistence of guilt feelings prove his Confession sacrilegious and the absolution worthless?

Then there is the girl trying to advance in holiness who approaches another priest, this time not one who disapproves of psychiatry but one who, on the contrary, dabbles in it. He asks her if she is neurotic. She comes away confused; she doesn't know if she is neurotic, but this reaction his question has provoked: she'll be on guard from now on; the priest won't get to know her as she is. She'll try to keep from him anything about herself that seems to her to indicate incipient neurosis. But what about the priest? Granted that, to say the least, his question indicates a certain ineptness, still if he is to give good spiritual direction it may be necessary for him to know whether his penitent is neurotic. However, is he confusing the purpose of direction with the aim of psychotherapy? And if his penitent is neurotic should he attempt to go beyond his depth into a field for which he has no training or competence? . . . Then there is the pious woman who tells her director how she is "persecuted" by her family. Should he tell her to bear wrongs patiently or should he be able to recognize the classic case of the paranoid? . . .

The Second Problem—Understanding Lay Life

Priests who are chaplains of lay groups or who are engaged in giving spiritual direction to lay people have shown great interest in understanding lay life. They have made a study of temporal problems; they show great sympathy with the problems facing young people and especially families. But this is another case where "a little knowledge is a dangerous thing." We lay people are all probably familiar with the example of the priest who clucks sympathetically over the financial hardships of a family with an income on which other families manage to live quite nicely! We can be amused by this sympathetic and naive over-identification while we are at the same time grateful to priests for making the effort to understand the manifold difficulties of lay life.

But there is an involvement of the priest in the temporal interests of his penitent that does represent a serious problem. Since the lay person should not (even if he could) live his spiritual life in a vacuum, it is to be expected that the circumstances and problems of his daily life are going to affect the state of his soul. He is going to present his problems, then, not in a disembodied state but in the context of this temporal situation. Since this is so, the lay person has the tendency to draw his confessor or director into his temporal life as an active participant. . . .

With all the emphasis on the necessity for lay people to develop personal responsibility and initiative, shouldn't the emphasis in spiritual direction be on the development of personal prudence in the penitent in order that he may solve the problems he meets in life as Christ would wish, rather than on having the director solve the problems for him? Is the director, even sometimes in the very act of trying to understand lay life, really applying to the situation the obedience of religious life?

The Third Problem—The Happiness Pitfall

The third problem is quite directly allied to the other two, for it concerns the temptation to make of spiritual direction not an assist to holiness but an assist to happiness. It reduces the spiritual director to an amateur psychotherapist who tries to make the lay person's life more agreeable than it is.

That this temptation exists is not surprising. The search for happiness—if one is to judge by the books on the best-seller list—is the focus of thought and action today. Everybody is trying like mad to be happy. Is it any wonder then that sometimes the goal of spiritual direction is shifted from holiness to happiness? . . .

Conclusion

It would seem then that the problem of spiritual direction for lay people reduces itself to the problem of how to integrate into the ancient science of the spiritual life the new knowledge of the human person attained through modern psychology, and further how to integrate this knowledge into the difficult art of spiritual direction, while making adaptations for modern conditions and the lay state. Neither lay people nor directors can be scornful of the tradition, nor can they refuse to use new insights which they have providentially received. This integration of the new and the old would be a hopeless task if the Church were stagnant but on the contrary it is the *living* Church, ever vivified and renewed by the Holy Spirit. It is because the writer is confident that this integration can be made that this article was written.

Women in Evangelical, Holiness, and Pentecostal Traditions

LETHA DAWSON SCANZONI
AND SUSAN SETTA

Historically, the broad category known as evangelicalism is rooted in the revivalistic movements of the eighteenth and nineteenth centuries and also reflects the influences of Puritanism and Pietism. In the early twentieth century, much of evangelicalism took on the particular coloring of the fundamentalist-modernist controversies over the inerrancy of Scripture, higher criticism, biological evolution, and the Social Gospel.[1] Holiness groups differ from other evangelical groups in their emphasis on sanctification as a second work of grace, separate from conversion. Pentecostal churches emphasize speaking in tongues as a sign of the Holy Spirit's infilling. Evangelical, Holiness, and Pentecostal traditions have in common their emphasis on personal conversion, biblical authority, evangelism, and lay involvement.

As the nineteenth century drew to a close, a number of prominent male evangelical leaders were speaking out on behalf of women's right to preach. Evangelist W. B. Godbey published in 1891 a booklet entitled *Woman Preacher,* in which he urged women to "get sanctified" and preach the gospel despite their churches' refusal to license them. He rebuked males for the harm they did by discouraging women. "The soul of a man must be wonderfully small," he wrote, "who, actuated by ignorance, prejudice, or egotism, would lay the weight of a straw on the dear sisterhood, whose hearts the Lord has touched, and whose lips he has anointed with a live coal from heaven's altar."[2] In that same year, B. T. Roberts, founder of the Free Methodist Church, argued for male-female equality in the home as well as in the church.[3]

Also speaking up for the ministry of women was A. J. Gordon, a Baptist who, with his wife Maria, established a training school that has developed into what is now Gordon College and Gordon-Conwell Theological Seminary. In 1894, Gordon wrote a forceful article after a woman missionary's scheduled presentation was canceled by certain male leaders who decided that public participation in the summer convention program should be limited to males only. Gordon was convinced that these leaders, who claimed women should not address assemblies where men were present, were wrongly interpreting Scripture. Gordon believed that the account of the Spirit's coming at Pentecost in Acts 2 provides evidence that women have been granted the right and power to prophesy.[4]

Gordon believed further that *human experience* must be taken into account in interpreting Scripture, and suggested that the Church's "spiritual intuition" may have been "far in advance of its exegesis in dealing with this subject." He pointed out the role of women in every great spiritual awakening and also provided examples of outstanding women of his own time who were serving Christ in public ministries. He told of men who, after observing God's blessing on such ministries, found themselves reexamining Scripture. "To many it has been both a relief and a surprise to discover how little authority there is in the Word for repressing the witness of women in the public assembly, or for forbidding her to herald the Gospel to the unsaved," he wrote. "If this be so, it may be well for the plaintiffs in this case to beware lest, in silencing the voice of consecrated women, they may be resisting the Holy Ghost."[5]

Fredrik Franson, founder of the missionary organization now known as The Evangelical Alliance Mission (TEAM), likewise argued that Scripture had been misinterpreted in its application to women. His essay "Prophesying Daughters," issued in Swedish by the Bible Women's Home Publishers in St. Paul, Minnesota, in 1896, provided the Scandanavian free churches in America with Franson's rationale for women's public ministry.[6]

On a similar note, Seth Cook Rees, founder of the Pilgrim Holiness Church, viewed the equality of the sexes as one of the marks of the ideal church. "No church that is acquainted with the Holy Ghost will object to the public ministry of women," he asserted.[7]

Numerous *women* were also urging other women to use their gifts in God's service on an equal basis with men. Near the turn of the century, a column in *Guide to Holiness,* a leading periodical of the Holiness movement, boldly stated that the limited role so passively accepted by large numbers of Christian women was actually an acquiescence to the prevailing societal mold rather than obedience to Scripture. "[The Christian woman] contents herself with shining, like the moon, with borrowed splendor, as the mother, sister, or wife of the great so-and-so," wrote columnist Mrs. J. Fowler Willing. Such a woman has "left her talent in its napkin while she is obeying the world's dictum by helping to make the most of his."[8]

However, considerable numbers of women were by no means hiding talents in napkins or lights under bushels. The dawning of the twentieth century found women engaged in many forms of public ministries— sometimes with church support and sometimes without it. "In my early evangelistic work, I met considerable opposition to woman's preaching," recalled Mary Cole, a traveling evangelist with the Church of God. "The Lord helped me to successfully drive these opposers out of their false positions and to show them that they were misusing the Scriptures."[9] Cole had sometimes been described as "Jesse James dressed as a woman and posing as a preacher" because of her fearless strength in handling the drunken rowdies who at times tried to disrupt her meetings.[10]

Another evangelist with the Anderson, Indiana-based Church of God was Lena Shoffner. During one memorable Alabama camp meeting, Shoffner preached for an hour and a half to an audience in which blacks and whites sat on opposite sides of the aisle with a thick rope running down the center. Shoffner's text was Ephesians 2:14—"For he is our peace, who hath made one, and hath broken down the middle wall of partition." As she decried the evils of racial prejudice and its inappropriateness among Christian believers, the audience was moved to tears and to action. White members and black members of the congregation looked across the heavy rope that separated them. They began loosening it together, letting it fall to the floor, where they trampled it on their way to the altar. There, women and men of both races wept and prayed together. Someone started to sing, and the others joined in; racial categories no longer mattered as voices blended in the words, "One heart, and soul, and mind we prove/ The union heaven gave us."[11]

Other Church of God women pioneered and carried on missions in impoverished and crime-ridden areas of cities, evangelized rural regions, established strategic urban congregations, engaged in foreign missionary work, conducted a publishing ministry for the blind, and were active in publishing other Christian literature.[12] They were also active in Christian education endeavors; and in 1922, the Anderson Bible Training School named a woman, Bessie Hittle Byrum, as head of the mission department.[13] A 1902 publication with photographs of Church of God leaders showed about one-fourth to be women, prompting a Church of God historian to conclude that "on the basis of this and other evidence, it is probably safe to say that no other movement either religious or secular in this period of American history, except the suffrage movement itself, had such a high percentage of women leaders whose contribution was so outstanding."[14]

In other Holiness groups, women also occupied a central role in the formative years. In the Church of the Nazarene, for example, women such as Mary Lee (Harris) Cagle, Lucy P. Knott, Mrs. A. F. Reynolds, and Mrs. Delance Wallas pastored churches, founded and taught in church schools, opened new areas to the gospel, and were active in formulating church doctrine and polity.[15] From its beginning, the Church of the Nazarene ordained women; and its leaders maintained that stance in spite of opposition from certain groups that refused to affiliate with it on that account.[16] Women who felt called to preach often recounted great inner struggles over answering that call, nonetheless. They knew that widespread general resistance to female evangelists and pastors existed. Therefore, in many cases, they first considered foreign missionary service or becoming a pastor's wife as a way to exercise their desire to serve God, while at the same time avoiding the criticism faced by women in the pulpit—only later to be persuaded that God had other plans for them (Documents 1, 2).

Nancy Hardesty, Lucille Sider Dayton, and Donald Dayton have suggested six factors that help explain the general receptivity to women's leadership and public ministry among Holiness groups: (1) a theology centered in experience (conversion and sanctification as a second work of grace); (2) biblical authority along with subjective interpretation of Scripture in line with experience; (3) an emphasis on the work of the Holy Spirit; (4) freedom to be experimental; (5) a reformist or revolutionary outlook that questioned the status quo; and (6) a tendency to form sects with organizational flexibility and that recognized a need for the gifts and leadership women offered.[17]

Specific aspects of the theology of the Pentecostal movement in its early stages also fostered the equality of the sexes. What has come to be called "classical Pentecostalism" (in contrast to the more recent charismatic or "neo-Pentecostal" movement) actually began with the experience of a young female student at Bethel Bible College, a school founded by the Holiness evangelist Charles Parham in Topeka, Kansas.[18] Agnes Ozman (Laberge) later wrote her own account of how she had prayed fervently for the baptism of the Holy Ghost and how her prayers were answered as she began speaking in tongues on 1 January 1901. She considered this experience to be a fulfillment of Acts 19:1–6. Three days after this occurrence, twelve others at Bethel also began speaking in tongues as a manifestation of the Spirit's baptism, and what became the Pentecostal movement was underway.[19]

Pointing out the variety of ministries carried out by women in early Pentecostalism, including prominent leadership roles as founders and pastors of some of the movement's largest churches, Charles Barfoot and Gerald Sheppard explain that such openness to gender equality was linked to an emphasis on the biblical *prophetic role*. Pentecostal theology laid great stress on (1) an individual's experience of a calling; (2) the group's confirmation of that call through its recognition of the Spirit's anointing; and (3) the group's conviction that the days of the "latter rain" had come, fulfilling Joel's prophecy that "your sons and your daughters will prophesy."[20]

However, according to Barfoot and Sheppard, the "prophetic Pentecostalism" that marked the period from 1901 into the 1920s gave way to an institutionalized "priestly Pentecostalism" that has continued into the present.[21] These scholars see this change as illustrative of the "routinization of charisma" and the insight of the social theorist Max Weber that the equality allotted to women in "the religion of the disprivileged classes" rarely continues beyond a religious movement's first stages. And even in those earliest stages, as Weber pointed out, certain minimal priestly (as opposed to prophetic) functions are usually reserved for males only.[22]

Those evangelicals not specifically aligned with the Holiness and Pentecostal movements also displayed a certain ambivalence toward women. There was, first of all, the inescapable tension between those evangelicals who saw the male-female relationship as hierarchical and those who viewed it as an equal partnership.[23] Second, the impact of cultural influences played their part. Sometimes women were simply ignored or disregarded, providing little more than a quiet backdrop against which the drama of life was acted out by men. Women's interests were often trivialized, their assumed nature regarded in sterotypical fashion. Again and again, they were not taken seriously (Document 3).

At the same time, many women in evangelical circles were taken very seriously indeed. It was the vision and persistence of a woman, Emma Dryer, who in 1873 had established a school of "Bible Work" in Chicago, which eventually gave rise to the school known today as Moody Bible Institute.[24] Dwight L. Moody recognized and encouraged the abilities and dedication of women like Emma Dryer and worked with them as equals in spreading the gospel.

Ninety years after its official 1889 founding Moody Bible Institute (MBI) fired one of its faculty members because of his and his wife's views on the equality of the sexes; but this action does not reflect the school's original posture.[25] One researcher, having carefully examined the school's offical publications from 1889 to 1945, has found hundreds of examples of women alumnae, staff members, and guest speakers who were serving with evident institute approval as evangelists, pastors, Bible teachers, pulpit supply preachers, instructors of Bible courses at Bible colleges, leaders of Bible classes for audiences of both men and women, evangelists and Bible teachers employed by Moody Bible Institute's extension department as official representatives of the school, and ordained ministers in several denominations. Women preached from the pulpit of Moody Church and were instructors for the summer Winona Bible School conducted by the extension department.[26] Janette Hassey suggests that this openness to women in public ministry, uncovered through her research, is related to the "fluidity in scope and functionalism in purpose" that characterized MBI in the early days. "Given the practical emphasis on evangelism and missions, and the overwhelming task of reaching the untouched 'masses' at home and abroad, *all* were enlisted (whether male or female) to teach, preach, and evangelize," she writes.[27]

Over the years, this openness to women in leadership positions gradually diminished. When the grandson of Salvation Army founders William and Catherine Booth attended Moody, he took issue with a professor's derogatory remarks about women as ministers, reminding him of Catherine Booth. "But there are not many Catherine Booths," the teacher answered. "You do not give them the opportunity to become Catherine Booths," was the student's retort.[28] In 1955, a class of students studying 1 Timothy 2:11–14 were told the passage "does not forbid a woman's teaching a class of children or of women, but does forbid her from being a pastor of a church or a teacher of doctrine in a school." According to the instructor, one major reason was that "Eve, the woman was completely deceived, whereas Adam sinned with his eyes wide open. The man, filled with the Spirit, is therefore a safer repository of doctrine than the woman."[29]

Elsewhere in evangelicalism, barriers to women's public ministry were also being erected both subtly and not so subtly. In 1930, in a spirit contrary to the practice of its founder A. J. Gordon, Gordon Divinity School imposed a quota system to ensure that "from that time no more women students should be admitted in any year than would bring the number of such students to one-third of the total enrollment.[30] Through a careful survey of yearbooks, one researcher has shown the impact of that quota system and the more restrictive attitude toward women that it represents. Whereas half the divinity school students in 1932 were women, by 1936 that figure had dropped to less than one-third. When male student enrollment was affected by the Second World War, the quota system was lifted; but women did not begin returning to the school in significant numbers until well into the 1960s. During much of the decade of the 1950s, in fact, no women enrolled as divinity school students at all.[31]

Holiness and Pentecostal groups also began showing signs of a dimming of their original vision for the equality of the sexes. The percentage of female pastors in the Church of the Nazarene declined from 20 percent in 1908 to 6 percent by 1973.[32] In the Church of God (Anderson), nearly one-third of its congregations had women pastors in 1925; but fifty years later, only 3 percent had women pastors. Further, the churches pastored by women throughout that half century were the smallest churches, having congregations of fewer than fifty members.[33] One observer from within that group writes, "In principle, the Church of God welcomes women ministers, but in practice we do not trust them." He sees the period between 1916 and 1940 as having been the most open to women leaders. "It is only at the end of the period, during World War II, that we see women losing their grip upon the ministerial office. Their desire to serve was as great as ever, and undoubtedly God was still calling women to the ministry," he continues. "But the mood of the times, both inside and outside the church, erected a difficult hurdle for any woman who wanted to enter the professional ministry."[34]

With the move toward more priestly and bureaucratic approaches to ministry, women lost privileges in the Pentecostal groups as well. Already, at its 1914 founding, the Assemblies of God had practiced a form of male-female hierarchy by reserving the highest office, ruling elder, for men—although women could be ordained as ministers and evangelists. By 1931, with the shift toward "priestly Pentecostalism" in full swing, an official resolution stripped ordained women of the right to administer the ordinances—a right restored by another resolution four years later, but which nevertheless served as a harbinger of a deterioration of the status and freedom women had enjoyed during the beginning stages of the Pentecostal movement.[35] Other Pentecostal groups, such as the Church of God in Cleveland, Tennessee, the Church of God in Huntsville, Alabama, and the Pentecostal Church of Christ, also limited the offices their female ministers were permitted to hold and the duties they were permitted to perform.[36] With declining support for women's equality, the percentage of ordained female ministers among Pentecostal groups has also declined—even in groups founded by women, such as the International Church of the Foursquare Gospel, founded in 1927 by evangelist Aimee Semple McPherson.[37]

WHY THE INCONSISTENCIES AND INCREASINGLY RESTRICTIVE ATTITUDES TOWARD WOMEN?

A number of factors help account for the ambivalence toward women's religious leadership in Evangelical, Holiness, and Pentecostal traditions, and the changes occurring in the first sixty-five years of the twentieth century.

First, with few exceptions, *even when the equality of the sexes was avowed, it was a limited equality*—an "equality" fenced with qualifications and reservations. We have seen this in the Pentecostal groups that recognized a woman's prophetic calling and right to preach, but restricted her exercise of priestly functions. Even more widespread was the teaching that, although a married woman could be a spiritual leader at church, she was under her husband's headship at home. A corollary view was the assumption that women were God's second choice, exceptions to the rule and called by God when men were unavailable. Women who agreed with such teachings found themselves more acceptable to male leadership than if they had questioned them. Thus, perhaps, it is not surprising that such ideas were expressed even by some of the century's most renowned and influential female religious leaders, such as evangelist-healer Kathryn Kuhlman, who preached to many millions throughout the world over her fifty years of ministry (Document 4).

Other eminent female preachers, such as Aimee Semple McPherson, who founded the International Church of the Foursquare Gospel, and Alma White, founder of the Pillar of Fire Church, found it difficult to reconcile their public ministries with expectations of female subordination in the home. McPherson was convinced that, had she not left her husband to begin her ministry as a traveling evangelist, he would have lost her anyway because she would have died of a broken spirit from not having followed God's call (Document 5). Throughout her ministry, she showed signs of conflict between patriarchal and feminist outlooks on the proper sphere of women, women's power, and feminine and masculine symbolism and imagery.[38]

Alma White spoke out forcefully for women's rights in the Church and larger society (Document 6), and was overjoyed at the 1919 passage of the Woman Suffrage Amendment, calling it "the triumph of the Cross in the liberation of women, who in their inequality with the opposite sex had worn the chains of oppression."[39] Yet, as Susie Stanley points out, "White's feminism faltered in the domestic realm," and both her life and her teachings showed contradictions over the years. White "felt that her husband was head of their home," but not head of her church. Her husband disagreed, persuaded "he was entitled headship status in all areas of life."[40] As a result, their marriage, which at one time had been a colleagueship in ministry, became increasingly marked by tension, including Kent White's demands that his wife not speak in public without his consent. (She reported that once he even put his hands over her mouth as she spoke.[41]) White's husband left her in 1901, and the couple remained separated until a few year's before his death in 1940. No doubt some couples who attempted to maintain a belief in authority in separate spheres found it difficult to ascertain where the home left off and the church began—especially when a wife's ministry kept her away for long periods of time or prevented her fulfilling traditional household duties in ways the husband considered his right. On the other hand, some women evangelists reported supportive, encouraging husbands who backed their ministries fully and gladly shared home responsibilities.[42]

One of the few people who dared to speak out for a Bible-based *total* equality between women and men was Katharine C. Bushnell, a medical doctor, missionary, reformer, linguistic scholar, and student of the Bible, who devoted years of painstaking study to the writing of the book *God's Word to Women,* first published in 1912. Bushnell was convinced that the Scriptures had been grossly misinterpreted and even distorted in translation and that God was *not* punishing women for Eve's sin nor insisting that wives be ruled by husbands (Document 7). Bushnell's carefully researched book was enthusiastically received and its message spread further through the efforts of Jessie Penn-Lewis, a leading speaker and writer in the deeper life movement who was associated with the ministries of such men as F. B. Meyer, Andrew Murray, and Dwight L. Moody. With Bushnell's permission, Penn-Lewis published in England in 1919 a simplified distillation of Bushnell's major points in a low-cost booklet called *The Magna Charta of Woman.*[43]

Moving on to a second factor involved in evangelicalism's attitudes toward women in the historical period under consideration, we need to be aware of *how various evangelicals reacted to societal changes.* Between 1900 and 1960, the percentage of women in the paid labor force had more than doubled (from 18.3 percent to 37.1 percent).[44] At the beginning of the century, slightly more than one out of twenty married women were employed; but by 1965, the figure was just over one out of three.[45] Women were granted the right to vote and were increasingly excelling in virtually every area of life. Religious leaders such as Alma White, Evangeline Booth, and Lee Anna Starr viewed such happenings with relish and challenged the church to appreciate its women more fully and cease restrictive policies that drove capable women away (Documents 8, 9). "This may be well called woman's age," wrote Fannie MacDowell Hunter, voicing the question in the minds of many: "If she has freedom to engage in secular employment, why not allow her freedom to engage her time and talents in telling the story of Jesus and His love?"[46]

Other leaders in evangelicalism viewed the changing political, economical, and social roles of women with disfavor. Suffrage was called a violation of God's will and a sign of women's lust for temporal power.[47] A domino theory held that changes in the traditional female role would mean the downfall of the home and the destruction of society. It was feared women were becoming "brazen" and putting aside their feminine nature and aspirations toward godly motherhood and developing other interests and career goals instead. Such allegations prompted M. Madeline Southard, founder of the American Association of Women Ministers, to tell the group's 1921 assembly that, in view of census figures showing the work women had long been engaged in, it seemed clear "that men were not disturbed when women washed the world's dirty clothes and scrubbed its dirty office floors. It was only when women ventured into higher realms that they became fearful of what would happen to their children and to their femininity."[48]

Some male leaders flagrantly disparaged women's accomplishments. One fundamentalist evangelist argued that, while "any woman" could become a physician by passing a medical course, few men would go to a female doctor; and few businessmen would choose a female manager over a large company. He said that men had some innate sense that God never intended women to be in authority over men, that it was "unnatural and inefficient."[49]

No doubt economic factors entered into the feelings of threat that some men experienced as educational and career oportunities opened to women, particularly in religious service. Even such a supporter of women's right to preach as Fredrik Franson made use of the pragmatic argument that women could "most inexpensively carry on the work" in pioneering missionary work.[50] The other side of such pay inequities is a point made by sociologist Peter Rossi in 1961:

> Women depress the status of an occupation because theirs is a depressed status in the society as a whole, and those occupations in which women are found in large numbers are not seen as seriously competing with other professions for personnel and resources. It is for this reason that professions such as education, social work, and librarianship develop within themselves a division of labor and accompanying status along sex lines.[51]

Perhaps such anxieties entered into male hesitancy over the possibilities of more women becoming members of the clergy, not only in evangelical circles, but elsewhere as well. (Even so prestigious a liberal publication as *The Christian Century* published an editorial in 1923 that, although supporting women in ministry, called attention to economic factors and urged women preachers to "enter into a 'gentlemen's agreement' not to appeal to the parsimony of churches by under-bidding the male ministry."[52])

A third factor contributing to tighter restrictions on woman's role was *conservative evangelicalism's penchant for order.* According to an entry in an evangelical dictionary of theology, "the important reason against women's ordination is that it offers a logical and psychological inconsistency to clear Bible teaching concerning home government and its relationship to higher institutions, and therefore strikes at the root of government and law and order."[53] Order, as defined by much of evangelicalism, meant a prescribed place for everything and everything in its place—especially in the case of women (Documents 10, 11). God's message to a wife was that she be lovingly subject to and supportive of her husband and acknowledge him as her head (Document 12). She could serve God admirably as a minister's wife (Document 13), but not as a minister herself, and should trust God to lead her to areas of service determined by her husband's career. Thus when Ruth Bell (Graham) was torn by intense struggles over not fulfilling her lifelong missionary aspirations, she was consoled by her sister's reasoning that God led Ruth to Wheaton College to meet her future husband rather than to prepare for the mission field. "Maybe God does want you over there in Tibet as an old maid missionary," she told Ruth, "but I doubt it. I think He wants you right here in this country—as Billy Graham's wife."[54] The "feminine mystique" ideals increasingly promulgated in the larger society during the 1940s and 1950s were given divine legitimation by the insistence that "God's order" decreed that woman's place was in the home.

One of the strongest indicators of the "order" mindset of much of evangelicalism was the rise of *premillenial dispensationalism,* a movement that taught that past, present, and future were divided into a series of stages in which God worked in specific ways. An extremely popular vehicle of the movement was *The Scofield Reference Bible,* used by millions since it was first published in 1909. James Barr has called it "perhaps the most important single document in all fundamentalist literature," point-ing out its influence on how the Bible came to be interpreted among vast numbers in evangelical student groups, churches, and schools.[55] *The Scofield Reference Bible* did not treat woman positively. The notes for Genesis 3 stated that "the entrance of sin, which is disorder, makes necessary a headship, and it is vested in man (1 Tim. 2:11–14; Eph. 5:22–25; 1 Cor. 11:7–9)." The notes on the Parable of the Leaven in Matthew 13 state, "A woman, in the bad ethical sense, always symbolizes something out of place, *religously* . . . In Thyatira it was a woman teaching (cf. Rev. 2:20 with Rev. 17:1–6)."[56] There is little doubt that *The Scofield Reference Bible's* notes and cross references have had a profound effect on conservative evangelical opinions on biblical teachings about women and men.

By the late 1960s and early 1970s, the appeal to a hierarchical order-ing of the sexes as God's plan was being based on other modes of reason-ing as well, most notably the ancient idea of the "great chain of being" allegedly found throughout nature and the "chain of command" method of running business corporations and the military.[57]

Other factors also entered into the limitations placed upon women in Evangelical, Holiness, and Pentecostal traditions. The growing profes-sionalization of the ministry, the bureaucratization and institutionaliza-tion of groups formerly more open and flexible, the move toward increased cultural accommodation and concern over "respectability" and greater acceptance in established ecclesiastical circles, and other factors associated with the classic sect-to-church transition no doubt played a significant part. Likewise, a rigid, mechanistic approach to Scripture and a zealous commitment to a particular understanding of biblical inerrancy came to be viewed as a badge of orthodoxy. Biblical criticism and inter-pretations that took into account the Bible's human element and cultur-ally specific applications were viewed with alarm and suspicion of apostasy.[58] In such a setting, to question the hierarchical ordering of the sexes was considered tantamount to questioning the authority of Scrip-ture and God's claim on human lives.

Even so, the voices of God's maidservants, heeding the Spirit's call to prophesy, were not entirely stilled (Document 14). And occasionally, a male voice—such as Russell Prohl of the conservative Lutheran Church, Missouri Synod—chimed in to call the church to task for its treatment of its daughters.[59] By the mid-1960s, the first stirrings of a new restlessness were being felt among a few scattered women in evangelicalism—women who would meet and band together and watch their numbers multiply over the years ahead as they worked toward fresh understandings of partnership and equality between the sexes in the church, home, and society. Such evangelical women and the men who share their vision

agree with Katharine Bushnell, who voiced her concern at the very
beginning of the twentieth century:

> We must continually improve our understanding of God's will, and this neces-
> sitates a continual improvement in our interpretation of God's Word. . . . At
> no point is faith in the entire Bible being so viciously and successfully attacked
> today as at the point of the "woman question," and the Church so far attempts
> no defence here of her children. It assumes that the interests of merely a few
> ambitious women are involved, whereas the very fundamentals of our faith
> are at stake.[60]

Evangeline Booth, Commander of
the Salvation Army in the United
States (1904–1934) and General of
the International Salvation Army.
[Photo frontispiece from her book,
Toward a Better World (Garden City,
N.Y.: Doubleday, Doran and Co,
1928).]

Kathryn Kuhlman, faith healer who
took her ministry to hundreds of
thousands beginning in 1946. [Photo
by Doug Grandstaff, from her book,
Nothing Is Impossible with God (Engle-
wood Cliffs, N.J.: Prentice-Hall,
1974); permission to reprint from the
Kathryn Kuhlman Foundation.]

Lee Anna Starr, ordained minister, Methodist Protestant Church, distinguished lecturer, champion of temperance reform. [Photo from her book, *The Bible Status of Women* (New York: Fleming H. Revell, 1926).]

Alma Bridewell White, founder, Pillar of Fire Church, 1901, in which she held the rank of bishop and editor of the magazine, *Woman's Choice*. [Photo from her book, *The Story of My Life* (Zarephath, N.J.: Pillar of Fire, 1938).]

Aimee Semple McPherson, founder, International Church of the Foursquare Gospel and one of the famous evangelists of the 1930s. [Photo courtesy Heritage Department, International Church of the Foursquare Gospel, Los Angeles, Ca.]

Victoria Booth Demarest, oldest daughter of the founders of the Salvation Army, whose career extended over seventy years, at one of her final preaching engagements, Evangelical Women's Caucus International, Saratoga Springs, N.Y., June 1980, at the age of ninety-one. [Photo courtesy Evangeline Booth Demarest.]

Documents: Women in Evangelical, Holiness, and Pentecostal Traditions

Document 1: Mary Cagle: "My Call to the Ministry"

Mary Lee Cagle was influential in the early years of the Church of the Nazarene. Her first husband, Robert Lee Harris, had founded the New Testament Church of Christ in 1894, shortly before his death. Cagle carried on his work and held revivals from Texas to Tennessee. After marrying the Reverend, H. C. Cagle, she continued as a powerful force in the western Holiness movement, serving as the only female officer and directing a school in Buffalo Gap, Texas. The New Testament Church of Christ united with other Holiness groups, and out of this merger came the Church of the Nazarene.[61] The following account of Cagle's struggles to follow God's call is typical of many women who faced doubts and opposition as they pursued ministerial careers.[62]

Early in life I had a longing desire to be a blessing to the world.

When fifteen years of age I was truly converted to God and with this change of heart, the longing to carry gladness and sunshine to darkened hearts and homes became more intense. I felt assured of a Divine call to engage in Christian work. On account of the teachings of that time regarding woman's ministry, I decided there would be no opening for me in my home-land. I came to the conclusion that my call was to the foreign field where I supposed a woman would have freedom in preaching Christ to the heathen. Many dreams I had of crossing the waters and preaching to them. . . .

Finally I became discouraged and a spirit to disobey the call came into my heart and thus I lost the joys of salvation. Although backslidden in heart my outward life was consistent and I kept up the form of religion but without power. My name was on the church record and my pastor considered me a true, loyal Christain.

While in this blackslidden condition, a preacher filled with the Holy Ghost came to our Church to conduct a revival meeting. Holy Ghost conviction seized my heart and the former joyful experience was restored to me. With the restoration came the old-time call to preach; but God by his Holy Spirit revealed to me that my work was not across the waters, but here in my home-land. What a struggle I had. I plead [sic] with God to release me from the call. It seemed it would have been so easy for me to say "Good-bye" to loved ones and native land and pour out my life among the heathen. The thought of remaining at home to preach the Gospel brought trouble to my heart. I knew there was not so much reproach attached to going as a missionary.

On my face before God, with tears, I would plead to be released. I knew to go out in this country as a woman preacher would mean to face bitter opposition, prejudice, slanderous tongues, my name cast out as evil, my motives misconstrued and to be looked upon with suspicion. . . .

While debating in my mind about the call, I became engaged to and married Rev. R. L. Harris, the Texas Cow-Boy Preacher. I married him thinking that by becoming a preacher's wife, I could more easily do the work God called me to. But instead of this, I found it so easy to shift the work upon him, and I thought by so doing that God would release me and I would conduct the singing and women's prayer meetings and would assist in the altar work in our revival meetings.

During all this time my heart was not satisfied. God still pressed upon my heart *the call to preach.*

After three short years of married life, my husband was seized with that dreadful disease—consumption of the lungs. It was a great source of grief to me.

After some months of suffering he told me his work was over and that God was going to take him to his home in Heaven. . . .

One day I went all alone with God to have a season of secret prayer. In my desperation I said: "Lord, if you will heal my husband, I will preach," and God answered me with these words: "Will you do what I want you to do whether I heal your husband or not?" These words came as a thunder clap to my soul.

There on my knees the inward struggle was long and heated. Finally by the help of God I was enabled to say from my heart: "Yes Lord, whether my husband lives or dies, I will do what you want me to do." What joy flooded my soul! From that hour to this, that question has been settled.

About two months after this my husband was promoted to Heaven. At the time of his departure God did a most gracious work in my soul. He sanctified me wholly, thus fitting me to go out on the battlefield as an Evangelist to win souls.

Document 2: Fannie MacDowell Hunter: "Women Preachers"

Edited by Fannie MacDowell Hunter, a Nazarene minister, Women Preachers *was published in 1905. It contained the stories of twelve women called to preach the gospel. In the book's conclusion, Hunter argued that Christ had restored to woman equal rights and privileges lost in the fall, and that "the objections to the equality of man and woman in the Christian Church are based upon the misinterpretation and misapplying of a few passages of Scripture." She called the Church to task for accepting women as foreign missionaries while denying women the right to preach.*[63]

In the face of the Bible teaching on the ministry of women, who would presume to silence *one* of the thousands of modest, Christian women, who are in homes, the Church, school, or in the W.C.T.U. [Women's Christian Temperance Union], and other organizations, being blest of God in using their voices in His service? And yet there are some ecclesiastics who form resolutions against their efforts to preach the Gospel.

The writer was once present when a large body of preachers were in annual session. During that year, one of their pastors had invited a woman preacher to assist him in the revival services on his charge. She was greatly used of God in bringing the lost to Him. This body of preachers were in very plain terms expressing their disapproval of his course and of a woman being allowed to fill any pulpit within "their bounds." Different suggestions and resolutions were offered in order to prevent the repetition of such a course. At last it was settled in this way: "It is the *sense* (?) of this body that no woman be allowed to fill any pulpit within our bounds." Later on, before the session closed, the Presiding Officer introduces his wife to the audience, who, *standing in the pulpit,* proceeds to make a speech in favor of the "_____ Society" of the Church, and from the pulpit very pathetically pleads with men and women to support it with their means and prayers. She met with the approval and applause of every member of that body. She was allowed perfect freedom to explain from the pulpit, *the plan of their society* (organization.) But a woman preacher must not be allowed the privilege of explaining the *plan of salvation* and plead with lost men and women to yield to Christ. This same body of men approve of women going as missionaries, for their Board of Missions is supporting some in the foreign field. "Consistency thou art a jewel."

Hunter concluded her book by reprinting a poem ("'T was woman!") published anonymously in 1891, which attacked woman. She then included a resounding reply that exalted woman:[64]

On the fly leaf of an old book the following was written:—

> Who hailed the first appearance of pride,
> And listened while the serpent lied,
> Consented to be deified?
>
> > 'T was woman!
>
> Who by the tempter first betrayed,
> Infringed the laws that God had made,
> And all the world in ruin laid?
>
> > 'T was woman!
> > 'T was woman!

REPLY (By someone identified only by the initials, N. B. C.)

> Who failed to tell his new made bride
> How Satan basely, foully lied
> About their being deified?
>
> > 'T was Adam!
>
> Who joined his wife in sinful pride,

Altho' he knew the serpent lied
About their being deified?

                     'T was Adam!

Who tried to charge upon his wife
The blame of his own sinful life
When God and men were set at strife?

                     "Old Adam!"

Who ever since has laid the blame
Of his own follies, sin and shame
Upon the wife who bears his name?

                     "Old Adam!"

Who viler than the serpent's hiss,
Betrayed his Savior with a kiss
And shipwrecked every hope of bliss?

                     "Not woman!"

Who vowed that he would sooner die
Than Lord and Master he'd deny,
And on that eve did curse and lie?

                     "Not woman!"

Who urged the rabble to deride
The Son of God, and crucified
Their Lord with thieves on either side?

                     "Not woman!"

Who nailed his Savior to a tree
And mocked His dying agony
When He expired to set man free?

                     "Not woman!"

Who used her place as ruler's wife
To intercede for Jesus' life,
When plots of enemies were rife,

                     " 'T was woman!"

Who, when her plea could not avail,
Stood near the cross to weep and wail
While murderers drove the cruel nail?

                     " 'T was woman!"

And when he bruised the serpent's head
And rose triumphant from the dead
What was the first word Jesus said?

                     " 'T was woman!"

When John on Patmos saw the sights
And glories of celestial heights
Whom saw he 'mid the heavenly lights?

                     " 'T was woman!"

Now, everybody say amen!

Document 3: Mrs. J. Ellen Foster: "Work for Women"

In this selection from a feature in a 1909 issue of the Moody Bible Institute publication, The Institute Tie, *Mrs. J. Ellen Foster rebukes those who trivialize women's concerns and fail to challenge women to stretch their minds and hearts.*[65]

I have first a complaint to make to you, brethren, who are teachers and preachers. In your public leadership you are inclined as a rule to emphasize that which is petty and small in woman's life and duties, and not to emphasize as much as you should that which is broad, wide and inspiring. By this I mean that you forget, or rather you overbalance, in your teaching the effeminacy of woman rather than her humanity. You ought to try more to lift woman to a comprehensive thought in Jesus Christ. There is neither male nor female, bond nor free, but we are all one in Christ Jesus; and it is eminently appropriate that I should say this from this platform, for if there was any thing for which D. L. Moody stood it was for this.

You need not exhort women to be true to their homes,—they are going to be anyhow, but they will be true just in proportion as you lead them to the higher planes of fellowship with Christ. A great deal that men say about women's duties, and all that, is perfect bosh! Do not emphasize the things which are small and petty; emphasize the things which are great and wide. What are they? That we all of us do the thing to which God puts us. If you had not emphasized so much the duty of woman to the home, men would not have shirked their duty to the home as they have. There are certain responsibilities which do fall to women, and which never can be passed to the father, but the responsibility of the father cannot be assumed by the mother.

What would I have you do with woman? I would have you enforce her responsibility to God for whatever He puts in her way to do. Sisters, what would I have you do? I would have you study, of all things, the higher Christian life. I would have you get away from the things which are small and transitory. Oh, I am so weary in my soul of associating with women who talk only of small things! . . .

Document 4: Interview with Kathryn Kuhlman: "Healing in The Spirit"

Known as a faith healer (although she herself disliked the term), Kathryn Kuhlman (ca. 1907–1976) was born near Concordia, Missouri. She began her ministerial career as a teenager, at first traveling with her sister and tent evangelist brother-in-law and later with her close friend, Helen Gulliford, a musician. The two young women were billed under the name "God's Girls." Kuhlman is best known for her healing services, attended by thousands, with an extensive further outreach through radio and television. Beginning in 1946, Kuhlman was based in Pennsylvania—first in Franklin, but headquartered in Pittsburgh after 1950—and from there she traveled throughout the world holding revivals and healing services.[66] Many contemporary charismatics credit Kuhlman with giving the new movement respectability in the eyes of mainline churches. Women's Aglow, a large interdenominational charismatic Christian women's organization, for example, believes that Kuhlman articulated biblical principles correctly.

Although Kuhlman believed in women's ordination, she also agreed with those who believed women were to serve only when men were unavailable. She believed that the Bible advocated female subjection, while at the same time emphasizing that Christianity had raised the status of women in the ancient world by freeing them from harsh domination by men.

The several books credited to Kuhlman were ghostwritten. Hence the following excerpt from an interview near the end of her life provides rare insight into her personal views on the ministry of women, male dominance, and female subordination.[67]

Q. Was Aimee Semple McPherson any kind of model or inspiration to you?

A. No, because I never met her. But several years after Miss McPherson died, Maggie Hartner and I visited her grave. There we found a young man and a woman who was probably his mother viewing the monument erected to the memory of Miss McPherson. The woman was telling how her preaching had made Jesus so real. "I found Christ through her life," the woman said. At this point Kathryn Kuhlman thought to herself that if after I am gone just one person can stand by my grave and say, "I found Christ because she preached the Gospel," then I will not have lived in vain. . . .

Q. Do you find that being a woman hinders your work in any way?

A. [Laughter] I don't know because I don't know what it would have been like had I been a man. When unpleasant things happen, I just act like it never happened. Let me bare my soul: I do not believe I was God's first choice in this ministry. Or even his second or third. This is really a man's job. I work hard, seventeen hours a day. I can outwork five men put together. I get little sleep. I stand at the pulpit four and a half hours at a time without sitting down once, and I can still leave the stage as refreshed as when I walked on. I have given myself completely to the Holy Spirit, and he gives me sustenance. God's first choices were men. Someplace man failed. I was just stupid enough to say, "Take nothing and use it." And he has been doing just that.

Q. Why aren't there more women preachers?

A. You will just have to ask God. I don't know. [Laughter] I really don't know but I wouldn't wish this job on any woman, I'll tell you that. If you think it's easy, try it.

Q. What do you think of women's lib?

A. You want to know something? Women's lib won't like to hear what I have to say. I'd give anything if I could just be a good housewife, a good cook. Oh, I'd like to be a good cook. I'd like to have about twelve children. It would be so nice to have a man bring in the pay check. I would just love to have a man boss me. It might not last long. But for a little while it would just be great. When it comes to women's lib, I am still as old-fashioned as the Word of God. I still think the husband should be the head of the family. I know how it was at our house: If Papa said it, it was just as though God said it. We never had any women's lib, but we had a mighty happy family. Papa did the work, and Mama ran Papa without Papa knowing it, and it was a beautiful situation. . . .

Q. How do you interpret Paul's and Peter's apparent injunction against women's speech in First Timothy 2:11 and 12?

A. Oh, this is a good one. Kinda looks like they didn't believe in women's lib. But if it were contrary to the will of God that women should preach, Paul certainly would have reprimanded Philip, in whose home Paul visited, for Philip had four daughters who were preachers. Now that's a house full of preachers, let me tell you.

Q. Isn't that an argument from silence?

A. All right, but take a look at Acts 2, talking about the last days: "Your sons and your daughters shall prophesy." I believe the reason Paul said what he did about women needing to be silent was because in the synagogues of that day women would sit in the balcony and would talk so loudly that the speaker could not be heard. Maybe John's wife or Saul's wife would call down and say, "Did I turn off the stove?" Or if they were voting, Elizabeth would call down and say, "Abe, say no. You know I don't like him." So Paul said, "Let the women be quiet." That did not mean they were inferior. The Bible teaches that both men and women have their proper places, each with responsibility. The man is the head of the house. That does not mean he is a tyrant. We all know there are differences, and thank God there are differences. But women are not lesser. Some of the great leaders of Hebrew history were women. Personally, I admire Golda Meir. What Golda wants, Golda gets; yet she is sensitive. There are some things that men naturally do and some that women do, but it was Christianity that freed women from their subservient role. I could never see how women could reject Christ, because he gave dignity to women.

Document 5: Aimee Semple McPherson's Call to Preach

One of the best-known evangelists of the twentieth century and founder of the International Church of the Foursquare Gospel,

Aimee Semple McPherson (1890–1944) had been converted to a form of Pentecostal Christianity through the man who became her first husband, Robert Semple. Shortly after the young couple's arrival in China for missionary service and one month before their first child was born, Robert Semple died. Extremely depressed, Aimee returned with her young daughter to her native Canada, married Harold McPherson, and moved with him to Rhode Island. In the following excerpt from her autobiography, Aimee Semple McPherson tells of her struggles to find contentment in homemaking and motherhood, her resistance to God's call to be an evangelist, the severe depression and physical illness she experienced, and her decision to pack up her two children, leave her husband, and begin an itinerant ministry.[68] The positive note on which the excerpt ends was short-lived. After a brief time ministering with her, her second husband returned to the world of business, divorced Aimee, and married someone else.[69]

A dozen times a day I would take myself to task as I would catch sight of my tearful face in the looking-glass saying: "Now see here, my lady, this will never do! What right have you to fret and pine like this? Just see those shining, polished floors, covered with soft Axminster and Wilton rugs. . . . Why aren't you glad to have a home like this for the babies, as any other mother would be?"

"Why, it's perfectly ridiculous for you to think of going out into the world again, and—remember if you found it hard with one baby before, what do you suppose you would do now with two?" . . .

But, Oh, the Call of God was on my soul and I could not get away from it. For this cause I had been brought into the world. With each throb of my heart I could hear a voice saying:

"Preach the Word! Preach the Word! Will you go? Will you go?" and I would throw myself on my knees, tearfully sobbing:

"Oh, Lord, You know that I cannot go. Here are the two babies and here is the home, and here is the husband, who has not the baptism and is not even seeking it. I will work here in the local mission, and that will do." But no, the answer still came back, clear from heaven:

"Go! DO THE WORK OF AN EVANGELIST; Preach the word! The time is short; I am coming soon." . . .

My nerves became so seriously affected that the singing of the teakettle upon the stove or the sound of voices was unbearable. I implored the little one to speak in whispers. I hated the sunshine and wanted to keep the shutters closed and the window shades drawn tightly. The doctors said I would lose my reason if something was not done. I became very ill in body and inside of one year two serious operations were performed. Each time, before going under the surgeon's knife and during many other times of critical illness, when it seemed as though I were going to die, I would call the saints to pray for me that I might be delivered, but each time they prayed and I could plainly hear the voice of the Lord saying:

"Will you go? Will you preach the Word?" I knew that if I said "Yes", [sic] He would heal me. But how could I say "Yes?" Difficulties rose like mountains in my path. . . .

About two in the morning the white-robed nurse, who had been stroking my hand, saying: "Poor little girl; poor little girl," seemed to be receding. Everything grew black—someone said:

"She's going." Just before losing consciousness, as I hovered between life and death, came the voice of my Lord, so loud that it startled me: "NOW—WILL—YOU—GO?" And I knew it was "Go", one way or the other. . . .

Oh, don't you ever tell me that a woman cannot be called to preach the Gospel! If any man ever went through one-hundredth part of the hell on earth that I lived in, those months when out of God's will and work, they would never say that again.

With my little remaining strength, I managed to gasp:

"Yes—Lord—I'll—go." And go I did! . . .

Mother now being in Canada, I telegraphed there for money; and when alone in the house one night, 'phoned for a taxicab, and at eleven o'clock bundled my two babies inside while the chauffeur piled the two suitcases on top, and away we sped to catch the midnight train for home and Mother. To make a new start and begin all over again it seemed the most natural thing in the world to go back to the starting place from which I had set out before.

God was with me and I was conscious of His leading and support at every step. With my little baby (Rolf McPherson) clasped in one arm and Roberta (Semple) sleeping in the other, I held them tightly to me as the immensity of what I was doing swept over me. The streets were dark and almost deserted as we rolled along toward the depot. . . .

I was obeying God, and although the enemy was still endeavoring to hound my tracks with accusations and forebodings of future disaster, he had someway lost his grip and his power to overthrow me. When he twitted me with the leanness and the barrenness of my soul, that hurt the most of anything because it was so true, my heart sang within me:

"Never mind, Rebecca's on her way to the well—to the fountainhead—to the sure source of supply—to the banqueting table of the King, and we'll soon be filled up now."

Upon reaching her parents' home in Canada, she was told they would care for the children so that she could attend a Pentecostal camp meeting. Before she left, she sent her husband a telegram saying, "I have tried to walk your way and have failed. Won't you come now and walk my way? I am sure we will be happy." McPherson continues with an account of what happened at the camp meeting.

Perhaps some of you can imagine my feelings at I sat in the audience looking up at the platform whereon sat different ones whom but a few years before I had prayed with when they came through the baptism. There they were, shaking and quavering under the power, faces radiant—hallelujahs ringing—and here I sat, dabbing at my eyes with a wet handkerchief and saying:

"Oh, Jesus, You used to bless me like that. I used to shake under the power and praise you just like that.

"Oh bless me now, my Savior;
I come to Thee."

... When the call for the altar service came I stole forward amongst the others and bowed at the altar, feeling utterly unworthy to touch even one of the rough planks which formed its floor. All I could do was bow my head and weep. . . .

"Oh, Lord, forgive m—" before I could finish the words I felt as though the Lord had put His hand over my mouth and said to me:

"There, my child, it's all right. Don't say anything more about it." This was so sudden and unexpected I could not comprehend it, but thought surely I must be mistaken. . . .

Well, the suddenness and the magnitude of this hearty reception completely bowled me over. It broke my heart and bound me to Him more than any whipping could ever have done. Such love was more than my heart could bear. Before I knew it I was on my back in the straw under the power, saying:

"Dear Lord, just let me be as one of your hired servants. I do not feel worthy to testify or work at the altar or preach but just let me love you and dwell in your house, my Saviour."

The next thing I knew the Spirit was speaking in tongues through me, giving me the interpretation. A brother from London had a message in tongues—the Lord gave me the interpretation of that— and he fell back under the power. I was laughing and weeping and shaking. A little knot of people gathered round to rejoice with me. The Spirit lifted me to my feet and I walked up and down praising the Lamb for sinners slain. Falling on my knees I worshipped the Lord again. . . .

The old-time power and the anointing for praying with seekers rested upon me. Many other instances, which I will not refer to here, took place. But Oh, the Lord did not let these wonderful answers to prayer, as I prayed for the seekers, come to puff me up, but to encourage me. It was balm to my wounded, troubled soul. . . .

Camp over I returned to my Mother's . . .

Within the house was a little pile of letters, demanding my immediate return "to wash the dishes," "take care of the house" and "act like other women." But I had put my hand to the Gospel plow, and I could not turn back. I was going through, and I had the assurance that the

Lord would bring my husband also. I certainly never could win him the other way and he would have had to have parted with me for good if I had died, which I surely would have done had I remained out of the work. I was going through: Jesus was with me and nothing in all the world mattered now. My heart was right with God.

A week later, McPherson attended another camp meeting in London, Ontario. Soon her own ministry was to resume.

The blessed London camp meeting over, the Lord strongly impressed me to accept an invitation from Sister Sharp of Mount Forest, Ont., to conduct Bible meetings there in a little hall called "Victory Mission." The power and the glory of the Lord came down in a precious way. The mission soon became too small to hold the people; we were obliged to hold the services on the spacious lawn between the Sister's home and the mission. Such a spirit of revival came down upon the people that soon a tent was bought, hungry people filled it night after night and those who could not get in stood in rings round its border.

It is not necessary for me to go on and relate the wonderful way in which Jesus worked in this meeting, to tell how the town was stirred, how our Sister has haled [sic] before the magistrate and liberated, how over a hundred were saved and scores received the baptism. . . .

However, I must tell you the best news of all, for right in the midst of one of the meetings which was held in Mount Forest, my husband landed with his suitcase, to attend the meeting.

So changed was I, so radiantly happy, so filled with the power of God and the unction of the Holy Spirit, that he had to admit that this was indeed my calling and work in life. Before many hours had passed he himself had received the baptism of the Holy Spirit, spoke in tongues and glorified God. How the Lord does vindicate and honor those who go through with Him! As my husband saw the workings of the Holy Spirit, sinners coming to the altar for salvation, believers receiving the Holy Spirit, and heard me delivering the messages under the power of the Spirit, for truly it was not I, but Christ that lived in me, he told me that he recognized that God had called me into this work and would not have me leave it for anything in the world. And through the succeeding years, though part of the time he is with me and part of the time elsewhere, the Lord has made him perfectly willing for me to go on whether he is along or not.

The Lord has wonderfully blessed and supplied my every need and the needs of the two children, for food, clothing and traveling expenses. We have lacked no good thing. The way has been growing brighter and brighter day by day. The harvest of souls is increasing month by month. The work is spreading out and the nets are filled with abundance of fish. Glory! Glory!! GLORY!!

Document 6: Alma White: Woman's Coequality Essential In Human Government

Alma Bridewell White (1862–1946) founded a Holiness organization called the Pentecostal Union in 1901. The group's name was changed to the Pillar of Fire Church in 1917, in part to disassociate it from the tongues movement that was increasingly assuming the title "pentecostal." Consecrated as the first American female bishop in 1918, White led the church until she died at age eighty-four. A strong supporter of equal rights for women in the Church and society, White believed that winning the vote was not enough. She believed that the oppression of woman was directly linked with many other kinds of societal evil and endeavored to raise consciousness through the magazine she launched in 1924, Woman's Chains.[70]

The following radio sermon, "Woman's Place," shows the political emphasis that characterized White's ministry.[71]

Woman's place of co-equality with man in the rulership of the world has been unjustly denied her since the fall in the Garden of Eden, and if the world is ever redeemed from its barbarity and crime, according to the plan of redemption wrought out on Calvary, she will have to occupy the place intended for her by the Creator at the beginning.

"So God created man in His own image, in the image of God created he him; male and female created he them. And God blessed them, and God said unto them, Be fruitful, and multiply, and replenish the earth, and subdue it: and have dominion over the fish of the sea, and over the fowl of the air, and over every living thing that moveth upon the earth" (Gen. 1:27–28). We see by this scripture that God gave man and woman equal dominion,—there was no distinction.

It is evident there is something woefully lacking in the machinery of government. It is failing to function properly, and only the great Master Mechanic can put it in order. Men may reject certain parts of the machinery and try to operate without them, but there can be nothing but failure and bitter disappointment in the end. They will have to acquiesce and accept the original plan if there is to be hope for this and future generations.

The powers of evil are fast getting beyond the control of the male sex, and complete destruction is threatening. There must be some opposing force to check these tendencies in both Church and State.

Has the Almighty left man in uncertainty, with no guiding hand or star of hope, after six thousand years of failure in trying to rule the world? There should be sincerity on the part of men in searching out the difficulty, and willingness to accept the truth and acknowledge mistakes. If men have the interest of humanity at heart and are not wholly given over to selfish purposes, they will rectify mistakes, make amends, and give woman her place in the administration of government.

True, some concessions have been made; but it has usually been only when the sword has done its deadly work, as in the case of the late war, after which woman received the franchise in England and America. These two great Protestant powers had withheld justice from her in the right to use the ballot, going against the light of progress and that of Holy Writ. They kept woman from having a part in making the laws that controlled her destiny. At the same time woman has held equally responsible with man for the breaking of the laws, penalties being meted out to her with the same severity, except in some instances when personal sympathy may have entered into the decisions of the judiciary, and clemency was extended.

Christain enlightment was too widespread for things to have gone so far. Adjustment should have been made long before the twentieth century was ushered in. Civilized nations should have given woman her place in their law-making bodies before they were compelled to do so. Schools for women have been neglected. Women have been barred from colleges and universities, scarcely any opportunity being afforded them in these higher institutions of learning to fit themselves for places they were intended to fill in the affairs of religion and of government.

There is now a great hue and cry about abolishing war, but this can never be while human rights on so large a scale are being denied and the reins of government held by men who have passed judgment on half the population contrary to the laws of God. The scripture says, "Promotion cometh neither from the east, nor from the west, nor from the south. But God is the judge. He putteth down one, and setteth up another" (Ps. 75:6–7). When anyone strives for honors or rulership in Church or State there should be no prejudice because of the sex of such person; otherwise we may expect the social fabric to go to pieces and the civic structure to break down under the strain of injustice.

For every great conflict in which nations have been involved there has been an underlying cause. Preceding the late war, the women of England were being arrested, imprisoned, and forcibly fed in their contention for the ballot. They had shed no blood, but had to suffer indignities from officers who were continually on their track. They were thrown into prison with common criminals, where they showed a willingness to die, if necessary, for human rights. After the war broke out they were released, and soon afterwards the leader of the suffrage movement was invited to sit on the platform with the Premier and other great men of the British nation.

The work carried on for the enfranchisement of women in England had a direct influence in favor of woman suffrage in the United States, and sentiment was created that finally led to the adoption of the Nineteenth Amendment to the Constitution.

The Constitution of the United States as originally written declared all men free and equal; yet for a hundred and fifty years women were denied the ballot and a citizenship worthy to be compared with that of their husbands and brothers. Property rights have been denied them in every state in the Union, and our lawmakers are still but little concerned about these things.

Woman has proved her ability to work by the side of man in all matters of education, scientific and literary research, as well as in the administration of government. Queen Victoria is ranked as the greatest sovereign of which Great Britain can boast. There are others whose names could be mentioned in the long list of women who have proved their ability to cope with questions of an international character where the destinies of nations have hinged on right decisions.

Down the ages woman has proved to be the more sincere, devout, and self-sacrificing in religion, whether a devotee of paganism or a true worshiper of Jehovah. She has tipped the scales against man's indifference and lack of fervency in the spirit. This was unquestionably proved at the beginning of the Christian dispensation, when, in so many instances, she proved her devotion to the Master and her loyalty to His Church. Whenever woman has failed to scale the heights of human progress it has been because man forged her chains and kept her in subordination and thraldom.

The old pagan religions exemplify man's unjust domination over woman and his tendency to penalize and enslave her. The old ecclesiasticisms are all permeated with the same leaven. Their policy, contrary to Scripture, has always been to give man the preeminence, however, unworthy he might be. When such violation of human rights is tolerated, what can be expected but an era of crime and bloodshed? The dark clouds of divine retribution are even now hanging over the horizon, and the question is, How long will the avenging hand of a just God be stayed while the innocent suffer and the guilty go free?

The pulpits are almost silent against immorality and the flagrant sins of the age. It is within the power of men, who hold the reins of government in both Church and State, to change these things. If they would only concede to women the rights accorded them by the Creator, there might yet be hope; but in all probability they will yield no ground except when compelled to do so. With the attitude toward women manifested in the present day her chains will not likely be completely broken without further divine intervention,—and who knows how soon it may come?

Little by little, by constant effort, woman has won back some of her rights, but the victory is not yet complete. The disposition to injustice is too strongly rooted in the hearts of men to open doors for her advancement and equal privileges in the legislative bodies.

It was said that Lucy Stone's father sent his sons to college, but when his daughter asked that privilege he said the girl must be crazy, and refused her a penny. However, she sold berries and paid her passage across the lake to Oberlin College, the only college in the country at that time to admit women. At her graduation the faculty demanded that her thesis be read by a man, but she refused to permit this, and it remained unread. Later when she appeared on the lecture platform she was repeatedly mobbed.

For many years women found almost every door of higher education closed against them. When Elizabeth Blackwell—the first woman physician in the United States—entered a medical school her garments were torn and her book defaced by male students. When at length woman made her way into the various industries she was discriminated against in the matter of wages, and it is to this day. Fannie Mendelssohn's musical compositions were credited to one of her brothers. Carolyn Herschel discovered eight comets and numerous clusters of stars, but these were listed as the discoveries of Sir William Herschel, her brother. Catherine Green was the true inventor of the cotton gin. She conceived the idea and communicated it to Eli Whitney, and came to his aid when he was about to abandon the enterprise; yet the invention was given out to the world as Whitney's. It was Mrs. Howe who convinced her husband that an eye could be placed in the needle of a sewing machine, near the point, thus bringing him success. Marie Curie was the real discoverer of radium, but she was denied membership in the French Legion of Honor. Many women writers of recent times have signed men's names to their works to get them before the public because of the prejudice against women writers.

The inspired Word says, "God sent forth his Son, made of a woman" (Gal. 4:4). He who condescended to be born of a woman will see that her sex is duly recognized in His coming kingdom, and will finish the work of bruising the serpent's head and removing the curse of her subordination.

Document 7: Katharine C. Bushnell: "Did God Curse Woman?"

Born in Peru, Illinois, Katharine Bushnell graduated in 1879 with the first medical class of Northwestern University. As a medical missionary, she established a children's hospital in China and later engaged in reform work in India. She was commended by the British government for her investigation of the China-India opium trade and for her recommendations for dealing with vice conditions affecting

*British soldiers stationed in India. In the United States, she engaged
in reform work with Frances Willard and the Women's Christian
Temperance Union. Bushnell caused a stir with her investigation of
the "white slave trade" in Michigan and Wisconsin. In spite of official
denials, she boldly (and with police protection) presented her well-
documented report before the Wisconsin state legislature, which later
passed a bill that came to be known as the Kate Bushnell Bill. Bushnell
died at her Piedmont, California, home in 1946.*

*Bushnell believed God had called her to a public ministry and was
convinced that the Scriptures used to inhibit women's ministry had
been either mistranslated, misinterpreted, or misapplied. A brilliant
scholar who spoke seven languages fluently and who had translated
an ancient Latin Bible into English, Bushnell undertook a painstaking
study of the Bible in its original languages in order to find "God's
word to women." She presented her findings in a mimeographed
correspondence course for women, and later in a book of the same
title.[72]*

*The following excerpt shows her conviction that the Bible had
been misused to keep women subordinate to men—something that
God had never intended and that the Scriptures, rightly understood,
did not teach.[73]*

98. . . . The teaching that God punishes Christian women for the
sin of Eve is a wicked and cruel superstition, and unworthy the intelligence of Christians. But in addition to this, the doctrine has laid a
blighting hand upon woman's self-respect, self-confidence and spiritual activity, from which cause the entire Church of Jesus Christ
suffers moral and spiritual loss, and therefore we offer no apology for
expending much time and thought in a thorough examination of
Genesis, third chapter. . . .

107. But the need of a different translation and interpretation of
Genesis 3:16 will scarcely be realized by those not familiar with the
usual teachings to be found in our Bible commentaries, which defy
principles of morality and justice, as well as outrage the sense of the
original words, as can be proved by the ancient versions. . . . Browne
says, "Desire here expresses that reverential longing with which the
weaker [woman] looks up to the stronger." Addis says "Woman is to
desire man's society, notwithstanding the pain and subjection which
are the result."

108. The assumption is more or less general that morbidly intense
sensuality, when it displays itself in the female character, is of Divine
manufacture. Knobel interprets God as saying, "Thou shalt be possessed by the passionate desire for him. " Keil and Delitzsch, "She was
punished with a desire bordering upon disease." Dillman comments
on the passage: "The special punishment of the woman consists in the
evils by which she is oppressed in her sexual vocation, in the position

she occupies in her relation to man," and yet, doubtless he would scarcely hesitate to pronounce such a relation, "Holy Matrimony!" Driver declares "She shall desire his cohabitation, thereby at the same time increasing her liability to the pain of childbearing." If this sensuality were the state of woman's mind in general it would not be necessary to starve women out of industrial lines, and put a check upon their mental development, lest they be disinclined to marry if capable of self support; yet these are the methods which have been used in order to maintain the "domestic" desires of women. Calvin says, "This form of speech is . . . as if He [God] said, 'Thou shalt desire nothing but what thy husband wishes.' She had, indeed, previously been subject to her husband, but that was a liberal and gentle subjection; now, however, she is cast into servitude." In other words, Calvin would have us believe God first ordained marriage, but afterwards substituted "servitude." Patrick, Lowth, etc., in their commentary declare of the husband that he shall have the power "to control thy desires," but we have never known of a husband who could control more than the outward acts of his wife. Poole elaborates this decree into, "Thy desires shall be referred to thy husband's will and pleasure, to grant or deny them as he sees fit." Dr. Adam Clarke says: "It is a part of her punishment, and a part from which even God's mercy will not exempt her . . . Thou shalt not be able to shun the great pain and peril of child-bearing, 'thy desire shall be to thy husband.' . . . Subjection to the will of her husband is one part of her curse; and so very capricious is this will often, that a sorer punishment no human being can well have."

109. But the astounding part of this teaching is, that these men fail to see that, if a wife must be under a "curse" because she is under a husband who exercises the cruelties that constitute that curse, this is equivalent to saying that God has ordained that man and marriage shall be a curse to woman. Such teaching relieves a husband of the duty to observe nearly the entire decalogue, if only the person he practices his transgressions upon happens to be the one he has vowed, before the marriage altar, that he willl [sic] "love and cherish."

110. But does this teaching accord with the general tenor of Scriptural morals? Not at all. Abraham, once upon a time, desired to maintain a polygamous household, and Sarah objected. Did God speak to her about the matter, and say: "Remember Eve, and the penalty: Thy desire shall be thy husband?" He spoke to Abraham, saying: *"In all that Sarah saith unto thee, obey her voice"* (Gen. 21:12). The word rendered, in English, "hearken unto," in this passage means obey, and it is translated "obey" in very many other passages,—such as Gen. 22:18. When Hannah centered all her "desire" upon a hoped-for son, her husband exhorted her to center it, rather, upon himself, saying, *"Am I not better to thee than ten sons?"* Hannah did not obey the

expositor's teaching as to Gen. 3:16, and God blessed her in this sort of "disobedience" to her husband, by sending the son. So we might go on illustrating the fact that God has shown no zeal in enforcing this supposed "law" of His. But one quotation is sufficient to entirely destroy the fallacious interpretation of Gen. 3:16, and that is the well-known Golden Rule, uttered by Jesus Christ: *"Whatsoever ye would that men should do unto you, do ye even so unto them."* We have never yet found the man who longed to be ruled by the will of his wife. All men led by the Spirit of Christ obey this Golden Rule, which sets at defiance the so-called "law" of Gen. 3:16, as interpreted by these expositors.

111.... Lev. 20:18 is a law which punishes the wife, with the husband, if she should yield her will to his under improper conditions. This law necessitates the view that God holds woman as a free agent in the marriage relation. Further, the Apostle Paul, 1. Cor. 7:4, makes the authority of the wife precisely equal to the husband's in the marriage relation, saying. *"The husband hath not authority over his own body, but the wife."* We are quite aware that this verse has been reduced to a mere sophism by Bible commentaries. But "authority" does not mean "authority" at all, unless it comprehends the idea of being able to act with perfect independence either one way or in the precisely opposite way....

272. Now we must proceed slowly to study O.T. "headship." Look at the O. T. reference in the margin [of 1 Cor. 11:3] (the only O. T. reference cited), where these words occur regarding the headship of the husband,—Gen. 3:16. The only other place where the husband is said to be the head of the wife, Eph. 5:23, refers in the margin also to Gen. 3:16 only. No other word can be found throughout the O. T. which seems to support the interpretation that men are to govern their wives. But we have already shown (par. 198) that at Corinth the church used the Septuagint Greek version and would read Gen. 3:16, *"Thou art turning away to thy husband, and he will rule over thee,"*—the same is true of those addressed in the Epistle to the Ephesians, for Paul's quotations are also from the Septuagint in this letter.

273. Now had we always read, as we should have read, *"He will rule over thee,"* instead of *"He shall rule over thee"* (Pars. 124,127; all the ancient versions testify that the verb is a simple future), ignorant, careless, or dishonest interpreters would not have thought to show that this "rule" was God-ordained. We remember seeing in a religious periodical, when a discussion of enlarging woman's activities in the Church was on, an editorial in opposition, which ended by quoting Gen. 3:16,—*"He shall rule over thee,"* Remember, woman,—shall, *shall,* SHALL!"

274. Prof. J. H. Moulton, in his *Grammar of N.T. Greek,* says: "The use of shall where prophecy is dealing with future time is often

particularly unfortunate. I have heard of an intelligent child who struggled for years under perplexity because of the words, 'Thou shalt deny me thrice.' " It could not therefore be Peter's fault, if Jesus had commanded him! The child's determinism is probably shared more widely than we think; and a modernized version of many passages like Mark 14:30—e.g., 'you will be renouncing Me three times'—would relieve not a few half-conscious difficulties.' How different women would have felt if, from the beginning, they had read, 'he will rule over thee!"

275. We question, then, the correctness of interpreting the words, "But of a wife the husband is a head," and meaning, "Of the wife the husband is the ruler." Gen 3:16 proves nothing of the sort; it only prophesies what has been only too true,—that ever since Adam fell, his male progeny has sought to subjugate woman: and it is further demonstrable that to the extent that grace works in the heart of the male he loses the love of the pre-eminence and the desire to rule his wife. . . .

289. No teaching of the New Testament has ever been more cunningly perverted than this concerning the "headship" of the husband. Does Christ jealously keep the Church from rising into His power: or does He say, "Behold, I give you power?" Does He say, "This is My throne, keep away!" to the Church; or does He say, "To him that overcometh will I grant to sit with Me on My throne?" Christ's delight and His constant exhortation is for us to share His throne-life with Him. If we fall short, it certainly is not because He has ever shut the door to our attainment of it. He is not jealous of His own exaltation; He only secured it (for He had it before He came to earth), in such a manner that He might bring it within our grasp also.

290. But are we not to obey Christ? Yes, most certainly; obey Him because He is God, because he is King of kings; and these a husband is not, and he should not usurp Christ's prerogatives. Christ said: "Be not ye called Rabbi: for ONE is your Master, even Christ; and all ye are brethren." . . . "Neither be ye called masters; for ONE is your Master, even Christ." Woman's spiritual Head is also her King; and so is man's spiritual Head. But woman's matrimonial head is not her king,—he is only a fellow-disciple and fellow-servant of the King; and the King has laid down His rules as to the conduct of fellow-disciples towards one another: "Ye know that the princes [rulers]—of the Gentiles exercise dominion over them, and they that are great exercise authority upon them. But it shall not be so among you: but whosoever will be great among you, let him be your minister: and whosoever will be chief among you, let him be your servant" (see Matt. 20:25; Luke 22:25).

291. When the Word says, "the husband is the head of the wife," by the pen of St. Paul, it merely states a fact; those were the conditions under which women lived at that time. The husband was, in those days,

the head of the wife simply because he held the superior place. In days when a man could divorce his wife *"for every cause"* (Matt. 19:3; and even Christ's own disciples demurred when Christ declared this was not right), there could be no doubt that women were compelled to be ignorant, inferior and very cheap. The rabbis taught that it was lawful for a man to divorce his wife if she even burned his food. Hence the Apostle says, "Be a head, as Christ is a Head of the Church,—to help your wife upward to your own level,"—for it is only as man imitates Christ in his conduct that he can remain in the Body of which Christ is Head. Therefore the woman should "imitate" (1 Cor. 11:1, R.V.) St. Paul, and the others in worship. And the man has certain duties to perform toward his wife which are analogous to what Christ purposes to do for His Church, for its elevation, until it shall *"reign in life with Christ Jesus."* This is the headship of the husband that Paul speaks of. He would never encourage the husband to imitate Adam and Antichrist in trying to be *"as God,"* to woman, and to interfere with Christ's authority over His own servant,—woman.

Document 8: Evangeline Booth: The Woman's Movement and the Salavation Army

Evangeline Booth (1865–1950) was the seventh child of Catherine and William Booth, founders of the Salvation Army. Having begun her evangelistic preaching career at age seventeen, Evangeline held leadership positions with the Salvation Army in England and Canada before serving as commander of the Salvation Army in the United States from 1904 to 1934. In 1934, she was appointed general over the International Salvation Army.

Evangeline Booth was one of the best-known female preachers of her time, drawing enormous crowds wherever she spoke. It was she who was asked to deliver the invocation at the 1932 Democratic Convention at which Franklin Delano Roosevelt was nominated for the first of his four terms as president of the United States.[74] Like her mother Catherine, who had persuasively set forth arguments for women's equality in her nineteenth-century booklet Female Ministry,[75] *Evangeline published in 1930 a booklet entitled simply* Woman, *which pointed out women's contributions to the world and the Church and urged women to fulfill their full potential by recognizing and seizing opportunities for service everywhere. In the following excerpt, she speaks of Salvation Army women as exemplifying this outlook.[76]*

As a woman, standing in the front lines of service to humanity, it is with an unbounded enthusiasm of gratitude that I hail the dawn of this long-awaited day of opportunity. The forces of prejudice, of selfishness, of ignorance, which have arrested the progress and curtailed the influence of womankind for centuries, are receding from the foreground of the future, and with astonished vision we look upon the limitless fields of progress. Across all oceans, however tempestuous, over all frontiers, however mountainous, into all countries, however remote and inhospitable, the women's movement is spreading, the exhiliration and invigoration of its spirit is in the very air we breathe, bracing the nerves, stimulating the will, and reinforcing the faculties. . . .

For what we call the woman's movement is not social merely, not political merely, not economic merely. It is the direct fulfilment of the gospel of the Redeemer. . . .

In the Salvation Army we see, as it were, the summation of the woman's movement, her equal status with man in social and spiritual and intellectual responsibility, her readiness to find a greater happiness in service than any selfish pleasure could have afforded. For if woman has been successful in inspiring men to great deeds and noble aims, it is because she herself abounds in enthusiasm. It is a mistake to attribute a woman's enthusiasm to excitement, to emotion. It is, rather, an utter abandonment to an aim, only to be carried to triumph by such devotion. *If woman loves, she worships. If she champions a cause, she will fight for it. If she gives, she gives all. If she lives for, she will die for.*

My Mother was an enthusiast. While retiring and blessed with that conservativeness that always has at its demand perfect control, she abounded in enthusiasm. The Salvation Army has revealed its spirit, its love, its sincerity, to the peoples of the world more than anything else through the service of its enthusiastic women. The world does not say of us that we possess much, or that we talk much (unless it is I); but the world has been kind enough to recognize that we love "not in word, but in deed"—achieved in the passion of the Cross.

Shallow and fickle, the mind of the public, bewildered by multitudinous impressions, is apt to seize upon some symbol, some sensation, and to suppose that this is the whole of the affair. Many people think that the women of the Salvation Army are lassies who, in the main, spend their time and energies on waving the tambourine and shouting their "Hallelujahs." During the War, our girls achieved a reputation scarcely less embarrassing. It was supposed that their whole energies were devoted to serving out the doughnuts to the boys in the trenches and daily welcoming bombardment as a shortcut to glory.

Of the courage of our women officers, I would be the last person in the whole world to utter a word of depreciation. 'Tis conscience that makes cowards of us all, and if shell fire no longer alarms, it is because hell fire has lost its terrors.'

But death and danger had not been the only trial of these women's faith. They had faced dirt, they had handled disease, they had not flinched before uttermost degradation, they had not been dismayed by the most awful defacements of God's image, imprinted on our race; there is no depth of misery, of despair, of iniquity that is concealed from the steady eyes of the women of the Salvation Army. The hospitals and homes for mothers, deserted by those who should have been at their side as partners in parenthood, the hotels for working women, the visitation of women in prisons, the bureaus of employment, the young women's residences, and the Home League in every corps for helping women to be better housewives, these are only some of the agencies which are conducted by the women officers of the Salvation Army.

Document 9: Lee Anna Starr: Determined Women and "Detached Service"

Dr. Lee Anna Starr was an ordained minister in the Methodist Protestant Church and pastored the College Church in Adrian, Michigan, and Avalon Park Church in Chicago. In addition, she was a distinguished lecturer and championed temperance reform. Her 1926 book, The Bible Status of Woman, *presented a thorough study of Scripture on the topic and showed how faulty interpretations had obscured the equality of the sexes that God had intended at creation. "The fallibility of human understanding in nowise alters the truth as revealed in God's Word," Starr argued. "Not Scripture, but our exegesis has been at fault."*

The following extract is taken from the concluding section of Starr's book, where she cites numerous examples of women who wished to serve God through the church but were turned away. Therefore they had found other avenues of service.[77]

The church afforded these women of ten talents no tasks commensurate with their ability, so they lifted their eyes and looked on the fields outside, and lo! they were "white already unto the harvest," and the laborers few. In the need, they read God's call to the larger service. The church lost, but the world gained when they responded: "Here am I: send me." Who can charge them with dereliction?

A new term has been coined by religious writers in these latter days—that of "detached service"—meaning Christian and humanitarian effort outside the pale of the church. The Woman's Christian Temperance Union; Salvation Army; Volunteers of America; Young Women's Christian Association and American Red Cross, all belong in this category.

It is a notable fact that three of the organizations above named were founded by women and in the establishment of the other two, the wife was an equal participant with her husband. This "detached service" might have been performed within, instead of apart from, the church, if prelates had read aright the Pauline declaration: "There can be no male and female: for ye all are one in Christ Jesus."

a bishop said recently: "The brainy women members of our churches are going more and more into club work, and more and more into politics, while they should be devoting themselves to the church." Commenting on this plaint of the bishop, Welthy Housinger says:

"This good bishop cannot see that the time has long since passed when the highly trained women, who are leaving our colleges, are willing to take up any work which does not enable them to see the possibility in the future of sharing in the administration of that work. . . . I do know that when a young woman of our church leaves college halls today, she has an intelligent idea of every vocation, from aviation to brokerage, and may enter every one except the ministry. She may become a policeman or a judge; she may be a mayor or a senator, but she may not be ordained as a minister of the Gospel of Christ. So the young women of trained intellect and talent, as they come out to take their share in the world's work, specialize, in increasing numbers, in law, and not a few have become Judges. (One is now the Assistant Attorney General of the United States.) They specialize in journalism and become editors; they specialize in education and become college presidents, but they may not, in the name of the Father, receive a child into the church nor administer the sacrament to the dying."

If the bishop here spoken of desires to enlist the "brainy women members of the Churches," he must advocate for them larger tasks than that of quilting and serving tables. God never entrusted man or woman with ten talents, or even five, and charged the recipient to trade with one, and to hide the others in a napkin. Tasks cannot be assigned the women of today after the measurements of the Church at Corinth nineteen hundred years ago. The types of womanhood are different and this difference must be reckoned with. If the authorities of the church persist in pouring new wine into old wineskins, the skins will burst and the wine will be spilled.

Apprehension has been expressed in some quarters that if women are allowed larger scope, the church will become "feminized." We remind these foreboders that for fifteen hundred years the church was masculinized, and while, during that period, it built up a powerful hierarchal system, its spiritual life was at lowest ebb. So long as we follow the Divine plan, the cause of God will not be disturbed, and the Divine plan is that the daughters, as well as the sons, "shall prophesy."

Document 10: John R. Rice: "Bobbed Hair, Bossy Wives, and Women Preachers"

The writings of John R. Rice are typical of the harsh tone with which some fundamentalist leaders addressed the roles and relationships of women and men. Rice was a southern evangelist and editor-publisher of The Sword of the Lord, *an independent weekly tabloid devoted to revivalism. His writings on various topics often included*

discussions on the proper role of women. In his book Prayer—Asking
and Receiving,[78] *Rice cautioned women that their prayers—even for
their husband's salvation—would not be answered unless the wives
were subject to their husbands. In* Bobbed Hair, Bossy Wives, and
Women Preachers, *Rice used three major proof texts to argue that
these practices were the result of rebellion against God's authority.*
The following excerpts are representative of Rice's views.[79]

"Thy desire shall be to thy husband, and he shall rule over thee."
Wives must be subject to the rule of their husbands if they fit into
God's order of things. Does some wife who reads this find her heart
rebellious against her husband? You do not want him to rule you? You
do not want to obey? Then you feel just like all the criminals in the
penitentiaries and jails feel. They, too, are rebels against God-given
authority. They, too, want to be independent and have their own way.
The very heart of the crime question is rebellion against authority.
And most criminals were first allowed to get away with rebellion
against the rule of parents in their own homes. Not being disciplined
and controlled and conquered as children, they were not willing to be
subject to the next authority God put over them, the authority of
government. Criminals are simply rebels against authority and every
rebellious wife has the same attitude of heart. You who read this do
not want to have that attitude and I trust you will carefully search your
heart and ask God to take away any rebellion against His will or
against those to whom He commands you to give obedience. . . .

"But my husband wants me to have bobbed hair, and you said for
me to obey my husband," some woman says. No, you are mistaken.
It was not I who said you were to obey your husband. It was the Lord,
and the Lord plainly promised that your husband would be won to
God by your obedience (1 Peter 3:1,2), and not that you would be led
into sin. And any woman who obeys her husband reverently and
lovingly in other matters, and explains her Christian convictions on
matters of pleasing God, will find that her husband will not want to
lead her into sin. I know that God's way always works, and any Christian woman can have God's help in doing right. If you explain why
you should have long hair, and obey your husband in other matters,
he will not want you to lose your glory by sinning in having bobbed
hair.

From a sermon to men only:

. . . God is a masculine God.
A man, then, is nearer like God than a woman, and in a sense, man
is in the image of God. . . .
Am I Christ's own personal representative? Do I represent Jesus
Christ in my home? The wife is to come to her husband to find God's
will. The wife is to glorify her husband and look to him as if in some

sense Christ dwells in your body in the home. I am, in my home, the image of God Almighty. . . .

The Bible plainly says that Eve was deceived but that Adam was not deceived. He knew better. He knew it would not make him wise. God never intended women to lead men around by their noses. . . .

Men, do you see how serious is your responsibility? If God is going to win this country, He must do it through men. It is a strange thing that people have got more sense in matters of government and business than in matters of religion. We would not elect a woman president, nor follow a woman in business, but we leave church work to the women! No wonder the Bible said, "The children of this world are in their generation wiser than the children of light" (Luke 16:8).

Preachers, are you willing for your church to be run by a handful of critical old hens who want to tell you where to head in? They have got to have their own announcements. You must not run past twelve o'clock or the dinner will burn! God bless women, but He never intended any preacher to be run by a bunch of women. God never intended the home to be run by women, and God never intended Christian work to be run by women.

Men are to lead out in music, in Bible teaching in the church, in personal soul winning in the church. God depends on men for leadership. Go to your Bible and try to find any contradictions to that. You can't do it. God has reserved the main place in the church for men.

Document 11: Donald Grey Barnhouse: "The Wife with Two Heads"

From 1927 until his death in 1960, Donald Grey Barnhouse was pastor of Philadelphia's Tenth Presbyterian Church and influenced evangelicalism throughout the United States and beyond through his books, lectures, films, radio and television programs, directorship over the Evangelical Foundation, and as editor of the magazine he founded, Eternity, *(formerly* Revelation). *The following editorial first appeared in the December 1958 issue of that magazine.*[80]

I am not talking about unsaved wives, but wives who are professing Christians. So often they come to us with home problems. The husband is not interested in the things of God, so the family drifts along without any spiritual cohesion. Perhaps they all go to church together on Sunday morning, and the wife goes to all the activities of the week, but the husband seems uninterested. Why?

Perhaps the wife has two heads.

"But I want you to understand," God tells us, "that the head of every man is Christ, the head of every woman is her husband, and the head of Christ is God" (1 Cor. 11:3). I can hear the outraged cry that goes up from many a woman, "But if I didn't use my head, where would we be?"

There are two ways in which a Christian woman can use her head. She can use it to think independently and for her own interests, or she can use it to think in the spiritual terms that God had laid down. With delight she learns the joy of knowing it is her husband's house, his home; the children are his; she is his wife. When a woman realizes and acknowledges this, the life of the home can be transformed, and the life of her husband also.

Nothing is better calculated to smooth the rough corners of a man than the realization that his wife loves him and that she loves him in the way God intended a woman to love a man. When a man sees his wife centering her whole life in him, he realizes that this is more than mere human love; there is a divinity in the daily round of chores and the providing for his comfort. When he understands what God has said, that the man was not created for woman but the woman for the man (1 Cor. 11:9), the husband will soon learn that in the Lord he is not independent of his wife (11:11).

And the woman who follows this spiritual direction will more than likely find that she is getting what she wants without taking it. A woman is never happy with what she takes, only with what she is given in love. By losing her selfish head she is no longer a monstrosity but what the Lord meant her to be. And therein she will discover all joy.

Document 12: Yvonne K. Woods: "The Wife God Uses"

The following extract is from an article republished from an earlier issue of His *magazine, an evangelical periodical for college students published by Inter-Varsity Christian Fellowship (IVCF). Written by Yvonne K. Woods, wife of the general secretary of IVCF in the United States, C. Stacey Woods, who had great influence among students, the article was included as a favorite for the February 1960 "editor's choice issue." (The original publication date was not provided.) This particular emphasis and interpretation of Scripture was common among evangelical groups working on college campuses.[81]*

What can be more emphatic than the words written to the church at Corinth, "Neither was the man created for the woman; but the woman for the man." Not that one was created inferior to the other, for God made man male and female and said to them, equally to woman as to man, "Have dominion over every living thing that moveth upon the earth." So just as the whole creation was brought into being by the Lord Jesus and exists for the accomplishment of His will and purpose, so the woman was brought into being and designed to be a fitting helper to man in his God-given responsibility on earth.

But the first woman failed to be a true helpmeet to her husband, failed to help him obey God. Then God decreed that the man should "rule over" the woman. It is at this point that the great divergence between God's order and present-day attitudes can be most clearly seen. God has never rescinded the law that the husband is to be the head of the home. It is distinctly repeated in the New Testament, but with this interesting difference of emphasis. Under the Old Covenant, God had said to the woman, "Thy husband shall rule over thee." Under the New Covenant, God says, "Wives submit yourselves unto your own husbands, as it is fit in the Lord"; and again, "Wives, be in subjection to your own husbands."

This is the heart of every message specifically addressed to married women in the New Testament. Why? Because in the willing, wholehearted submission of the wife to her husband God wants the world to see a picture of the attitude that should characterize the Church in relationship to His son the Lord Jesus Christ. Therefore, the call is, "Wives submit yourselves unto your own husbands, *as unto the Lord.* For the husband is the head of the wife, even as Christ is the head of the church."

Document 13: Catherine Marshall: Identity Through Marriage and a Husband's Career

Catherine Marshall is best known for her biographies of her husband, the Reverend Peter Marshall. Born the daughter of a Presbyterian minister, Catherine attended Agnes Scott College, had lined up a teaching position, and then became engaged to Peter. At first, she found his ideas on marriage much too stringent; but later she came to agree with him. As a minister's wife she performed all the tasks expected of her, as she tells us in her biography of her husband, A Man Called Peter, *and in her autobiography,* To Live Again. *When her husband died she had to reconcile reality with former attitudes about the role of women in the society and in the Church. Finally, she came to believe that she was called by God to continue her husband's work by editing his sermons.*[82]

"He still places women on such a pedestal," I confided in my journal, "much as my father's generation did, and he seems quite old-fashioned in some ways—especially toward marriage and the home.... Yet, yet, I wonder if I shall ever meet anyone whom I admire so much—?"

Like the rest of young America, I would never have taken the philosophy of marriage Peter advocated from any of the older generation, but we took it from him, liked it, and came back for more.

Was it possible, I wondered, under the stimulus of his thinking, that women in seeking careers of their own, were seeking emancipation from their own God-given natures, and so were merely reaping inner conflict? Could this be one of the basic reasons for the failures of so many marriages today? Could God have created us so that, ideally, we achieve greatest happiness and greatest character development as our husband's career becomes our own, and as we give ourselves unstintingly to it and to our homes? I was not sure, but it was worth pondering deeply.

In marriage I had found my identity, my answer to the question, "Who am I?" As a woman, much of my orientation in life had been centered in my relationship to one man. It is this way with most women.

Then when death cleaves the marriage partnership, the woman left alone feels that her whole basis for living has been washed out. She must begin all over again . . . "Who am I now?"

Document 14: Victoria Booth Demarest: "I am Thy Prophet Still"

Victoria Booth Demarest (1889–1982) was the daughter of Catherine Booth-Clibborn, oldest daughter of the founders of the Salvation Army, William and Catherine Booth. Like her mother and grandmother, Victoria was a gifted preacher and held evangelistic campaigns in Europe, the United States, Canada, and Newfoundland.

The preaching career of Victoria Booth Demarest extended over approximately a seventy-year period. One of her final preaching engagements was the conference of the Evangelical Women's Caucus International held at Saratoga Springs, New York in June 1980, when Victoria was ninety-one years old.

In this poem, composed when she was seventy-four, she prays that age will not stop her ministry.[83]

> O Lord, O Lord, the fire burns—
> I am Thy prophet still!
> Thy Word within me all pent-up
> is straining at its bonds of flesh
> and would burst forth in fiery speech;
> but now, alas, the Spirit's thrust
> too oft is stayed by man's conceit.
> Ah, must Thy Word be smothered still,
> as womb-ed child must it be killed?
> Thou mad'st me woman,
> Thou mad'st me prophet,
> And Thou canst not belie Thyself.
> That which to God is good
> why should man contradict?
> What then is sex but flesh and blood?
> Shall God be bound by His own making?
> Shall cell or gene be more than CALL
> or Spirit's urge in man or woman?
> Nay, God forbid!

'Tis well His right to speak through man
or ass, through child or woman—
let pride, in guise of flesh, not rise
and say to God, "What doest Thou?"
I am Thy prophet still,
and laugh at man's forbidding.
But now alas 'tis not by sex
alone that I am held in thrall.
The years, the years—and people say,
"Too old, you are too old."
'Tis strange and wrong—
just when her soul
matured by knowledge and by pain
beneath thy Spirit's sway,
just when her suff'ring healed,
her weakness changed to strength,
Thy prophet most has strength to give and
balm to those in pain,
that she, by circumstance of years
must hold her wealth and not impart
her given strength to those in need!
This shall not be!
As long as breath and health are mine
to serve—I must and can.
I am Thy prophet still!
The "must" is mine, the "way" is Thine.
Have I unknowingly
betrayed my trust?
Have I, some place, some time,
sidestepped Thy will?
Have I, a woman, wife and mother,
allowed life's daily claims and clamor
to hush the Spirit's Voice?
If so, dear Lord, forgive—
I am Thy prophet still!
Perhaps 'tis not in hallowed church
or in a public place
that now my voice must rise—
who knows Thy plan?
Thy servant blindly follows.
Perhaps 'tis in the written word
Thy Voice shall speak through me—
perhaps 'tis through the silence—
can it be? I do not know—
But come what e'er the years may bring,
Thy Will be done—
I am Thy prophet still.

Patterns of Laywomen's Leadership in Twentieth-Century Protestantism

ROSEMARY SKINNER KELLER

Increasingly wide participation and leadership in all structures of Protestant churches has characterized the experience of Protestant women in the twentieth century. Laywomen's status has been marked both by expansion of movements pioneered in the nineteenth century and by entrance into new fields in the twentieth century.

A host of ecumencial women's structures were initiated by females in the early twentieth century. Simultaneously, in denominational mission work, women participated both in separatist female societies and sought equitable status in mainline church mission boards long run by men. Laity voting rights were won for women in most denominations by the first part of the twentieth century, and larger numbers of single females gained professional status as missionaries, often significantly affecting the nature of mission work. Women also gained entrance onto seminary faculties, and today their presence has become an accepted part of most schools for ministerial training in this country.

More women have become involved in the structures of Protestant churches than in any other type of institution in the United States. This participation has awakened women to new possibilities for their own lives and has enabled churches to function in a scope impossible without their voluntary and professional service.

Yet, only a handful of women in various movements stand out as leaders whose vision led to consequential changes. They provided the inspiration and leadership models that enabled countless women to follow after, becoming vital movers in denominational and interdenominational structures at lower levels. The experience of these primary leaders often illustrates the realities of sexism present in wider areas of the Church. Finally, their leadership patterns offer notable insight for women today who are molding new lifestyles and roles in the Church out of a consciously feminine perspective.

This chapter focuses on case studies of major female leaders in four areas of women's work in twentieth-century Protestantism. These women, avowed heroines of major movements, were selected because their names and experiences need to be recovered, and because they provided lessons in effective leadership for large numbers of pioneers of their own day—and of ours.

PROFESSIONAL VOLUNTEERS: HELEN BARRETT MONTGOMERY AND LUCY WATERBURY PEABODY

The experience of Helen Barrett Montgomery and Lucy Waterbury Peabody provides insight into the leadership qualities and personal lifesytle that made them a unique team in their day and a useful model for late-twentieth-century ministry. Beyond their innovative leadership as lifelong lay members of Northern Baptist churches, "These two women were ecumenical pioneers. They were involved in the founding or in the early nurture of almost every major interdenominational achievement of Protestant women in America. These include the World Day of Prayer, summer schools of missions, united missionary study, union schools of higher education for women overseas, and Christian literature of women and children."[1] Their legacy is carried on today by women who have made a profession of voluntarism in interdenominational and denominational agencies throughout Protestantism.

Lucy Waterbury Peabody exhibited a notable personal change during her two marriages. She wed Norman Waterbury immediately after his graduation from seminary. She entered her first marriage with a traditional understanding of a minister's wife's role, and expected to live her life through his by assisting him in pastoring a local church. Shortly before their marriage, however, he changed his career plans and decided to enter the foreign mission field, leading Lucy to conclude that "unless one were willing to go anywhere a man might be called, it would be better to drop the engagement." She began married life in 1881, as a twenty-year-old missionary bride, by sailing to India one month after their wedding. This calling of marriage and ministry was fulfilled only briefly, however, for five years later Norman Waterbury died in India.[2]

For the next twenty years, Lucy Waterbury gave herself to full-time voluntary missionary society service in close teamwork with Helen Montgomery. She understood herself as an independent woman whose identity was found primarily through her work and sisterly alliances. At age forty-five she entered a second marriage, to Henry Peabody, twenty years her senior. Peabody was a highly successful businessman, a widower of many years, and active in the Church as national president of the Board of Managers of the Baptist Missionary Union. Again, marriage and ministry were brought together, but this time each person entered the union with a clear, tried-and-tested personal identity. Their short marriage, concluded by his death two-and-one-half years later, demonstrated equality and self-conscious interdependence of partners.[3]

Helen Barrett and William Montgomery lived a long and full married life. From the early years of their marriage, she combined the roles of housewife, church leader, and civic crusader. Today she, like Lucy Peabody, would be seen as a professional volunteer. Montgomery apparently was able to hold together a successful personal life and a demanding public career. While active in local church work and chair of the board of trustees of Colgate-Rochester Divinity School, William Montgomery was a businessman who purposely stayed in the background of Helen's public life. Their spheres were separate, though their support was mutual. He gave her behind-the-scenes help and seemed proud of her contribution and wide public recognition, affirming her as qualified and committed. William Montgomery consciously gave his wife an unusual amount of space and support in a marriage of that day; the professional team of Waterbury and Peabody would not have been possible without it.[4]

Unique precedence for working relationships of women are found in the model of Helen Montgomery and Lucy Waterbury Peabody. Commitment to the mission cause provided the base for their lifelong teamwork. Both women demonstrated many of the same leadership qualitites. They met the public well. They were strong speakers and able administrators. Both could envision new ideas and were not afraid to take risks to enact them (Document 1).[5] Their qualities appear so similar that it is perhaps surprising that competitiveness and conflict, rather than cooperation, did not develop. A high level of self-confidence and mutual trust enabled them to esteem each other's abilities, rather than to be threatened by one another's recognition. Their vision of a larger cause superseded egocentrism in their working relationship.

The prime movers of a score of organizations for missions still in existence today, Peabody and Montgomery understood themselves as pioneers in a unique place to change the nature of women's work and of the church. Both women forsaw that one new movement opened more and larger opportunities for involvement, rather than limited the circle of leadership. Often one woman would take primary leadership in a project for a time, while the other supported and advised from the background.

While most of their energy centered in women's mission work, Helen Montgomery became the first woman to head a national governing body of a Protestant denomination when she was elected president of the Northern Baptist Convention for 1921–1922. Her presidential address, delivered at the conference over which she presided, reveals her ability to inspire, lead, and motivate (Document 2). Montgomery always recognized that her elevation to leadership of the entire denomination resulted from the support of women in its missionary organizations. In her post-convention letter "to the women of the churches" she expresses her appreciation for that longstanding indebtedness (Document 3).

LAITY RIGHTS CHAMPION: BELLE HARRIS BENNETT

The struggle for voting rights for women in the Methodist Episcopal Church, South, was neither the first nor last drive in the late nineteenth and early twentieth centuries to open the governing power of mainline denominational church structures to laywomen. The issues raised in this movement and the leadership role of Belle Harris Bennett were mirrored in various degrees throughout Protestantism.

Belle Bennett stands as the most distinguished woman in the history of the Methodist Episcopal Church, South. In 1887, she founded the Scarritt Bible and Training School, one of the earliest institutions for preparation of deaconesses—pioneer professional women of Protestantism—in the United States. Further, Bennett presided over both the Woman's Home Mission Society and the Woman's Board of Home Missions, which grew out of it at the turn of the century. She also bore primary responsibility for the struggle and final victory of laity rights for women in the General Conference of the Methodist Episcopal Church, South. Patterns of compromise and confrontation characterize her leadership of this movement.[6]

Success of the Southern Methodist church women in expanding their missionary society organization caused the male-dominated General Conference of 1906 to pass measures restraining women's work and autonomy. Four years later the conference reorganized all women's mission work under one general board on which women would be given one-third representation, and which unified both the foreign and home mission work of women under one Woman's Missionary Council. The issue was confronted within all denominations. Promise to women of a wider sphere of influence was often a means of subordinating them, by taking away their direct decision-making authority and power of the purse. Bennett's public and private responses to the general church's move illumine her understanding of the complex political realities. Publicly, she accepted the General Conference's mandate, expressing assurance to women that their home and foreign branches of missionary work could still function independently and that women had gained power to legislate on the full mission policy of the church. No longer would they be restricted simply to a "woman's sphere."[7]

Bennett was not naive, however. She recognized the seriousness of criticism lodged against her. Mary Helm, editor of the Woman's Home

Missionary Society journal, *Our Home,* contended that women would be a helpless minority on the general mission board; one-third female representation was a meaningless gesture of an agency dominated by bishops accustomed to holding absolute sway. Belle Bennett's statement made in private demonstrates her own fear of the truth of such an allegation: "I am a unionist, but I did not believe in the union of the Woman's Board with the General Boards on the basis which we were compelled to accept. I accepted what they gave, fearing something worse—complete subordination."[8]

While Bennett moved toward conciliation and compromise on the status of women's missionary work, she was simultaneously mounting a direct attack of confrontation on the laity rights issue. She recognized the connectedness of the two strategies, as suggested in her 1909 president's message to the Woman's Home Missionary Society: "Any disturbance of the autonomy of the Woman's Missionary Societies, more especially any annulment of the administrative rights, which have been vested in their Executive Boards for the last thirty-two years, will bring about such a disturbance of relationships in the Church as Methodism has never known."[9]

The inability Bennett experienced in maintaining independence of Women's Missionary work impelled her to mount an uncompromising movement for laity rights for women in the legislative body of the Church. From 1910 until 1918, women under Bennett's leadership developed well-organized grass-roots campaigns in each geographical area to gain votes for passage of women's voting rights at the General Conference. Their strategy also enabled local women to make the connection between passage of women's suffrage on the national political scene and in the Church. Women's power of organization was mobilized to effectively implement Belle Bennett's rhetoric.

Bennett was granted significant speaking time on the laity rights issue at both the 1910 and 1914 conferences (Documents 4, 5). Her words were unequivocal. In her 1910 speech she stated boldly: "My Brethren, this is not a matter of reason with you. You do not protest against this with your reason. It is a matter of prejudice, it is a matter of sentiment. You are burning incense to an ancestral tablet. Methodism has been doing a great deal of that."[10]

She appealed, first, on the basis of the rights of women in the church. "Today, seven-tenths of the Sunday School teachers are women, and yet you say you don't think women ought to sit on Boards of Education." Women's participation in all areas of the Church's program demanded their voting representation.[11]

Bennett realized, however, as did leaders of the national women's suffrage movement in secular society, that appeal to women's rights alone would not gain the vote for them. With strategy similar to secular suffrage advocates, she spoke to the need of the church for women in legislative decision-making positions. Bennett drew persuasive comparisons of the government of the Church to that of the home:

> After twenty centuries we stand knocking at the door of the Church of God, saying yet, "My brothers, brothers, won't you take us in?" God made man and woman coordinate. Without the coordination of man and woman there is no reproduction of life, no perfect government of the home. Let the father die, and the mother and the little children all along through the years miss that government. They miss in the home what makes the perfect home. Let the mother die, and again the government of that home is broken. The Church is the house of God and the mother of God's people. You need the perfect government of the man and woman in the Church."[12]

APPLIED THEOLOGIAN: GEORGIA HARKNESS

In 1939, Georgia Harkness received the appointment of professor of applied theology at Garrett Biblical Institute. In accepting this position, created especially for her, she became the first woman to teach in a major theological seminary in the United States in a field other than Christian education.

Harkness's background prepared her well for this pioneering role. With impetus from an article in the *Christian Advocate* to enter a new profession for women, she first began graduate study in Christian education at Boston School of Theology. Desiring, however, to teach in higher education rather than to be a religious educator in a local church, she sought admission to the Ph.D. program in philosophy at Boston University. Evaluating Harkness's admission, Dr. Edgar Brightman contended she had the brains but not the "stick-to-itness" necessary to complete such a rigorous program. Brightman's admonition was challenge enough for Georgia Harkness. She gained her Ph.D. in 1923, with the distinguished philosopher as her mentor.[13]

Harkness had over fifteen years of teaching experience in higher education in philosophy and theology when she began her appointment at Garrett Biblical Institute. Her previous appointments had been limited to two women's colleges, Elmira and Mt. Holyoke. Beyond her academic training and teaching background, Georgia Harkness had taken courageous stands on social issues, the needed "field experience" for applied theology.

Many of those positions would be innovative for the institutional church in any age, but in the 1920s and 1930s they were often radical, unpopular, and inflammatory, to the point of creating suspicions of her national loyalty. Her primary social concern was world peace. She remained a firmly committed pacifist throughout her entire life, which spanned two world wars and the Korean, Vietnam, and Middle East conflicts. After the First World War, she took issue with the popular position of the conquering allies that Germany should bear total guilt for the atrocities. She challenged the allied nations to bear their guilt in stripping Germany of its colonies and leaving it burdened with poverty and unemployment, too weak to contribute substantially to its own recovery (Document 6). She recognized the evils that industrialization brought on the working classes, among them child labor and prostitution (Document 7). Harkness called the churches, through Jesus' example, to stand against class stratification in its own institution and in society. A champion for the full ordination of women in the Methodist Church until finally granted in 1956, Harkness delivered the strongest possible appeals for full rights of women in the church, including ordination, in the early 1920s (Document 8).[14]

Harkness's model and experience foreshadowed that of scores of women who entered seminary teaching in the 1960s, 1970s, and 1980s. Early in her career she had experienced sexual discrimination, applying for positions in theology and religion "to be told that only a man could be considered." One such experience came when Professor Ernest Hocking, for whom she had graded papers on her Ph.D. program, sought a teaching post for her at Radcliffe. She returned to Elmira, however, because Radcliffe hired only Harvard professors, who could only be male.[15]

Because she was a woman, her forthright positions on social issues and high visibility in world religious organizations made her stand out more than her male colleagues. Harkness had been one of the few women active in the World Council of Churches and related international ecumenical movements since the mid-1930s.

When she began teaching at Garrett Biblical Institute, Georgia Harkness was a mature scholar almost fifty years old. In a sense, she was one colleague among a field of notables, distinguished for their scholarship and publications. She valued the collegiality of many, some of whom were members along with her in the Methodist Federation of Social Action. She attributed any resentment from faculty more to the initial attention she received than to her presence as a woman.

Covert, if not overt, sexism was present, though. One student stated: "She may be a woman, but she thinks like a man." Harkness was not flattered; her response was "what man?"[16] Some students described her as theologically thin, believing that because she could be understood with ease she lacked depth. Such a critique misses the genius of Georgia Harkness, however. Her lifelong involvement in the local church and issues of the world led her to write for laity and to train students to preach and teach for lay consumption.

Her exchange with Karl Barth at the 1948 meeting of the World Council of Churches at Amsterdam demonstrated that she could debate with leading male theologians without deference. Describing the encounter, in which Barth asked Harkness to state the theological basis for the life and work of women in the Church, she recalled:

I said briefly in the Old Testament it is stated that male and female are created in the image of God; in the New Testament, Jesus assumed always that men and women were equal before God, and in our Christian faith is the chief foundation of sex equality. Barth claimed the floor; said that this was completely wrong, that the Old Testament conception of woman is that she was made from Adam's rib and the New Testament, that of Ephesians 5, that as Christ is the head of the Church, so man is the head of woman. There followed a lively interchange in which I did little but to quote Gal. 3:28, but the room buzzed. Barth convinced nobody, and if I have been told he was trying to have some fun with the woman, his joke back-fired. A year later, when a friend of mine asked him if he recalled meeting a woman theologian from America, his cryptic reply was, "Remember me not of that woman!"[17]

During her ten years on the faculty, she succeeded as a distinguished theologian, almost the lone woman in a man's field. Her great disappointment came when she was not offered the chair held by Harris Franklin Rall in systematic theology when he retired in 1945. Instead, the young recent graduate, Gerald O. McCulloh, received the position. Harkness was deeply hurt personally, judging that the seminary president "understood 'applied' theology to be inferior to 'real' theology of systematics. She took it personally, judging that [in the president's eyes] a woman could be an applied theologian because it was inferior. However, when it came to systematics, even a man with no teaching experience was better than a woman."[18]

When invited to teach at Pacific School of Religon in 1949, Harkness accepted. Garrett-Evangelical Theological Seminary, which grew out of the former Biblical Institute, corrected its error in 1975 and established a lasting tribute to its pioneer female professor by endowing the Georgia Harkness Chair in Applied Theology, held today by Rosemary Ruether. In a broader sense, the chair distinguishes a particular quality that women may bring to seminary teaching today in closely relating theological inquiry to issues of social justice and the practice of ministry.

MEDICAL MISSIONARIES: ANNA KUGLER AND IDA SCUDDER

By the beginning of the twentieth century, all denominations of Protestantism responded to the necessity of recruiting women physicians for foreign missionary service. The direct need was pronounced: native women in continents of Asia, Africa, and South America could not be treated by male physicians. Powers of superstition and false religion reigned forcefully. Unless the churches sent women physicians, rampant disease would overcome women.

Though a small corps of male doctors had been sent to mission fields by the 1860s, that number had increased to over 700 physicians—including 222 women—by 1900. In 1910, there were 667 men and 348 female physicans serving in missionary stations. The entrance of women doctors brought a significant change in the status of medical missions: Only then did medicine become "regarded as an essential Christian ministry and a legitimate mode of proclamation of the gospel of the Great Physician."[19]

While the primary purpose was to provide medical treatment for women, the leadership of Anna Kugler and Ida Scudder suggests that the immediate aim became an avenue for wider purposes of Christian witness and service to women.

Anna Kugler, a pioneer female physician in South India, began the first organized medical work for women in the India Mission of the United Lutheran Church. Kugler applied to the Board of Foreign Missions of the Lutheran Church for a medical appointment in 1882, when only a handful of women served as medical missionaries under any denomination. Though the Lutheran women felt unable to undertake medical work immediately, they sent her to India as a teacher. Two years later she was commissioned for full-time medical work.[20]

Her assignment presented an overwhelming task: She was placed in the midst of twenty million Telugus, for whom no medical work or hospital for women had ever existed. During her first term of five years, she met only three other women doctors. Her Guntur Hospital opened in 1898. It's quality of medical care, administered by her staff of missionary personnel and medically trained native women, appears to have been excellent.[21]

A primary question, at the heart of the missionary movement since its origin, applies directly to Anna Kugler's leadership of the Guntur Hospital: should Christian missions be directed primarily toward evangelism or toward meeting physical needs of persons without seeking their conversion? Without detracting from the importance of medical care given, the Guntur medical mission was, as most missionary enterprises of the early twentieth century, an instrument for evangelism. When she became superintendent, Kugler adopted as the motto for the hospital: "Ourselves your servants for Jesus' sake" (2 Cor 4:5). In Kugler's own words, this was the purpose of the hospital: "Some who heartily approve of medical work, as far as it pertains to the body, hold that it is not proper to do anything to disturb the faith of the Hindus. But no apology is offered for presenting Jesus Christ to patients as a personal Saviour" (Document 9).[22]

Kugler stressed that persons of all ages and conditions, of high or low castes and even outcastes, be admitted to the hospital. Equality of treatment was to be given to all patients. This was one conscious way in which they sought to communicate "the universal nature of the Gospel."[23]

Doctors and nurses were expected to witness directly to the salvation which Christ had worked in their own lives. Morning prayer groups were conducted for all employees. Preaching services were held on Sunday mornings, as well as Sunday school for women and children. Kugler instructed native women in ways of explaining scriptural texts to patients in the wards. Many patients were baptized while in the hospital. Whether converted or not, upon leaving the mission they were encouraged to buy Bibles and continue studying the teaching learned while in the wards (Document 10).[24]

The birth of babies enabled the most direct and dramatic witness to the aim of evangelism in the hospital. Helen Barrett Montgomery described Anna Kugler's activity:

> It is easy for Dr. Kugler to do things that in another would have given serious offense. For example, when the little *rani* (Hindu princess) had given permission for us to enter her private room, Dr. Kugler picked up her baby, saying: "You know, *Rani,* this is a *Yesu Christu* baby, for it was born in a *Yesu Christu* hospital. You will never teach it to worship idols, will you?"[25]

The stress on evangelism basic to Anna Kugler's leadership became less prominent in Christian global mission strategy by the mid-twentieth century. Emphasis was placed on greater development of indigenous native leadership, service in the spirit of Christ, and tolerance of the plurality of religious faiths. In mission work directed toward females, concern had been placed on advancement of the status and rights of women since its beginnings in the late-nineteenth century. As the twentieth century progressed, Christian missions increased efforts to train native women for leadership in their own countries.

The development of Asian colleges for women, one of the major projects of Helen Barrett Montgomery and Lucy Waterbury Peabody among others, became a primary means of training females in eastern countries. In medical missions, Ida Scudder's work illustrates the shift from Christian evangelism in women's hospitals to the training of women doctors to assume leadership in the medical field in India. Scudder, founder of the first school of medicine for women in India, was the daughter of a medical missionary, granddaughter of the first medical missionary to India. Born at her father's mission station, she grew up in the United States, resistant to mission work for herself. After returning to aid her parents in a new and isolated mission post during her mother's illness, Ida experienced a dramatic conversion. Called upon to aid three women in childbirth, all of whom died during one night, she then committed herself to full-time medical missionary work for women in India.[26]

After training in the United States and being commissioned by the Christian Reformed Church, Scudder returned to India and gained funding for the Mary Taber Schell Hospital for Women in 1902. As needs mounted rapidly, the hospital expanded and the Vellore Medical School opened in 1918.

Ida Scudder dreamed, and in time succeeded, in raising the school to a medical college. The status was gained due, in no small measure, to the record of excellence compiled by early students awarded the degree of Licensed Medical Practitioner, lower of two medical degrees given in

India. "Of the fourteen young women who finished the course, everyone passed the final examinations given by the Madras Medical College at the end of four years. One received the gold medal in anatomy and another in obstetrics. Of the four hundred men who took the examinations, only twenty percent passed."[27]

Scudder's leadership of these first students "suggests an Indian guru and his followers. They lived and worked together, the students literally sitting at her feet, for she taught many of the courses herself, and with excellent results" (Document 11).[28] Her style grew out of the conditions and needs under which she worked. With no other trained female doctors to share responsibility, Scudder had to assume strong and total authority herself. By 1916, she was joined by Gertrude Dodd of New York who became treasurer and financial manager of the Medical School and College for twenty years and a trusted confidante.

The women students idolized and idealized Ida Scudder. They saw her as a mother hovering over and concerned for their every need. They also valued her closeness to them, describing her as "more a part of them" than would ever again be possible. If Ida Scudder's leadership style evidenced strong matriarchal qualities, it also evidenced determination to raise her students to stand on their own feet as pioneers in their own country in a previously all-male field. Her address to the first graduating class of Vellore Medical School in 1922 is a remarkable blend of the lofty idealism and hard pragmatism which she instilled in the women graduates (Document 12). It leaves no doubt why Scudder was long remembered as the beloved "Dr. Ida."

CONCLUSION

Women in the late twentieth century are experiencing their "day in the sun" in many areas of institutional church work. More positions of greater responsibility and authority are being opened to them than ever before. For the first time in history, a woman often receives preferential consideration for posts of leadership in volunteer and professional capacities. The response within any one woman is likely to be complex. She may feel valued and honored, while simultaneously realizing that her lack of experience will increase possibilities of failure.

Models from prefeminist generations of history raise difficult but essential concerns of personal lifestyle and public leadership for today. Biographical study can help us avoid pitfalls and envision new styles of life and leadership growing out of other's experience. This chapter has lifted up cameo portraits of a few such women and issues that may address our own condition, directly or indirectly.

Insights that arise from this study include the following. First, women must take responsibility to bring their personal and professional lives together into one integrated whole. Many are juggling traditional patterns of wives and mothers alongside new models of equality in public work roles. To challenge this historical mode of woman as primary nurturer within the home is often highly threatening to personal relationships and perpetuates the "superwoman" mentality. Lucy Peabody and Helen Montgomery were middle-class women of traditional upbringing who became liberated in both their private and public lives. It was necessary for them, along with their husbands, to develop strong independent identities that led them, not in separate directions, but to stand on their own feet in interdependent relationships.

Similarly, their public roles as women in "team ministry" were equally challenging to cultural prescriptions. Their pattern of shared authority succeeded because they related to each other in a noncompetitive and genuinely supportive manner. Women today often verbally affirm noncompetitiveness more readily than they practice it, too busily stepping on other peoples' feet as they climb the ladder.

Belle Bennett's experiences teach the necessity to "choose our battles." Bennett was a political strategist who decided that winning laity voting rights was more important than maintaining autonomy of women's missionary societies. Her decision is debatable. Perhaps she should have confronted both issues and not compromised on the latter. It was a political calculation, however, born out of her decision that the choice was essential or both would be sacrificed.

Throughout each of the women's stories runs the underlying theme of indebtedness to other females and support of sisters. Political realism and individual advancement must not be held over against the special call of "Women's Work for Women," as much a responsibility of females today as when envisioned by women's society leaders a century ago. It is a part of women's particular evangelistic task, combining the goals of Anna Kugler and Ida Scudder.

Finally, Georgia Harkness, a precursor of contemporary liberation theologians, challenges women and men today to recognize the interconnectedness of issues of social justice. Classes, sexes, and races cannot be set over against each other if the vision of Christ's new age is to be experienced on this earth. Harkness and other women in this chapter applied their faith radically to daily decisions. They are important to us, not so much because they were extraordinary women, but because of the precedents they set for women of feminist persuasion in church leadership positions in the late twentieth century.

Helen Barrett Montgomery was a pioneer in Baptist and ecumenical women's missionary society leadership. She was the first woman to head a national Protestant denomination. [Photo from *Missions Magazine*, July 1922.]

Belle Harris Bennett gained laity rights for women in the Methodist Episcopal Church, South, and founded the Scarritt Bible and Training School, the first deaconess training center in her denomination. [Photo courtesy of the United Methodist Church Archival Center, Drew University, Madison, New Jersey.]

Helen Barrett Montgomery, delivering the presidential address at the Northern Baptist National Convention, Indianapolis, 1921. [Photo from *Missions Magazine*, July 1922.]

Dr. Georgia Harkness, leading female theologian of the mid-twentieth century and first woman to teach theology at the seminary level. She is shown here as professor of Christianity at International Christian University, Tokyo, in 1957, at a farewell tea given for her. [Photo courtesy of the United Library, Garrett-Evangelical Theological Seminary, Evanston, Illinois.]

Ida Scudder founded the first school of medicine for women in India, the Vellore Medical School, in 1918. [Photo from *Dr. Ida: The Story of Dr. Ida Scudder of Vellore* (New York: McGraw-Hill, 1959).]

Graduating class of early female doctors in India. [Photo courtesy of Vellore Medical College, India; Archives, Garrett-Evangelical Theological Seminary.]

Documents: Patterns of Laywomen's Leadership in Twentieth-Century Protestantism

PROFESSIONAL VOLUNTEERS: HELEN BARRETT MONTGOMERY AND LUCY WATERBURY PEABODY

Document 1: "College Days": The Campaign for Higher Education of Asian Women

The vision and organization of ecumenical women's society movements at the turn of the century came from such pioneers as Lucy Waterbury Peabody and Helen Barrett Montgomery. Lucy Peabody's leadership of "College Days," the year-long campaign to fund Asian women's colleges, demonstrates the essential ability of both women to conceive new movements, to administer broadly based programs, and to mobilize support. A description of "Dollar Day," the last major project, which brought the campaign to successful completion, dramatically illustrates Peabody's personal ability, the highly developed organizational network, and the legacy to "professional volunteers" for generations to follow.[29]

The last lap of the race, as Mrs. Montgomery expressed it in a recent number of *Missions,* for the Seven Union Christian Colleges of the Orient is on, and Washington's part in the event is to be of a decidedly signal character. It will be remembered that the race started in Washington last year at the time the College Day luncheons were inaugurated, which are still being given in the leading cities of the country. At that time the churches of the Capital City, of nearly all denominations, united in a campaign for the seven Union Christian colleges and succeeded in raising $25,000. Now Washington is having its full share in the closing triumphs that are being staged in all parts of the country.

Mr. Rockefeller's gift of $1,000,000 from the Laura Spelman Rockefeller Fund to the Union colleges, provided the women of the United States would raise $2,000,000, is too well-known to be repeated here. More than $2,000,000 of the $3,000,000 has been secured, and to attain the remainder of the amount before the time limit on the Rockefeller gift expires, January 1, 1923, Mrs. Peabody, chairman of the building committee for the colleges, devised plans for inaugurating a day of dollar gifts, which by a Nation-wide popular movement would bring in all money that is still lacking. She selected Saturday, December 9, as the date of the Dollar Day, and the project is in full swing all over the country to make the day a success.

A short time ago Mrs. Peabody came to the Capital City and laid before one of the Government officials of high authority the greatness of this adventure in international friendship—whereby the people of the United States were putting $3,000,000 in educational institutions, seven high standard colleges and medical schools—for the girls of India, China and Japan. "Mr. Secretary," said Mrs. Peabody and a member of her committee who was with her, "we have secured $2,000,000 of the $3,000,000 necessary to put up the building and equip these colleges. There is no question but what the people of the country will give the other million, provided we can give the plan the publicity it needs to reach them. Now, how could publicity be obtained in a better way than by a radio broadcasting that would be Nation wide?"

"It is an international adventure in education as well as friendship, my dear madam," replied the courteous Secretary. Then after much thought and consideration, much planning and munipulation, it was finally arranged, through Commissioner of Education John J. Tigert, that there would be sent out through the Arlington radio, the largest radio broadcasting station in the world, save the one in Paris, a story of the seven colleges and the plan of the Dollar Day.

As the matter eventually developed there will be two evenings devoted to a Nationwide broadcasting of the Dollar Day plan for the union Christian colleges. On Monday evening, December 4, the broadcasting station at Arlington will be used. Mrs. Coolidge, the wife of the Vice-President of the United States, will introduce the speaker, who will represent Dr. Ida Scudder to the people of the Nation in the interest of the colleges. Then over the Arlington radio the story of the seven colleges will be told, as well as some of Dr. Scudder's experiences as president of one of the seven colleges—the Women's Medical School at Vellore, India.

On Saturday evening, December 2, the radio broadcasting will be done through the courtesy of Woodward and Lothrop, who generously offered their big radio broadcasting station for the colleges. The well known and beloved Methodist bishop, Dr. William F. McDowell, will there make an introductory address, introducing the colleges and presenting Dr. Scudder. That missionary physician will then tell the people of the country the wonderful story of the seven women's union Christian colleges—three in India, three in China, and one in Japan. On that same evening, Saturday, December 2, Dr. Mott will speak for the colleges at a New York broadcasting station. Dr. Robert Speer will speak in the same manner at a station in New Jersey, and at the same time well-known speakers will "broadcast" the story of the colleges from Pittsburgh, Chicago, Denver, Seattle and San Francisco.

In addition to this Mrs. Peabody has secured the Associated Press, and announcement of the plan and a story of the Dollar Day will be sent out by that far-reaching medium. In very many of the States the daily papers will keep that plan before their readers during the week beginning December 3, and leading weekly papers will publish the story of the colleges in full at that time.

On Sunday, December 3, Dr. Scudder will speak for the colleges at several important places in Washington. At the Sunday school hour in the morning she appears before the Burrall class of Calvary church.

During the morning service she will speak at Foundry Methodist church. In the afternoon, a large mass meeting will be held at Mount Vernon place Methdist church, where many of the leading official church, business and club women will be present and where an audience of 1,500 people will greet her. In the evening she will be honor guest at the famous Episcopalian school for girls, the Cathedral, on the heights of Georgetown, and where at an evening service she will again present the colleges.

Do you ask, How is the plan for the Dollar Day to be worked out? In the same way that has been used by the Red Cross and the Near East Relief—dollar gifts from the millions! Every one who reads these lines is going to give on Saturday, December 9, at least $1 toward these seven wonderful union Christian colleges. Moreover, will not everyone try to get someone else to give also in order that the

DOLLAR DAY

will become

THE MILLION DOLLAR DAY?

Document 2: Helen Barrett Montgomery's Presidential Address to the Northern Baptist Convention

Elected president of the Northern Baptist Convention for 1921– 1922, Helen Barrett Montgomery became the first woman to lead a national church govening body. Portions of her address, given here, demonstrate the vision of her message and her power to speak with authority. She presses the Baptists to value their own denominational heritage and to commit themselves to the broader purposes of religion, civic freedom and evangelism to win the nation and world for Christ in the aftermath of the First World War.[30]

The delegates to the Northern Baptist Convention of 1922 face the most serious condition and the most momentous questions that have ever confronted a Northern Baptist Convention. I am sure that we are all sobered by the weight of responsibility that is ours. Our children's children will look back to this hour and judge us by what we do. If we are small, or weak, or cowardly; if we are swayed by passion or prejudice or take counsel of our fears they will write down our failure with shame and sorrow. We must not disappoint the present; we must not fail the future; the times summon every delegate to draw on his resources of spiritual power. The occasion summons him to lay aside childish things and really to be, during the days just ahead of us, the man he longs to be.

We meet as Baptists. We have a great history. We are trustees for great principles. We face great opportunities. We are not sufficiently conscious of our history and the notable contribution we have made to the cause of individual liberty, civil and religious. There was dedi-

cated in Washington, recently, a memorial to Roger Williams. The
president of the United States turned the first spade full of earth
when they laid the foundation of the Roger Williams Memorial
Church. . . .

We Baptists may be proud of our history. We are trustees of some
great principles, never more needed by the world than now. Let us
not betray them. We Baptists are the recognized democrats of the
Protestant world. The local church is our depository of ecclesiastical
authority. The association has no authority over the local church; the
state convention has no authority over the association; and the Northern Baptist Convention has no authority over the state convention. All
these are voluntary cooperative associations created for the sake of
greater effectiveness in the business of the kingdom. But as democrats
we regard the right to cooperate as equally sacred with the right to
differ. It is ours to prove that without abandoning our democracy we
can learn to stand shoulder to shoulder in the cooperative prosecution
of the great tasks of the Kingdom. . . .

We face great opportunities, too great for us rightly to measure them.
One hundred million people in Europe, as a result of the war, have
religious liberty for the first time. Our distressed brethren in many
lands need us to help them set up the standard of a free church in
a free state. In Latvia, Poland, Belgium, France, Czechoslovakia,
Russia, Spain and Italy there are opportunities such as had not entered into our fathers' hearts to conceive, waiting for us to enter in
and possess them. But we need to ask ourselves soberly a question.
Have we ourselves a firm hold of the principle of toleration and
religious freedom so that we can help them to establish it? Are we free
from religious intolerance and bigotry? Pray God that we may purge
ourselves of any root of bitterness and rise to the fullness of this great
opportunity.

From all sections of our mission fields come the news of rising tides
of evangelism that are lifting our missionary enterprise in their
mighty arms. Is this a time for us to diminish our aid when from
Assam, from Burma, from India, from Africa, from China and Japan
and the Philippines come tidings of nations in commotion prepared
for Zion's war? If we look to our own beloved America the prospect
is the same. The time demands of us such a program for home
missions and city missions as shall enable Baptists to do their share in
making America truly Christian. The Sunday-school world is awakening to a new sense of responsibility for the moral welfare of our
nation. To our Publication Society we have entrusted our most precious possessions—our children. To it we commit religious education
and to it we must also give the funds for a tremendous advance. The
only limit to the opportunity is the spirit of the churches. . . .

One of the good heritages that came to us out of the war was the consciousness that we must either, as a soldier boy expressed it, "put up or shut up," that we could not continue to sing "The Light of the World is Jesus," "Jesus Shall Reign Where'er the Sun Does His Successive Journeys Run," and contribute only our loose change to make him King and Lord. We must either abandon our claim of His supremacy and our devotion to His cause or square our gifts with our claims.

Every one of the great denominational crusades has fallen on evil days. Each one of them is halted with the vision only partially realized. The voice of criticism is heard, deceit and distrust and disloyalty have their say. Greed speaks only too loudly in many of the objections that are made; but in spite of all, the movements move, the cause goes on, the standards of giving of the church are raised, a new vision of the supreme value of Jesus and His Gospel to the world is gained. . . .

Brethren we are in a great campaign. We have a war to fight for our Lord Jesus Christ. We must not disagree! We must not fight each other! We must unite to win.

Let this Convention be founded and proceed and end in prayer. Satan is here. He longs to divide us. He rejoices when he sees Christian brethren in dissension. Nothing but prayer can defeat him. Let us gather in little groups and in our own closets and pour our hearts before God.

"Oh, send out Thy light and Thy truth; let them lead me; Let them bring me unto Thy holy hill, And to Thy tabernacles. Then will I go unto the altar of God, Unto God my exceeding joy; And upon the harp will I praise Thee, O God, my God, Why art Thou cast down, O my soul? And why are Thou disquieted within me? Hope Thou in God; for I shall yet praise Him, Who is the help of my countenance and my God."

Document 3: A Postconvention Message to the Women of the Churches

Immediately after presiding over the Northern Baptist Convention, Helen Montgomery penned the following letter to women of the missionary societies of her donomination. She expresses the bonds of sisterhood which she feels with these women. While serving the entire church, she recognizes the special support given to her by other women and her deepest responsibility to them.[31]

Dear Women of the Churches:

The Indianapolis Convention has held its last session and I am sitting in my hotel room waiting for my train. I want to write you a brief and personal letter of what is on my heart.

First let me thank you all for the wonderful support that you have given me. I know that I was your representative; that my selection was a recognition on the part of the denomination of the effective work done by the women's organizations at home and abroad. All the year I have felt behind me your loyal cooperation upholding me. For all your letters and telegrams, for all your resolutions adopted in local and in state meetings, I thank you. I shall be a better and more courageous woman because of your support.

Then I want to recognize publicly the stay and support that your prayers have been. I know that you have been praying for me because you have told me so; but I know it also because of the present power of your prayers in my life. Never was there a Convention where so many people both in groups and in their closets were carrying it to God in prayer. Those prayers God has answered. His presence could be felt in our Convention. There was earnest conviction on both sides, but there was also courtesy and fairness and a spirit of mutual forbearance and helpfulness. God has been speaking through this Convention. He has preserved us from schism. He has enabled us to emphasize the things on which we do not differ.

Above the Convention platform were the words spoken by a Chinese Christian at the recent conference in Shanghai,

"AGREED TO DIFFER, BUT RESOLVED TO LOVE."

These words expressed the spirit of unity and faith that bound us.

I feel that the past year has seen a wonderful revival of true prayer among us. God has still greater things to do for and through us if we will adventure ourselves in Him in prayer.

I want to congratulate you on the outcome of the Continuation Campaign. Here, too, prayer had its great enabling part. I know that is is a disappointment to you that you cannot know the exact amount of your gifts, as can the World Wide Guild and the Children's World Crusade. Our inability to tell the exact amount is due to the misunderstanding of local church treasurers who failed to report separately the amount given through the Continuation Campaign. We do know that very large amounts were given and in due time we will report on that part of the total that can be credited.

While the amount given will be credited to the whole New World Movement and is not at all raised solely for the two woman's societies, yet it is a great spur and stimulus for the women to know what they have achieved. This year careful plans will be made to have the amounts given toward the Continuation Campaign collected in each local church by a key-woman who will turn it over to the treasurer and secure from him a receipt. This will enable us to know what we give.

I have a great hope that you will continue to put spiritual things first in our great cooperation crusade for the New World Movement. Continue the prayer groups. Pray definitely for the things you need: that obstacles may be removed, that hearts may be opened, that the goals may be reached. God will work through and for you. Emphasize the great, deep, fundamental and eternal motives in all your work.

Appeal to the highest and best. Uphold the cross of Christ in all that you do and say. It is His cause that we present. It is His needs that we urge. It is His glory that we seek.

So many have quoted to me that great text in Esther—I am not sure; I cannot tell; I am grateful if in any way God has used an instrument so weak and so unworthy. But of you all, Baptist women, I do not doubt—I *know* that you can save us out of our present difficulties. I am sure that you "Are come to the Kingdom for such a time as this." Faithfully yours,

HELEN B. MONTGOMERY.

LAITY RIGHTS CHAMPION: BELLE HARRIS BENNETT

Document 4: Speech to the 1910 Convention of the Methodist Episcopal Church, South

After yielding on the autonomy of Woman's Missionary Society work in the Methodist Episcopal Church, South, Belle Bennett took an uncompromising stand on voting rights for lay women. She exposed long-ingrained prejudices against women's participation and made a strong appeal based on the rights of women and the church's need for their contribution.[32]

MISS BENNET SPOKE AS FOLLOWS: Brethren, I am not unmindful of the very great courtesy you are doing me in giving me the time to speak before you here, and I believe I can convince some of you at least, that what we have asked from you in this amendment is neither unwomanly nor unreasonable.

The women who ask this of you are the same women who sit beside you in the pew every Sunday morning. They are the same women that kneel beside you at the altar to take of the body and blood of Jesus Christ. They are the same women that go out into the hard places, the lanes and by-ways of towns and cities; the very same women. I never heard one of you say that a deaconess by doing that work can become unwomanly. I never heard one of you say that these women who go out into the dark, hard places of the foreign field, who work beside the most degraded in the heathen lands, and the home fields, have become unwomanly because of the work they have done.

I stand here this morning to say that the great Church of God that you represent today needs the womanhood of the Church in the councils of the Church. Four years ago, this great body, assembled at Birmingham, helped to pass the law concerning the Woman's Home Missionary Society, which, last year, raised $246,000, a restrictive law saying that these women should not without the consent and approval of the General Board of Missions take more than $5,000 of money which they raised for buying property, etc. Men! if one woman had been on this floor, and had risen to protest against that, or to explain to you that which was hard to understand, or if there had been one woman to whom you had looked to explain this provision, you would not have done it. If there had been a woman at that time in your General Board, and could have counciled with your Missionary Committee at that time, who could have taken some control of the work in the foreign land, you would not have done that thing. It was not that you meant to do that unkind thing. At that time you passed a law that the missionary women should have two years of training school, and two years of testing, before such one went out to the field, and should look to your General Board for supervision and instruction. You need us in the council of the Church.

Objection has been made that so few women want this thing. May I ask you, my brethren, when any great forward movement of the world event went forward with a majority vote. Always in the beginning of great events, or in great movements, the beginning must be with a few. This I say to you today. It is not a few who believe that the fullness of time has come. A great part of every household of men and women are feeling your sisters should sit on terms of equality in the Conference of the Church. . . .

I believe the minority report says that we do not want to put on our women this great additional work. Today I look around this house, and I see women here from all parts of the world, from far off Seattle, from San Francisco, from everywhere. Are not these the mothers of the land, the very mothers that you say cannot leave their duties at home. I wonder if there are any babies at home today whose mothers are here, who will not accept these additional burdens. . . .

I speak not for the women who it in their parlors, with carpeted floors and curtained windows, with the tenderness of love of brethren and friends and little children around them. I do not speak in their behalf. . . .

Today in Dallas, Texas, as for the last twelve years, we have had a little, though unworthy home, where the poor unfortunate girls of that section have been gathered in, and mothered. It is for the three hundred thousand such girls in the State of Texas alone, those poor fallen girls,—I stand in the councils of Church to speak for them.

And I stand here to speak for the seven millions of wage-earning women who are in this land today.

My brothers and friends, Mr. George Stuart said to me some years ago, in speaking of these women: "I would put them all back into their homes, and let them have the comfort of their homes."

Gentlemen, if you had been in some of the homes where we have been! I stood in one of the great packing houses of Kansas City, and saw all those women; I have been in the cotton mills of all these various sections, and seen these women with their little children who had no other way of earning their living, earning their daily food, and we have these mothers whom I saw going back to their wretched homes, where they were huddled, three, five, yes, fifteen, in rooms only fifteen feet square, and I say is God pushing them out of their homes, and has the Church taken no step to protect these women by going down into the great cities and giving them sanitary homes. I do not plead for those to whom you give love and affection, and kindness, but I do ask you to let us into the councils of your Church, and bring before you the need of these women down in the hard places. Why should we not sit beside you in the Boards of Education? Seventy years ago there were less than a hundred women who taught school. Seventy years ago they had no part in higher education. Today seven-tenths of the Sunday School teachers are women, and yet you say you don't think your women ought to sit on the Boards of Education. . . .

As I look over your arena here today, I could see that the sentiment back of you all of these years is such that you would say, "This is hardly a place for a woman." But in the Conference the question is not one of the loudest voice, but it is the question of the speaker on the stand. Don't you think women could be seen as well as men if she had on a white dress, and a blue ribbon and flowers?

Now my brethren, I believe that our voices are just about as good as most of yours. I have strained my ears as I sat back there, and it is just occasionally that a man could be heard at the rear of this hall, and I believe our voices could penetrate as far as the men's do sometimes.

My brethren, this is not a matter of reason with you. You do not protest against this with your reason. It is a matter of prejudice, it is a matter of sentiment. You are burning incense on an ancestral tablet. Methodism has been doing a great deal of that.

But there are so many things I would like to say in behalf of those who stand for this. I know that there have been plenty of silly women, of gossiping women, and plenty of idle women. But you may remember what the old Yorkshireman said in Adam Bede, I believe, "God Almighty made them to match the men." I have seen many women that I thought had met more than his match.

According to the ruling of the Church, to which I listened eagerly, this matter cannot come under four years. If you put this measure on its passage, and let it go down to the Annual Conference, it must come back, and it will be eight years before some women might possibly sit in this General Conference. I do not believe you would object if there was a little corner of women over there, and I think that, if such a woman as Miss Laura Haygood sat in this body, and some question as to the foreign field came up, you would be glad to hear her. There are not a great many of our women who would sit in your Annual Conferences or General Conferences, but our contention is this, I repeat it again, you need the women in the councils of the Church,—the Church needs it, the world's evangelization needs it, and we believe that the fullness of time has come for this thing. I hope you will put this measure on its passage. If you do not, we are to have four years of education. You must have that because there are plenty of men, as well as women, who need to be educated on it. Put this act on its passage, and it will come back to another General Conference to be ratified, and even then there would not be many of you here in the Conference. A great many of us will be gone home to God. We have not done this work in our own strength. We have gone to our boarding houses to ask God to guide us. Week after week we have said we thank Thee, O Lord, that I stand here today, after seventeen years of work guided by the same commission that brought me into the Church, and the Master has said "go." Bishop Hendrix said look at the men on this platform—one here from Asia, another from China, another from Korea, represented on this platform, and I said a woman is not considered worthy to stand on this platform.

Not yet can the women sit on the platform of the Church of Christ with her brothers. After twenty centuries we stand knocking at the door of the Church of God, saying yet, "My brothers, brothers, won't you take us in?" God made man and woman coordinate. Without the coordination of man and woman there is no reproduction of life, not perfect government of the home. Let the father die, and the mother and the little children all along through the years miss that government. They miss in the home what makes the perfect home. Let the mother die, and again the government of that home is broken. The Church is the house of God and the mother of God's people. You need the perfect government of the man and woman in the Church. Put this measure on its passage, and let it go down to the conferences and come back to you; and eight years from now perhaps there will be one or two women in the General Conference. I thank you again, my brethren.

Document 5: Forceful Debate at the 1914 Convention

Belle Bennett's unyielding stance finally led the Methodist Episcopal Church, South to grant laity rights to women at the 1918 Convention. Her arguments reprinted here from the 1914 Conference build upon those of her 1910 address.

The opposition to laity voting rights for women, presented by Mrs. T. B. King of Memphis, was shrill. Her position echoes the continuing strain of the "Cult of True Womanhood"—and sounds familiar even today.[33]

MISS BELLE BENNETT SPOKE IN FAVOR OF LAITY RIGHTS AS FOLLOWS: Brethren of the General Conference, for the thousands of women who desire that this action shall be taken by this General Conference,

I thank you for this privilege. Gentlemen, this is not a class question. This is a great Church question and one which has been decided by the largest bodies of Methodism all over the world long ago—by the English Church, by the Irish Church, by the Australasian Church, and in nearly all the Methodist Churches. The women for whom we are acting are the most loyal, the most intelligent, the most devout women in the Church. These are the women who pay their assessments over and over again. I have known the women all through the missionary societies of the Church, and they are invariably the women who pay their assessments to the Church.

Now, my brethren, the Church is a divine institution; but you who sit here to-day and every day making and unmaking the government of the Church know that this is a very human institution. One of the arguments brought against us is that our Lord did not appoint any women in the college of the disciples; that he did not send out any women in the seventy. Neither did our Lord ordain or appoint the bishops of the Church. He did not establish Sunday schools; he did not establish Epworth Leagues. It is you, my brethren, who make the government of the Church; and in the Church home, as in "our own home," is not the woman a great factor in the government in that home?

It is not that we want to have authority. We meet very often this argument. For instance, the one which you meet in Paul's letter; "Let the women keep silence in the Churches." Brethren, may that not have been the highest wisdom in the sixteenth or seventeenth centuries? There are no Sunday schools; they were not presidents of the Epworth League or superintendents in the Sunday school. All those things were not in the Churches then.

Again, another argument is that it will release the men from the care of the Churches. I have an opinion of my own that only a comparatively few will get into the Quarterly Conference, so that men will not be released from care of the Churches. I was brought up in a home with six brothers and a father, and all were taught to work. Now, brethren, if this appeal is granted, and it should go down to the Churches, it would be four years before it would be ratified in this General Conference as an integral element. We have lost an intelligent element of the Church and should have taken it the first time. The common people are in the Church as an intelligent element.

Now we think that we have a great body of women who have lived the shut-in life who do not want to assume responsibility, but they pay their dues and the woman who pays her dues even by proxy will not have as vital an interest as the woman who pays her own Church assessments. But if you send it down, it will be four years before it can be ratified, and then another four years before a woman can sit in this Conference, and fifty years before fifty women will sit in this great body. And yet Christian women constitute more than half of the Church membership and do half the work of the Church. We sit here to-day with this our appeal that the time may come, though it may take eight years, and we hope this appeal will pass this house. The case is this: that we raise $250,000; but if we want to expend more than $5,000 we ask permission of the General Board of Missions. You cannot send out the women without first bringing them before the General Board of Missions. The General Conference of the Methodist Episcopal Church granted this privilege to women twenty-five years ago, and yet in all that time there have not been more than thirty women who have sat in the General Conference of that body.

All down through the ages we have had and do have to-day somewhat of Oriental residuum in our Southern Methodism, and it is the sheltered woman in her home that opposes taking responsibility. You have the women in this opposition who hesitate about any great change in domestic life; and yet, as I have said, you ought to have these women, the most intelligent, the very brightest women, who are doing the greatest amount of work, to sit with you and take a part in the great work of God in the Church, and we ask you to let them sit with you as we suggest. The woman sees the side that the man does not see, and the man sees the side that she does not see.

Once more that old argument, "When all the women want it," If all women wanted it, they would have it and have it quickly. If all the men want any great reform, they will have it quickly. I say to you, in the name of these women whom I represent, you do need the women in the councils of your Church. As the great volume of prayer goes up from the congregations to the Father, "Thy kingdom come," you pray for this measure which will surely come. I have not met a man among you who does not say it will eventually come. Then why not let it come now?

MRS. T. B. KING, OF MEMPHIS: It is my distinguished privilege this morning to represent the motherhood of the Church. I am not a mother myself, but my own precious mother is living, and I can conceive of no greater honor than to represent her and speak for her this morning. I come before you to speak not only for my mother but for thousands and multiplied thousands of women all over Southern Methodism; and I declare to you we do not want laity rights.

The very movement, from its beginning, has been utterly repugnant to us. And I represent the interest of the Christian Church. We are doing just as much work as the women who want laity rights, we are contributing just as much money as they are; and we do not feel that we have been circumscribed in any particular. We do not ask for any more liberty or latitude; and certainly not for emancipation, for there is nothing to be emancipated from. If there is a highly honored class on this earth, it is Southern womanhood, warm, happy, exalted,

honored, beloved. No queen upon her throne has held a more royal
sway or exercised more undisputed sovereignty. Our splendid, noble,
chivalrous men would give their last ounce of strength and every drop
of blood for our defense and protection. O, it was a sad day for
American womanhood, and she received a most cruel blow, when
"women's rights" was raised.

This whole question of laity rights is the suffragist question. You
read the literature that has been sent out by this movement; and if you
do not find that one point coming right through, from start to finish,
the question of women voting, I do not see what else you can find in
it. It is their desire to vote. It is the Church wing of the suffrage
question. I have never talked to one who favors this, with one execp-
tion, who was not a suffragette.

When God created the sexes he made woman for man's helpmeet
and not for his competitor. One was to be the complement of the
other. He gave us different endowments, different graces, different
talents, and different spheres to operate in. I come to you this morning and ask you if it is right that men's work, shall be put on the
shoulders of women. If you grant that, I think it will be a question of
women's wrongs instead of women's rights. We cannot do your work
and you cannot do ours; and we do not want to do yours. We have
more than we can well do now, and we ask you that you do not put
your work upon us. We do not want to act as men. We do not want
to be men. We want to be womanly women, with all the sweetness and
the gentleness that God has endowed us with.

Suppose you do let the woman come in to do all your work, to be
stewards and members of all the Conferences? What is going to happen? You emasculate your Church in one sense, and you masculinize
it in another. The Church needs men. Let the men come and take
their place, and let the woman stay where they belong and where God
has intended them to be.

They say it is Scriptural; and they give this passage of Scripture,
"There is neither male nor female, bond nor free, but all are one in
Christ Jesus." You know full well that is not a question of administration at all. That is a question of justification by faith and of our
relation to Christ. If it is Scriptural, when the seven were elected in
the Church why was not a woman elected one of the deacons? Why
was not a woman sent out with the seventy? Or made one of the
apostles of the Lord? Christ is the head of the Church, and man is the
head of the woman. They bring up the cry "of taxation without
representation." Our offerings are free will offerings, and nobody is
taxed in our Church. They say they cannot administer their own
affairs. But the women appropriate every cent of missionary money
they raise, at their Council meeting. There are ten women who are
on the Board of Missions. Is there anything unjust about that? Why

should these women ask to act independently of the Church and set up a government of their own? I feel like that is disloyal, and as one of the women who has a large part in this work and has helped to raise all this money I say it is disloyal. Think of the confusion and anarchy in our Church if the women are allowed to act independently of the rest of the Church.

So I hope you will let it stand just as it is. They say that most of the other Churches have answered this call to the women. At the last Ecumenical Conference it was stated that Methodism had made an increase of 1,109,000 members, and that one-third of this was in our Church. One-half of the increase in American Methodism was in the Methodist Episcopal Church, South. Why should we follow the example of others when we are taking the lead? It would be better for them to follow our example, I think. Mr. Taft, I think it was, said that the South is the conservator of our great nation. When radicalism comes up from the North and the East and the West, there is ballast enough in the South to keep the grand old ship of state steadily moving on her way in the boundless expanse of governmental high seas. So I say to you about the Methodist Episcopal Church, South. Her feet are planted on the rock. Amid the wildest storms she stands undaunted, nor heeds the violent shock, her eye is upon omnipotence, and she sounds out the challenge to Methodism all over the world.

Faith of our fathers, holy faith,
We will be true to thee until death.

APPLIED THEOLOGIAN: GEORGIA HARKNESS

Document 6: Theological Realism Applied to War and Peace

Georgia Harkness pioneered as a female seminary professor, asking hard theological questions regarding pressing social evils of the day. Writing in 1925, she holds the Allies responsible for their own guilt in the First World War and in the peace settlement at Versailles.[34]

Germany's Place in the Shadow

Berlin has been, and still is, a city of beautiful buildings. One does not see in the physical aspects of the city the cruel vestiges of war which strike horror to one's heart in Rheims and the battlefields of France. We say, perhaps, that it was Germany who wrought this desolation, and she ought to suffer. But we are so much in the habit of thinking of Germany as the insensate aggressor bringing suffering to the rest of the world that we forget something very important. We forget that *we starved the Germans.* During the war over three-quarters of a million civilians in Germany (763,000 the statistics say) died from the effects of Allied Hunger Blockade. Among those who survived, the blockade has everywhere left its traces in weakened constitutions and stunted growth, in rickets and tuberculosis. The extent to which it struck to every walk of life is evidence by the fact that Dr. Deissmann, great New Testament scholar and authority on the Mediterranean world, fainted, on his way to the university one day during the blockade, from hunger and undernourishment. Conditions are better now, for in addition to relief sent from without, Germany from her own slender resources has done much to relieve the suffering of her people. But though the immediate crisis is past, the chalky faces of the German students whom I saw gathered at a university convocation and the undersized bodies of three thousand German children whom I saw being fed by the Quaker relief, still haunt me, and make me wonder.

Remember—it was the Allies, America included, who starved the Germans. A necessary war measure we called it, and lulled our consciences into acquiescence. But the Germans say that the invasion of Belgium was also "a necessary war measure." Which is right? Or are both wrong? I wonder if we can call ourselves Christians and justify either.

Germany sits in the shadow of difficulty, and distress, and doubt. Her future rests largely in the hands of the Christian people of other nations, for only through brotherly understanding and mutual trust can the shadows be banished. Shall the fires of prejudice and hatred enkindled by the war psychology continue to enflame us? Until these fires are quenched, the shadows will linger.

Germany and the War-Peace

I shall not attempt to apportion the responsibility for the provisions of the treaty. But wherever the fault may lie, no fair-minded person can deny that Germany was forced to sign a document a long way removed from the Fourteen Points and the Armistice terms on which she laid down her arms—a document which was forced upon a broken nation too weak to resist but not too much cowed to rankle under its severity, a document which has in it the seeds of future wars. The leaders of Germany admit that she lost the war, and by all historic precedent she ought to settle for it. But ought she to have been stripped of all her colonies? Ought her agricultural and mineral resources to have been treated as free plunder by her victorious enemies? Ought she to have been dismembered by the Polish Corridor, which cuts her territory in two and leaves the eastern section isolated? These are, at least, debatable questions. Probably Germany has exaggerated, and the Allies have minimized, the injustice done through the provisions of the treaty. But that economic imperialism played a considerable part in the shaping of the treaty can hardly be denied. Land-grabbing is an old game, and a widely practised one; yet this scarcely justifies the vigor with which it was played around the so-called Peace Table at Versailles.

I hold no brief against the French, though I believe the demands imposed by France at Versailles were an error of tactics, if not of ethics. France was then, and still is, dominated by the psychology of fear. When the demand for international security outstrips the machinery for providing this security, somebody must suffer. Both France and Germany have suffered in the past for this reason. But whatever real sympathy we may have for France—and after seeing the battlefields I have a good deal—we must recognize that there is more real security to be won by moderation than by retaliation. One cannot discipline successfully by overpunishing; and the Hohenzollerns are not the only ones who have failed to observe this bit of practical psychology. It is to the credit of the Herriot Government that it has recognized, much more than the Poincaré party, the economic and protective value of good-will.

There is some justice in the charge that Poincaré and his followers have been expecting of Germany an impossible thing, namely: to be weak and strong at the same time. France wants Germany to be too weak to attack, yet strong enough to pay. This is a perfectly natural attitude, for which I do not condemn France. But it is a hard matter to execute! Nor has the "war-peace" helped in its execution. Germany can pay her debts only by maintaining such industrial prosperity that her exports exceed her imports, and when the raw materials and markets afforded by her colonies were taken away and her trade was crippled by heavy traffics, the possibility of such a surplus of exports was greatly reduced. . . .

The question of the war-guilt is a vital one. For the terms of the peacy treaty are based on the assumption that Germany alone was guilty, and in signing the treaty she was forced to subscribe assent to a statement of sole guilt to which she has never assented in spirit. A large part of our popular thinking rests on the same assumption. "Good enough for them. The dirty dogs deserved all they got. Too bad we didn't kill off the whole bunch"—repeatedly we have heard such gracious sentiments!

That Germany was guilty in a measure is unquestionable. The better element in Germany admits this. But to say that she was *solely* guilty is a very different matter.

The war-guilt evidence cannot all be presented in a paragraph. But the examination by historical experts of the diplomatic papers made accessible since the war has shown that Austria, Russia, and France were as much embroiled in the outbreak of the war as was Germany, and that not even England can be fully exonerated.

. . . I have no desire to exonerate the Kaiser. I think Germany's guilt may be higher than fourth in the scale—in fact, it is a rather futile task to attempt to apportion the responsibility. But no one who has any conception of the maelstrom of European politics in 1914 can, with any pretense at fairness, attribute to Germany the sole guilt for the war. Yet the peace terms were laid down and the reparation debts assessed to her on this basis, and on this basis public sentiment has condemned her. Tales of German atrocities have been heralded abroad, while equally atrocious acts committed by the Allies have been passed over in silence. Hatred has been fostered under the guise of religion, and we have forgotten the message of the Prince of Peace. I am not trying to defend Germany; but I am asking for a fairer judgment—for a truer appreciation of the viewpoint of this country which sits in the shadow. Instead of placing all the blame for the war on Germany, we had better blame economic imperialism, secret diplomacy, and the whole war system. Until we who call ourselves Christians can bury our grudges and learn to love our enemies, there is not much hope of peace on earth, good-will toward men.

Document 7: Evils of Industrialization and War Buildup

Throughout her lifetime, Harkness prophetically called churches to stand against social evils of all kinds. Again, this commitment is demonstrated early in her career through her article, written in 1925, "The One and the Many." [35]

As I write, I glance at the morning paper and see headlines stretching across the page which tell of the progress, or lack of progress, in the attempted rescue of one Floyd Collins entombed in a cave in Kentucky. For two weeks it has been so. By the time the article I am now writing gets into print, Collins will be half forgotten and some other spectacular event will fill the headlines. But for the present, his misfortune is the leading news time and the principal topic of conversation throughout the United States.

The misfortune of one individual calls forth the sympathy of the nation. This is well. But what about the thousands of children who are entrapped in factories, not dying outright, but surrendering to the claims of Mammon the vitality that makes for years of usefulness? In every industrial center we find them—thousands of them who are being permanently stunted in mind and body and are being robbed of the precious heritage which is their due. Their captivity lasts, not days, but years. We want to rescue Collins from his plight. But a measure is before us to release these children from captivity—and we vote it down.

What about the rest of the exploited toilers of the world who live close to the margin of existence and who spend their days remote from the sunlight of opportunity and true freedom? What about the thousands who surrender their lives each year in industrial accidents, and other thousands whose lives are shortened by the crushing grind of an industrial system in which they are but cogs in the great machine? Not all industry is depersonalized, but too much of it is—the victims of the system are all too numerous. If the life of one man is precious, is theirs less so?

What about the girls who are drawn into lives of shame by lack of a living wage—girls who are entrapped in a living death and who kill their souls that their bodies may live? What about the thousands who become the victims of men's lust because, in our homes and schools and churches, we have failed to train our boys and girls in ideals of righteousness? What about the traffic in life and character which goes its way almost unchecked because political corruption, and bribery, and the double standard have ordained that it should prosper? If one person caught in a cave can arouse so much comment, perhaps we had better be a bit concerned about the thousands who live daily in a plight more horrid.

Doubtless some reader is saying, "The cases really are not parallel —these people may be unfortunate, but they are not dying." Yet they *are* dying, in body as well as in soul. There are statistics in plenty to prove it. But we need not pore over statistics to know that child labor, and industiral exploitation, and prostitution shorten the lives of their victims, and do so in no very pleasant fashion. They may die in their beds, but they are none the less the victims of destructive forces. If these destructive forces arise from men's greed and lust rather than from God's physical laws, the more shame on us that we fail to bestir outselves! Some day perhaps we shall decide that the wholesale murder which extends over a period of years—the murder which we now conceal under a cloak of respectability by calling it "business enterprise"—is a murder as heinous as the sudden taking of life, which we consider man's gravest crime.

But if one wants a parallel in which the death of many is real, and sudden, and horrible, it is not far to seek. For what about the millions who laid down their lives in the World War? It is not my purpose to question the purity of the motives for which they fought, but only to face the ugly facts. The war statistics tell us of ten million soldiers dead, three million others missing and presumably dead, thirteen million civilians dead—a gruesome total of twenty-six millions claimed by the gods of war! When we add to this list an estimate of twenty million wounded, nine million war orphans, five million war widows, and ten million refugees, the total is too staggering for the human mind to grasp. Twenty-six million dead, forty-four million more bereft of life's most precious values, uncounted millions thrust into the depths of suffering and despair!

Yet a good many people in America are talking very calmly about getting ready for the next war. And we are advocating a policy of greed, of suspicion, of selfish isolation, of increased armaments, of insult to other nations—which cannot fail to furnish fruitful soil for the growth of the seeds of war. To be sure, nobody wants another war. But how many of us want to avoid it sufficiently to bestir ourselves? I venture to say that at this moment many people in the United States, many people in Christian churches, yes, in Methodist churches, are more concerned about how to get one man out of a cave than about how to avert a world-destroying catastrophe!

I am not suggesting that any one should be any the less concerned about Collins. We ought to be concerned about him. While the newspapers have undoubtedly made much of the spectacular elements of the case for commerical reasons, the fact that the value of one life has called forth such a nation-wide response is very significant. It indicates that we have the capacity for sympathy, and that we realize something of the intrinsic worth of human personality. Since this is true, it is time for us to wake up to the fact that the tragedies being enacted in the lives of millions through child labor, exploitation, prostitution, and war are not less serious than the sufferings of one man.

The great difference between the two kinds of tragedy lies in the fact that one is common, the other is unusual. The events connected with evils we have mentioned are not spectacular; they are not "news." If the newspapers would concentrate for a while on the rescue of the victims of these great human evils, something might happen.

It costs us nothing to sympathize with Collins, for most of us can do nothing to help to rescue him. But if we genuinely sympathize with these millions who are surrendering their lives as victims of forces more real and more terrible than a landslide in a cave, it will cost us a great deal. It may cost us something in taxes and loss of profits. It will cost us much in time, in energy, and perhaps in popularity. Is it worth the cost? One man's life is worth saving; so are the lives of millions.

Document 8: Advocacy of the Ordination of Women

Georgia Harkness led in the struggle for ordination of women in the Methodist Church until it was finally granted in 1956. In this 1924 article, she presents the strongest possible case for ordaining females. Her arguments are as timely and pertinent today as when they were written.[36]

. . . But while nobody questions the value of the volunteer service rendered by women to the Church, there are many who still seem to consider that a special dispensation has been granted to men to fill most of the paid positions within the Church. They are willing enough, to be sure, that a woman should be a missionary or a deaconess or a church secretary. But for a woman to preach—impossible.

Not Many Are Called

Now lest some ministerial brother be alarmed for fear a feminine aspirant may be seeking to usurp his legitimate place, let me say at the outset that I do not think many women at present are likely to attempt to enter the ministry. The wall of prejudice is too strong for any except the most courageous. A few remarkably gifted women such as Maude Royden have been able to make a place for themselves in the ministry, but the Church which would not choose a mediocre man in preference to a superior woman is one among a thousand.

I do not maintain that this prejudice can be attributed exclusively to the ministers themselves, for most of them are more broadminded than their congregations. There is, however, a deep seated relic of medievalism in the attitude of the Church at large which the clergy has not done all it might to eradicate. Such is the shortage of ministers that in many denominations almost any man of good moral character and religious convictions can get a pulpit. But when men are permitted to preach whose education does not extend beyond the eighth grade, and women college trained and sometimes theologically trained, are denied that privilege, something is wrong.

Margaret Slattery tells of an experience wherein she was requested to address a large church audience, not from the pulpit, but from a little oak table down by the register, because, as the church officials told her, "No woman's foot has ever stood in this pulpit." It was only when she firmly gave them the option of permitting her to speak from the pulpit or cancelling the engagement that they reluctantly capitulated. This may be an extreme case, but the fact that it can occur at all in this enlightened age affords food for thought.

One does not need to be an ultra-feminist to recognize that such a state of affairs ought not to exist. The Church has a task on its hands big enough to demand the consecrated talent of both sexes, and many of us believe that it is neither wise nor Christian deliberately to reject the assistance which trained women would gladly render in its ministry if given an opportunity. When it is announced that in our largest Protestant denomination twenty-seven per cent of its ministry have had less than a full high-school education and that in this same denomination there has been a net loss of 613 ministers during the past four years, one wonders if it is not time to bring about a change in established traditions.

Why Women Are Excluded

In these days of many investigations, would it not be well to investigate the causes of the exclusion of women from the ministry? The reasons generally given are as follows: (1) that according to Scripture women must "keep silent in the churches," (2) that the ministry would take woman out of her natural sphere, (3) that she is by nature unfitted for success in such work, (4) that she would not be apt to make it a permanent occupation, (5) that increased competition would tend to interfere with the tenure or salaries of men, (6) that the Church would lose in public esteem by the general admission of women to its ministry.

The first argument can be disposed of without much controversy. One does not have to be a very profound biblical scholar to recognize the difference between our modern social regime and conditions in wicked, conservative Corinth in the days of Paul, when Christian women must walk warily lest they be confused with the brazen women of the street. A prudent bit of advice to the Corinthian women of the first century ought scarcely to be made a stumbling block to progress in the twentieth. The prayer meeting and the Epworth League and the Sunday school would have a sorry time of it if we were to take Paul's words literally as a permanent injunction!

The second objection has more supporters, for from time immemorial we have heard that "woman's sphere is the home." Undoubtedly it is true that for the majority of women the care of the home is the first duty, and we are not advocating that the preacher's wife exchange places with the preacher (though we may have known cases where such an arrangement would not be disadvantageous!). But in spite of the fact that the "woman's sphere" argument has been urged against every movement for the political and professional advancement of women, an increasing number of intelligent people have come to recognize that woman has also a legitimate sphere outside the home. It is not our purpose here to enter into a discussion of the whole feminist controversy; but if it is granted that woman has a rightful place in business and professional life, there is no more reason why she should be excluded from the ministry than from medicine. Practically every avenue of leadership today is open to woman save in the Church, and there she must content herself either with rendering volunteer service or working in a subordinate capacity.

Try and See

To those who fear that we women would not make a success in the ministry, we reply, "Try us and see!" Is there anyone who really believes that a woman with proper training cannot preach as good a sermon as a man? Our voices to be sure may not carry far, but there are few churches where this would be a serious obstacle and we are not likely very soon to get a chance to preach in those churches. And as for what our voices say, we invite you in all modesty to compare the sermon of the average woman preacher with that of the average man—take the best of each, or the poorest of each, or use any standard you wish so long as it is impartial—and examine the result. We are not afraid to submit to such a comparison. Are you?

But of course preaching is not the only work a minister has to do. A minister must be a pastor, an executive, an educator, a financier—a host of other things. But is there any one of these capacities in which women have not proved their ability? If women are strong enough in physique, intellect and personality to pursue successfully every other profession, why not the ministry? We are not claiming for women any sexual superiority, but it seems a matter of plain common sense that equality of ability ought to bring with it equality of opportunity.

The argument that the ministry ought to be a life job and that a woman might relinquish it to marry after a few years is a more tenable objection. But suppose she should! Does this nullify the value of her work in the years before her marriage? And does it interfere with the continuance of her work during the second leisure of middle life after her children have grown to maturity. Furthermore, while most women with professional interests regret the necessity of having to choose between a home and a career while a man can have both, there are many capable women who in full sincerity decide they can render more service to the world by remaining unmarried; and if the Church does not offer an opportunity to invest their talents some other and perhaps less worthy agency will.

Competition

The argument that women might supplant men in the ministry or lower their salaries is not very often publicly advanced by the clergy themselves. However, in the eyes of many people who argue from the general conditions of woman's participation in industry, this seems an important factor. They seem to anticipate a great influx of women at whose advance the present occupants of the pulpit must courteously rise and withdraw to give the ladies their pulpit chairs. There is about as much soundness in this argument as in that of the anti-suffragist who feared that if women were given the vote, Congress would be overrun with them and a woman might (horribile dictu!) be seated in the Presidential chair! Women will find a place in the ministry only so fast as their ability and training win them a legitimate place, and the demand for ministers is such that if any man is crowded out in the process, it will be because he is unfit for survival.

To those who say that the standing of the Church in the eyes of the public would be lowered if women were admitted to its ministry, we reply that if it would, then it is time for public opinion to be remodeled. Does anyone think any the less of the medical profession because women may enter it on an equal footing with men? The public expects and desires men to do its preaching—simply because men always have. The Church is probably our most conservative institution. There are many within its fold who, perhaps unconsciously, adopt as the guiding motto of their lives, "Not so, Lord, for I never have. . . ." It is obvious that if the Church is going to keep abreast of the times and meet the spiritual challenge of the new age it must relinquish some of its conservatism; and whatever our theological convictions may be, it might not be a bad idea to introduce some "modernism" into our conceptions of the function of women in the work of the Church.

Ordination Desirable

Some denominations, to be sure, are willing to ordain women, and it is easy to say that if women want to preach they should enter those denominations. But the issue does not lie wholly in ordination. Not many more women are preaching in those denominations where ordination is possible than in those where it is denied. The crux of the matter is, to put it baldly, is that women cannot enter a field where they are not welcome. Ordination is desirable, I believe, to put the stamp of the Church's approval upon the admission of women to its ministry. But what is needed even more is a general recognition by pulpit and pew of the legitimate place of trained women in this field. Women will never find a welcome in the ministry until the press and our present religious leadership have a remolded public sentiment. Ordination is a step in this direction, but it is a step—not the final goal.

I am not blind to the fact that some other religious vocations are open to women. In fact, I am in another myself. Every year I have the privilege of directing a good many young women who are thinking seriously of religious or social work as a vocation. But I never advise any of them to prepare for the ministry, though I consider it the highest religious calling. Under present conditions it would be futile for them to think of it, for they might take three years of theological training beyond their college work, only to find themselves superseded by men with high-school training or less. If there are men enough in the ministry to do the work and do it well, we are willing to let them. But are there? We wonder if the advancement of the Kingdom is not more important that the maintenance of an ancient prejudice.

MEDICAL MISSIONARIES: ANNA KUGLER AND IDA SCUDDER

Document 9: Purpose of the Guntur Mission Hospital

Anna Kugler, first female medical missionary of the United Lutheran Church to India, dreamed from childhood of entering the mission field. She decided to become a medical missionary in her late

teens after enrolling in the Women's Medical College of Philadelphia.
Here she states the primary purpose of medical missions to be evange-
lism in the name of Christ.[37]

Very early in our Medical Mission work certain well-defined principles were laid down. In the Report of 1900 some of these are
mentioned:

1. As far as possible the work should be carried on in accordance with the best
   and latest scientific teaching of the day.
2. Extravagance should be avoided, but the main object should not be to carry
   on the work with the least possible money.
3. As a mission hospital is both philanthropic and evangelistic in its object, the
   work should not be entirely gratuitous but the payment of fees should be
   encouraged.
4. While believing thoroughly in stated and regular religious teaching, it is
   held that the most effective preaching in the wards is often that done by
   the doctors and nurses in their daily ministrations.
5. A well-organized hospital with a well-qualified staff of doctors and nurses,
   doing work of which they are not ashamed professionally, aiming after
   self-support, and actuated by a love for Christ and a desire for souls—such
   an institution placed in the midst of a Hindu and Mohammedan community will attract patients and will afford opportunities for Christian work
   that will make it one of the most powerful evangelistic agencies of the
   present day. . . .

Emphasis has always been laid upon having the doctors take an
active part in the evangelistic work. The patients soon detect a doctor's
indifference to the Bible teaching. The Jesus religion must be of value
if the doctor recommends it, and the patient listens with reverence as
the doctor prays by the bedside.

"Alas, you were not here when my little one died! I wanted you
to pray that it would go to Jesus," said a young Brahmin mother as
she wept over her child. Essential as it is that the physicians show their
interest in this work, they are very dependent for the regular Bible
teaching upon the Bible women, of whose blessed ministry too much
cannot be said.

Reference has been made under "Patients" to the fact that a number of adults and many infants have been baptized, but these are only
a few of the spiritual results of the years. It is not unusual for a Hindu
woman to go to sleep on the operating table with the name of Jesus
on her lips. During her delirium a young Brahmin woman rehearsed
time and again the account of the death of Christ, maintaining that
it was for her He had died. When she went out she was still a Hindu,
but hidden away in her subconscious self was the teaching that she
probably had received in a mission school. There are thousands in the
villages who, though secret believers today, will some day confess
Christ, and not when they are delirious, as the result of a living faith

in Him of whom they have heard, perhaps in the school or zenana or hospital.

Document 10: A Tribute from a Hindu Friend

A letter to Anna Kugler from a Hindu rajah testifies to the acceptance of the evangelistic goals along with the medical service. Kugler's evangelistic thrust characterized the entire mission enterprise through the early twentieth century.[38]

The medical work which several of the Christian missionaries are engaged in is by far the most successful and productive one by reason of the facilities which lady medical missionaries have in getting access into the homes of the most highly placed and Gosha (secluded) families in India. The lady doctors do not only get an opportunity of treating the bodies of their patients, but also infuse a Christian spirit by constantly placing the Gospel of the Lord Jesus Christ before them. This may not be possible to the ordinary lady missionaries, as they will not be sought after as the medical ones.

Mission hospitals for women and children are doing wonderful work in this land, to alleviate the temporal and spiritual condition of the unfortunate women whose customs preclude them from any contact with the outside world. The Rainy Hospital at Madras, the A.E.L.M. Hospitals at Rajahmundry and Guntur, and the Bethsaida Hospital at Pittapuram are a few amongst such institutions personally known to me. My family is frequently visiting the A.E.L.M. Hospital for women and children at Guntur for medical relief for the last twenty years. Before our first visit to this hospital my wife and children never heard the name of the Good Shepherd—no, not even once. After their acquaintance with this hospital, though we are not converts in the strict sense of the term, my family regularly pray every morning and evening in the name of the Lord, read their Telugu Bible and meditate on some passage or other. We do not now feel ashamed if people call us Christians to mock at. It is needless to say that this change in my family is mainly due to the saintly character of the most able physicians in charge of the hospital.

Not less than a hundred thousand women of the surrounding districts received physical benefits within the walls of this hospital, and all of them had, side by side, the benefits of knowing the life and teachings of the Lord Jesus Christ. Numbers of Bible women, engaged for the purpose, pour into the ears of the patients and their relations that go to the hospital the wonderful message of love. The beautiful buildings of the hospital that attract the attention of the passersby from a distance speak with diverse tongues the saving power of the Cross of Christ. It is a blessing in disguise, for people that enter in to obtain physical relief come out with not only a cured body, but also with a cured soul. They enter in with a dilapidated body and a sin-sick soul and exit with a healthy physical frame and a clean conscience. Many members of my family, friends and relations were saved from physical death within this hospital and obtained spiritual benefit as well. I can say with confidence that it is the case with many thousands of families. Volumes can be written on the good work that is going on in the Guntur Mission Hospital, but I close this testimony with these few words for want of space. May God bless and mutiply such institutions and the saintly physicians for the spread of the Gospel among the Indian people.

RAJAH M. BHUJANGA RAO.

Vellore, South India
9th May, 1927

Document 11: A Student's Description of Ida Scudder's Leadership

Ida Scudder founded the first medical school for women in India. Though born at her father's mission station in India, she grew up in the United States. Resistant to a career in mission work for herself, she experienced a dramatic conversion after returning to India to aid her parents in a new and isolated mission post during her mother's illness. Scudder was called upon to aid three women in childbirth, all of whom died during one night. She then committed herself to full-time medical missionary work for women in India. A student at the Vellore Medical School tells of Ida Scudder's leadership and concern for her pupils.[39]

With just one or two books and one microscope, and a few bones, it was real fun to begin the school. We used to sleep with the bones under our pillows, and steal them out at night from under the pillow for study. But with all these difficulties, it was Dr. Scudder's courage and the wonderful lectures she gave that brought such good results at the beginning of the school. Weekly she used to give examinations, and unless we got 90%, back came the paper with a page full of criticism. Each week, we used to take turns in groups of four at a time, having dinner with the family; and enjoy a social bit from life. Each evening there were the basketball and badminton games in which she took part with us; and then after that, rides for all of us in the Ford car; we used to be seated on the mud-guards, bonnet, and in double rows inside; and the trip was usually down to the mission compound. She was more a part of us then than she can be with the students now.

Regarding the food, she had great difficulty. She wanted to give us the best food prepared in the best way; and we used to give her a lot of trouble in that line, it was something like a mother worrying over the feeding of her first child due to inexperience.

On Sunday, after going to church, we were made to do more work at the hospital and the reason that she gives was that it was God's work, and so it should be done thoroughly on His day. Each and every patient would be sent to on that day, and each nurse's work would be supervised. In the early days, we used to have to run from patient to patient, because when she walked her steps and movements were so quick. She never liked to see us standing idle for one moment in the hospital and she was sure to make some work for us, so we remember how we used to get busy the minute we'd see her on the steps.

Music, prayers, and especially the Bible study about Paul, was a great help indeed. She was our ideal in most of our lives, and we were sure to be recognized as her followers by so many of her patients when we went to work.

Any doctor, any new treatment, any specialist, never passed by Vellore without being called in to give us a lecture or a clinic.

Then we remember one day which was a Government holiday and it happened on a Saturday too; we all planned to ask her to let us have the day off, when she wanted to teach us so much! Our aim was to use the holiday for study, too, but not in the classroom, but she didn't understand that, and so she got up and walked out saying that she would have no more class. But we made up for it by sending our class president to her, and later on having a lecture and tea party! To any place of interest to which she was invited, we were sure to follow her and each patient of particular interest would be shown to us without the least embarrassment to the patient.

One thing she never liked in us was our getting sick. She was an example of one who never got sick, so it was natural, I should say.

Her morning rounds were sometimes done before she came to the early morning class, and the night rounds were done at about 10 o'clock; then she used to work at her desk until about twelve in the night.

Document 12: Ida Scudder's Address to the First Graduating Class, Vellore Medical School, 1922

Scudder's own goals in training her students for full womanhood, as well as excellence in medical care, are projected to her first graduating students.[40]

Today we stand on the mountain top of achievement. The seemingly insurmountable obstacles lie below us. As we glance back four years and see that group of rather timid girls we rejoice with you as we realize that in spite of all the hard things you have overcome and the struggles you have had, you have kept on climbing and overcoming. . . . There will probably never be a time in your lives which will hold the same meaning that today holds; the thrill of having accomplished much gives you joy, but much lies before you of work to be done; . . . as among the mountain ranges, so in life, there are still greater heights in the distance, more stony paths to climb; and you will realize you have made only a beginning.

You will not only be curing diseases, but will also be battling with epidemics, plagues and pestilences and preventing them. You will be teaching mothers how to nurture their children so that they will make more efficient reliable citizens to take their rightful places in their nation. The practice of medicine affords scope for the exercise of the best faculties of mind and heart.

You must learn to be cool, collected and quiet, to have presence of mind; rapid thought and action in the most trying circumstances. You must learn to have wise judgment in moments of great peril; you must train your tempers until you have complete control, for your temper will often be taxed by exasperating patients and their friends. You must learn never to betray indecision and worry, for if you become flustered and flurried, you will lose the confidence of your patients. Practice and experience will train you to have firmness and courage.

Do not always look for gratitude, for sometimes when you are most deserving, you will get the least. Do not expect too much of your patients, do not betray surprise or be aggravated if you find they are taking medicine from half a dozen doctors.

There will be disappointments; your pet theory will be dashed to the ground; your most painstaking laborious work, unsuccessful; there will be cares, anxieties, failures which are very common to a professional life. These are the valleys into which you descend, but stand up bravely, be true and keep on climbing.

Face trials with a smile, with head erect and a calm exterior. If you are fighting for the right and for a true principle, be calm and sure and keep on until you win. . . .

The aim of the Vellore Medical School has been (as you have realized) enthusiasm, love for your work and for the subjects you are studying, a thorough knowledge and mastery of your subjects. The future will need even greater enthusiasm on your part, and the greater knowledge will come by living experience.

If you find yourself in a small hospital in some out of the way place, set yourself to work it up, study to perfect yourself whenever you have time to study. Some of the greatest names in the medical world are of those who have toiled for years in some obscure spot and by their faithfulness to small details have so perfected their knowledge that the world at large stops to listen to what they have to say.

Never stand aloof from your colleagues. Be true to them and to yourself. Give them the experience of your best talents, and take from them what they have to give. Never have an attitude of superiority and indifference. . . .

We have watched you during the past four years with interest; we have rejoiced as we saw you developing, becoming stronger, more self-reliant and finer women. Your characters have been moulded and deepened, your sympathies widened. You have been prepared for what lies before you. . . .

Have gentleness, forbearance and courtesy when dealing with the sick. May the blessing of quietness, and assurance and of wisdom which is pure, peaceable, gentle, full of mercy and good fruits be yours always.

And last and greatest of all, may you follow always and closely in the footsteps of the Great Physician, Christ, who went about doing good, healing the sick, outpouring His wealth of love upon a sinning, sorrowing world, encouraging, uplifting, and carrying joy wherever He went.

Study to know the will of God. Make yourselves workers that need never be ashamed.

To those of you who will be successful in the finals, I bid you farewell as students, and extend to you the right hand of fellowship as colleagues; and in the future may we together help India to take her rightful stand among the great nations of the world. To you, my beloved students, farewell, and may God's richest blessings be upon you one and all.

Women in Religious Education Pioneers for Women in Professional Ministry

DOROTHY JEAN FURNISH

The contribution of women to religious education has been poorly chronicled, partly because religious education is a recent field of endeavor which has had as yet few historians; partly because it is assumed that the contribution of women is scarcely news, since "everyone knows" it is a women's profession. In its broadest sense religious education is not new. All religious groups seek in some way to pass on the tradition from generation to generation. From the beginning of the Christian church there has been concern that the story be shared; first, with Jews who had not heard of Jesus; then with the converted gentiles who needed to understand the Hebrew Scriptures; and finally with the young. This chapter, however, is primarily concerned with the modern religious education movement, which is a uniquely twentieth-century phenomenon. Therefore its historical time frame coincides with the time frame assigned to this volume—the twentieth century. Furthermore, the assumption that religious education has always been a women's field deserves some scrutiny.

Significant new insights marked the turn of the century in America, and directly or indirectly they led to the creation of a new profession and a new field of study called "religious education." At the University of Chicago Dr. DeWitt Burton, Dr. Shailer Matthews, and president Rainey Harper were convinced that the perspective and methods of historical criticism were relevant for biblical interpretation, not only in the graduate schools, but in the Sunday Schools of the land. This called for a new breed of curriculum writers and teachers. At the same time, John Dewey was advocating the use of the scientific method in education. The new confidence in science brought new hope that "proven teaching methods" could be discovered that would guarantee the successful transmission of knowledge and the assurance of morality among the young. This called for experimentation. The liberalism of nineteenth-century theologians such as Ritschel, Rauschenbusch, and Schleiermacher was firmly planted in the mainline Protestant denominations. Its emphasis on growth and Christian living was compatible with new understandings in educational philosophy. Liberal theology, scientific method in education, and new methods of biblical interpretation seemed to be made for each other. Furthermore, the revival as a means of ingathering for churches was waning, and although somewhat reluctantly in many quarters, the clergy was willing to give "modern religious education" the opportunity to show what it could accomplish.

THEOLOGICAL CONFLICT: THE OLD VERSUS THE NEW

The Sunday School as a movement had achieved great organizational advances during the nineteenth century. Thousands of people attended national and international Sunday School conventions. Teacher training institutes were established for Sunday School teachers. A system of International Uniform Sunday School Lessons was created.

Although they embraced new structural and organizational concepts for religious education, many educators were reluctant to accept the liberal theological stances, with its reliance on new methods of biblical interpretation. Rather, they held fast to their conviction that the aim of religious education was conversion, and that the primary means for bringing about conversion was an urgency on the part of committed Christians as they told the story of salvation.

Henrietta Mears (1890–1963) was one such person. As a director of Christian education for thirty-three years, she emphasized the importance of using the most progressive educational methodology. On the other hand, her belief in the inerrancy of the Scriptures did not require the use of the newest critical insights of modern biblical scholarship. For her the Bible was the authoritative revelation of God, just as it was written. The knowledge it contained was important, but only to the degree that its acquisition would lead to personal salvation. Henrietta Mears never sought ordination, but in her years as director of Christian education, she had a special interest in the training of young men who themselves were aiming for ordination. Young women who showed special promise were expected to prepare to become ministers' wives. Only one or two women followed in her footsteps to do the work of Christian education (Documents 1, 2).

Many men and women who chose the profession of director of religious education (or director of Christian education) espoused a liberal theology and followed the historical-critical hermeneutic of the University of Chicago group. The Religious Education Association, organized in 1903, and of which John Dewey was a charter member, became a theologically liberal home for most religious educators in the so-called main-line denominations.

Sophia Lyon Fahs was as liberal as Henrietta Mears was conservative. As writer, editor, and teacher she was influenced by the educational philosophy of John Dewey. Subject matter was not as important to her as the goal that children never cease to learn. Whatever the content, it must be appropriate for the child's level of development. Especially must the Bible not be taught until children can understand the historical setting in which it is placed. Furthermore, the goal of Bible teaching was not personal salvation. The growing person's own life experience was to be the basis for religious faith. Part of that life experience would be exposure to religious literature and thought of all of the religions of the world including, of course, the primary literature of the Christian religion, the Bible (Document 3).

Her understanding of the Bible is in striking contrast to the inerrancy view held by Henrietta Mears.

> In order to understand the ... Bible realistically, one must accept it as a collection of books all of whose authors were human like the rest of us, and wrote of things as they saw them. Biblical scholars recognize frankly that the sixty-six books of which the Bible is composed do not express a consistent point of view regarding either God or man. They realize also that ancient historical records, such as these, usually contain inaccuracies; that myth, legend, and historical fact are often presented without any distinction made between them. Scholars also point out that the entire collection is mainly about one ancient people and their great leaders and prophets, and that not infrequently the writers show a biased attitude toward other nations.[1]

In 1959, when she was eighty-two years old, Sophia Fahs accepted ordination in the Unitarian Church. In her ordination sermon she took occasion to support the ordination of women, and to urge that seminaries employ women for their faculties (Document 4).

LOCAL CHURCH DIRECTORS OF RELIGIOUS EDUCATION

In its earliest days the profession of director of religious education (DRE) attracted both laymen and laywomen, as well as some ordained men who found a special ministry in the work of religious education (Document 5). In 1929 there were an almost equal number of men and women in this field (Document 6). However, due to the effects of the depression, by 1938 only 26 percent of the directors were men. Women were willing to work for less money, and thus began the myth that it was inherently a women's profession (Document 7). It is interesting to note that even when 75 percent of the DREs were women, most pastors reported their preference for a man in this position. Following the Second World War, men began to return to the profession.

One of the major tasks of the DRE has always been to improve the quality of religious instruction that takes place within the local church. Sometimes this has meant writing curriculum resources; always it has meant planning and implementing leadership training events for volunteer teachers. It included devising and carrying forth a plan for selecting and recruiting leaders, and ideally provided for classroom observation and supervision by the DRE.

The other major task of the DRE was to coordinate all of the educational aspects of the church's total program. This included organizing the Sunday school, planning for church-home cooperation, working with community agencies involved in character building activities, participating in ecumenical events, and working with all church groups that had programs for children or youth (e.g., women's societies, choirs, Boy Scouts and Girl Scouts).

The profession was of such a nature, however, that individual directors were able to personalize it to fit their own interests and abilities, as well as to meet the needs of the local congregation. For example, Sophia Fahs limited her work in the local church to children, while Henrietta Mears specialized in work with college young people, even while maintaining direction of the entire religious education program. Most religious educators, in spite of their personal interests, found that they were called upon to be generalists, sometimes specializing in one age group, and sometimes in another.

BEYOND-THE-LOCAL-CHURCH EXECUTIVES AND STAFF

Many denominations created large national staffs whose task was to develop education programs for the denomination. The degree of direct involvement by national staffs in the work of the local congregation varied according to the denomination and to the decade. Although not always the case, it was the usual custom for such positions to be filled by people who had first had experience in the local church. Local church DREs who were upwardly mobile might, therefore, aspire to such a job. In addition to national staffs there also existed in most denominations regional administrative structures, which employed staffs of their own and served as counterparts to the national staff and liasons with the national denomination and the local church. Mary Louise Woodson Crane (1899–1982) is typical of such educators (Document 8). Furthermore, beyond the denominational lines were interdenominational networks; for example, the International Council of Religious Education and later, the National Council of Churches. Women with expertise in children's work found most ready acceptance for these national level positions. Men filled most of the positions in youth work, adult work, and as general executives. In addition to extensive travel, speaking engagements, and leadership of workshops and other training events, many of these women were writers of children's books or books for teachers, and many of them were editors of curriculum resources.

Mary Alice Jones (1898–1980) was an example of one who combined staff work with writing. She began her career as a regional director of children's work for her denomination, and subsequently moved to a staff position with the International Council of Religious Education; later she became children's book editor for Rand McNally & Company, and finally returned to her own denomination as director of children's work for the Division of Local Church of the Board of Education (Document 9).

Typical of many national staff positions, her job was described in this way:

[She will be] responsible for the general supervision of the Christian education of children in the Methodist Church, comprising 105 annual conferences in every part of the nation, in most of which there is a conference director of children's work. The broad program of Christian education of children includes such phases of work as the Sunday School, missionary education groups, vacation church schools, weekday religious education, kindergarten, work with nursery children, laboratory schools for the training of children's workers.[2]

The first black woman to receive a doctor's degree in religious education was Olivia Pearl Stokes (1916–). Soon after receiving her Ed.D. from the joint graduate program at Union Theological Seminary and Teacher's College, Columbia, in 1952, she became the director of the department of religious education for the Massachusetts Council of Churches, where she remained until 1966. She then joined the staff of the National Council of Churches, where she was associate in educational development, with special assignment as "urban consultant." In addition to her national staff positions she has published, and at this writing is serving as adjunct professor of religious education of New York University. She has referred to herself as an "ecumaniac," taking the best liberal insights from all of the major denominations.

Another "first" was Emily V. Gibbes (1915–), the first black woman to serve as a field director of religious education for the Presbyterian Church. She began this work in New York in 1949, and later became an associate general secretary for the National Council of Churches, with special responsibility for leadership in the division of education and ministry. Typical of other religious educators before and since, she found opportunity to work in a variety of arenas. In addition to her national denominational and ecumenical staff work, she has also been sought as an educational consultant for churches in Africa, and in her retirement teaches at New York Theological Seminary.

CURRICULUM WRITERS, EDITORS, PUBLISHERS

Much like denominational executives and staff, women found a place in religious education journalism, especially when writing for or about children. One fertile field for women writers has been in the area of curriculum resources, where they have served as both writers and editors. It was the work of a late-nineteenth-century woman, Mrs. J. Woodbridge Barnes, that inspired the rapid development of curriculum resources in the twentieth century and the subsequent need for writers and editors (Document 10).

Henrietta Mears saw as one of her major responsibilities as DRE the writing and eventual publishing of curriculum resources. Beginning as a local church need, the work has grown to become known as the Gospel Light Curriculum.

Sophia Fahs may be best known as editor for the progressive Beacon Series of resources for the Unitarian-Universalist Church. In this capacity she also became well-known as a writer of books for children.

In addition to her work as a national denominational staff worker, Mary Alice Jones is best known for her children's books. When asked by Rand McNally to publish in hardback the series that was to become her best known, the "Tell Me . . ." series, she struck a bargain. She would agree to these "expensive editions"—$3.95 each—if at the same time the publisher would agree to make some of her small, inexpensive books available for sale in supermarkets for nineteen cents. She insisted that parents who would not spend dollars, but who felt they should do something about the religious training of children, would drop one of the smaller books into the grocery cart along with the peas and corn. And this they did, causing her books to sell well over twenty million copies.

PROFESSORS OF RELIGIOUS EDUCATION

The emerging profession of DRE created a need for academic training in psychology, Bible, and education, with special emphasis on the implications of these disciplines for local church practice. In 1907, the call went out for people serving such a function to make themselves known to the Religious Education Association. The first meeting of these specialists in religious education was held in 1910. In April of that year, B. S. Winchester wrote: "It may be expected that the colleges, the theological seminaries, and the universities will soon perceive their opportunity and will prepare for it by founding and strengthening departments of biblical literature, comparative religion, pedagogy and kindred subjects. . . .[3]

In 1911, the Boston School of Theology at Boston University established a chair of religious education. In 1919, Adelaide Teague Case (1887–1948) became an instructor in the religious education department of Columbia University's Teachers College. She earned the rank of professor in 1935 and became head of the department. Later, she taught at the Episcopal Theological School in Cambridge, Massachusetts, where she remained until her death.

In 1926, Edna Baxter (1890–1985) began a long teaching career at

Hartford Theological Seminary Foundation. She was the first woman at Hartford to achieve the rank of a professor, and the first to head the department of church education. She retired in 1960 after teaching thirty-five years. In 1984, at the age of ninety-four, she published her autobiography (Document 11).

In 1927 Sophia Fahs and one other woman became the first two women on the faculty at Union Theological Seminary. Fahs remained in this position for eighteen years, until 1944.

It was reported that Henrietta Mears was sought by Fuller Theological Seminary to teach in that department of religious education. She declined this invitation, wishing to remain with her work in the local church.

Other early women professors included Hulda Niebhur, Iris Cully, and Clarice Bowman. It is important to note that a profession that was to become known as a "woman's profession" at the local church level was almost exclusively male at the graduate school level. In fairness, it must be added that religious education departments were usually the first to employ women, probably because women seminarians, unable to anticipate ordination, were traditionally expected to enroll in the religious education department.

SUMMARY

Religious education in the twentieth century has been noticeably enriched by a select group of women who have served on college and graduate school faculties, and by those who have achieved recognition because of national exposure—those on denominational and interdenominational staffs, and those who have published. Less noticeable are those thousands who have directed religious education programs at the local church level. Those whose expertise is most readily accepted have been the ones who have specialized in work with children, although at the local church level DREs are typically expected to possess skill in working with all ages, as well as special abilities in administration.

The future of women in religious education is uncertain. Now, as more and more women feel acceptance by the Church and seek ordination, fewer women see religious education as the only viable option. Although there are more women in seminaries now than at any other time in history, fewer women are enrolled in the departments of religious education. Many who choose religious education as a specialty do it within the context of ordination, indicating that there will be an increasing number of people holding the title of Minister of Christian Education. As the size of denominational staffs and graduate school faculties is reduced, there will be fewer opportunities for the upwardly mobile local church directors.

This chapter has documented and described the work of some of the outstanding women who have made contributions to the field of religious education. This is recognition they richly deserve. But in addition to these whose names we record are the countless thousands who have worked on local church staffs, always in a subordinate position as compared with the pastor. These are the ones who receive the curriculum resources and read the theory books written by others, who finally are called upon to implement the denominational programs created by others, and who are asked to do this with excellence in the real world of limited financial resources and fewer and fewer volunteers.

Edna Baxter, in garb of the Methodist Episcopal deaconess, April 25,
1917, head of the department of
Christian education at Hartford
Seminary and first woman to achieve
the rank of professor in a U.S. Seminary. [Photo courtesy of Edna Baxter.]

Mary Alice Jones, leading editor of
children's religious curriculum for
the International Council of Religious Education. She is showing curriculum materials to children, circa
1940. [Photo courtesy of United
Methodist Information Service,
Nashville, Tennessee.]

Sophia Fahs, leading religious educator of the Unitarian Church, of
worldwide reputation as a writer, editor, and teacher. [Photo taken on
Mother's Day, 1963, by Editta Sher-
man; courtesy of Dorothy Beck, New
York City.]

Henrietta Mears with her long-time assistant, Ethel May Baldwin, at the First Presbyterian Church, Hollywood. [Photo courtesy of Gospel Light Publications, Ventura, California.]

Henrietta Mears, director of Christian Education at First Presbyterian Church, Hollywood, California, 1928–1963, and founder of the Gospel Light curriculum publications, pictured here with Donn Moomaw and Billy Graham. [Photo courtesy of Gospel Light Publications, Ventura, California.]

Documents: Women in Religious Education: Pioneers for Women in Professional Ministry

---

THEOLOGICAL CONFLICT: THE OLD VERSUS THE NEW

Document 1: The "Old": Henrietta Mears

Henrietta Mears (1890–1963) was director of Christian education at First Presbyterian Church in Hollywood, California, from 1928 until her death in 1963. One of the giants of the field, she represented those who combined the "old" evangelical approach to theology and biblical interpretation with the "new" methodologies of twentieth-century education. One of the achievements for which she is best known is as founder of Gospel Light curriculum publications.[4]

In Minnesota she had been a successful teacher, but as Director of Christian Education in Hollywood, Miss Mears would have to organize and train others to teach. With reliance on God and allegiance to his Word, she mapped out the course she was to take. What she often said to her fellow teachers thoroughly characterized her own ministry:

Two things Joshua had to do to qualify him for his great work: To be strong and of good courage, and to make the Book of the Law his continued study. God's Word must be our only infallible guide. In keeping it there is great reward. To reject his Word is to be rejected.

Miss Mears insisted that Christian education must be Christian. Every lesson, each meeting must honor [Christ]. And this implied—what she never doubted—that the Christian teacher must be faithful to the Bible. "Christian education recognizes the inspired Word of God," she would say, "not only as its text and the sum of its message, but also as the source of the principles by which successful Christian education may be carried on." And throughout the ensuing years of her career, no one ever thought of Henrietta Mears as being anything but absolutely loyal to the Bible as the authoritative revelation of God. . . .

One day Miss Mears picked up a student's manual in the primary department and read the lesson title: "Amos Denounces Self-Indulgence." "What!" she thought. "How can any child grasp that?" Other lessons showed her how irrelevant this Primary Sunday School material was to the six-seven and eight-year-olds. Then the shocking news came to her ears that the lesson material being used in the junior department was to be discontinued. Moving immediately to find out what could be done, she questioned the possibility of purchasing the type so that a printer could print books for their own use, but the lead had been scrapped. The last resort was to purchase as many lesson manuals as possible, and this resulted in knowing that at the end of three years it would be necessary to find other lesson material for the juniors. The time had come. Miss Mears could delay the decision no longer.

Never one to dally, she immediately asked Dr. MacLennan [the minister], "Do you mind what materials we use in our Sunday School?" "Use anything you want as long as it teaches the Bible," was his reply. . . .

Motivat[ed] by the impression that the Bible was the most poorly taught book in the world, she faced the task before her. . . . Miss Mears and her educators worked out a prospectus, determining the accomplishments expected at each age level. The die was cast and the writing begun. There was absolutely no thought of ever printing and selling the lessons. Miss Mears just saw a need in her own Sunday School and answered it to the best of her ability. To keep ahead of the week-by-week demand for lesson materials for a Sunday School that was growing out of all bounds of anyone's experience or the realm of reason was a full time job in itself. But the administrative tasks also remained constant in their demands, to say nothing of speaking and teaching responsibilities, which consumed hours and hours of preparation. True, it was not humanly possible, but God intervened and was lavish with His might and power and strength. This can be the only answer!

Document 2: A View of Scripture: Henrietta Mears

Another of Miss Mears's biographers tells of her view of the Bible[5]*:*

Miss Mears has never felt it safe to take anything out of the Word of God, for two reasons. There is always something, literally and figuratively, on both sides of the page, in the Bible. Cut something out on one page of the Bible and there will be something on the other side that you will lose, too. . . . You must believe all Scripture with the same faith or you will have as many different versions of the Bible as the Bible has readers. . . .

Miss Mears' second reason for feeling it is dangerous to remove things from the Bible is that many people begin to take things out of their Bibles because they seem incompatible with certain current beliefs. Then, as science makes new discoveries, and new scrolls are unearthed, and history substantiates the very things that have been taken out of the Bibles, there is a mad scramble to get them back in again!

"But I'm very calm when all this scrambling takes place," smiles Teacher, "because I never took them out in the first place."

Document 3: The "New": Sophia Lyon Fahs

Sophia Fahs (1877–1978), one of the women giants in religious education in the twentieth century, was the representative par excellence of the "new" approach to theology and biblical interpretation. Although raised as a daughter of Methodist missionaries, her position eventually took her to leadership in the religious education program

of the Unitarian Church, and it was there that she gained her world-
wide reputation as writer, editor, and teacher. Edith Hunter, her
biographer, writes about her early school years, her desire for a
career, her decision to attend theological seminary, and her philos-
ophy of religious education, which would be reflected later in the
Beacon Series of curriculum resources she would edit.[6]

In June 1893, she was valedictorian of her class in the Wooster
High School. In connection with her valedictory speech there was a
bit of controversy. The principal had told the girls who were to have
a part in the graduation exercises that they would be expected to read
their essays while the boys could give theirs as orations. Sophie, convinced that girls were just as capable as boys, was sure that a girl's
memory was just as good as a boy's. She rebelled at the ruling and the
principal finally yielded, saying that Sophie might give her address
without a manuscript, but that he would hold it and prompt her if
necessary. The necessity did not arise.

Sophie wrote her fiancée of her desire for further study, not
simply to satisfy her own eager mind, but to equip herself as a missionary and a missionary wife. She was aware of the problem which is
supposed to be unique to women of the second half of the twentieth
century but which actually has faced some women in every period of
history; that is the conflict between the home and a career. Her words
have a very familiar ring. "I am too ambitious to serve the women of
some heathen land to be the nonentity for the direct work of foreign
missions that some wives seem to be. I am too ambitious to give my
life in direct foreign missionary work to give twenty years of the
strength of my life in service at home as my mother has done. Such
lives count a great deal, but I long for the other." . . .

In a letter to her parents, Fall 1923:

"Now prepare for a shock when I tell you what I am doing this
winter. The decision was made only a few days before I acted on it.
I am registered at Union Theological Seminary as a candidate for the
Bachelor of Divinity degree—a three year course—and have begun
work as a regular student, being a classmate of my nephew, Scovil . . .

"My purpose in doing this is to get a thorough going training for
work in religious education. If I work as a director, I need to have the
advantage of an equal standing with the pastor in the church. If I
should take a little community church someday myself, then I could
organize the church on a democratic basis and we could together work
out an entirely new program of church activities in which preaching
would be merely an occasional feature of the program. At any rate,
I am starting out on the adventure at the age of forty-seven." . . .

For thirty-three years then in her writing she had been wrestling
with the problems related to the two questions: What to teach in
religious education and how to teach it. By 1937 she was more than

ready to help develop new materials needed to implement a new philosophy of religious education. . . .

Asked to list and discuss what [the liberal religious educators] would insist upon in the religious education of their children, Mrs. Fahs cited four items; the first was an awareness on the part of the teacher that no *particular* subject matter was essential. She did not mean that there was no subject matter, no content in religious education, but that in religious education "there are many gateways . . . More important than *what* children learn is . . . how they learn it." Second, . . . "I object to giving stories from the Bible until children are old enough to have achieved sufficient appreciation of the long ago to place the characters portrayed . . . in their historical settings. I object to having little children told Bible stories simply because they prove interesting or mystifying or have a sweet moral influence." . . . Her third point was that the children should have the opportunity all through the religious education process to build their faith on their own experience . . .

And finally, she asked that whatever is taught not be limited to one religious heritage . . . If only one heritage is presented, richness and diversity of viewpoint is lost, and it is all too easy to identify partial insight with "the truth." . . . "I believe that the coming generation should build a nobler religion than has as yet been embodied in any tradition . . . A liberal's child should come to realize that finding God is his own job and not one which he may relinquish to any adult or to any traditional revelation."

For twenty-seven years between 1937 and 1964 Sophia Fahs worked with the Unitarian denomination to produce the religious education materials that might help the next generation of liberal children in the building of that nobler religion.

Document 4: Sophia Fahs Preaches Own Ordination Sermon

Against all custom, Mrs. Fahs was given the opportunity to preach her own ordination sermon. At age eighty-two, at the Montgomery County Unitarian Church in Bethesda, Maryland, on February 9, 1959, Mrs. Fahs spoke of the place of women in the general ministry of the Church, and of her continued concern for curriculum development.[7]

It is because as a church you have discovered that all ministers are educators, and all religious educators are preachers and priests in a broad sense, that you have ordained me to "the ministry" in general. Through this ceremony you are inviting me into full fellowship with them all. This is a truly cherished honor.

. . . I wish to express my satisfaction over the fact that this public ceremony was not intended primarily for the purpose of promoting the cause of women in the general ministry. Yet the thought has inevitably been in all your minds. The ordination of a woman to the ministry in any Protestant church in America is still a rare occurrence. And in our American Unitarian Association, it has been outstandingly rare. Of the 539 ministers listed in the latest Unitarian Year Book, there are but six women, and of these six one only is now active. The other five have all retired.

The resistance to women as pulpit ministers and as heads of churches is still strong, and perhaps for some good reasons. Yet in these modern times, when women are successfully entering a number of professions that have long been filled predominantly by men, it would seem that the latent possibilities in our American womanhood for church leadership might well be more adequately tested. Some of our theological seminaries in the liberal fellowship are now advertising that they seek both men and women students. Yet the number who take the full three year course is exceedingly small. At present, I understand, there are only two women enrolled for the B.D. degree in all our five theologically liberal seminaries. There are doubtless a number of complex reasons for this small registration of women. Two at least are quite apparent. The churches do not expect women to take any special work in religion in order to direct the education of the children. And second, the two oldest and best known of our presumably liberal theological seminaries do not even have one professor on their own faculties who offers courses in religious education. . . .

Even though I am glad that the feminist element in this ordination has not been primary, yet I find an exhilaration tonight in being a woman, and in being able therefore to act as a kind of representative of all the other women who are now ministering faithfully week by week in our liberal churches.

The curriculum materials we are using in our liberal church, and the processes of learning on the part of the children that we advocate are different from those expressed in any other denomination series that I know of. It is of equal importance to note that our goals also are different. We are not trying to persuade children to accept a salvation we ourselves are assured is needed and available. We are not even trying to condition them toward a love for Jesus or the church. What they may become eventually—whether Christian or Unitarian or Universalist—is not our concern during these early years at least. Our immediate hope is to sensitize them to the opportunities their present experiences afford them for their own nurture, and to encourage them and suggest to them how they can gather up out of their own direct relations with the universe, their own lessons and patterns for living. . . .

All this does not mean, of course, that the study of Biblical or other history is neglected in our religious education. The truth is that in our philosophy more, rather than less, historical knowledge is called for than is demanded when the goals are more narrowly determined. Simply stated in our philosophy, all books, all knowledge, all story materials become but records of the actual experiences, the acts and thoughts and feeling of other persons. We distinguish between the bible as presenting the great Christian Epic of salvation—a unified body of beliefs to be accepted as a divine revelation—and the Bible as a collection of ancient records of the history of the Hebrew people, together with their myths, legends, poetry and sermons. To revamp these supernaturally interpreted events in order to ferret out the actual historical experiences behind them requires the most thorough Biblical criticism and scholarship. It calls for the honest best from our Biblical professors, and that expressed in clear and simple language.

LOCAL CHURCH DIRECTORS OF RELIGIOUS EDUCATION

Document 5: A Profession for Both Men and Women

The beginnings of the profession of director of religious education date to the first decade of this century. Initiated by the Religious Education Association, the records of that group document both the early presence of women in the profession, and the fact that from the very beginning it was seen to be a profession that might expect both men and women members.[8]

This is the first meeting of those men and women who are employed in churches and other institutions as "Directors of Religious Education," or in any like capacity engaged in supervision of such work. The Problems of Co-ordinating the Educational Activities of a Church; The Creation of Curriculum Material; The Functions of a Director of Religious Education, and other topics of special interest of employed Superintendents, to leaders in the educational work of the church, will be discussed. . . .

. . . Does this not point toward a new profession for which there will be a great demand in the near future, the expert in religious education? Here is a large and varied field, offering to the young men or women great usefulness and influence. It may be expected that the colleges, the theological seminaries, and the universities will soon perceive their opportunity and will prepare for it by founding and strengthening departments of biblical literature, comparative religion, pedagogy and kindred subjects; by establishing experimental Sunday Schools; and by themselves conducting winter institutes, correspondence courses, and summer schools for the better training of Sunday-School teachers and the discussion with the churches of their common problem of religious and moral education. Perhaps in this way the standards of Sunday-School instruction may be raised and established.

Document 6: The Constituency of the Profession

No record has been discovered citing the names of those who attended the first meeting of directors of religious education in 1910, but a review of the members of the Religious Education Association (REA) in 1910 does not indicate that there were any women among its membership who considered themselves to be religious education professionals. By 1912, however, the presence of women was evident. In 1917, a woman was secretary of the group, and by 1920, a woman was "chairman." [9]

While at St. Louis, in connection with the R.E.A., a meeting was called and was opened at 9:30 in the Y.M.C.A. building by Chairman Boocock, Barkley, Hubble, Young, Davies, Miss Chamberlin, Evans, and Erb. The chairman then read the suggestive *[sic]* topics which had been sent in by different directors. The first subject called for was "The Position of the Director of Religious Education in the Church." It was then suggested that different men [sic] give a review of the work of the year. . . . Miss Chamberlin reported on the work in the Hyde Park Baptist Church . . .

Active members in the association must have a college degree or its equivalent, and in addition either a full three years' theological course including courses in religious education, or two years of study in an approved school of religious pedagogy. Those without the college degree are eligible to associate membership. In any case members are salaried workers either in churches or in denominational positions on a full-time basis. . . .

J. W. F. Davies, President
Mary Lawrence, Secretary, 25 Beacon St. Boston
Herbert W. Gates, Chairman Program Committee . . .

[26 members are listed, 4 of whom are women]:

Miss Georgia L. Chamberlin, American Institute of Sacred Literature, Chicago, Ill.
Mrs. Henry W. Hunter, Congregational Training School for Women, Chicago, Ill.
Miss J. Gertrude Hutton, Hillside Presbyterian Church, East Orange, N.J.
Miss Mary Lawrence, Formerly, First Congregational (Unitarian) Church, Providence, R.I.

One of the departments of the Religious Education Association is maintained for and by those persons whose vocation is that of religious education. A majority of the members are directors of religious education in churches though many are associated with community enterprises and educational institutions. The officers of this department are:

> Chairman, Mrs. Henry W. Hunter, Oak Park, Ill.
> Vice Chairman, Rev. Fred L. Brownlee, Cleveland, Ohio
> Secretary-Treasurer, Miss Mary Lawrence, Montclair, N.J.

The January, 1920, membership is as follows: *[There follows 131 names, of whom 31 are women.]*

Document 7: The Work of the Profession: Elizabeth Miller

The profession of director of religious education (DRE) was a new one in this century. In the midst of industrialization and a technological revolution, the director was in every sense a pioneer, exploring an unmapped terrain. Some of the rigors of that adventure included charting the course of a task that was little understood by both laypeople and clergy; working long hours with little pay; maintaining high standards even when economic depression forced the DRE to become a church secretary in addition to educational responsibilities; and discovering, living with, and sometimes solving the problems of team ministry with male, ordained clergy. In February 1968, Elizabeth Miller wrote of her early years as a director of religious education[10]:

Dear Dorothy:

When I went to Boston University School of Religious Education in 1923–25 Religious Education was becoming very popular. In fact it was so popular that there were many more openings for D.R.E.'s than persons. Churches in many cases didn't know what a D.R.E. was for when employed. I had the advantage over some of the post graduate students from my public school experience as a teacher and supervisor in the elementary grades. Some without experience went out into churches and tried to do all the things they learned in the classroom in a year when it would take four or five. I knew one had to build up confidence before completely reorganizing the entire church school.

I had splendid cooperation in my first position as D.R.E. in Riverside, California. However, there were financial difficulties about raising the budget so they let me go after 2 years and got a young seminary student (green!) to do part time. I had made very careful records of my two years and in commuting he lost all the records within a few weeks, so I was told. The Associate pastor at the First Methodist Church (also from B.U.) and I worked together along with the Presbyterian minister in getting some Leadership training classes started. I did only my own secretarial work which included getting the

Sunday Church bulletin ready for the printer. I did calling connected with my educational program.

My next home was St. Paul, Mininesota where I spent ten very happy years. The Ramsey Co. Council of R.E. was one of the livest centers of R.E. I have ever known which meant the selling job was done and the people were quite well educated as to the requirements for a good program. A D.R.E. got so involved with the whole city program that she had to protect her local church program. Every church I have served has had first and foremost in mind a good and big youth program. My first love was children's division so I worked on that very hard along with building a youth program. At that time there was not so much stress on Young Adults.

My years in St. Paul (1927–1937) were during the depression period. These years meant salary cuts when salaries were small to begin with. Our part time secretary was discontinued which meant I got out a weekly mimeographed church bulletin. It took me HOURS to put out a NOT TOO GOOD bulletin. Finally, I went to the powers that be and said, "You better let me go; you are paying me to do work which I am not fitted to do and the work for which I am here is being neglected." They got a part time secretary at once. I have never been asked to have any part in the financial end.

During the war years (1940–47) I was in a large downtown church in Seattle. Much time was given to the transient youth; military, navy [sic] and the hundreds who came to work in the shipyards and Boeings [sic] Aircraft. We served them well and we were benefitted as much as they. We got wonderful leadership especially from the young men who worked at Boeings [sic]. In spite of the long hours and hard work those were rewarding years.

My last work, or you might say my swan song, was strenuous but I had a chance to do what I had dreamed of. I had worked with the minister a short time in Duluth and seven years in Seattle, and now in Des Moines, Iowa. The church needed everything and was in debt. At once the minister appointed a marvelous building committee with several members from the Drake University faculty. For three years we worked diligently on plans for remodeling the sanctuary and building a new educational building. This was completed and furnished before I retired in 1957; a three story building for the Children's Division. We had five marvelous choirs with choir directors who appreciated the entire church school program.

I must say how very important I think staff meetings are . . .

With love and happy memories,
Elizabeth

BEYOND-THE-LOCAL-CHURCH EXECUTIVES AND STAFF

Document 8: The Work of the Profession: Mary Louise Woodson Crane (1899–1982)

This is an article about one director of Christian education who was much more than that; but it is also about scores of other courageous women who worked for little monetary compensation because they believed in the work they were called to do. This document tells about one director, but the last three paragraphs speak eloquently of hundreds of other unnamed women.[11]

When Mary Louise Woodson Crane died at the age of 83 on 3 July 1982, at Westminster-Canterbury House in Richmond, Va., her home for her last years, she was far from those scenes of her early life which seem to have shaped her remarkably useful career. . . .

Pacesetter

While Texas was setting the pace for the rest of the church, the program in Central Texas Presbytery set the pace for the rest of Texas. From 1927 to 1937, Mary Louise worked like a beaver. Her annual reports show how the job is done, when it is done: year after year, over and over, endless meetings with teachers of children and youth; miles of travel to committee meetings and conferences; detailed and personal attention to small (and larger) churches and their teaching programs, leadership schools . . . conferences with pastors; training for Vacation Church School workers; youth retreats and summer conferences; reports to presbytery, getting folks to . . . the conference center . . . year-in, year-out; meeting the oncoming tide of each generation for training in discipleship. Her report for a typical year showed an average monthly travel mileage of 840.

She started in 1927 with a promise of $125 a month and expenses. By 1933, the record showed a hope (not a promise) of $1310 [a year] and $300 for expenses "provided this can be raised." They did a little better; $1,419 and $275 for expenses. In Central Texas she got the experience which enabled her to do what she did so well.

The Crucible

From 1937 to 1944 she was director of youth and student work for the Synod of North Carolina, and streams of solid and substantial members of the church today recall with deep affection what came to them from those days . . .

She joined the Queens College faculty in 1944, where she directed a major citywide leadership training program. In 1947, when she married one of the church's ablest and best-known missionaries, Charles L. Crane, she went to the Belgian Congo (now Zaire) for nearly four years. In that situation all that she knew about recruiting, training and encouraging leaders could be used.

Back home—in Richmond—she and her husband were caught up in the significant movement that brought into being the pioneering, interracial All Souls Church. There, she continued to work as a member after her husband's death. The congregation found that it had for itself, and for free, one of the church's ablest and most experienced Christian educators. It was Mary Louise Woodson Crane as much as anybody who was responsible for the high level of this church's teaching program in its early years and the informed and willing dedication of its members to a quality enterprise.

She joined the Richmond staff of the Board of Christian Education for six years, with responsibility under two directors of leadership education and on her own twice between directors. Her final employment was as an associate in the office of the regional director of Christian education for Virginia, William B. Sullivan. Here came a repetition of the early days, with concern for children's work and leadership education cross the synod. "Lab Schools" were the feature of the day, with local teachers of small children brought into centers for a week where the ablest available people tried to show them how to do it. Mary Louise took these, like everything else she had a responsibility for, with absolute seriousness. It was important, the time and opportunity were limited and people needed to give themselves completely to the task at hand. One woman wanted to miss one day. Might she have permission? Not from Mary Louise, whose judgment was that the opportunity was short and if anybody had been sent from a church for this special and important task, then to miss one day out of five was unthinkable.

She was no seeker of personal recognition. She held on to the abiding values. Her last act was typical—the contribution of her body, which had been beset by disease and hospitalized for almost a year, to medical research. . . .

She is made the subject of this brief sketch not only because of what she was and contributed, but also because she was typical, extraordinarily typical, of countless others, similarly trained and motivated, who have given themselves without stint to the church's mission and program, establishing Sunday Schools and new churches, conducting training classes, guiding youth leaders and children's workers, on and on, year after year.

Why Did They Do It?

Over much of this time they did it with slight remuneration—sometimes disgracefully little. They did it because they were, themselves, committed Christians with a vision and understanding of selfless service. They did it for love of Christ and his Church.

Sometimes, they were taken for granted. They did not receive even the best that words can do, though they doubtless were thanked profusely and were deeply appreciated by individual pastors and others. (A standing vote of thanks by a presbytery at the end of 10 years of sacrificial, life-draining service is not much. Maybe some church governing bodies have better and more imaginative and lasting ways of doing this than others.) Some people can recognize that many of the best of these devoted servants have worked harder and more effectively, with more to show for it and with less remuneration than many, if not most, of the pastors.

However that may be, the DCEs, the employed trainers of teachers and workers with youth, the pioneering founders of Sunday schools and churches—the ones who do the really hard and basic work of the church, without which there would be precious few to hear our great and persuasive sermons—deserve our abiding thanks in every way that we can demonstrate it.

Document 9: A Representative: Mary Alice Jones (1898–1980)

Before assertiveness for women was acknowledged to be a virtue, Mary Alice Jones modeled it. With flashing brown eyes, Dr. Jones tackled inequities in salary scales; in the community she decried certain popular styles of child evangelism; and in the church she challenged the clergy to practice what they preached. At her memorial service it was stated that her uniqueness resided in the quality of her certainties. Some of these certainties were expressed by her at a retirement dinner honoring her in Dallas, Texas, on January 7, 1964[12]:

If we are to be used of God to communicate the Christian faith to children, we must develop a divine discontent with the tendency we seem to have glibly to verbalize our faith. Too often we substitute a formulation in words for an experience of meaning. We make beautiful words into a sort of boat which enables us to skim over the surface in comfort and to protect us from entering into the depths of meaning in our Christian faith.

... It is, I think, primarily because we—the theological and biblical scholars to whom [children] have the right to look for basic insights, and the pastors and parents and teachers who directly teach them—all of us do too much skimming along in our verbal boats. Thus we are unprepared to deal with the rising questionings that come from the depths of actual present life experience.

... The church has no choice other than to prepare herself for a much larger and much more effective approach to Christian nurture. The children are here. There is no question at this point. The only question is whether the church can move with the devotion, understanding, and discipline necessary and with the speed required to minister to them in accordance with their need, real and present, not our middle-aged brought-over-from-yesterday notions of what those needs should be.

But beyond the teaching, learning, nurturing experiences of the Christian community . . . lie the secular community, the nation, the world. Children of today cannot be protected from the world. They live in the world. Technology exposes them to it in detail. Christian nurture which attempts to segregate them from the total life of which they are a part cannot communicate the Gospel to them where they live.

The children of our own household of faith must be related to the total ministry of the church. There are, therefore, some inescapable burdens of shared suffering which our children must bear even while they are yet children if they are to experience the meaning of the Christian faith, not just say words about. It is of the essence of being human beings called to be sons of God in the midst of the present world. Christian nurture is not just for the exaltation of the good and the beautiful. It must also equip children to recognize and know how to deal creatively with the ugly, the disruptive in their own lives and in the lives of others and in the life of institutions and nations.

CURRICULUM WRITERS, EDITORS, PUBLISHERS

Document 10: The Struggle for Graded Lessons: Mrs. J. Woodbridge Barnes

Before the turn of the century Mrs. J. Woodbridge Barnes, along with other women active in Sunday school work, began to plead for the cause of graded curriculum materials, noting that children need different levels of content at each age. The struggle that began in 1896 finally culminated in graded lessons in 1909. The story of that effort is told by historian Arlo Ayres Brown. This letter to the International Lessons Committee is a model of both tact and persistence.[13]

At the New Jersey School of Methods for Sunday-School Workers held at Asbury Park, New Jersey in the summer of 1896, Mrs. J. Woodbridge Barnes proposed to her students the following question: "What do we wish our children to know about the Bible before they are twelve years of age?" Together they worked out on the blackboard an outline which became the basis of the Graded Supplemental Lessons of the Elementary Department of the Sunday School, and which were approved by the International Sunday-School convention of Denver in 1902. The success of these supplemental lessons proved to be a stimulus to creating a demand for international graded lessons because teachers soon began to ask, "Why can we not make this graded supplemental material (usually taught for ten minutes) the main lesson material?" . . .

The International Sunday-School Association at the International Convention in Louisville, Kentucky, June 18–23, 1908 voted to prepare a thoroughly graded course, following the work of Mrs. Barnes and her committee. . . .

March 27, 1907
TO THE INTERNATIONAL LESSON COMMITTEE:

Gentlemen:

As members of the Graded Lessons Conference, now in session, we desire that you may be fully advised of our plans, our work, and our relationship to the International Sunday-School Association; particularly as your cooperation is essential to the complete fulfillment of our purpose.

Our desire is to see the present beginners' course of two years suitably revised, and followed with a three years' primary course and a four years' junior course; the whole constituting nine years of graded-lesson material, to the completion of the average pupil's twelfth year. We desire to secure from the International Convention, as was done in the case of the Beginners' lessons, a vote of approval and reference of the matter to you, and either before or after such a vote, as you may deem wise, we desire you to consider the plan of lessons which we hope ere long to be able to submit, and issue them with your approval, with such modifications as to your wisdom may seem needful.

We are all of us strongly on the side of the International unity; we believe in our Sunday schools working together; we recognize the continued necessity for an Ungraded International Course; but we know that a proportion of schools far too large to be longer neglected demands graded material for regular lesson work. We feel that it is vital that this material should come to them from the International Lesson Committee, that it should be such as actual teachers of the classes, and grades concerned can use under present circumstances, that it should conform to truth in child study and represent the best available methods in teaching practice, and that its end and idea should be the salvation of the pupil and the upbuilding of his character.

In 1902 at Denver, as you recall, the conference of elementary grade teachers petitioned the Convention for a two-year Beginners' course to be issued by you. Similarly at Toronto in 1905, the representative elementary conference, heartily, and without one dissenting vote, expressed its appreciation of the Beginners' lessons and asked for a Primary Course as soon as the way opened to issue it. The matter again came up at the meeting of the Editorial Association in July, 1906, when our chairman by request of that Association presented a paper showing how not only a primary but also a junior graded course is absolutely essential to the present movement for adapted and effective work in the elementary division of the Sunday school.

We as a Conference, were called together by our Chairman, Mrs. J. W. Barnes, with the approval of the International Executive Committee, on the ground that the demand for graded lessons should be led and not merely yielded to by the International Association. The effort was made to secure as members all the lesson writers, State elementary leaders, and specialists in Sunday school pedagogy within practicable distance from Newark, the chairman's city. Several who were earnestly desired found it impossible to attend. The Conference first met in October 1906, and meetings have since been held about once a month, each meeting lasting two days. We have worked in two sections, primary and junior . . .

We have agreed upon the needs and interests of pupils in the grades concerned, and the corresponding truths to be embodied in the lessons selected. The choice and arrangement of these lessons is progressing as rapidly as is consistent with a close following of our ideal. We hope ere long to complete a working outline of at least the first year primary and the first year junior, and then to introduce the lessons thus outlined into a number of selected schools for experimental use, before agreeing on our final draft of the course, either in outline or detail.

We rejoice to observe the many other efforts now being made in this same direction, and believe that God's hand is clearly leading us to better and higher things. We believe, too, that when the right material has been found and arranged in the right order the reasons for it will appear. We respectfully ask your sympathy in our efforts and your cognizance of our existence and our purpose.

With great respect, we are yours,
The Graded Lessons Conference.
Mrs. J. W. Barnes, Chairman.

To which Dr. Schauffler sent the following reply:

New York, April 1, 1907.
My Dear Mrs. Barnes:

Yours of the 30th together with communication to the Lesson Committee of March 29th is at hand. It will be placed before the committee at our meeting in April in Boston, and I presume will also come up before the Joint Committee Meeting in London.

The program that you outline is somewhat surprising, for it involves practically a nine years' course of graded lesson material. I shall be exceedingly interested to see where your workers find material for a nine years' graded course that shall be in any true sense graded material. I cannot myself conceive where such material really graded can be found from Genesis to Revelation. However, it may be that the combined intelligence of skilled workers can produce such a course. The graded lessons that I have seen so far have been graded more in name than in fact as to material. Of course, the Lesson Committee will take no action in this matter until after the Louisville convention, for we are under instructions from the Denver Convention which we are bound to carry out without material deviation.

With very best wishes,
    Yours sincerely,
        A. F. Schauffler

PROFESSORS OF RELIGIOUS EDUCATION

Document 11: A Worldview: Edna Baxter (1890–1985)

Three convictions have characterized the life of Professor Edna Baxter: The scholarly study of religion, and especially the understanding of the Bible as history, is foundational for religious education; to teach, one must understand the culture from which the student comes; and, although she recognizes that as a woman she was a pioneer in all phases of academia, she wants it to be clearly understood that her motivation for her life has come from her dedication to God. The following excerpts—the first two from conversations and the third from her autobiography—illustrate these three convictions.[14]

In my church, the Methodist Episcopal, we had an order much like the Catholic Church called "deaconesses," and I decided to dedicate my life to God and the church. I went to Waverly, Pensylvania near my home to be dedicated by Bishop Berry at the meeting of the Wyoming Annual Conference. I took vows of celibacy. As a deaconess I wore a black costume with a little white hat and white linen ties.

They wanted to ordain me when I was out at Garrett teaching in the summer of 1957 . . . but I had already been consecrated by a bishop as a deaconess and my vows were much more severe than the ministers' vows. I didn't need any more. . . .

The president of Hartford found that missionaries were ignorant of world cultures, and he thought he would cure that by starting what became the Kennedy School of Missions. He brought world scholars from different continents. So through the ages I had these ministers, missionaries, and a wide variety of students in my classes; they came from all over the world. I immediately began to realize that these people must have education that suited their culture, not American culture; I began to travel in order to learn about world cultures. I didn't go on tours; I stayed with the people. I can think of a woman from India who came to me after she finished her education and before she went back to India. She said, "I can never thank you enough for what you've done for me. For the first time in my life I've learned to appreciate my own culture, and now I can go back and help my own people. . . . Travels helped me in my teaching more than I can tell you. I could enter into the lives of my students."

One of the things that disgusts me is giving little children Bible stories, hit and miss, random; they have no meaning because they have no history. I believe that young children in the early grades ought to start looking at the world they can see, and connect it with God . . . G-O-D . . . not Christ, not Holy Spirit, but God. Begin helping them to see the greater working of God who has order and system and values. You can't use any of these words with children, but you can help them see nature and think of God, and to use prayer as thanksgiving for beauty. . . .

Some have said, "What a pity you had no children." But I say, "I have hundreds all over the globe. They are my best friends, even to my great age." Their friendship is my compensation and reward. No money could buy this experience. . . .

I grew up when women were chiefly housewives and cared for their families. They could become servants, nurses, or elementary teachers. In some churches women entered orders. . . . Women had to do things largely in women's organizations.

I think I was not too self-conscious about being a woman. I was not aware of "equality." I did not strive to be a man. Yet, with dedication to God and His service, I was motivated to study, to become educated, and finally to become a professor of Christian Education. My dedication led me to do the impossible. Without my planning it, I taught hundreds of ministers and other men, as well as women. I was at times the only woman in some of my seminary classes. I think my progress was due to vision and great emphasis in my early life in my church on service to others, as well as consideration for people. As I studied about Jesus, I learned that his central message was a way of love. This affected my way of adjusting to my work in Seminary days when I came to work with an all-male faculty.

About this time four of us [who are residents of Avery Heights Retirement Center] had been placed on the Board of Directors. One day I met with the president. I told him my wish for more education

Winning Ordination for Women in Mainstream Protestant Churches

BARBARA BROWN ZIKMUND

From 1800 to 1860, American society was strongly influenced by a coalition of political and intellectual leaders rooted in (1) Congregational, Reformed, and Presbyterian traditions; (2) the legacy of Episcopalian and Lutheran state churches; and (3) indigenous evangelistic groups of Baptists, Disciples, and Methodists. This mix produced a so-called "evangelical consensus," which became known as "mainstream Protestantism." To be sure, "mainstream" sometimes stretched to include numerically marginal groups such as Quakers, Brethren, and Unitarians, but the common definition primarily included the above groups.

Mainstream Protestantism depends upon voluntarism. Local congregational life and denominational structures thrive on the volunteer energies of millions of church members. Through voluntary service these Christians launch missions, sustain local congregational life, and support clergy. For mainstream Protestant men and women, especially women, church work has great appeal. By the end of the nineteenth century, therefore, it was not surprising that women began to question some of the unexamined assumptions surrounding their membership and leadership in the churches. Women lacked equality of influence and opportunity. Eventually, this meant that women sought ordination.

Before examining the specific debates and arguments on ordination, it is important to note that the ordination of women is integrally connected to patterns of lay equality in the church. In most mainstream denominations no progress is made towards the recognition of women clergy until women gain significant power and influence as laity. The journey begins with basic citizenship rights in the local congregation. Are women allowed to speak up in church meetings? Do women have a vote? Eventually, the issue expands to deal with questions of lay leadership. Can women serve on the vestry, the session, the official board, the church council? Can women represent their church at regional, diocesan, or national meetings? Sometimes certain lay responsibilities call for "ordination" as deacon or ruling elder. Mainstream Protestant churches rarely take up the question of women's ordination (as clergy to preach and lead worship) until questions of lay leadership have been resolved.

Among Congregationalists, Baptists, and other denominations with congregational polity, most battles over lay citizenship were finished long before the twentieth century. If women served their churches as lay leaders, it was not difficult to support the idea of women as clergy. Most scholars believe that the first ordination of a woman in mainstream Protestantism was carried out by Congregationalists in 1853. The one exception in this pattern is the Disciples. They ordained a woman to preach long before there was general acceptance of female lay elders. This is because lay elders exercise important liturgical roles in the Christian Church (Disciples of Christ).

Denominations following presbyterial or episcopal polity went much slower. Some justification for women as ruling elders or members of the vestry was necessary before the question of women clergy became appropriate. Once that question was answered, however, the issue was more practical than theological. How could a married woman do it? What was the relationship of ordained ministry to mission and educational work? What if local churches did not want women pastors? Could anyone envision women bishops? Cautious church leaders did not want to take this step if it was impractical. In connectional churches, where clergy belong to a regional structure beyond their status in a local congregation, ordination was actually one step away from total equality. Methodist women could not rest until they had gained membership in annual conference.

Winning ordination in mainstream American white Protestantism, therefore, begins with basic lay suffrage in the local church and moves to full equality of opportunity for clergy throughout a denominational system. Many denominations with congregational polity progressed quickly through this cycle in the nineteenth century, even though legal equality did not always mean the end of injustice.[1] Methodists, Presbyterians, Lutherans, and Episcopalians started the cycle later. Therefore the struggle for women's ordination or equal clergy status in the twentieth century is most clearly documented by an examination of these four groups.[2]

METHODISTS

In the 1880s several women were elected to the General Conference of the Methodist Episcopal Church (ME), North, but the Conference refused to seat them. Four years later, female delegates appeared again; this time they were seated. Also in 1880, two women, Anna Howard Shaw and Anna Oliver (who already held licenses to preach), came before the General Conference seeking ordination. The Conference refused to act.[3] Furthermore, it rejected the unofficial practice of licensing women, declaring that "no member of the church shall preach without a license." Anna Howard Shaw left the Methodist Episcopalians to be ordained by the smaller and more progressive Methodist Protestant Church. Anna Oliver stayed to press her case, albeit unsuccessfully.[4] The Methodist Episcopal Church, South also refused to license or ordain women.

From 1880 to 1920 the status of women evangelists and leaders in the ME Church, North was ambiguous. However, in 1920 the General Conference received a memorial from the Kansas conference supporting the licensing and ordination of women. The Conference voted to license women, but referred the question of ordination to a Commission for study. In 1924 Commission recommended that women be ordained as local preachers, but not admitted to membership in the annual conferences (Document 1).[5] Without conference membership, ordained women could only serve those churches left open after every male member had received his appointment. During the debate efforts were made to remove the word "local" from the recommendation, thereby giving women full status and equality as clergy. According to Madeline Southard, a licensed preacher and founder of a new ecumenical association for women preachers, the debate never dealt with ordination, but concerned itself with the practical ramifications of "conference membership."[6]

At approximately the same time, the ME Church, South granted lay rights to women. This denomination never did license or ordain women until forced to do so by the reunion of Methodism in 1939.

Every four years, from 1924 to 1956, the General Conference of the Methodist Episcopal Church, North, and later, the reunited Methodist Church considered the question of full ecclesiastical standing for female ordained Methodist preachers. When the Methodist Church came into being in 1939, the three uniting churches struck a compromise on women's status: southern ME churches were forced to accept women as local preachers; northern ME churches retained ordination without conference membership; and Methodist Protestants, who ordained women and gave them conference membership, were given assurances that already ordained women would not lose their conference membership even though full status would no longer be available to women. It was a close vote, with only seven votes preventing the new Methodist Church from granting full ecclesiastical equality to women (Document 2).[7]

Finally, in 1956, prodded by two thousand memorials on the issue, the General Conference acted. The badly divided Committee recommended that women be admitted to conferences, but that that "only unmarried women and widows may apply"; thereby they avoided the problem of appointments for married women. A strong minority report argued for no change at all. An amendment tried to reserve the decision to each annual conference. The debate was practical and administrative, not theological. In the end the General Conference acted decisively, rejecting the qualified recommendation of the Committee and voting full access to the "travelling ministry" (and conference membership) to all ordained Methodist women (Document 3).[8]

In 1968, the Methodist Church merged with the Evangelical United Brethren (EUB) Church. The EUB Church was itself a 1947 merger of two German Methodist bodies. One side of that union, the Church of the United Brethren in Christ, went back to eighteenth century.[9] Beginning in 1841, it appears that the United Brethren licensed many women to preach at the local level. By 1889, the General Conference officially endorsed granting a license to a woman, "provided she complies with the usual conditions required of men."[10] That same year a woman was ordained by the Central Illinois Conference.

The Evangelical Church and its predecessor bodies, however, never ordained women. During conversations leading up to the EUB union, "women's ordination" was rarely discussed. Yet in 1947, when the newly constituted EUB General Conference reviewed the policies of the new denomination worked out by the bishops, they discovered that the union would not take away "the ministerial status of any man or woman," but there would "be no ordination as ministers granted to women" in the EUB Church.[11] As time went by, however, the question never became a controversial issue. Certain bishops continued to ordain women, but these "isolated instances neither provoked any recorded objections nor inspired any generally accepted practice."[12] In 1968, the Methodist Church merged with the Evangelical United Brethren Church. It was clearly stated that women would have full ecclesiastical standing in the resulting United Methodist Church.

PRESBYTERIANS

Presbyterian concerns about the ordination of women relate even more closely to issues of lay status because Presbyterians commonly ordain lay deacons and ruling elders. In the early 1920s, overtures authorizing women to these lay offices came before the General Assembly of the Presbyterian Church in the USA (northern). In 1923, the decision was made to ordain women as deacons.[13] This was also the time period when the strong independent women's organizations in the church were absorbed into a unified denominational structure through reorganization.[14] Many women were dissatisfied with this development and raised questions about women's role in the church.[15] By the late 1920s, northern Presbyterians were asked to vote whether women should be ordained as ruling elders (local lay leaders) and/or teaching elders (clergy responsible for the ministry of word and sacrament) (Document 4).[16] The General Assembly sent three overtures on women's status to the presbyteries. The first one was in support of total equality. The second and third approved women as ruling elders and licensed evangelists. Only the overture authorizing women to be ordained as ruling elders passed. By asking for full equity, which was not voted, women nevertheless gained increased power as lay leaders.[17]

Eventually, however, pressure for a recognized status for women serving the church through professional ministries of mission, evangelism, and education mounted. To meet this need, in 1938 the General Assembly established a category of "commissioned church worker." It was clearly stated, however, that this status did not "confer any ministerial rights and privileges." Women could now prepare for full-time service in local congregations, but they remained unordained.[18]

After the Second World War, the question of women clergy again confronted the General Assembly. Another overture approving the eligibility of women to the ordained ministry of Word and Sacrament was sent to the presbyteries, but it did not even receive majority support, let alone the required two-thirds vote.[19] A *New York Times* article summarized the debate with tongue in cheek (Document 5).[20]

Finally, in 1953, the Presbytery of Rochester (New York) raised the issue again. A committee was appointed to study the question. By 1955, it recommended that women be ordained as teaching elders (clergy) (Document 6).[21] This time it passed by an overwhelming majority.[22] In the religious enthusiasm of the 1950s, women clergy were no longer a threat. Those who voted for women clergy, however, did not think that great numbers of women would seek ordination. Women would serve in education, in rural settings, in the urban crisis, and as assistants to established clergy. People refused to see women's ordination as an invitation to real equality (Document 7).[23]

Obviously, women's ordination could not be ignored in the conversations that led to the merger of the Presbyterian Church in the USA and the United Presbyterian Church of North America (UPNA) in 1958. The smaller, conservative UPNA had ordained women as deacons in 1906. However, United Presbyterians had never ordained women as ruling elders or ministers, although a number of women had served as recognized evangelists. In the new church it was decided that women would have full equality, at least in principle. But no one was enthusiastic. In spite of their commitment to principle, Presbyterian church leaders from all sides did little to break down the *de facto* inequality that continued.[24]

The Presbyterian Church, US (southern) could not even affirm the principle, having never ordained women to any office even though women did serve on national committees and boards. In 1952, the issue was hotly debated at its General Assembly with no action. In 1957, the assembly sent a measure to the presbyteries approving the ordination of women only as deacons and ruling elders. It was voted down. Finally, in 1964, almost a full decade after northern church action, southern Presbyterians approved women as deacons, elders, and ministers all at once.[25]

Actually, the small Cumberland Presbyterian Church, which broke away from southern Presbyterianism on frontier issues in the early nineteenth century, led all other Presbyterian groups in its acceptance of women as lay elders and ministers. Not all Cumberland presbyteries applauded this openness, but in 1889 the Nolin Presbytery (Kentucky) ordained the first Presbyterian woman to the full work of the gospel ministry.[26]

LUTHERANS

Lutheranism in America began the cycle of concern about women's role in the church even later than the Presbyterians. During the first half of the twentieth century, American Lutheran church bodies remained fragmented and psychologically tied to their various European traditions. Women in American Lutheran churches organized into women's guilds and societies, but concern for equal lay leadership and clergy rights rarely developed before 1940. At that time, several things brought the issue forward.

First of all, the incredible changes in women's role in American society could no longer be avoided. The isolation of first generation immigrants was breaking down. Lutheran women actively engaged in many aspects of political and social life.

Second, American Lutheranism was strongly influenced by European developments. In the aftermath of the Second World War, Lutheran churches in Scandinavia began to change. The Norwegian state church had the right to appoint women pastors in 1938. After the war there was great need for pastors; women were no longer attracted to the deaconess role; and, because many Lutheran churches were state churches, political movements for human rights had an impact upon church policies. In 1948, the Danish parliament opened ordination to women. By 1950, a Swedish church commission recommended ordination, but because of the controversy over church-state relationships and the ecumenical ramifications of such action the decision was delayed until 1958. Three Swedish women were finally ordained in 1960.

Changes in American practice began with the question of vote and voice for women at several levels of the church. In 1907, Augustana Lutherans decided that women could vote in their local churches and, in 1930, they were seated as delegates to judicatory meetings. In 1934 United Lutherans approved women as delegates, members of the church council, and members of boards and commissions. The American Lutheran Convention seated its first woman delegate in 1944.[27]

Meanwhile, the Lutheran Church-Missouri Synod (LC-MS) delayed the question. Finally, in 1954, they authorized a study of "women's suffrage in the church," only refusing to grant local voting rights to women in 1956.[28]

Lutherans were also very influenced by developments in biblical scholarship and the ecumenical agenda of the World Council of Churches. In the late 1950s, many Lutheran bodies were preoccupied with church union. In 1960, the American Lutheran Church (ALC) consolidated midwestern Lutheranism. And in 1962, four other groups united to form another even larger Lutheran body, the Lutheran Church in America (LCA). Throughout this period the question of women's ordination was raised, but not resolved. Scholars debated the biblical, theological, practical, and ecumenical issues. Many concluded that there were no biblical or theological reasons against women's ordination (Document 8).[29] Missouri Synod Lutherans objected that the question was not being dealt with correctly. They published an English translation of a German book on the subject to show that the ordination of women would be a "practical invalidation of the proclamation concerning woman's subordination" (Document 9).[30] By the late 1960s, the three major American Lutheran churches (LCA, ALC, and LC-MS) held in Inter-Lutheran Consultation on the Ordination of Women. They agreed that it was possible (and even Lutheran) to disagree. It was only a matter of time before the LCA and ALC acted to ordain women. They argued that "although the Gospel does not change, conditions do. New situations, differing customs, continued research, the on-going work of God, and the promptings of the Spirit demand constant reconsideration of previous assumptions."[31]

EPISCOPALIANS

The Protestant Episcopal Church in the United States sees itself in continuity with worldwide Anglicanism. Consequently, Episcopal efforts to deal with the question of women's ordination were strongly influenced by what happened in England and among other Anglicans.

In 1920, the Lambeth Conference (a regular meeting of all Anglican bishops held every ten years) declared that "the ordination of a deaconess confers upon her holy orders." But, by 1930, the bishops changed their interpretation. Ordination was only for male priests, deaconesses were appointed.[32]

This confusion prompted one thoughtful Anglican scholar to write a book supporting the admission of women to full priesthood. As the Dean of Emmanuel College at Cambridge, he argued that "to perpetuate habits of mind and methods of organization suited to the period when women's subjugation was axiomatic is under the circumstances of today to invite failure; it is to prefer a stage coach in an era of motorcars and aeroplanes." The book was reprinted on this side of the Atlantic with an introduction on "The American Situation." Although ignored by Episcopalians, it was an inspiration to women in many denominations (Document 10).[33]

Most American Episcopalians became aware of questions surrounding women's role in the church in the 1940s. In 1947, the diocese of Vermont approved the election of women to local vestries. Many dioceses, however, continued to keep women off vestries and to question the validity of women delegates to the Triennial Convention. By 1950, reports from the World Council of Churches and a controversy caused when the Bishop of Hong Kong ordained a woman made many Episcopalians aware of the issue. Methodist and Presbyterian action in the mid-1950s exacerbated the situation.[34]

Finally, in 1964, the General Convention changed the canon on deaconesses to "ordered" rather than "appointed." Within the year Bishop James Pike interpreted that to mean that an "ordered" deaconess had the authority of Holy Orders and could be in charge of a parish. The House of Bishops met in 1965 to deal with the furor and commissioned a study on the larger question of the role of women in ministry.[35] The Committee reported a year later that the burden of proof was on the opposition to show "that the unique character of the ordained ministry makes that ministry a special case and justifies the exclusion of women from it" (Document 11).[36]

The struggle for ordination in the Episcopal Church went well into the 1970s. Several times the House of Bishops voted in favor of women priests, only to have the vote defeated by laity in the House of Deputies. It was not resolved until unauthorized ordinations (1974) forced the church to deal with the issue after the fact. Even then, concerns for mutual recognition and ecumenical unity continued to undermine Episcopal commitments to full equality for women.[37]

MAINSTREAM PROTESTANTISM IN CONTEXT

During all of these years of Methodist, Presbyterian, Lutheran, and Episcopalian activity, women in denominations that had ordained women many years earlier watched with interest. They began to ask each other why they failed to reap the benefits of their "equality." They asked their denominations to clarify long-standing practices concerning women. They pressed for better placement and representation for women clergy. Female seminary admission to master of Divinity programs rose as increasing numbers of women openly prepared themselves for pastoral ministry.[38]

These same years also caused conservative Protestants to become more and more defensive. After the modernist-fundamentalist controversy, which raged during the first few decades of the twentieth century, hard-line conservative evangelical Protestantism withdrew from the mainstream. Relying upon a network of Bible colleges and independent nonsectarian mission organizations, conservative evangelicals ignored the question of women's ordination.[39] From time to time, some zealous soul would write a small pamphlet deploring the changing role of women and defending "old time religion." All efforts to reinterpret scriptural admonitions against women speaking in church were dismissed as the work of the devil.[40]

In the 1970s, however, this isolation began to crack. Ecumenical theological education made it difficult to do theology by "proof text." Neo-evangelicals generated a spirit of self-criticism and concern for social justice. Electronic evangelism sought respectability. Biblical scholarship discovered that Jesus was a feminist. By the 1980s, the problem of women's ordination had become so relevant that the Southern Baptist Convention acted to condemn it.[41]

The more important context for mainstream Protestantism was the ecumenical movement. By the 1940s and 1950s, any examination of women's ordination had to be approached with geographical and denominational sophistication. In some denominations the question concerned women preaching, in others it involved sacramental authority. It was not uncommon for younger mission churches to ordain women, in spite of the policies of parent denominations. Social and cultural differences raised questions about the authority of the Bible for all times and places. Theologians examined the nature of the church and called for a new appreciation of the laity. By 1964, the ordination of women was a major ecumenical issue (Document 12.)[42]

Finally, important political, economic, and social factors influenced twentieth-century developments surrounding ordination for women in mainstream Protestantism. In 1920, the women's suffrage amendment was ratified and women became voting citizens. Church women began to wonder, If women can go to the polls to vote for the president and congress, why can't we vote and serve as leaders in our churches?

Economic patterns of supply and demand also had an impact upon the situation. During the 1920s, the economy was expanding and there were more pastorates than clergy. But during the depression and wartime, churches did not feel the same pressure to ordain women. Only in the postwar religious revival of the 1950s, did Methodists and Presbyterians finally grant equal ecclesiastical status to women. It is no accident that the periods of greatest advancement for women clergy in mainstream Protestantism always came when there was an undersupply of trained clergymen.

More than politics or economics, however, the social context of women's lives invited twentieth-century women to consider ministry. Compared with their grandmothers, women were living longer, staying healthier, benefiting from more education, and spending a major portion of their lives employed outside the home. It was only natural that these women, nourished by the Christian church, began responding to God's call in new ways (Document 13).[43]

But recognizing the call, and getting the ecclesiastical structures to honor and support that call, was only the beginning. It was true that women did seem to have an advantage in certain pastoral situations, especially in their ministry with and to other women. But the framework for their ministry was rarely supportive (Document 14).[44] Women were forced to make their own way without the social and institutional acceptance so readily available to men (Document 15).[45]

Winning ordination in mainstream Protestantism was and is a process, not an event. It began when women spoke up in their local churches and voted their concerns. It progressed when women accepted church leadership responsibilities at home and in denominational structures. It became more complicated when women felt God's call to serve in ordained ministries of Word and Sacrament. It was advanced when ecclesiastical bodies recognized the ministerial authority of women and men as equal. And it will be fully won when women find appropriate recognition and support for their theology and their ministries throughout church and society.

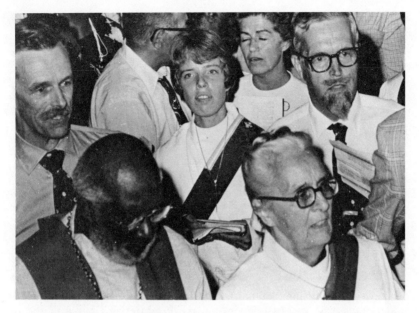

The Reverends Carter Heyward and Jeanette Piccard, shown surrounded by supporters at their "irregular" ordination to the priesthood of the Episcopal Church, July 29, 1974. [Photo courtesy of the Rev. Carter Heyward.]

The Rev. Marjorie Matthews surrounded by clergy at the United Methodist General Conference, 1984. Matthews was the first woman to be elected to the episcopacy of any major denomination. [Photo courtesy of the General Commission of Archives and History, United Methodist Church, Madison, New Jersey.]

The Rev. M. Madeline Southard, founder of the American Association of Women Ministers and its journal, *The Woman's Pulpit,* begun in 1922. [Photo courtesy of Carol Lynn Yellin, from the Rev. M. Madeline Southard Biographical Collection.]

The Rev. Letty Russell in her office in the Presbyterian Church of the Ascension, East Harlem Protestant Parish, New York City, shortly after her ordination on September 19, 1958. [Photo taken by *The New Mirror,* courtesy of the Rev. Letty Russell.]

Maud Keister Jensen, first woman to receive full clergy rights in the Methodist Church in 1956, shown speaking at Drew University, Madison, New Jersey. [Photo courtesy of the General Commission on Archives and History, United Methodist Church, Madison, New Jersey.]

Documents: Winning Ordination for Women in Mainstream Protestant Churches

Document 1: A Methodist Report on Licensing and Ordaining Women (1924)

From 1880 to 1920, the Methodist Episcopal Church, officially refused to "license" women ministers. In 1920, the General Conference approved licensing women as local preachers and asked for a study on ordaining and admitting women to Annual Conferences. The Commission reported to the 1924 General Conference that it was too early to make the decision about Conference membership. Women should be ordained as local preachers.[46]

On May 25, 1920, the General Conference of that year adopted a report of the Committee on Itinerancy, referring to a commission of seven, the expediency of granting to women ordination and admission to the Annual Conference. After careful individual study and common discussion, your Commission found itself with three definite convictions:

First—That the validity of a woman's call to preach is not involved in any action which the General Conference may take in respect of the ordination of women and their admission into the Annual Conference;

Second—That, inasmuch as the ordination of women and their admission into the Annual Conference would inaugurate far-reaching social and spiritual issues, such action ought not to be undertaken either as an administrative expedient to meet the emergency created by a temporary decrease in ministerial supply, or as an economic expedient to adjust ministerial supply to inadequate financial support;

Third—That in the connectional polity of Methodism, the ordination of women and their admission to the Annual Conference would introduce peculiar and embarrassing difficulties. In non-connectional churches, in which, alone, ordained women have been admitted to settled pastorates, the relation can be terminated at will by either party to the contract. In Methodism our connectional polity guarantees to every effective minister a church and to every self-supporting church a minister; and the pastoral relation is established by appointment of constituted authority, and properly terminated only with the consent of constituted authority.

Your Commission, also, after wise and careful exploration of both the mind of our own Church and the experiences of other Churches, has been led to conclude that the indifference of the Church at large to the matter of the ordination of women and their admission to the Annual Conference, is in itself evidence that no imperative demand for such ordination and admission exists; that Methodism had had altogether too limited experience in licensing of women as preachers to provide a basis upon which a final decision ought to be reached, and furthermore, that the knowledge and experience of other churches, in which women have served and are still serving as settled pastors, are too fragmentary and insufficient to justify the Commission in offering a final decision.

However, the very evident and acute need for an effective sacramental ministry on the part of women, in certain home and particularly in the foreign fields, has seemed to your Commission to indicate clearly an expansion of service which the Church, with reason and propriety, can open to them.

Your Commission, accordingly, taking into consideration these and other factors of significance, unanimously recommends that the General Conference enact such measures as shall provide for the ordination of women as local preachers under the conditions and satisfactory to the requirements which the Discipline has determined and maintains for ordained local preachers.

Document 2: Reflections on the Status of Methodist Women Preachers

"I want to get in touch with some women who are preaching, like myself. I know so few, and there must be others." With these words a Kansas woman, Madeline Southard, organized the American Association of Women Preachers to support women ministers in their search for equality in mainstream Protestantism. Initially, members were drawn from Methodist, Congregational, Northern Baptist, Disciples, and Presbyterian churches. In more recent years Lutherans, Episcopalians, and Roman Catholics have joined.

From 1922 to the present, the association has published a small journal entitled The Woman's Pulpit. *Reports and reflections on the ecclesiastical status of women fill its pages. In the thirty-two years that elapsed between the ordination of Methodist women as local preachers and full membership for women in annual conferences, there were many articles in* The Woman's Pulpit.[47]

How the Opposition Helped at the 1924 General Conference.

A group of the strongest men signed a substitute for complete equality and gave arguments that I wish we had space to quote. The other side seemed to become fearful that the substitute might carry, and closed with a strong plea on the ground that it would imperil unification with the M. E. South Church. That carried great weight, and the report was adopted. One curious thing was that not one single voice in that whole assembly, in the hours of debate, was raised against ordination. Some of the people who fought it so four years ago, stood for it this time. By our keeping the whole attention centered upon what was not granted, and so opposing the report, our opponents themselves did all the talking for ordination. Some did not know just what they had done when it was over, they felt they had defeated us. In reality it is a great victory, incomplete as it is.

Madeline Southard

"... how the double standard works when women are not members of annual conference."

To have this background, to see how every step woman has taken in the church has been against stubborn resistance, is necessary if we would consider the matter of admitting women to membership in the Annual Conferences. For the same arguments are now advanced against all the others. But before considering them let us see what conference membership means. For it has been said that with license and ordination granted, woman has about as much opportunity as she would have as a member of Conference.

In answer to this we simply say, ask any young man who is entering the Methodist ministry if he intends sometime to become a member of a Conference. He will certainly answer yes. Ask him why. If he knows his church at all, he will tell you that unless he becomes a member of a Conference he will go through life as a supply pastor, and that no young man of the right sort would dream of going through life as a "supply" unless terribly hampered by hopeless limitations.

But this state that Methodism desires her keen alive young men to reject with scorn, this it is that she offers to her keen, alive young women, saying to them: "See how generous I have become to you. I am willing that you should go and preach in any of my difficult fields that can not or will not support a man as pastor. I am willing that you shall build them up for me. I have always held that you were delicate and needed protection, therefore I will send you to circuits where there are no modern conveniences, where there are long trips to make to distant outpoints, where the income is small and uncertain, and the community indifferent or torn by church quarrels. If you will work hard and build this up for me so that it will be a desirable charge for some man, a member of my Conference, I will say many lovely words about your consecration, your feminine humility—and I will send you to another difficult point to do the same thing over again. Of course you will not have money for books and magazines and contact with the big movements of the day, but it is very wrong and worldly to desire these things. I teach my sons to desire them, they run a neck-to-neck race for them, but to you my daughters I give the high privilege of living a meek and humble life."

How the Arguments Are Never Theological.

You have heard arguments against the admission of women to the annual conferences. Seldom is it argued on Biblical grounds in our denomination today for the sound scholarship of our leaders and the fact of women's ordination would preclude such arguments. The so called "practical grounds" are the basis of the arguments usually advanced.

That practical problems would be incurred, in the admission of women to the annual conferences, no one can deny. The great Methodist church with her genius for organization can meet every such problem and solve it. In fact at the present time, she has the disciplinary provisions in the articles on location and supernumerary relations to handle any special problems which might arise.

How Parenthood Should not Cause Problems.

Parenthood does not deter either men or women from being good ministers. In fact, parenthood is an asset, for family problems of the parish are better understood by those who have children of their own. There is no place in the world where children can be better nurtured intellectually and spiritually than in a parsonage and the problems involved in bringing children into the world and caring for them can be met by the parents if common sense, consecration, and prayer are brought to bear on each situation.

The conference need not worry about the fate of the husband of a woman minister. If both husband and wife are thoroughly Christian, even though their vocations may differ, they will work out their problems in harmony and good faith with no loss to their family relations or to the annual conference.

How the Spiritual Integrity of the Church is Threatened By This Inequality.

The Church makes bold, glorious, and fearless pronouncements on temperance, ecumenical relationships, need for ministers, rural problems, education, missions, church union, international situations, racial injustice, nationalism, the emancipation of labor, and other causes, proclaiming in these pronouncements that "We judge practices by the Christian gospel." In spite of the pleas of the underprivileged the same Church ignores the liberating gospel which declares that "in Christ Jesus there is neither male nor female," by keeping the doors of the annual conferences barred to qualified women. Such a church needs an awakening, a repentance and works meet for repentance.

This prevailing condition threatens the spiritual integrity of the church, for how can a church preach justice and deny it to some of her own members, and remain utterly sincere? It is not surprising that more and more of our most brilliant women are turning to secular organizations for places of leadership, since they cannot find them in the church. This entails the loss of talent and ability that should be used directly for Christ and the church.

How can a church preach against class legislation and continue to legislate against sex without losing spiritual power?

Document 3: The Methodist Church Debates Equality for Women Ministers (1956).

In 1956, during the last debate surrounding the question of whether women should have full status in the Methodist Church, the issues were practical, not theological. A halfway measure was proposed by the Committee whereby only widowed and single women would have Conference membership, but even this was unacceptable to some. J. Dewey Muir presented a minority report.[48]

The ability to preach and to give leadership in the Church is not in any sense determined by sex. This is acknowledged. That some women have done excellent and outstanding work and service, is recognized. Ability to preach, to give leadership, have little to do with the real issue of granting Full Ministerial Rights to Women.

The General Conference has been deluged with a multiplicity of Memorials dealing with this question. Not all of these Memorials were in agreement that Full Clergy Rights should be granted to women. Without examination, however, one might assume that the multiplicity of these Memorials is a mandate from the churches and Conferences.

Upon examination of these Memorials, because of their similarity of statement, one may well conclude that they have come from a limited segment of the Church. Since the burden of these Memorials has to do with Full Clergy Rights For Women, let us raise this question: what are Full Clergy Rights and how are they constituted?

Ministerial rights we believe are vested in ordination rather than in Conference membership. Ordination is now available to the women of Methodism. We remind you that ordination, either as Deacon or elder, gives to every recipient thereof, male or female, traveling preacher or local preacher, exactly the same rights, privileges, and prerogatives. There is no ministerial function or service which can be performed by an Ordained Elder who is a member of an Annual Conference, which cannot be performed by a Local Elder, man or woman.

The issue than becomes the sole matter of Ministerial Membership in an Annual Conference. It is the judgment of the Ministerial Members of the Committee on the Ministry that such request as has come before The General Conference is based upon a general theory that basically no privilege should be granted one sex which is denied to the other. In that noble sentiment we share. However, we are facing the realistic problems of administration of the law of the Church. It is at this point that our conclusion differ from the Majority Report.

We submit to you that the proposed legislation is an admission of the administrative problems involved, for it proposes that admission to Conference Membership shall be restricted to unmarried women and widows, and further provides that upon marriage, Conference Membership of a traveling woman preacher shall be discontinued.

We remind you that our traveling ministry operates within an appointive system in which [pastors minister] to churches where appointed, and churches accept pastors appointed to them. If the proposed legislation is enacted, let us not assume that women preachers will be sent to little churches, to undesirable churches, to undesirable circuits, or places no one else wishes to fill.

Rather, let it be assumed that any church to which a Bishop sees fit to appoint a Minister will accept that appointment without raising any question as to the sex of the Minister. In other words, admitting women to the traveling ministry ought never to be restrictive as to appointment, but open the way for appointment of a woman Minister to any church in Methodism.

We remind you that when any person is admitted as a Ministerial Member of an Annual Conference, the presiding Bishop must appoint that person to a pastoral charge. If our Charges operated upon a Call System, the proposed legislation would present no problem, for under such a system a church would issue a call only to a minister whom the congregation desired.

Under our appointive system, every Ministerial Member of an Annual Conference must be appointed to a Pastoral Charge or some Special Appointment of the Conference, whether there is a Charge that wants that Minister or not.

I am keenly aware of the problems involved in appointing some men to churches, yet no church has said, "No, we just do not want a man preacher." Yet in trying to appoint even good women ministers —and I remind you that I come from one of the Annual Conferences of Methodism which has in its ministerial membership a woman member, plus our quota of women who are Approved Supply Pastors—yet in trying to appoint good women pastors, ministers, it is not uncommon for the answer to be, "We just do not want a woman minister."

In this, if they are—which we agree to, aside from the fact of the differences dependent of the fact that God created his children male and female, there ought to be no differences of standard or privilege based upon differences of sex.

Practically, until those demanding such legislation are committed not only to the legislation but to the receiving of women traveling preachers, not in general but in particular as Pastors of their own particular Charges, we are of the opinion that our present legislation, which does provide for ordination of women with all the rights appertaining thereto, but without membership in the Ministerial Membership of an Annual Conference, is best for our particular Church.

I trust that The General Conference, not out of any spirit of division, not out of any spirit of ill-will, but only with a sense of the importance of the problem of administration, will see fit to adopt the Substitute Report.

Thank you.

Although many laywomen's organization supported the proposed change, some women did not agree. Mrs. Henry D. Ebner spoke for the Minority Report; Mrs Edwin S. Anderson spoke against it.[49]

For: Bishop, first of all I would like to say that I think this is a very serious question that is before us, and although we have had some funny things happening, I think we should consider it in a very serious light.

I would also like to say that as a woman, as a Local Preacher in my Church, I have never felt that my Church has discriminated against me, but that wherever I wanted to serve, there seemed to be a door opened to me, to be able to serve.

I would remind you all of the many times that you have sat in a meeting where you have been privileged to see great groups of Missionaries coming to the platform, as well as groups of Deaconesses, and we have been impressed by the great number of years of service that they have given to our Church. But we have also been impressed with the fact that many of these women are beyond 50 years of age and we do not seem to be able to attract the younger women to fill up the ranks.

Now, if I were a young woman and God was calling me into full-time Christian service, I feel that the Ministry would be a very attractive field for me. I won't go into all of the details as to why it would; but if we open up another field of service for our younger women, when at this time we do not have enough Deaconesses to work in our institutions and when we are bereft of those we need to fill up the ranks of the older Missionaries, I feel that we are making a big mistake.

I am not impressed, Bishop and Members of The Conference, Brothers and Sisters included, by the number of Memorials that have been sent in regard to this question, because I feel that many of them were sent in without the people realizing all that would be involved if this legislation were passed. I do know that of those that I have interviewed, and some in this very Conference, they said, "Yes, we are in favor of Full Clergy Rights For Women, but I don't want a woman minister serving our church."

Now, we do not want to discriminate further against our women, but if we enact such legislation we will find ourselves in the very embarrassing position of belittling many of our women who would be very glad to serve.

Now, there is an opportunity in our great Church for women to preach and we are very thankful for that. But before we vote on this question, those of us who might be tempted to vote to change our *Discipline* would have to answer yes to three very important questions, and I submit them in all seriousness.

First of all, if I voted yes, I would be able to say to my District Superintendent, "Yes, send me a Woman Pastor."

Secondly, the Ministers as well as the Laymen would have to say, "I am willing to serve under a woman District Superintendent," for if this goes through, we are not going to discriminate.

I do not like even to use the word "discrimination" because in my mind it has always been connected with unhappiness and discontent. I have never felt that I needed as a woman to fight for equal rights with men. I feel I have more rights than the men will ever have.

Furthermore, Bishop, my last question that I believe the Delegates of this Conference would have to answer in the affirmative if they vote yes, would be this: We are willing to elect a woman Bishop. Now, you may think that is rather exaggerated, but, believe me, it is not. You have had the reference to the power of womanhood. I leave that to your own thinking.

I would urge that this be considered very seriously, that no more joking about it be passed around, and that you vote no when it comes to the Majority Report and that you support the Minority Report for the sake of the women of our Church.

Against: I am President of the Conference Woman's Society of Christian Service. In considering women's place in the Church, since the early days when she was not even permitted to sit in the pew with the men of her family, to say nothing of having a voice in Church policy, to the turn of the century when she was gradually given more recognition, the present time finds women being given more recognition in all areas of service and meeting the same standards as men.

Membership in our Methodist Church has increased by nearly two million in the past fifteen years, and as a result is far short of ministers to stock adequately the churches and expand its Program. The reserve of well-trained women ministers is ignored because of tradition, thus losing valuable and much needed leadership.

Women are accepted as candidates for the ministry and are permitted to graduate from seminaries. They are permitted to perform all the services that men ministers perform, and they are required to attend the sessions of Annual Conference. The Lay Delegate is permitted to sit within the bower of the church and has the privilege of the floor; but the woman minister has no privileges. Much of the opposition, I believe, to Full Clergy Rights is based on difficulties which may arise, should women become Conference Members. I believe that most of these difficulties are hypothetical and are magnified out of all proportion to their importance.

I should like to comment very briefly on one or two of them. We hear that the churches will not accept women ministers; but we know that some Conferences are already using them most satisfactorily. The Maine Annual Conference, for instance, has Mrs. Margaret Henrichsen, who started out with two small churches and is now serving five additional churches which had no Pastors. There are many other instances which I might cite, but time does not permit.

A woman Conference Member is guaranteed an Appointment is another one of the objections. But why not for women as well as for men, if they have equal opportunities and equal qualifications?

Occasionally a member has taken the Supernumerary Relation because for one reason or another he was not willing to accept the Appointment offered. A woman Member of a Conference would have the same privilege. A woman joining a Conference would understand the difficulties which might be encountered, and I feel sure that these difficulties would be in some way satisfactorily solved.

The churches which have given Full Clergy Rights to women have been greatly pleased with the results. The Methodist Church has always been able to adapt itself to change and should set an example in granting equal rights and opportunities of service to all its members, regardless of sex.

There is a definite trend toward giving Full Clergy Rights to qualified women, and I believe that Methodism should join that trend. After discussion with some of the District Superintendents, I am, of course, well aware of the difficulties involved in Full Clergy Rights. However, I feel that this Majority Report should be accepted and, therefore, I am speaking against the Minority Report.

Document 4: Presbyterians Debate: Expediency Versus Principle

In the late 1920s, Katherine Bennett, a powerful laywoman, wanted the General Council of the Presbyterian Church in the USA to deal constructively with the relationship of women's organizations to the church. It chose instead to raise the question of women's ecclesiastical status. In corresponding with Robert E. Speer, Katherine Bennett argued that it was time to deal with the principle of women's equality in the church and set expediency aside.[50]

The question being opened I am not willing to have an overture asking that women be admitted to the eldership: I ask that expediency be set aside and the principle be faced by the church. I quote Miss Royden, p. 249, and rest my case on her statement. If it be right that women have equal place with men in the church, then it should be given to them: if it is not right, then let them not be given the elder-ship. Miss Royden writes:

"It is the whole of my difference with most of the opponents of the further development of women's ministries in the Church that to me it seems a question of vital and fundamental principle—to them a matter chiefly of expediency. As in the beginning with Paul so today, the duties, the liberties, and the sphere of women are too often decided with a view to practical expediency, and the question asked whether the Churches 'need' them or not; whether their coming into the industry might not create practical difficulties; whether it would promote or postpone reunion; and so on. But we claim that the question cannot be decided in this way. We claim that it is a question of principle, and that expediency must follow, not lead, when a principle is involved. If on a question of principle we are right, then our claim must be granted, and it will be found expedient to grant it. Let those who oppose us equally on grounds of principle agree with us at least in this—that on questions of principle nothing need or ought to be considered but whether they are the principles of God, divinely ordained, and proclaimed by Christ our Master and our Lord."

One reads the above: then one reads from the Resolutions of the General Assembly of the Presbyterian Church of England: "The Assembly declares that there is no barrier in principle to the admission of women to the Ministry . . .

"The Assembly has affirmed that there is no barrier in principle to the admission of women to the ministry. The point remaining to be considered is this: Are there any considerations of a practical nature which make it advisable to open the ranks of our ministry to women?
(a) It is inconsistent with the uniform tradition of the Christian Church.
(b) Another objection, less general in its application, is the strain which might be laid on the relationship between different branches of the Presbyterian Church which extend to each other 'mutual eligibility' should one of them introduce women into their ministry.
(c) More serious is the opposition which is based on differences between men and women, which are felt by some to be fundamental to this issue. This aspect of the question is attached sometimes (1) to the exclusive claims of the home on women; and sometimes (2) to inherent dangers connected with their intimate exercise of the functions of a ministry which includes both male and female members.
(d) Opposition has been offered to any proposal to include women in the regular ministry of the Church on the ground that the severe and unre-mitting demands upon the modern pastor are such as women must often find impossible of fulfilment."

The Assembly could not agree as to the expediency of the action and the Overture to admit women to the Ministry was denied.

Personally I was not prepared to see this matter of status opened when General Council proposed it: it is opened and my conviction is that the fundamental rightness or wrongness of the matter must be faced, and action taken accordingly. Let the Church deny further "rights," or remove restrictions and inhibitions that are based on sex. It is thus that I would like to see our Committee report to General Council.

I should perhaps add that in my own thinking each privilege accorded may bring increasing embarrassments unless the differences in privileges between the sexes are all removed. A woman may, let us say, become an elder: are there any rights connected with the privileges of this office in the entering upon which there would be further obstacles?

Women's position is so equivocal today, so constantly to be explained or interpreted that I am prepared to risk all on asking whether the Church is willing to accept them as members, as workers, without discrimination, allowing them to take their place in the course of the years in any positions for which they are fitted, and to which the church may call them. Let discriminations be obliterated and the future will care for itself.

Document 5: The New York Times on Women in Ministry

The question of ordination for women clergy was voted by the General Council of the Prebyterian Church in the USA in 1947 and sent to presbyteries for action. Although the overture was not approved, it was noticed by the secular press. As the New York Presbytery prepared to vote, the following article appeared in the New York Times, *outlining the arguments on both sides of the issue.*[51]

. . . Let me first present the main reasons advanced against women in the ordained minsitry.

The first is a matter of women's emotional balance, which many feel is not as stable as men's. They believe that the record of women in public life, especially in politics, sustains this judgment. The word "globaloney," coming at a time when it did, was an emotional blurb that had its natural emotional reaction in the life of the woman who uttered it.

Now the pulpit has lived through a century of over-emotionalism, say the folks who feel that today restrained and accurate teaching is desperately needed. The world sits on a powder keg, and not sparks but sober and judicial advice is needed. This they feel, by and large, and with exceptions, men can better deliver.

At the Presbytery meeting I joked about how a woman pastor might come home from church with a couple of elders to dinner. Who else, under the economic status of an average minister (not yet like the teachers under the wing of AFL), could or would be there to greet them at the parsonage door but a beruffled husband, hot and anxious from his vigil over the kitchen range, stamping his delicate number twelve shoe when he got the good parson aside because the post-service meeting had taken longer than the roast lamb to get done?

This may be an exaggeration, like the musical moment before the sermon for the preacher to powder her nose, but what about the young married pastor and her children? Must the church be closed for three months for a number of years while the pastor gets her own little flock? Or will the vows of celibacy be ordered as in the Church of Rome? Even birth control has not been developed enough to synchronize births with the summer vacation.

Others think that there is a feminine overbalance in the average congregation now. They feel that women pastors would so feminize the church that men would frequent it in even smaller numbers. Women will listen to men "tell them off " for their sins, but men will not seriously do the same for women. A man who has been taken over the coals on Saturday night or Sunday morning in his own house by the little lady will not lightly enter a church to hear another woman continue the rebuke. For that matter, say these folks, neither will a woman sit and let another woman preach to her for half an hour with no chance for rebuttal.

Again, the inability of women to keep confidences is advanced by those who think that even a pastor, be she of the feminine sex, would flit from home to home like a busy bee with "the dirt" instead of pollen and what would germinate in no time might not be rosemary for rememberance but poison ivy for the congregation.

Of course, the most conclusive argument for those who believe each admonition of the Holy Writ is timeless in its application, are such passages as 1 Timothy, ii, 11–12, "Let the women learn in silence with all subjection. But I suffer not a woman to teach nor to usurp authority over the man."

Those who favor women being admitted to the regular ordained ministry have very different ideas. They take the negative arguments and pull them to pieces. Women, they say, have in a short time of greater freedom taken their place by men in fields where emotional balance and discretion are prime considerations. They practice as famous physicians, they work as famous scientists, they sit as judges, are Congressional Representatives and will soon get their full political rights to occupy the nation's highest office. It is an insult to her whole species to say a woman cannot keep a confidence as well as a man, say both men and women of the affirmative.

Of course, there are physical difficulties in connection with motherhood, but these are gradually being overcome as in the case of school teachers.

As for the female overbalance in churches it might be that a few attractive personalities with goodness and eloquence plus personal charm would attract many more men than now attend. Perhaps that is just the reason for any real imbalance in the sex proportion of attendance. Who can say that every male preacher does not exert any personal magnetism he possesses? And, in fact, some overplay this appeal shamefully, as some women might do also.

There is a strong point made by those who say that God combines the virtues of both mother and father. It might be that a woman could better depict the former. Just as in the home the balance of family influence is disturbed by removal of either mother or father, the church may be lacking that balanced ministry. Perhaps, say those who believe this, the heavy hand of punishment would be modified in the preaching, by the wooing and winning side of God's love, as the mother's patient understanding in the home sometimes tempers the father's stern unyielding discipline.

As for the scriptural admonitions against women speaking in churches, we must distinguish between timeless truth and local admonition. Again and again Jesus brought the commands of Moses up to date.

Women kept veiled and silent in many other places than the synagogues in the time of Paul, but today they are vocal in all these other spots such as the forum, the market place and the theatre. "Time makes ancient good uncouth." Why not admit them to the pulpit also?

To these protagonists there is one practical reason advanced for ordained women pastors. Many if not the majority of women are home all day. Male pastors are not too welcome or in place visiting these mothers and housewives in the daytime. Their husbands, away at business, at times resent it. But women ministers and pastors could do so and get close to the problems besetting the housewife, counseling her with the knowledge and understanding of a women's point of view. How fine, too, her tender touch in sickness or in emergencies where a man, no matter how well trained in theology and good intent, would be fumbling and awkward.

I have tried to express the opinions of both sides as judicially as possible. I cannot keep a gleam of humor out of my eye when I speak for the negative. I feel that women get what they want, given time, and will get the privilege of the pulpit and the pastorate in the Presbyterian Church as they got the vote in the affairs of the nation.

Of course, the same arguments hold in the case of the Negroes from the South and immigrants from the underprivileged sections of the world. We deny them equal rights because they do not prove they have the requirements that can and will only come to them by the possession and use of those rights.

The vote in the New York Presbytery will not be so close, I predict, as it will in the whole country, allowing for the backward sections. Women may not win this year, but win they will, and God bless them. But also, God keep too many of them from taking up this new field all at once. Letting folks learn new things, even in a democracy, is a necessary nuisance. It's like the baldish head I am just beginning to acquire. It's not a pleasant process and some think not a nice thing to have put on us, but I'll fight to keep it.

Document 6: Shall Women Be Ordained? (1955)

In 1955, the Presbyterian Church in the USA appointed another committee to study the question of women's ordination. Mrs. L. Irving Woolson, secretary to the committee, reported why "every member of the committee was convinced that the privilege of ordination ought to be extended to women as well as to men."[52]

The matter seemed to center basically around four questions: What does the Bible say about it? What does the theology of the Presbyterian Church say about it? What bearing does the historical and traditional attitude of the Church have on it? What has the present-day sociological status of women to do with it?

It seemed, therefore, that any decision the committee might reach should be thoroughly grounded theologically and philosophically. The committee felt that it should study statements already published on the position of women in the Church and in the world, and further that additional studies by our own theologians were needed. Therefore, it asked two outstanding men to prepare statements—one on the Biblical basis and one on the theological basis for ordination of women. These statements were carefully studied as were others that delineated the historical and traditional position of women in the Church, the sociological status of women in the world, and the instances of increasing co-operation between the sexes, particularly in opportunities for service in many fields. Some of the findings that influenced the committee follow:

The Bible teaches us that in Christ Jesus *there is neither male nor female.* The New Testament certainly supports the view that before God men and women are equal—neither sex is inferior to the other in access to God's grace and gifts. Women did serve as deaconesses in the Apostolic Church and did hold other positions of authority. Old Testament writers tell of many women who were prophetesses— women clearly chosen and inspired by God. Acts 2:17 implies that at Pentecost women as well as men received the Spirit and prophesied or spoke with tongues. God has spoken and speaks today through both men and women.

If we interpreted the Bible literally, we would never have approved ordaining women as elders. For there is just as much and just as little basis for ordaining women as elders as there is for ordaining them as ministers! It is true that women were never mentioned as priests or bishops in the Old Testament or the New. But the fact that they were prophetesses brings up the crucial question whether prophecy may be regarded as a regular ministry of the Church, and opens up the whole field of our reformed understanding of the ministry. This leads to a consideration of the theological or reformed doctrinal view of the place of women in the Church.

Two major theological issues are involved: first, the relation between men and women from the point of view of their divine creation, their redemption in Christ, and their coexistence in the Christian faith and life; and, secondly, the whole doctrinal interpretation of the Church and the ministry. In its report to General Assembly the committee stated "that it is proper to speak of equality of status for men and women both in terms of their creation and their redemption; that it is proper to speak of equality of status for men and women in the Church and its ministry; that there is no theological ground for denying ordination to women simply because they are women ... that there is no theological barrier against the ordination of women if ordination would contribute to the edification and nurturing of the Church in its witness to the Lord of the Church."

These are only some of the arguments and considerations that the committee studied—only one more may be mentioned here. The ministry is today becoming more and more diversified. Ordained ministers are working in many new fields, such as radio and television; in social agencies; as chaplains in industry; in psychotherapy; as counselors; as directors of Christian education. Plainly, to be a minister is not necessarily to be a preacher, and both men and women have varied and unique qualifications for varied and unique ministries.

Women may be doctors, lawyers, engineers, professors, architects, even ball players and bus drivers. If, then, God calls a woman to preach the gospel and chooses to speak through her, dare man or the Church question his choice? In Christ *there is neither male nor female.*

Document 7: The Experience of Women Pastors

When the Presbyterian Church in the USA finally approved the ordination of women ministers in 1956, there was much conjecture about how women pastors would serve the church. The following article appeared in Monday Morning, *a weekly magazine for clergy. It reflects the attitude that women pastors will do special ministries to "relieve or supplement" the work of male pastors.*[53]

Secularism and sin are entrenched in the cities. There is allure for all ages and stages of human beings. Our city churches must be correspondingly and intensively organized with leadership adequate to serve our Great Leader. As go the cities and churches, so goes the world. Spiritual leaders in the city work well nigh around the clock. They are faithful men, seeking to meet the challenge within and without the church. To adequately meet the spiritual needs of these congested memberships and communities there is an urgent call for additional spiritual leaders adequately trained and consecrated.

Here is where the call for ordination of women already competent, and younger women, confronting a changing society, seems most urgent. The women, old and young, should have leaders with training equal to that of men. An ordained woman, among many other specializing tasks, can conduct junior congregations, relieve or supplement the pastor in calling, assist in the pulpit, take the sacraments to the sick and aged, perform certain types of personal work, counsel with young women on personal problems, even marry them, and lay away those of their sex.

We pay builders of church plants salaries running into six and seven figures. Shall we do less in passing years in training and retaining builders of spiritual likeness to Christ in each and all taken into our communion?

Following up the action of our church, should not our overburdened pastors be supported in a search for commitment for training of a quota of at least 400 women of the above estimated 839? Most of the women would probably come from the 509 churches in our cities. And should these women, after ordination, marry or become disabled they would still remain an asset to the city church.

Document 8: Lutherans Discuss Women in the Church

While Methodists and Presbyterians seemed more concerned with practical questions, Lutherans examined the question of women's ordination theologically. In 1957, the Reverend Russell C. Prohl asserted that the Bible and the law of creation recognize the husband as head of his wife, but this does not mean that men in general are the head of, or superior to women in general.[54]

The church has a vast reservoir of talent in her devoted and highly qualified women. To keep this treasure in storage is poor stewardship. It is time for the church to put to use, to the fullest extent, the mission potential she has in her women.

There is no Scriptural reason why the women, who are in many cases the backbone of the congregation, should not have the right to help make decisions through voting membership. Contrary to the traditional stand of many church bodies, thousands of Sunday Schools have women as superintendents. The congregations which have selected these women should be congratulated rather than reprimanded. It would not be contrary to God's Word to help solve the parish day-school teacher problem by granting the same call to a teacher regardless of sex, and thus, for the first time in the history of the church, to offer some reasonable security to those women who have dedicated themselves to the public ministry of the Word in our schools. It would not be anti-Scriptural to permit our women missionaries and deaconesses at home and abroad to publicly teach the Word to men as well as to women and children. Many congregations have women who are better qualified to act as delegates to church conventions than the men whom congregations choose for this important Kingdom work. Why not send the best qualified members regardless of their sex? Just one example. There is a devout Christian woman, active in church affairs, whose knowledge of parliamentary law is recognized throughout the United States. Why should she not be seated in an official capacity next to the president of Synod at church conventions ready with professional advice on matters of parliamentary procedure? And finally, why not open the theological seminaries to qualified young women as ministerial students? God alone knows how many outstanding prophetesses and ministers, how many Annas and Deborahs and Phoebes there would be devoting their full time to "making disciples of all nations."

The time has come to declare that since the public activity of a woman is no longer considered as a breach of the marriage vow and since the law of the land no longer denies to woman the right to act independently in promiscuous gatherings, women are eligible candidates for any office in the Church of Christ if, of course, they have qualifications equal to those of the male candidates for the office. In other words, it is time for Christian churches in general to support the 1955 resolution of the Presbyterians that "there is no theological ground for denying ordination to women, simply because they are women." Emil Brunner offers excellent advice when he says that "it is absolutely impossible to put down in black and white, as a universal rule, which spheres of activity 'belong' to woman and which do not. This can only become clear through experience, and for this experience first of all the field must be thrown open."

Moses once expressed the wish, "Would God that all the Lord's people were prophets and that the Lord would put His spirit upon them." May God speed the day when these words become true; when, as Joel foretells, our sons and daughters shall prophesy; when, as David pictures the New Testament times, the host of women preachers will be great indeed, and when, as Isaiah predicts, it shall be our privilege in Christian pulpits everywhere to hear a woman herald of Good Tidings lifting up her voice to tell the Lord's Zion, "Behold your God!"

Document 9: Lutheran Church-Missouri Synod on the Office of Women in the Church

Lutheran hesitancy about women's ordination found expression among German scholars. In 1955, a book by Fritz Zerbst was translated into English and published by the Lutheran Church-Missouri Synod. Unlike biblical fundamentalists, the author looked at the entire question of subordination, rather than specific texts, and argued that the ordination of women would violate the order of creation. Subordination, however, should not be equated with inferiority.[55]

The subordination of woman which, as emphasized previously, must not be confused with the concrete forms which it may assume in the course of history, is a constituent part of the New Testament proclamation that cannot be argued out of existence. However, under the assumption that the orders of creation and of redemption must remain in harmony with each other, one must inquire of Paul whether it is and must remain necessary that the content of the New Testament proclamation concerning woman's subordination must be expressed in just this manner, that the church denies "the office" unto woman. More generally formulated, the question reads thus: Must, then, the full content of the proclamation, both with respect to creation and to redemption, be in force also in church practice, in practical theology, and, specifically, in the matter of calling persons into the office? Should not the church simply give governing prominence to the thought that it may do any and everything which serves to "edify the congregation"? And does not the ordination of woman to the holy ministry serve in our day to edify the congregation?

Whether or not the regulations of the church must conform to its proclamation (kerygma) is in our estimation an important question for practical theology. The concern of the church cannot be merely to copy in false biblicism the regulations of New Testament congregations with respect to their offices. But it is indeed the task of Lutheran theology to exercise watchful care, lest a practice develop in the church which is in conflict with its proclamation. In this connection it is extremely important to take note of the fact that an emerging practice in the life of the church frequently arises out of a more or less consciously held conviction which needs to be thoroughly examined. Practical theology has the watchman's task of proving the practice of the church by the touchstone of the Gospel message and of providing it with determining guidelines.

Not every momentarily expedient practice can be justified upon careful reflection. Paul detected in the teaching office of woman a desire "to usurp authority" over the man, an annulment of woman's subordination, and a peril to the marriage institution. At first thought it is difficult to understand the reason for these fears; but are they wholly unfounded? Although the proclamation of the Word and the administration of the Sacraments do not *per se* imply an exercise of rule, but a rendering of service, it is true nevertheless that by these functions rule is exercised over the congregation. Paul rightly sensed this. Rule is exercised over a congregation not only through conduct of its business affairs, through leadership in its meetings, or through maintenance of an external apparatus, but primarily through preaching and the administration of Sacraments. The responsible choice of texts, their responsible exposition with application to the existing concrete situation of the congregation, encouragement and admonition pointed according to need, consolation and warning, the forgiving and retaining of sins in confession, the practice of church discipline—all these and other functions are essentially functions of rule over a congregation. In the last analysis, of course, such rule is exercised through the Word and the Holy Spirit, not through any power inherent in man. Nevertheless the Holy Spirit rules through human agencies, the witnessing office-bearers. Therefore Paul strives to set forth clearly that wherever the authority to rule the congregation is conferred upon woman, there the subordination of woman is nullified. The order of creation, however, cannot be nullified in one area of church practice without consequences for the proclamation of its whole message and for the life of the congregation. The fear is not unfounded, therefore, that there is something hidden behind the demands for the ordination of woman into the office. Practically all arguments drawn in support of these demands from church history and from theology give foundation to such fear. The opening of the full ministry to women is to express the nullification of differences between the sexes; it is to indicate that the order of creation has been annulled already in the world—if not generally, then at least in the ecclesiastical domain. Resistance at this point to all tendencies toward dissolution of the order of creation is never merely a matter of expediency determined by the circumstances of the times, but it is a matter of principle. Therefore also the thought that everything is permissible which serves to "edify the church" cannot be superimposed as governing principle in this matter. Whether or not the ordination of woman into the office actually or in the long run serves to edify the church cannot be determined, either theoretically or through references to practice. Furthermore, this question must not be placed at the center of reflection. If that were done, then one could also with equal justification regard as normative the assertion that the ordination of woman into the office would cause the men of the congregation to withdraw from public services and result in the development of a "woman's church."

The determining principle, then, in this: Whereas rule over the congregation is exercised through the proclamation of the Word and the administration of the Sacraments, the ordination of woman into this office is a practical invalidation of the proclamation concerning women's subordination. The demands that the office be opened completely to woman must be resisted, because they are essentially an attack upon the order of creation, which must be preserved.

Document 10: Anglicans on the Advantages of Ordaining Women

When Charles E. Raven, a progressive Anglican writer, wrote a small book arguing for the ordination of women in the 1920s, it was reprinted in America with an introduction by an American woman, Elizabeth Wilson. In the following selection, she lists the gains the church might anticipate if women were ordained.[56]

The fear has long been expressed that much would be lost by the removal of the prohibitions against ordaining women and calling them to pastorates. The fear is now being expressed that something is being lost by not removing these prohibitions. Speaking in terms of gain instead of loss, what is it reasonable to suppose might be the gain to the cause of Christ and His Righteousness in the United States if Canon Raven's premises should be agreed to and his conclusions acted upon?

Would it not be this: First, a return to the practice of Jesus Christ and the early Church in welcoming women to the fellowship of the Gospel and in using their ministry *in accordance with the social customs of the day.* Second, recruits for the ranks of preachers from among the young women who have been classmates in colleges and theological seminaries of the young men candidates who have been presenting themselves in less than sufficient numbers—a dearth which we hear constantly lamented. Third, the employment of women's inherent gifts, not competing with the ministry of men but supplementing it. Canon Raven's comment on the English war workers, "They brought with them what few men possess: the personal touch, the sense of personal values, which we with our concern for problems and abstract principles so easily lose," is only half of the case. The other half is that women with their resourcefulness may work out new forms of preaching, new avenues through which the soul may find God, just as the English situation led to the introduction of the Pilgrims. Fourth, a general increase of interest in religion and in religious education among women and girls, as it is recognized that the churches allow and expect women to take a full share in their leadership: at present the disabilities attaching to women's work react unfavourably upon the whole attitude of women towards the study and service of Christianity. Fifth, the adoption of a more Christlike outlook upon personal, social, and political problems on the part of the churches as these, by taking women into full partnership in their councils, assume a more human because less purely masculine character. The absence of women's distinctive contribution weakens and to some extent distorts the witness of the Church on many prominent moral and spiritual issues. Those who have had full experience of it will realize most easily the advantages that equal cooperation between men and women might give. Women may sew together the new wine skins which will hold fresh revelations of the truth as it is in Christ Jesus and of His power to resolve the perplexities of thinking, praying Christians today. But such mental processes are now too often inhibited.

Document 11: Anglicans Critique the Reasons Against Ordaining Women

When the Committee to Study the Proper Place of Women in the Ministry of the Church reported to the Episcopal House of Bishops in 1966, it indicated its belief that the burden of proof lay with the opponents of women's ordination. To oppose the ordination of women was to assert that the whole trend of modern culture was wrong, or that ordained ministry could justifiably exclude women. Why? [57]

Reasons Given Against the Ordination of Women

Mental and Emotional: The alleged mental and emotional characteristics of women are said to make them unsuitable to serve as clergymen. Such arguments are never very clear, consistent or precise. Sometimes, the weaknesses of women is stressed, despite the fact that women are healthier and live longer than men. Or, it is claimed that women think emotionally rather than rationally and that they over-personalize problems or decisions.

The same sort of arguments could be used to show that women are unfit for almost any business, professional, or public responsibility. They were used against the admission of women to higher education, to the practice of medicine and law, and against women suffrage. They are still being used against the admission of women to the House of Deputies of the General Convention.

None of these negative arguments has been borne out in any other walk of life. Women have proved to be capable, often brilliant, lawyers, statesmen, scientists, and teachers. They have enriched the practice of medicine, and politics have neither been redeemed nor debased by their participation.

As experience has demonstrated, only experience can show the extent to which women might fulfill a useful role in the ordained ministry, as well as ways in which their role might be different from the role of men. Here, as in other callings, women would need to be better than men in order to compete with them.

Emil Brunner states, "It is absolutely impossible to put down in black and white, as a universal rule, which spheres of activity 'belong' to women and which do not. This can only become clear through experience; and for this experience, first of all the field must be thrown open."

Because the field has not been thrown open, any judgment based on the Church's experience with professional women workers is limited and inadequate. With the highest respect for the contributions these women are now making, the Committee is convinced that an absolute bar at the level of ordination has a deterring effect upon the number of women of high quality who enter professional Church work or undertake theological study, and that the same bar places theologically trained women in a highly uncomfortable and anomalous position.

Marriage Versus Ministry: There is alledged the impossibility or impracticality of combining the vocation of a clergyman with domestic responsibilities, with marriage, as well as the bearing and care of children. Would it be possible for a wife and mother of a family to bring to the priesthood the required degree of commitment, concentration, and availability?

First, it must be said that many women choose careers and never marry, others combine marriage and careers. The Church recognizes that the latter is an entirely legitimate vocation, both in the secular world and in the Church itself

Secondly, the question of married women is partly answered by the fact that married men are permitted to serve as bishops, priests and deacons in the Anglican Communion. Such permission implies an acknowledgment of the strong claims that the wife and family of a married clergyman rightfully have upon his time, his money, and the conduct of his vocation. All would grant that a clergyman has a duty, as well as a right, to take into account his wife's health, or his children's education, in consideration a call, in negotiating about his salary, in determining his standard of living and the amount of money he will give away.

While other, and perhaps more serious, problems might exist for a woman who wished to combine ordination with marriage, the Commission is by no means convinced that such a combination would not prove practical in many instances. Even such demanding professions as teaching and medicine are finding ways of using skilled and trained married women with children, both on a part-time and a full-time basis. Many intelligent women find that they are better wives and mothers by combining an outside calling with the care of a family. Many also can look forward to years of full-time professional work after their children are grown.

The Commission would ask whether the leadership of the Church does not possess resourcefulness and imagination similar to that displayed by other institutions in using married women, if not often as ministers in charge of parishes, yet as assistants, or for the specialized types of ministry that are sure to develop much more rapidly in the future. It is thought unlikely that any great number of women would seek ordination, considering the very real difficulties involved. But difficulty is not impossibility, and at the least there need be no fear that women will "take over" the Church.

Theological Arguments: Then there are certain theological objections which seem to the Committee to present a strange mixture of tradition and superstition.

Biblical: Some of the objections rest on a rather literal approach to the Bible and fail to take into account the degree to which the Bible is conditioned by the circumstances of its time. It is not necessary to dwell upon the Creation Story, in which woman is created after man and taken from him, nor be influenced by the fact that women were excluded from the covenant-relation of God with Israel, any more than one would support polygamy or slavery because both have clear sanction in the Old Testament. Nor is one moved by the familiar argument that our Lord chose only men to be his apostles. Any sound doctrine of the Incarnation must take full account of the extent to which Jesus lived and thought with the circumstances and environment of his own time. To deny such facts is to deny the full humanity of Jesus and to subscribe to a grotesque Docetism. Our Lord did choose women as close associates, even if he did choose men as the transitional leaders of the new Israel. The Committee also believes that St. Paul, as well as the authors of Ephesians and the Pastoral Epistles, were sharing in the passing assumptions of their own time, as well as advising wise strategy for the First Century Church, in recommending that women keep silent at services, cover their heads, and be subordinate to their husbands; just as St. Paul thought it wise to send a run-away slave back to his master. Much more permanent and basic are St. Paul's words, "There is neither Jew nor Greek . . . slave nor free . . . male nor female; for you all are one in Christ Jesus."

Image of God: Then, there is a cluster of theological objections based on the assumption that the female is a less true or complete image of God than the male; and that, therefore, woman is less capable, or is quite incapable, of representing God to man and man to God in the priesthood, and of receiving the indelible grace of Holy Orders.

This line of reasoning has a number of curious sources. In the Bible, God is thought and spoken of as "he," for the most part, as would be entirely natural in a culture first militant and war-like, always patriarchal, and with a developing monotheism. Even so, God can be compared with a mother who comforts her child.

Jesus Christ was born a man. Obviously, God's unique child would need to be born either a man or woman; and again, in a patriarchal culture, only a man could fulfill the role of Messiah, Lord, or Son of God. When one calls God personal, one can mean no more than that human personality is the best clue we have to the nature of God. Perhaps male personality is a better clue than female personality in a masculine-dominated society, but who would presume to project such sexual differentiation upon the very nature of God. The first of the Anglican Articles of Religion states that God is "without body, parts, or passions." To call God "he," implies no more than to call the entire human race "man" or "mankind."

The view that the female is a less true or complete image of God than the male is sometime still supported by a tradition coming from Aristotle and St. Thomas Aquinas, which holds that woman is an incomplete human being, "a defective and/or misbegotten male." This tradition was based upon the prescientific biology which held that woman was an entirely passive partner in reproduction. On this subject, the Rev. Dr. Leonard Hodgson has commented, "We should be unwise to base our theological conclusions on notions of a prescientific biology which has never heard of genes [or] chromosomes."

Emotional and Psychological Pressures: The Commission is also aware that all the intellectual arguments against the ordination of women are connected with and reflect strong emotional and psychological pressures. These pressures *may* point to profound truth about men and women and their relationship to each other. Or, they *may* reflect magical notions of priesthood and Sacraments that linger on in the most sophisticated minds. Or, they *may* reflect the fact that our deepest emotional experiences in the life of the Church, experiences often associated with the birth and baptism of children, maturity and Confirmation, ownership and Sacraments, the pastoral ministry in times of crisis, joy and sorrow, are all closely associated with an episcopate and a priesthood that is exclusively male. Or, they *may* illustrate the sad fact that historical and psychological circumstances frequently make the Church the last refuge of the fearful and the timid in a changing world and that, the more rapidly the world changes, the stronger become the pressures to keep the Church safe and unchanged. Or, they *may* represent a threat to the present ordained ministers, to their wives, to lay men or lay women. The Commission is disturbed by the scorn, the indifference, the humorless levity, that is occasioned by the question of seating women in the House of Deputies, let alone their admission to ordination.

Finally, one cannot place much weight upon the common opinion that women themselves do not wish to be ordained. Who knows? Most women obviously do not, just as most men do not wish to become clergymen. But some women do. Kathleen Bliss has written, "This is not a woman's question, it is a Church question." The Church's answer must be determined, not primarily by what is good for woman, but what is good for the Church.

Document 12: Women's Ordination as an Ecumenical Issue (1948 and 1964)

In 1948, a Committee on the Life and Work of Women in the Church of the World Council of Churches (WCC) conducted a survey to examine all facets of women's role in Christian churches. It simply listed the common arguments for and against women's ordination. Fifteen years later, the WCC Commission on Faith and Order held a consultation on the ordination of women, arguing that regardless of differences the question had serious ecumenical ramifications. The following excerpts are from the 1948 report and the 1964 report.[58]

The Enquiry has noted that the full ordination of women to the ministry is indeed a controversial subject. Perhaps no subject related to women in the Church stands in such great need of full, ecumenical study as this one, not because of the great number of women who at this moment are seeking ordination, but because in certain groups throughout the world there is great interest and concern with the principles involved, and because it raises questions related to the unity of the churches.

A few of the reasons set forth against the ordination of women are:

1. The nature and God-given functions of women preclude their being called to this high office.
2. Specific injunctions such as "let a woman learn in silence with all submissiveness. I permit no woman to teach or have authority over man, she is to keep silent."
3. The authority and tradition of the Church have not included the possibility of women serving as clergy.
4. The fact that certain churches consider this a closed issue would make the reunion of the churches more difficult—perhaps impossible.
5. There would be resistance in parishes to having a woman clergyman. In part, this might be because of sex prejudice, and in part because churches of the Reformation have put a high value on the Christian parsonage and the contribution of the pastor's wife. In this connection it would be presumed that most women coming forward for the Ministry would be single women.
6. There would be especially difficult problems for a woman clergyman to face in case she married and had family and home responsibilities.
7. If women should be admitted to the full ministry, it might deter men from answering the call to it.

A few of the viewpoints of those favouring the ordination of women are as follows:

1. Women are now satisfactorily thus serving in some Communions.
2. The problems which they face in the Ministry have been met and largely overcome in other spheres of work.
3. The full ministry of women is required by the Christian doctrine of human nature.
4. "In Christ there is neither male nor female; for ye are all one in Christ Jesus."
5. Under the stress of danger and trouble the Church has been thankful to use them to the full.

6. In the present godlessness and indifference to religion throughout the world, the Church needs the joint service and leadership of men and women.

7. In some of the Younger Churches where women missionaries have been relatively free from traditional restrictions, there is a desire for women to serve the Church in the fullest way.

Two observations perhaps may be allowed concerning the foregoing. First, that important as the subject of "women clergy" is, in its need for further exploration, it represents only one phase of the life and contribution of women in the Church and should not be allowed to overshadow the whole. Second, that further study should be freed from fear, pride, resentment and prejudice, relying on the promised assistance of the Holy Spirit to lead the Church into all truth.

Many churches welcome women to the ordained ministry and have found the policy advantageous. Others, having adopted this policy, face serious internal tensions. In others, the policy is under discussion and provokes heated debate. The matter frequently becomes acute in negotiations for church unity. And even apart from formal negotiations, it affects the mutual relations of churches which ordain women to those which do not. It would be wrong, therefore, to view this issue as a result of feminist demands or agitation by a few enthusiasts. It concerns the total understanding of the ministry of the church and therefore has deep theological significance.

The range of the discussion and the urgency of the problem is something new in Christian history; it has been occasioned by social and cultural movements, although the solution of the problem requires theological decision. Social and cultural movements have their proper place as a challenge to translate Christian doctrine into possible new forms of church live and church order. It is true that the danger must be avoided of accommodating Christian truth to the current ideology, but we must also say that God may use secular movements for showing his will to us.

In our day there has been a rediscovery of two theological factors particularly relevant to our present study: a new insight into the nature of the wholeness of the body of Christ and a better understanding of the meaning of the partnership of men and women in God's design.

a) It is a basic tenet of the New Testament that the whole body is called to witness to the name of Christ; all members—men and women —have therefore their appropriate ministry to which they are called by him. This basic Christian truth was for many centuries overlaid. It has been rediscovered in our own day by all parts of Christendom.

b) It is an essential element of the Christian message that men and women are created in the image of God and are therefore of equal dignity and worth before him. The developments in our time have shown us that this truth has not always been sufficiently understood and emphasized. All the churches are confronted with the necessity of finding a new expression for this basic truth.

It is in this context that the question of the ordination of women is raised. Even the churches which oppose such ordination will realize that these new theological emphases have a relevance for them. The question involves many controversial points of exegesis, of dogmatic formulation and of ecclesiatical life.

Document 13: "Why I Entered the Ministry": A Personal Testimony

In the final analysis, the most significant factor in a woman's decision to seek ordination was her faith and her sense of calling to ministry. In 1944 one Methodist woman put it this way.[59]

Frequently and sometimes very directly, the Christian minister is asked the question: "Why did you enter the ministry?" I think that this very natural inquiry is made of the woman minister even more often than of the man, simply because her position in the church and community is unusual and unique enough to stimulate a greater curiousity in the minds of observers. As a minister I have often been asked why I chose a field which was almost closed to women, when there were so many other good vocations which one might follow.

I count myself most happy to bear witness to the faith that is in me, by having this privilege in a definite way.

Perhaps I can make the why of my entering the ministry clearer and more vivid by mentioning first some of the factors that did not enter in to the making of my decision to enter so challenging a field of endeavor.

First of all, I was not unduly urged, influenced nor persuaded to become a minister—quite to the contrary, I was discouraged, gravely advised against taking such a serious step by my nearest friends, co-workers, and pastoral advisers. Preachers and evangelists whom I had heard plead with tears in their eyes for young people to come forward and dedicate their lives to the ministry, seemed shocked and horrified when a young girl stepped forward to answer the invitation and they were frank to tell me so. By no stretch of introspective imagination can I attribute my choice of vocation to undue influence on the part of others.

Furthermore, I did not enter the ministry because the way was open, and it would be the line of least resistance to walk therein. The way was not open. The only ecclesiastical authority which would be granted me for preaching the gospel would be a local preacher's license, and the only opportunity would be a run-down church which no one else wanted to pastor. No, at the peak of my highest flights of optimism I could not say I entered the ministry because it was the line of least effort.

Nor did I enter because of the inducements of large salary nor for the hope of advancement in my chosen field. Of course no minister enters upon his sacred calling with the hope of a large salary, but it should be the normal and natural thing for the young to dream of recognition and advancement in position as a reward for work well done. Had I thought of either salary or promotion as an inducement, I would have turned back before I started.

While the service motive entered into my thinking, I would not call it the main and decisive factor in my choice, for the service of human kind would have entered into any vocation which I might have chosen.

What then was my one principal reason for entering the ministry? It was the compelling, urgent feeling within the innermost depth of my being that my soul's integrity could not be maintained unless I answered what seemed to me to be God's call to preach. To be true to the truth within me I must undertake the task which my heart's longing dictated. So strong and definite was this inner urge that I felt with Paul of old, "Woe is me if I preach not the gospel." Even before I was ordained by the Methodist Church I felt I was "allowed of God to be put in trust with the gospel."

As the years have gone by that important urge, or call, or consciousness of God's leading has not diminished, and although opportunities in other lines of work have beckoned, the conviction that the ministry is my vocation has been like a gleam which needs I must follow, no matter how strange the paths over which it has led. I thank my God for this continued, ceaseless, burning conviction within me that made my ministry a possibility in spite of the limited ecclesiastical status afforded me by the Church.

Document 14: "Don't Go into the Ministry Unless You Can't Stay Out of It."

Sometimes women clergy acknowledge that being a woman has some advantages, especially in ministries to and with women. Here the first ordained woman in the Evangelical and Reformed Church (now the United Church of Christ) explains how that works. Everything aside, however, she advises young women not to go into ministry unless they can't help it.[60]

From time to time the question has been asked of me—"Do you feel that there is any area of the ministry where an ordained woman can serve, not only as well as, but possibly even better than a male minister?" An affirmative reply can be given in regard to the large area of counselling with families with domestic problems. A substantial portion of my counselling has been in this area with an almost even ratio of men and women having taken the initial step to seek me out. Another area of great effectiveness for a woman is the ministry and work among the shut-ins, and the aged, both men and women, who need not only a sympathetic friend for their loneliness, but a patient and gentle spiritual counselor and advisor.

I have already mentioned the effectiveness of a woman minister counselor among women, but allow me to return to it in order to cite an example to illustrate my point. We have within our congregation, as do most congregations, certain persons who rather enjoy the attention their chronic illnesses bring them. In this case it was a woman—a Mrs. X. One of my visits to her occurred shortly after she had returned home from the hospital where she had undergone a rather minor and not particularly painful operation. However, part of the prescribed post-operative treatment was the wearing of a specially designed, custom-built Spencer foundation garment. The sympathetic ear which I lent to her rather lurid description of the intricate construction and sinister purposes of this masterful creation simply must have been too much for her, for without a word of warning, she disrobed faster than a seasoned burlesque queen and treated me to a grandstand view. I felt that at that moment I had served the Kingdom of God in a capacity safe for no man. Later, Dr. Alspach heartily concurred with judgment on the matter.

Consideration of my topic would indeed be incomplete were I not to dwell for a moment on a description of the very real problems that are peculiar to the role of the ordained woman. In my judgment, one of the most stubborn problems she faces has grown out of the very fact that in the past, the church has denied woman a wide, dignified, and official area of service. For a number of years our educational institutions have encouraged women to gain a higher education and to enter the professions. Yet, when thus prepared, it has limited its own opportunities except in niggardly ways. There has resulted the creation of a "caricature" of the type of woman who does church work and the type of work which she is pictured as doing. Where I have met and worked with ministers and laymen on a professional level, traditional factors such as this have rapidly faded away, but in my personal social life I have experienced its full force.

The normal, sentimental prejudice against a woman minister simply because of her female sex at no time has been a serious problem to me. The only reasonable explanation I can give for this can best be put into a statement. Any sensible woman knows that she will be faced with such prejudice, spoken or unexpressed. She can either feel persecuted and sorry for herself, create an issue of it, and argue against, or in a genuine Christian fashion she can work all the more diligently for the Kingdom in silent and unruffled dignity. There are some things one simply must take.

Still another problem that could be more frustrating than serious is the danger that a woman may type her ministry. That is, if she serves as an assistant or an associate minister, she may find herself becoming known as a young people's minister or a specialist in women's work, or a preacher of the children's sermon. Her hope is always for a complete ministry. I might say that this problem is not always entirely a result of her sex but more likely the result of the position of associate or assistant minister, male or female; for I believe that I can say without disloyalty or unkindness that one of the most serious problems I have encountered has been the lack of specific definition of division of duties of a senior, co-minister relationship.

Thus far I have spoken from my experience as co-minister. What the actual possibilities of being accepted as the senior pastor of a church in the Evangelical and Reformed denomination are, I can only surmise from certain observations. I do not believe that it is an impossibility, neither do I believe that it is a vague probability that an Evangelical and Reformed church might call a single woman by herself. Strides have been recently made to some degree in the placing of Mrs. Kissinger. On the other hand I do not believe that there will be a great rush to call women ministers. But neither do I believe that standing and arguing for the "emancipation" of women in the church will produce any better results than the same procedure has produced results in the realm of race prejudice. A woman must be able to show what she can do. She must display her abilities and possibilities, not in a covetous sense of "I want to do these things too," but as a matter of her own integrity, if she knows the call to be genuine, she must exercise the powers and abilities God has given her.

She asks only that she be given an opportunity—not prestige, not glamor, not honor, and esteem, only a chance to serve the cause of Jesus Christ in a dignified, complete way, in her own right as a complete person.

A little while ago, a young woman about to enter college came to see me—for she was seriously considering a pre-theological course and the seminary course leading toward the fully ordained ministry. She wanted some first hand information and advice. I answered her questions as honestly and realistically as I felt I must, describing as I had found them—the satisfactions—the personal inner struggles—the lonely moments—possible incompleteness of family life—the great glories of service—the frustrations. I found that the only counsel I could give her was "As you pursue the next years of study, think it over very often, very carefully, and very prayerfully, and when the time comes for you to make a mature decision, don't go into the ministry unless you simply can't stay out of it."

If God can use even the "wrath of man to praise him," I suppose he might even accept the preaching of a woman!

Document 15: "Can Women Make their Way into the Ministry?"

Inner motivation and some gender-related advantages did not diminish the fact that women in ministry found the calling difficult. The following article, published in 1929, outlined various ways women approached ministry: going to small churches, serving in staff positions in large churches, working in the YWCA, or teaching religion in colleges. It was time to support the fullness of their ministry. Women, however, were becoming conscious of their need to serve women. Yet the author believed that only when women and men are able to serve the church together will the church be able to meet the challenges of the day.[61]

However it is attacked, the main problem about the entrance of women into the ministry is the finding of ways and means to deliver her message and build up pastoral contacts with men and women. It means a struggle at the present time, and one which demands much courage and self-sacrifice. What has woman to contribute to the life of the churches that makes it worth while to strive so hard for the chance to give it? I am not of those who sentimentalize about woman's gift for religion. Not every women is a prophetess of God just because she is a woman, with the much-lauded woman's intuition, any more than every woman is an ideal mother just because she is a female with the famed maternal instinct. Women have a right to minister, first of all, because the Spirit of God can and has spoken through members of either sex. There is another reason also. Woman is needed in the leadership of the church today as she never has been at any other time in its history. The life of women is expanding in every sphere as it never has before. With the increase of privilege and opportunity for self-expression freedom and economic independence have come a host of new problems that women are just beginning to see, and responsibilities that they do not yet know how to bear. The whole ideal for woman is changing so that even the concept of what is womanly and ladylike, so clear-cut and well-defined to past generations is in a state of flux. Time-honored and hoary traditions are collapsing all about us. The modern woman is bewildered by all this; she is making mistakes; often she is headed for tragedy because she does not yet know what to do with her new freedom.

Who can show women the way out of this maze? Surely not a ministry made up entirely of men. They are not in the same situation, and therefore cannot contribute the solution. But there are some women who believe that the Christian gospel has in it the power and the principles along which a solution to the vexing problems of the new woman can be worked out. They are working out this solution in their own lives, and wish to share with their sisters what they have found in Jesus Christ that aids them in their difficult situation. Therefore they wish to enter the ministry, and try to gain the chance to do this. The church should give them this opportunity. The difficulties of the new woman cannot be met by women working in isolated groups. Life cannot be so conveniently simplified. Hence the church can only hope to be of help on the problems of life as she has an enlightened ministry of men and women striving together to guide the souls of men and women in the life they face together. The position of women is acute at present, but it affects the position of men and of children. The church, for ages, has tried to solve the problems of men and women through a ministry composed exclusively of men. This is no more adequate to redeeming the world at present than an exclusively feminine ministry would be. The church must quickly make room for trained women fitted to work on the problems of women on a Christian basis. That contribution alone would justify the hard struggle that women must make at the present time in order to win a place in the ministry.

Notes

Introduction

1. See Rosemary Radford Ruether and Rosemary Skinner Keller, eds., *Women and Religion in America, Volume 1; The Nineteenth Century, A Documentary History* (San Francisco: Harper & Row, 1981); and *Women and Religion in America, Volume 2; The Colonial and Revolutionary Periods, A Documentary History* (San Francisco: Harper & Row, 1983).
2. For example, Lois Scharf, *To Work and to Wed: Female Employment, Feminism and the Great Depression* (Westport, Conn.: The Greenwood Press, 1982); Rosalind Rosenberg, *Beyond Separate Spheres: The Intellectual Roots of Modern Feminism* (New Haven: Yale University Press, 1982); D'Ann Campbell, *Women at War with America* (Cambridge, Mass.: Harvard University Press, 1984); Susan W. Ware, *Beyond Suffrage: Women in the New Deal* (Cambridge: Harvard University Press, 1981).
3. Ruether and Keller, *Women and Religion in America, Volume 1*, pp. 1–41.
4. See Lillian Ashcroft Webb, "Black Women and Religion in the Colonial Period," in Ruether and Keller, *Women and Religion in America, Volume 2*, pp. 233–259.
5. Mary Ewens, "The Leadership of Nuns in Immigrant Catholicism," in Ruether and Keller, *Women and Religion in America, Volume 1*, pp. 101–149.
6. Barbara Brown Zikmund, "The Struggle for the Right to Preach," in Ruether and Keller, *Women and Religion in America, Volume 1*, pp. 193–241.

Radical Victorians: The Quest for an Alternative Culture

1. Franz Boas (1858–1942) turned anthropology away from large comparative studies of culture, within schemes of universal evolution of society, and sought to make it an exact social science by studying the meaning of particular elements of culture within a specific social context.
2. J. J. Bachofen (1815–1887), *Das Mutterrecht* (Stuttgart: Krais and Hoffman, 1861). It has never been translated into English in its entirety. An abridged English translation appeared as *Myth, Religion and Motherright*, Ralph Manheim, trans., Joseph Campbell, Introduction (London: Routledge and Kegan Paul, 1967).
3. Matilda Joslyn Gage, *Woman, Church and State* (New York: Arno Press, 1972). A more recent feminist publication appeared with Persephone Press, 1980, with an introduction by Mary Daly.
4. Lewis H. Morgan(1818–1881), *Ancient Society: Research into the Lines of Human Progress from Savagery through Barbarianism to Civilization* (New York: H. Holt, 1877).
5. August Bebel (1840–1914), *Die Frau und der Sozialismus* (Zurich: Volksbuchhandlung, 1879). It was translated into English by Meta Stern (New York: Socialist Literature Co., 1910).
6. Frances Willard, 1897 address to the National Women's Christian Temperance Association Assembly; see Mari Jo Buhle, *Women and American Socialism, 1870–1920* (Urbana: University of Illinois Press, 1981), pp. 108–109.
7. Edward Alexander Westermarck (1862–1939), *The History of Human Marriage* (London: Macmillan, 1891).
8. Robert Briffault, *The Mothers*, abridged, with introduction by Gordon Rattray Taylor (London: George Allen and Unwin, 1959), p. 431.
9. George Mosse, *The Crisis of German Ideology: Intellectual Origins of the Third Reich* (New York: Grosset and Dunlap, 1964).
10. Charles Samuel Braden, *Spirits in Rebellion. The Rise and Development of New Thought* (Dallas: Southern Methodist University Press, 1963). Also *These Also Believe. A Study of Modern America Cults and Minority Religious Movements* (New York: Macmillan, 1949).
11. Myrtle Fillmore (1845–1931) was the cofounder of Unity Christianity. Her chief literary contribution was the writing and editing of *Wee Wisdom*, a children's Unity publica-

tion. Her role in founding Unity is told be James D. Fillmore, *The Household of Faith: The Story of Unity* (Lee's Summit, Mo.: Unity School of Christianity, 1951).

12. Emma Curtis Hopkins (1853–1925) broke with Mary Baker Eddy in 1886 and came to Chicago, where she founded her own seminary and disseminated her views through the *Christian Metaphysician* (1887–1897). Among her books are *High Mysticism: A Series of Twelve Studies of the Wisdom of the Sages of Ages* (Baltimore: Williams and Wilkins, 1920).

13. Harriette Emilie Cady (1848–1941); her primary influence was through her often-republished *Lessons in Truth* (Kansas City, Mo.: Unity Tract Society, 1897).

14. Helena Blavatsky (1831–1891), *Isis Unveiled: A Master Key to the Mysteries of Ancient and Modern Science and Theology* (New York: J. W. Bowton, 1877); also *The Secret Doctrine: The Synthesis of Science, Religion and Philosophy* (London: The Theosophical Publishing Co., 1888).

15. Emmett A. Greenwalt, *The Point Loma Community in California, 1897–1942: A Theosophical Experiment* (Berkeley: University of California Press, 1955).

16. Aleta Baker's many books include *The Biune Corpus-Christi* (Washington, D.C.: n.p., 1938); *The Causal Essence Personified* (Boston: n.p., 1928); *The Luminous Doctrine of the Spiritual Heart* (Boston: n.p., 1929); *Man—and His Counterpart—Woman* (Boston: n.p., 1931), and *She, the Woman-Man* (Boston: n.p., 1935).

17. Among Harriette and Homer Curtiss's many books are *The Divine Mother* (San Francisco: Curtiss, 1921); *The Coming World Changes* (Washington, D.C.: Curtiss, 1926), *The Key of the Universe* (San Francisco: Curtiss, 1915); *The Message of Aquaria* (San Francisco: Curtiss, 1921), *The Mystic Life* (Washington, D.C.: Curtiss, 1934), *Prayers of the Order of Christian Mystics* (Washington, D.C.: Curtiss, 1934); and *The Voice of Isis* (Washington, D.C.: Curtiss, 1926).

18. Sir Arthur Evans (1851–1941) was the chief archaeologist for the excavation of ancient Crete and the Palace of Knossos. Influenced by matriarchal theory, he described his findings in Crete through that interpretative framework. Other important interpreters of preclassical Greek culture, from this perspective, were Jane Ellen Harrison (1850–1928), *Themis: A Study of the Social Origins of Greek Religion* (Cambridge: The University Press, 1921), and *Prolegomena to the Study of Greek Religion* (Cambridge: The University Press, 1903). Also Martin P. Nilsson (1874–1967), *A History of Greek Religion* (Oxford: Clarendon Press, 1925).

19. James George Frazer (1854–1941), *The Golden Bough. A Study in Comparative Religion* (London: Macmillan, 1890). E. O. James (1886–1972): His chief work on female religious symbols is *The Cult of the Mother Goddess: An Anthropological and Documentary Study* (New York: Barnes and Noble, 1959).

20. Students of comparative mythology influenced by the Jungian school of psychology have been primary writers in this area, publishing particularly in the Bollingen series, Princeton University Press. One example of such interpretation of the development of Goddess symbols is Erich Neumann, *The Great Mother: An Analysis of the Archetype* (Princeton University Press, 1963). So pervasive has been the Jungian school of interpretation of ancient myths that there has been little effort by other scholars of myth to look at the ancient texts and symbols from the context of the original culture and to ask whether these Jungian interpretations are accurate, rather than projections of a European romantic culture.

21. On the side of "Goddess religion" against biblical religion, see, for example, Carol Christ, "Why Women Need the Goddess" in Carol Christ and Judith Plaskow, eds., *Womanspirit Rising: A Feminist Reader in Religion*, (San Francisco: Harper & Row, 1979), pp. 273–86; and Naomi Goldenberg, *The Changing of the Gods* (Boston: Beacon, 1979); also Charlene Spretnak, *The Politics of Woman's Spirituality* (Garden City, N.Y.: Doubleday, 1982). In defense of an integration of biblical and nonbiblical sources for feminist theology, see Rosemary Ruether, "Goddesses and Witches: Liberation and Countercultural Feminism," *The Christian Century* (September 10–17, 1980): 842–847; also *Sexism and God-talk, Toward a Feminist Theology* (Boston: Beacon, 1983), esp. pp. 38–41.

22. Matilda Joslyn Gage, *Woman, Church and State* [1893]; reprint (Watertown, Mass.: Persephone Press, 1980), pp. 8, 21, 23, 337, 339, 345–346.

23. Catherine Gasquoine Hartley, *The Age of Mother-Power: The Position of Woman in Primitive Society* (New York: Dodd, Mead and Co., 1914), pp. 326–328, 303–305, 334–337, 340–341, 342, 344–345.

24. Carrie Chapman Catt, "A Survival of Matriarchy," *Harpers Magazine* 128 (April 1914): 738–748.
25. Buhle, *Woman and American Socialism, 1870–1920,* pp.145–172.
26. Josephine Conger-Kaneko, *The Progressive Woman* 5, no. 55 (December 11, 1912): 8; Theresa Malkiel, *The Progressive Woman* 6, no. 68 (February 6, 1913): 6, 15.
27. "The Social Evolution of Woman," probably by the editor, Henry Mills Alden, *Harpers Magazine* 120 (January 1910): 313–316.
28. Robert Briffault, *The Mothers: A Study of the Origins of Sentiments and Institutions* (New York: Macmillan, 1927), vol. 1, pp. 433–436; vol. 2, pp. 45–48, 51.
29. Mary Renault, *The King Shall Die* (New York: Pantheon, 1958). Other such novels by Renault are *The Bull from the Sea* (New York: Modern Library, 1962); *The Last of the Wine* (New York: Modern Library, 1956); *The Mask of Apollo* (New York: Pantheon, 1966), and *Fire from Heaven* (New York: Pantheon, 1969).
30. Marion Z. Bradley, *The Mists of Avalon* (New York: Knopf, 1983).
31. James Frazer, *The Golden Bough* (London: Macmillan, 1922).
32. Robert Graves, *The White Goddess: A Historical Grammar of Poetic Myth* (New York: Farrar, Straus, and Giroux, 1948), pp. 24, 386–390, 475–486.
33. Charlotte Perkins Gilman, *Herland,* serialized in *The Forerunner* 6 (1915); reprint (New York: Pantheon, 1979).
34. Charlotte Perkins Gilman, *His Religion and Hers: A Study of the Faith of the Fathers and the Work of Our Mothers* (New York: The Century Co., 1923), pp. vii–viii, 37–43, 45–47, 50, 226, 248–249, 251, 270.
35. Ella Wheeler Wilcox, *The Heart of New Thought* (Chicago: Psychic Research Co., 1902), pp. 33, 34–35, 88–90.
36. Katherine Tingley, *The Voice of the Soul* (Point Loma, Calif.: The Aryan Theosophical Press, 1928), pp. 82–83, 54, 233–235, 237.
37. Harriette Augusta Curtiss, *The Voice of Isis* (New York: Edward J. Clode, 1917), pp. xxvii, 253–255, 336–340.
38. The phrase occurs on the back jacket of the 1971 Putnam edition of Davis's book, (note 39)
39. Elisabeth Gould Davis, *The Fist Sex* (Baltimore: Penguin, 1971), pp. 68–69, 336–339.

American Indian Women and Religion on the Southern Plains

1. The southern Plains is an area bounded by the Rocky mountains and the Mississippi River on the east and west, extending north from central Texas to the northern border of Kansas.
2. C. F. Voegelin, "North American Indian Languages Still Spoken and Their Genetic Relationships," in L. Spier, ed., *Language, Culture, and Personality: Essays in Memory of Edward Sapir* (Menasha: Sapir Memorial Publication Fund, 1941), *pp. 15–40.*
3. Grant Foreman, *The Last Trek of the American Indian* (Chicago: University of Chicago Press, 1946), pp. 14–15.
4. James Mooney, *Myths of the Cherokees: Nineteenth Annual Report of the Bureau of American Ethnology* (Washington, D.C.: Government Printing Office, 1897–1898), pp. 125–135. Angie Debo, *The Road to Disappearance: A History of the Creek Indians,* 2d ed. (Norman: University of Oklahoma, 1967), p. 103.
5. Ake Hultkrantz, *The Religions of the American Indians,* English ed. (Berkeley: University of California Press, 1980), p. 9.
6. Ruth Benedict, "The Concept of the Guardian Spirit in North America," *Memoirs of the American Anthropological Association* (Lancaster, Penn.: 1923, vol. 29), pp. 28–43.
7. An extensive ethnographic study of Sanapia is found in David Jones, *Sanapia: Comanche Medicine Woman* (New York: Holt, Rinehart and Winston, 1972).
8. The giveaway is an institutionalized aspect of tribal ceremonies which rests upon the principles of sharing and reciprocity. Material goods and money are exchanged in friendship and for prestige. The most needy people are always large recipients.
9. Gustavus E. E. Lindquist, *The Red Man in the United States: An Intimate Study of the Social, Economic and Religious Life of the American Indian* (New York: G. H. Doran, 1923) pp. 428–430.
10. *Historical Statistics of the United States: Colonial Times to 1970.* vol. I (U.S. Department of Commerce: Bureau of the Census, 1975).

11. Gustavus E. E. Lindquist, *Indians in Transition: A Study of Protestant Missions to Indians in the United States* (New York: National Council of Churches of Christ in the USA, 1951).

12. Lindquist, *The Red Man in the United States*, p. 428.

13. Henry Warner Bowden, *American Indians and Christian Missions: Studies in Cultural Conflict* (Chicago: University of Chicago, 1981), p. 201.

14. James Mooney, *The Ghost Dance Religion, Fourteenth Annual Report of the Bureau of Ethnology, 1892–93* (Washington D.C.: Government Printing Office, 1896), vol. 14, pt. 2, pp. 663–746.

15. Omer Stewart, "Origin of the Peyote Religion in the United States," *Plains Anthropology* 19 (1974): vol. 19, 211–223.

16. Hazel Hertzberg, *The Search for an American Identity: Modern Pan-Indian Movements* (Syracuse: 1971).

17. Carol Hampton, "The Native American Church: A Religion for Twentieth Century Indians," unpublished master's thesis, department of history, University of Oklahoma, 1973, pp. 69–76.

18. Interview, Reverend Hazel Botone to the author, September 27, 1983.

19. Interview, Myrtle Lincoln to Julia Jordan, December 22, 1969, Doris Duke Collection, Norman, American Indian Institute, University of Oklahoma, vol. 1, T-607, pp. 2–4.

20. Interview, Mary Poafybitty Neido to David Jones, October 19, 1967, Doris Duke Collection, vol. 26, T-173-1, pp. 6–7.

21. Interview, Mary Poafybitty Neido to David Jones, June, 15, 1967, Doris Duke Collection, vol. 27, T-52, pp. 10–15.

22. Interview, Richard Manus to B. D. Timmons, February 8, 1969, Doris Duke Collection, vol. 16, T-417, pp. 7–8.

23. Interview, Annie Hawk to the author, January 17, 1977.

24. Interview, Rose Birdshead to the author, September 24, 1983.

25. Interview, Mrs. Amos Stovall to Lillian Gassaway, 1938 (Works Progress Administration, Federal Theatre of Oklahoma), Oklahoma Historical Society, Oklahoma City.

26. Sharon Fife, "Baptist Indian Church: Thlewarle Mekko Sapkv Coko," *The Chronicles of Oklahoma* vol. 48 (1970): 451–466.

27. Interview, Myrtle Lincoln to Julia Jordan, July 30, 1970. Doris Duke Collection, vol. 2, T-613, pp. 2–28.

28. Interview, Reverend Hazel Botone to the author, September 14, 1983.

29. Interview, Leonard Maker to Katharine Maker, December 12, 1968, Doris Duke Collection, vol. 47, T-344, p. 6.

30. Interview, Jess Rowlodge to Julia Jordan, December 5, 1967, Doris Duke Collection, vol. 5, T-170, pp. 16–18.

31. Interview, Alice Apekaum to David Jones, October 7, 1967, Doris Duke Collection, vol. 33, T-177-2, pp. 1–4.

Something Within: Social Change and Collective Endurance in the Sacred World of Black Christian Women

1. Several sources describe the "rise of Jim Crow" and the "betrayal of the Negro." Some of the most helpful are Rayford W. Logan, *The Betrayal of the Negro: From Rutherford B. Hayes to Woodrow Wilson* (New York: Macmillan, 1965); John Hope Franklin, *From Slavery to Freedom: A History of Negro Americans* (New York: Random House, 1969); Manning Marable, *How Capitalism Underdeveloped Black America: Problems in Race, Political Economy and Society* (Boston: South End Press, 1983); C. Vann Woodward, *The Strange Career of Jim Crow* (New York: Oxford University Press, 1974).

2. W. E. B. DuBois, "Of the Dawn of Freedom," in *The Souls of Black Folk* (Greenwich, Conn.: Fawcett Publications, 1961), p. 23.

3. Angela Davis, *Women, Race, and Class* (New York: Random House, 1981).

4. In addition to the majority of black churchgoers who are Baptist, Congregationalists, Pentecostals, and Apostolics, all practice adult believer's baptism.

5. Minna Davis Caulfield, "Imperialism, the Family, and Cultures of Resistance," *Socialist Revolution #20.* 4, no. 2 (October 1974): 67–85.

6. Cheryl Townsend Gilkes, "Together and in Harness: Women's Traditions in the Sanctified Church," *Signs: Journal of Women in Culture and Society* 10, no. 4 (Summer 1985).

7. Frances Ella Watkins Harper's poem—"We soon got used to freedom/ Though the way at first was rough/ But we weathered through the tempest/ For slavery made us tough"—is quoted in Dorthy Sterling, *We Are Your Sisters: Black Women in the Nineteenth Century* (New York: W. W. Norton, 1985), p. 331.

8. Elizabeth Lindsey Davis, *Lifting as They Climb: A History of the National Association of Colored Women* (Washington, D.C.: Moorland-Spingarn Research Center, Howard University, 1933), p. 19. Ida B. Wells Barnett, *The Autobiography of Ida B. Wells* (Chicago: University of Chicago Press, 1970), p. 121.

9. Davis, *Lifting as They Climb*, p. 19.

10. Gerda Lerner, ed., *Black Women in White America: A Documentary History* (New York: Random House, 1972), pp. 458–497.

11. Davis, *Women, Race, and Class;* Sharon Harley and Rosalyn Terborg-Penn, eds., *The Afro-American Woman: Struggles and Images* (Port Washington, N.Y.: Kennikat Press, 1978).

12. Lucy Campbell, "He Understands, He'll Say 'Well Done!' " *The New National Baptist Special* (Chicago: H. & T. Music House and Publishers, Inc., n. d., circa 1950), p. 11. The last copyright date for a particular song is 1949.

13. Wyatt Tee Walker, *"Somebody's Calling My Name": Black Sacred Music and Social Change* (Valley Forge, Pa.: The Judson Press, 1979).

14. Tony Heilbut, *The Gospel Sound: Good News and Bad Times* (Garden City, N.Y.: Doubleday, Anchor Books, 1975), pp. 224–232.

15. National Baptist Convention, *Gospel Pearls* (Nashville: Sunday School Publishing Board, 1921). Rev. E. W. D. Isaac, Miss L. E. Campbell, and E. W. D. Isaac, Jr., eds., *Inspirational Melodies* (Nashville: National Baptist Training Union Board, n.d.).

16. Heilbut, *The Gospel Sound*. Donald Vails, "Gospel Music: A Black Tradition," A workshop and series of lectures presented at Boston University School of Theology, 1981.

17. Heilbut, *The Gospel Sound*, pp. 252–253. Herbert Brewster, "Our God Is Able" (Chicago: Martin Morris Music, Inc. [1949] 1975), pp. 2–4. The androgynous theology is Clara Ward's addition to the composed text.

18. The overwhelming impact of women on the growth and development of gospel music is obvious from a cursory reading of Heilbut's *The Gospel Sound*.

19. W. E. B. DuBois, "Votes for Women," in Daniel Walden, ed., *W. E. B. DuBois: The Crisis Writings* (Greenwich, Conn. Fawcett Publications, 1972), p. 340.

20. Emma L. Fields, "The Women's Club Movement in the United States, 1877–1900" unpublished master's thesis, Washington D.C., Howard University, 1948, pp. 66–79.

21. Barnett, *Crusade for Justice*, pp. 69–75.

22. Such terminology can be found in a picture of some "leading preachers and educators of the formative period of the National Baptist Convention. . . ." J. H. Jackson, *A Story of Christian Activism: The History of the National Baptist Convention, U.S.A., Inc.* (Nashville: Townsend Press, 1980), p. 62.

23. W. E. B. DuBois, *Black Reconstruction in America: An Essay Toward a History of the Part Which Black Folk Played in the Attempt to Reconstruct Democracy in America, 1860–1880* (New York: Atheneum, 1979 [1935]), pp. 637–669.

24. The dates of their births and deaths were taken from Harry A. Ploski and Roscoe C. Brown, *The Negro Almanac* (New York: Bellwether Publishing Company, 1967).

25. Frank T. Wilson, Sr., ed., *Black Presbyterians in Ministry* (New York: Consulting Committee on Ethnic Minority Ministries, United Presbyterian Church in the USA, 1977), pp. 8–10.

26. The role of black women in education is described in several sources. One of the most helpful is Marianna W. Davis, ed., *Contributions of Black Women to America: Volume II; Civil Rights, Politics and Government, Education, Medicine, Sciences* (Columbia, S.C.: Kenday Press, 1981), pp. 261–356.

27. Evelyn Brooks, "The Feminist Theology of the Black Baptist Church, 1880–1900," in Amy Swerdlow and Hannah Lessinger, eds., *Class, Race, and Sex: The Dynamics of Control* (Boston: G. K. Hall and Company, 1983), pp. 31–59.

28. Robert Mapes Anderson, *Vision of the Disinherited: The Making of American Pentecostalism* (New York: Oxford University Press, 1979), pp. 62–78.

29. Walter J. Hollenweger, *The Pentecostals* (Minneapolis: Augsburg Publishing House, 1972), p. xvii. Leonard Lovett, "The Black Origins of the Pentecostal Movement," in Vinson Synan, ed., *Aspects of Pentecostal-Charismatic Origins* (Plainfield, N.J.: Logos

International, 1975). James S. Tinney, "Black Origins of the Pentecostal Movement," *Christianity Today* 16 (1971): 4–6.

30. Anderson, *Vision of the Disinherited,* pp. 63–78.
31. Such attempts to "regularize" the worship of black men and women who were formerly slaves are described in Leon Litwack, *Been in the Storm So Long: The Aftermath of Slavery* (New York: Alfred A. Knopf, 1979), pp. 450–501; and in Daniel Payne, *Recollections of Seventy Years* (New York: Arno Press/The New York Times, 1969), pp. 233–257.
32. James Shopshire, *A Socio-Historical Characterization of the Black Pentecostal Movement in America,* unpublished Ph.D. dissertation, Evanston, Ill.: Northwestern University, 1975.
33. Such activities are described in the biographical sketches throughout Lucille Cornelius, *The Pioneer History of the Church of God in Christ* (Memphis: Church of God in Christ Publishing House, 1975).
34. Teressa Hoover, "Black Women and the Churches: Triple Jeopardy," in Gayraud S. Wilmore and James H. Cone, eds., *Black Theology: A Documentary History, 1966–1979* (Maryknoll, N.Y.: Orbis Books, 1979), pp. 377–388.
35. James S. Tinney, "The Religious Experience of Black Men," in Lawrence E. Gary, ed., *The Black Male* (Beverly Hills: Sage Publications, 1981), pp. 269–276.
36. Sister Mary Roger Thibodeaux, S.B.S., *A Black Nun Looks at Black Power* (New York: Sheed and Ward, 1972). The Liturgical Conference, *This Far By Faith: American Black Worship and Its African Roots* (Washington, D.C.: The National Office for Black Catholics and The Liturgical Conference, 1977). Nathan Jones, *Sharing the Old, Old Story: Educational Ministry in the Black Community* (Winona, Minn.: Saint Mary's Press, 1982).
37. Black Catholics I have encountered have invariably described attending both their Catholic congregations as well as local Protestant churches of their relatives. One black priest vividly described his mother's insistence that his parochial school teacher's admonition not to attend Protestant churches was the kind of teaching that he would have to learn to ignore.
38. A participant in this meeting described this experience to me in a conversation.
39. Arthur St. George and Patrick H. McNamara, "Religion, Race, and Psychological Well-Being," *Journal for the Scientific Study of Religion* 23, no. 4 (1984): 354.
40. Albert Raboteau, *Slave Religion: The Invisible Institution in the Antebellum South* (New York: Oxford University Press, 1978). Mechal Sobel, *Trabelin' On: The Slave's Journey to an Afro-Baptist Faith* (Westport, Conn.: Greenwood Press, 1979).
41. Two colleagues, one from Memphis, Tennessee, and another from Mobile, Alabama, described Christian Methodist Episcopal (CME) and African Methodist Episcopal (AME) congregations in which they grew up, where "believer's baptism" by immersion was the only form of baptism practiced.
42. Jackson, *A Story of Christian Activism,* p. 62.
43. Some hint of this emerges in the tensions between Washington and the Club Movement discussed in Paula Giddings, *When and Where I Enter: The Impact of Black Women on Race and Sex in America* (New York: William Morrow, 1984), pp. 102–108.
44. Brooks, "The Feminist Theology of the Black Baptist Church," p. 36.
45. Evelyn Brooks Barnett, "Nannie Helen Burroughs and the Education of Black Women," in Sharon Harley and Rosalyn Terborg-Penn, eds., *The Afro-American Woman: Struggles and Images* (Port Washington, N.Y.: Kennikat Press, 1978), pp. 97–108.
46. Elizabeth Maddox Huntley, *Faith of Women on a Mission: A Pageant in Three Episodes* (Detroit: The Women's Convention/Harlo Press, 1976). Jackson, *A Story of Christian Activism,* pp. 87–88.
47. Charles Pleas, *Fifty Years of Achievement (History): Church of God in Christ* (Memphis: Church of God in Christ Publishing House, n.d., circa 1957). Rev. J. O. Patterson, German R. Ross, and Mrs. Julia Mason Atkins, eds., *History and Formative Years of the Church of God in Christ with Excerpts from the Life and Works of its Founder, Bishop C[harles] H[arrison] Mason* (Memphis: Church of God in Christ Publishing House, 1969).
48. Respondents in a study of urban community workers cited this ideology as representing black male resistance to female leadership. Cheryl Townsend Gilkes, *Living and Working in a World of Trouble: The Emergent Career of the Black Woman Community Worker,* unpublished Ph.D. dissertation, Boston, Northeastern University, 1979.
49. Lucie E. Campbell, "He Understands, He'll Say Well Done!' " and "Something Within,"

National Baptist Special, pp. 11 and 22. "Something Within" was written in 1919 and "He Understands" was written prior to 1949.

50. Rev. Charles Walker, "Lucie Campbell Remembered," *National Baptist Voice* (July/August 1983): 11.
51. St. Clair Drake and Horace Cayton, *Black Metropolis: A Study of Negro Life in a Northern City* (New York: Harcourt, Brace, and World, 1945), p. 394.
52. Rackham Holt, *Mary McLeod Bethune: A Biography* (Garden City, N.Y.: Doubleday, 1964), p. 45.
53. Davis, *Lifting as They Climb,* pp. 200–202.
54. Howard Thurman, *With Head and Heart: The Autobiography of Howard Thurman* (New York: Harcourt, Brace, Jovanovich, 1979).
55. National Council of Negro Women, *Women United: Souvenir Yearbook, Sixteenth Anniversary* (Washington, D.C.: Moorland Spingarn Research Center, Howard University, 1951).
56. Holt, *Mary McLeod Bethune, pp. 287–289.*
57. Sara J. Duncan, "In Vindication of Vital Questions" in John T. Jenifer, *Centennial Retrospect History of the African Methodist Episcopal Church* (Chicago: Sunday School Union, African Methodist Episcopoal Church, 1916), p. 141.
58. *Ibid.*
59. C. L. Tshabalala, "A Litany for African Women," *Voice of Missions* 42, no. 4 (August 1940): 1.
60. For a discussion of this cultural relationship, the following essay by Zora Neale Hurston (written around 1928) is helpful: Zora Neale Hurston, *The Sanctified Church* (Berkeley, Cal.: Turtle Island Press, 1982). Robert Mapes Anderson's *Vision of the Disinherited* contains an extensive discussion of the racial split in the Pentecostal movement (pp. 176–194), but does not consider the cultural influences of black people. In general, there is a real failure to appreciate the powerful role of racism in the shaping of American religious bodies and the failure of white churches, especially those whose origins lie in the revivalism of the American South and West, to acknowledge their cultural debts to the Afro-American religious experience. See also James S. Tinney, "Black Pentecostals: The Difference is More than Color," *Logos Journal.* 10, no. 3 (1980): 16–19.
61. The tensions between perceptions of Holiness and Pentecostal churches and perceptions of other religious organizations are evident in the research of Arthur Huff Fauset, *Black Gods of the Metropolis* (Philadelphia: University of Pennsylvania Press, 1944).
62. Delores Causion Carpenter described to me in a personal conversation the systematic exclusion of "nonmainline clergy" from an urban clergy survey in an area where the majority of the clergy (pastors) were "nonmainline" and women.
63. Pleas, *Fifty Years Achievement,* pp. 1–5.
64. Church of God in Christ, *Official Manual with the Doctrines and Disciplines of the Church of God in Christ* (Memphis: Church of God in Christ Publishing House, 1973), pp. 158–160.
65. Gayraud S. Wilmore, *Black Religion and Black Radicalism: An Interpretation of the Religious History of Afro-American People* (Maryknoll, N.Y.: Orbis Books, 1983).
66. At one point, the founder of the Church of Christ (Holiness), Elder C. P. Jones (cofounder with Mason of the Church of God in Christ in 1895) attempted to insist that church clerks within the denomination be men. While this was a minority viewpoint, it is indicative of the feelings of the times. Church of Christ (Holiness) USA, *Manual of the History, Doctrine, Government, and Ritual of the Church of Christ (Holiness) U.S.A.: True Holiness* (Norfolk, Va.: Guide Publishing Company 1926), p. 27.
67. Pleas, *Fifty Years Achievement,* pp. 12–16.
68. Sister Anna Smith, National Recording Secretary, "Minutes: 24th Annual Convocation," *The Whole Truth* 18, no. 1 (January 1942): 1.
69. Lucille Cornelius, *The Pioneer History of the Church of God in Christ* (Memphis: Church of God in Christ Publishing House), pp. 22–23.
70. Church of the Living God, Christian Workers for Fellowship, *Glorious Heritage: The Golden Book—Documentary and History* (N.C.: Church of the Living God, C.W.F.F., 1964), p. 22.
71. *Ibid.*
72. *Ibid.,* pp. 22, 24, 35–37, 39.

73. Telephone interview, New York City, 1984.
74. Typescript, unpublished document, National Conference of Black Sisters, 1968.
75. Lethia L. Craig and Edna B. Bronson, *A Handbook of Stories: Young People's Department of the Woman's Convention* (Nashville: Sunday School Publishing Board), p. 10.
76. W. E. B. DuBois, "The Woman," in Daniel Walden, ed., *W. E. B. DuBois: The Crisis Writings* (Greenwich, Conn.: Fawcett Publications, 1983), pp. 337–339.
77. *Ibid.*, pp. 338–339.
78. Craig, *A Handbook of Stories*, p. 11.
79. *Ibid.*, pp. 8–12.
80. Craig, "Nannie Helen Burroughs: She Knew What She Wanted to Be," in Craig and Bronson, *A Handbook of Stories*, pp. 83–86.
81. W. E. B. DuBois, *The Gift of Black Folk: The Negroes in the Making of America* [1924] (New York: Washington Square Press, 1970, pp. 178–190. Nannie Helen Burroughs, "With All Thy Getting," *The Southern Workman* 56, no. 7 (July 1927): 299–301, is excerpted in Gerda Lerner, ed., *Black Women in White America: A Documentary History* (New York: Random House, 1972), pp.550–551.
82. Lerner, *Black Women in White America*, p. 133.
83. Lerner, *Black Women in White America*, p. 133. Barnett, "Nannie Helen Burroughs and the Education of Black Women."
84. Nannie Helen Burroughs, *Who Started Women's Day?* (Washington, D.C.: Nannie H. Burroughs Publications/Nannie Helen Burroughs School, 1968). This is the 1968 version of a pamphlet that Miss Burroughs wrote and published before her death in 1961.
85. Nannie H. Burroughs, *The Slabtown District Convention: A Comedy in One Act* (Washington, D.C.: Nannie H. Burroughs Publications/Nannie Helen Burroughs School, 1979). This is the twenty-second edition of a play that Miss Burroughs wrote fairly early in her career.
86. Lerner, *Black Women in White America*, p. 32.
87. Thurman, *With Head and Heart;* Holt, *Mary McLeod Bethune;* Barnett, *Crusade for Justice.*
88. Brooks, "The Feminist Theology of the Black Baptist Church."
89. Nannie Helen Burroughs, *Role Call of Bible Women: Men Wrote the Highlights of their Lives* (Washington, D.C.: Nannie H. Burroughs School, n.d.).

Between Synogogue and Nation: Tides of Change for American Jewish Women

1. Henrietta Szold, *Hadassah Bulletin* I, no. 12 (July 1915): 7.
2. Zena Smith Blau, "In Defense of the Jewish Mother," in Peter Rose, *The Ghetto and Beyond* (New York: Random House, 1969).
3. General accounts of Jewish immigration to America include Irving Howe, *The World of Our Fathers* (New York: Simon and Schuster, 1976) and Moses Rischin, *The Promised City: New York's Jews, 1870–1914* (Cambridge: Harvard University Press, 1962). On Jewish women see Charlotte Baum, Paula Hyman, and Sonya Michel, *The Jewish Woman in America* (New York: The New American Library, 1977), Anita Libman Lebeson, *Recall to Life* (New York: Thomas Yoseloff, 1970); and Rudolf Glanz, *The Jewish Woman in America: Two Female Immigrant Generations, 1820–1929* (New York: KTAV, 1976), Jacob R. Marcus,*The American Jewish Woman* (New York: KTAV, 1981), and June Sochen, *Consecrate Every Day* (New York: SUNY Press, 1980).
4. Anzia Yezierska, *Salome of the Tenements* (New York: Boni and Liveright, 1923), p. 65.
5. Rischin, *The Promised City*, pp. 93, 85; Deborah Dash Moore, *At Home in America: Second Generation New York Jews* (New York: Columbia University Press, 1981), p. 3.
6. Anzia Yezierska, *Bread Givers* [1925] reprint (New York: Persea Books, 1975), p. 8.
7. Lillian Wald, *The House on Henry Street* (New York: Holt and Co., 1915), p. 21.
8. Mary Antin, *The Promised Land* (Boston: Houghton Mifflin Co, 1912), p. 277.
9. Moore, *At Home in America,* p. 90.
10. See also Elizabeth G. Stern, *My Mother and I* (New York: Macmillan, 1917), and Anzia Yezierska, "The Fat of the Land," in *Hungry Hearts* (Boston: Houghton Mifflin, 1920).
11. Laura Z. Hobson, *Laura Z: A Life* (New York: Arbor House, 1983), p. 12.
12. "Penalizing Parenthood," *Independent* 74 (March 20, 1913): 605.
13. Anzia Yezierska, "My Own People," in *Hungry Hearts,* p. 248.

14. Wald, *The House on Henry Street*, p. 185.
15. Polly Adler, *A House Is Not A Home* (New York: Rinehart, 1953), p. 27.
16. Paula Scheier, "Clara Lemlich Shavelson: 50 Years in Labor's Front Line," *Jewish Life* (November 1954): 7, reprinted in Marcus, *The American Jewish Woman*, p. 568.
17. Meredith Tax, *The Rising of the Women: Feminist Solidarity and Class Conflict, 1880–1917* (New York: Monthly Review Press, 1980), Ch. 8.
18. Alice Kessler-Harris, "Organizing the Unorganizable: Three Jewish Women and Their Union," *Labor History* XVII: 5–23, reprinted in Marcus, *The American Jewish Woman*, p. 581.
19. Theresa Malkiel, *Diary of a Shirtwaist Striker* (New York: The Co-Operative Press, 1910).
20. Eleanor Learner, "Jewish Involvement in the New York City Woman Suffrage Movement, *American Jewish History* LXX (1981): 442–461.
21. David A. Shannon, "Rose Harriet Pastor Stokes," Edward James, Janet James, and Paul Boyer, eds., *Notable American Women* (Cambridge: Harvard University Press, 1971), vol. III, pp. 384–386.
22. Richard Drinnon, *Rebel in Paradise: A Biography of Emma Goldman* (New York: Harper & Row, 1961).
23. Vivian Gornick, *The Romance of American Communism* (New York: Basic Books, 1977), pp. 6–7.
24. Marshall Sklare, *Conservative Judaism: An American Religious Movement* (Glencoe, Ill.: The Free Press, 1955), pp. 86.
25. Yezierska, *Bread Givers*, p. 95.
26. Emily Solis-Cohen, Jr., *Woman in Jewish Law and Life: An Inquiry and a Guide to the Literary Sources of Information Concerning the Nature of Jewish Law and the Status Accorded to Women* (New York: Jewish Welfare Board Publications, 1932), p. 1.
27. Solis-Cohen, *Woman in Jewish Law and Life*, p. 2.
28. The faculty of the Jewish Theological Seminary of America voted to ordain women on October 24, 1983, after the completion of this essay. See below.
29. Sklare, *Conservative Judaism*, pp. 86–88.
30. Umansky, "Women in Judaism: From the Reform Movement to Contemporary Jewish Religious Feminism" in Rosemary Ruether and Eleanor McLaughlin, eds., *Women of Spirit: Female Leadership in The Jewish and Christian Traditions* (New York: Simon and Schuster, 1979), pp. 340–344.
31. Rabbi Samuel Gerstenfeld, "The Segregation of the Sexes," *The Jewish Forum* VII (1924): 188.
32. Rabbi David Goldberg, "Women's Part in Religious Decline," *The Jewish Forum* IV (1921): 871–875.
33. Gilbert Klaperman, *The Story of Yeshiva University: The First Jewish University in America* (New York: MacMillan, 1969), pp. 179–180.
34. James Barron, "A Nylon Cord Is a Constitutional Issue," *New York Times* (May 10, 1983): B1; Saul Berman and Shulamith Magnus, "Orthodoxy Responds to Feminist Ferment," *Response* XII no. 4 (1981): 7.
35. Solis-Cohen, *Women in Religion*, p. 13.
36. For a provocative account of the Jewish identities of several female children of survivors, see Helen Epstein, *Children of the Holocaust* (New York: Bantam Books, 1980).
37. Rebekah Kohut "Jewish Women's Organization in the United States," *American Jewish Yearbook 5692*, vol. 33 (Philadelphia: Jewish Publication Society of America, 1931), p. 165.
38. Sochen, *Consecrate Every Day*, Ch. 1.
39. Goldie Stone, *My Caravan of Years* (New York: Bloch, 1945), pp. 150–157.
40. *Ibid.*
41. Henrietta Szold, "If This Be Politics!" *Hadassah Newsletter* VIII, no. 8 (May 1, 1928), p. 1–2.
42. *Hadassah Newsletter* (September, 1917).
43. Nick Mendelkern, "The Story of Pioneer Women," *Pioneer Woman* (September 1980), p. 21.
44. "Apprenticeship is Boon to Girls," *Women's American ORT Reporter* IV (December 1953): p. 6; "Report on Jewish Women in Training," *Women's American ORT Reporter* V (1954): p. 10. Sophie Udin, "The Working Woman Speaks," *The Pioneer Woman*

(August 1931): p. 1; Marie Syrkin, "The Women's Colonies of Palestine," *The Pioneer Woman* (February 1926): p. 3.

45. "Momentous Peace Conference," *The Jewish Woman* IV (1924): p. 14; Gertrude Weil, "The Woman Voter and the Nation's Conscience," *The Jewish Woman* VI (1926): pp. 10–11. Freda R. Bienstock, "Women's Mission is Peace Declares Mrs. Sternberger," *The Jewish Tribune* (June 12, 1925): p. 8; "Editorial" on International Women's Day, *The Pioneer Woman* (April, 1938): p. 1.

46. Henrietta Szold, *The Maccabaean* (July 1903): pp. 5–10.

47. A reference to the rabbinic saying that "he who teaches a woman Torah teaches her obscenity."

48. Marvin Lowenthal, *Henrietta Szold: Life and Letters* (New York: Viking Press, 1942), pp. 92–93. "The *Kaddish*, a sanctifiction of God, is recited by children in mourning for their parents at synagogue services during one year. By tradition, only male children recite the prayer. If there are no male survivors, a stranger may act as a substitute."

49. Isaac Metzker, *A Bintel Brief* (New York: Balantine Books, 1972), pp. 50–52; 66–67; 104–105; 126–128; 141.

50. A. Irma Cohen, "Judaism and The Modern Woman," *The Jewish Woman* 4 (October 1924): pp. 11–12; 45–46. On A. Irma Cohen, see "Samuel S. Cohon," *Who's Who In World Jewry*, Harry Schneiderman and Itzhak J. Carmin, eds. (New York: Who's Who In World Jewry, Inc., 1955), p. 141.

51. Martha Neumark, "The Woman Rabbi," *The Jewish Tribune* (April 17, 1925): p. 5.

52. Rabbi Moshe Tendler, *Pardes Rimonim: A Marriage Manual for the Jewish Family* (New York: The Judaica Press, 1979), pp. 20ff.

53. *Bedika*—internal examination by careful swabbing of the vaginal tract with a cloth, or a cotton-wrapped finger. (from Tendler, *ibid.*)

54. The letters reproduced here are in the Seligsberg Correspondence in the Rose Jacobs Papers, microfilm edition, Hadassah Archives, New York, N.Y. Alice Seligsberg to Herman Block, March 15, 1919; Alice Seligsberg to Rose Jacobs, November 27, 1932; Alice Seligsberg to the Hadassah Convention, October 20, 1936; *Hadassah Newsletter* II, no 11 (1922).

55. Aaron David Gordon (1856–1922) was a spiritual leader of the early Jewish settlers in palestine. He advocated the spiritual regeneration of the individual through agricultural labor.

56. "Action, not Charity," from *Alert!* issued by Pioneer Women, I (March 1946): p. 3.

57. *The Pioneer Woman* (October 1933): 4–5. Biographical information on Tamar Shultz supplied by Zelda Lemberger. See also "Isaac Levitas," in Harry Schneiderman and Itzhak J. Carmin, eds., *Who's Who In World Jewry* (New York: Who's Who In World Jewry, Inc., 1955).

Women Struggle for an American Catholic Identity

1. Williston Walker, *A History of the Christian Church,* 3d. ed. (New York: Charles Scribner's Sons, 1970), p. 527.

2. James Hennessey, *American Catholics: A History of the Roman Catholic Community in the United States* (New York: Oxford University Press, 1981), p. 173.

3. Mary R. Ryan, *Womanhood in America: From Colonial Times to the Present,* 2d. ed. (New York: New Viewpoints, 1979), p. 189. See also "The Breadgivers: Immigrants and Reformed: 1865–1920," pp.118–150.

4. Mary Ewens, O.P., "The Leadership of Nuns in Immigrant Catholicism," in Rosemary Radford Ruether and Rosemary Skinner Keller, eds., *Women and Religion in America; Volume 1: The Nineteenth Century* (San Francisco: Harper & Row, 1981), pp. 101–149.

5. Hennessey, *American Catholics,* p. 187.

6. For a consideration of the directives for Catholic hospitals and Catholic medical codes in this regard, see David F. Kelly, *The Emergence of Roman Catholic Medical Ethics in North America* (New York: Edwin Mellen, 1979).

7. To cite only one example, in 1926 the Sisters of St. Joseph in Baden, Pennsylvania, a diocesan congregation, sent four sisters to China as missionaries.

8. James Cardinal Gibbons, "Pastoral Letter of 1919," in Raphael M. Huber, ed., *Our Bishops Speak* (Milwaukee: Bruce, 1952), pp. 3–45.

9. Marie Hall Ets, *Rosa: The Life of an Italian Immigrant* (Minneapolis: University of Minnesota, 1970), pp. 172–174.

10. Mrs. Francis E. Slattery, "The Catholic Woman in Modern Times," *The Catholic Mind* 28 (March 22, 1930): pp. 124–131.

11. Katherine E. Conway to William Cardinal O'Connell, January 31, 1910, O'Connell Papers 3:15 (Archives, Archdiocese of Boston).

12. Kate Chopin, "Madame Celestin," in George N. Schuster, ed., *The World's Great Catholic Literature* (New York: Macmillan, 1942), pp. 331–335.

13. Minutes, National Catholic Women's Council, March 4–5, 1920 (Washington, DC: Archives of the National Council of Catholic Women).

14. Dorothy Weston, "Why Maternity Guilds?" *The Catholic Mind* 23 (August 22, 1935): pp. 316–320.

15. Rt. Reverend John Ireland, "Our Catholic Sisterhoods," *The Catholic Mind* 1 (January 8, 1913): pp. 105–118.

16. Sister Gonzaga to William Cardinal O'Connell, June 15, 1908 Records of Institutions, Hospital Correspondence 6:1 (Archives, Archdiocese of Boston).

17. Sister M. Madeleva Wolff, "Educating Our Daughters as Women," in *My First Seventy Years* (New York: Macmillan, 1959), pp. 125–130.

18. Mother M. Katharine Drexel, Letter of February 17, 1905, in Sister Consuelo Marie Duffy, *Katharine Drexel: A Biography* (Cornwall Heights, Pa: Mother Katharine Drexel Guild, 1965), pp. 257–258; Pope Pius XII, Address of April 6, 1941, in *Ibid.*, pp. 405–407.

19. Martha Moore Avery to William Cardinal O'Connell, January 4, 1918 and May 13, 1918 Chancery Central File M-1747 (Archives, Archdiocese of Boston).

20. Mary H. (Mother) Jones, *The Autobiography of Mother Jones*, Mary Field Parton, ed. [1925] reprint (Chicago: Charles H. Kerr, 1972), pp. 202–204.

21. Dorothy Day: "A Human Document," *The Sign Magazine* 4 (November 1932): 223–224; "Aims and Purposes," in *By Little and By Little: Selected Writings*, Robert Ellsberg, ed. (New York: Alfred A. Knopf, 1983), pp. 91–92; and "Our Country Passes from Undeclared to Declared War: We Continue Our Christian Pacifist Stand," in *By Little and By Little*, pp. 261–266.

22. Janet Kalven, "Woman and Postwar Reconstruction," *The Catholic Mind* 43 (February 1945): pp. 78–82.

23. Marguerite T. Boylan, "International Cooperation in Catholic Social Welfare," *The Catholic Mind* 47 (June 1948): pp. 398–404.

24. Dorothy Dohen, "Spiritual Direction," *Spiritual Life* 4 (September 1958): pp. 199–204.

Women in Evangelical, Holiness, and Pentecostal Traditions

1. George M. Marsden, *Fundamentalism and American Culture* (New York: Oxford University Press, 1980).

2. W. B. Godbey, *Woman Preacher* (Louisville, Ky: Pentecostal Publishing Co., 1891), p. 13.

3. B. T. Roberts, *Ordaining Women* (Rochester, N.Y.: Earnest Christian Publishing Co., 1891).

4. A. J. Gordon, "The Ministry of Women," *Missionary Review of the World* VII, no. 12, New Series (December 1894): 910–921. Reprinted as Gordon-Conwell Monograph No. 61, with introduction by Pamela J. Cole.

5. *Ibid.*, p. 12.

6. Fredrik Franson, "Prophesying Daughters," translated from the 1896 Swedish edition by Sigurd F. Westberg and reprinted in *The Covenant Quarterly* XXXIV, no. 4 (November 1976): pp. 21–40.

7. Seth C. Rees, *The Ideal Pentecostal Church* (Cincinnati: M. W. Knapp, 1897), p. 41, as quoted in Lucille Sider Dayton, "The Rise of Women in Evangelicalism" (Paper delivered at the national conference of the Evangelical Women's Caucus, Washington, D.C., November 29, 1975), p. 12.

8. Mrs. J. Fowler Willing, "Woman and Pentecost," *Guide to Holiness* 69 (September 1898): 87. Quoted in Dayton, "The Rise of Women," p. 11.

9. Mary Cole, *Trials and Triumphs of Faith* (Anderson, Ind.: Gospel Trumpet Co., 1914), p. 85. Quoted in Sharon L. Sawyer, "Women Pastors in the Church of God," *Colloquium* 8 (July/August 1976): p. 7.

10. From photo caption in *Vital Christianity* 22 (June 1980): p. 16.

11. Joseph D. Allison, "Heroines of the Faith," *Vital Christianity* 2 (May 1976): p. 12–13.

12. *Ibid.*, p. 13.

13. Joseph D. Allison, "An Overview of the Involvement of Women in the Church of God from 1916," for the series, "The Role of Women in Today's World: Six Study Papers," prepared for the Commission on Social Concerns, Church of God, Anderson, Indiana, 1978.

14. John W. V. Smith, *Heralds of a Brighter Day* (Anderson, Ind.: Gospel Trumpet Co., 1955), p.126. Quoted in Sawyer, "Women Pastors in the Church of God," p. 1.

15. Timothy L. Smith, *Called Unto Holiness: The Story of the Nazarenes—The Formative Years* (Kansas City, Mo.: Nazarene Publishing House, 1962).

16. *Ibid.*

17. Nancy Hardesty, Lucille Sider Dayton, and Donald W. Dayton,"Women in the Holiness Movement: Feminism in the Evangelical Tradition," in Rosemary Ruether and Eleanor McLaughlin, eds., *Women of Spirit* (New York: Simon and Schuster, 1979), pp. 241–248.

18. Sidney Ahlstrom, *A Religious History of the American People* (New Haven: Yale University Press, 1972), p. 820.

19. Agnes Ozman Laberge, *What God Hath Wrought* (Chicago: Herald Publishing, n.d.), p. 28.

20. Charles H. Barfoot and Gerald T. Sheppard, "Prophetic vs. Priestly Religion: The Changing Role of Women Clergy in Classical Pentecostal Churches," *Review of Religious Research* 22, no. 1 (September 1980): pp. 2–10.

21. *Ibid.*, pp. 10–17.

22. Max Weber, *The Sociology of Religion*, E. Fischoff, trans. (Boston: Beacon Press, 1968), pp. 104–105.

23. Swartley uses the terms "hierarchical" and "liberationist" interpreters in describing the ongoing debates within evangelicalism over sex roles today. See Willard M. Swartley, *Slavery, Sabbath, War, and Women* (Scottdale, Pa: Herald Press, 1983), Ch. 4.

24. James F. Findlay, Jr., *Dwight L. Moody* (Chicago: University of Chicago Press, 1969), pp. 321–336. A clash of personalities and disagreements on organizational details resulted in Emma Dryer's resignation from the Chicago Evangelization Society just five months before the October 1889 official opening of Moody Bible Institute (then called the Chicago Bible Institute).

25. In connection with the 1979 firing, the Moody Bible Institute administration issued a statement saying the school had held "a consistent position" over the years against the endorsement or encouragement of the ordination of women. For an account of the dismissal of Professor Stanley Gundry, see Anne Bowman Folis, *"I'm Not a Women's Libber, But . . ."* (Nashville: Abingdon, 1981).

26. Janette Hassey, "Moody Bible Institute: 1889–1914," and "The Role of Women as Fundamentalist Leaders 1914–1945: Moody Bible Institute, a Case Study" (Papers prepared for doctoral studies in history of Christianity, University of Chicago Divinity School, 1979–1980). Hassey's book, *No Time for Silence: Turn-of-the-Century Evangelical Women in Public Ministry* is scheduled for 1986 publication by the Zondervan Publishing House.

27. Hassey, "Moody Bible Institute: 1889–1914," p. 16. Quoted by permission.

28. Victoria Booth Demarest, *Sex and Spirit: God, Woman, and Ministry* (St. Petersburg, Fla.: Valkyrie Press, 1977), p. 100.

29. Kenneth S. Wuest was the instructor of the course on "The Prison and Pastoral Epistles." Mr. Wuest dictated notes to be memorized in a specific way for examinations. These notes were recorded by Letha Dawson Scanzoni, April 20, 1955.

30. Nathan R. Wood, *A School of Christ* (Boston: Halliday Lithograph Corp., 1953), p. 155, as quoted in Candace Waldron-Stains, "Evangelical Women: From Feminist Reform to Silent Femininity," *debarim* (Student Journal of Gordon-Conwell Theological Seminary) 3 (1978–79): p. 67.

31. Waldron-Stains, "Evangelical Women," pp. 67–68.

32. Donald W. Dayton and Lucille Sider Dayton, "Women as Preachers: Evangelical Precedents," *Christianity Today* 19, no. 17 (May 23, 1975): p. 7.

33. Sawyer, "Women Pastors in the Church of God," p. 7.
34. Allison, "An Overview," p. 28.
35. Barfoot and Sheppard, "Prophetic vs. Priestly Religion," pp. 8–11, 14.
36. *Ibid.*, pp. 12–13.
37. *Ibid.*, p. 15.
38. Susan M. Setta, "Patriarchy and Feminism in Conflict: The Life and Thought of Aimee Semple McPherson, *Anima* 9, no. 2 (Fall 1983): pp. 128–137.
39. Alma White, *The Story of My Life and the Pillar of Fire*, vol. 4 (Zarephath, N.J.: Pillar of Fire, 1938), p. 237.
40. Susie C. Stanley, "Alma White and Pillar of Fire Church," master's thesis, Iliff School of Theology, 1982, pp. 47–48. Quoted by permission.
41. *Ibid.*, p. 13. See also Alma White, *Story of My Life*, vol. 3, pp. 144–148, 209–213.
42. See Demarest, *Sex and Spirit*, pp. 121–133.
43. Jessie Penn-Lewis, *The Magna Charta of Woman* [1919], reprint (Minneapolis: Bethany Fellowship, 1975).
44. W. Elliot Brownlee and Mary M. Brownlee, *Women in the American Economy: A Documentary History, 1675 to 1929* (New Haven: Yale University Press, 1976), p. 3.
45. U. S. Department of Labor, Bureau of Labor Statistics, *Families and the Rise of Working Wives—an Overview*, Special Labor Force Report 189, 1976, pp. 13–14.
46. Fannie MacDowell Hunter, ed., *Women Preachers* (Dallas: Berachah Printing Co., 1905), p. 96.
47. Hassey, "Role of Women," Appendix A.
48. M. Madeline Southard, "The First Fifty Years," *The Woman's Pulpit* 47, no. 2 (April-June, 1969; reprint from 1959), p. 7.
49. John R. Rice, *Bobbed Hair, Bossy Wives, and Women Preachers* (Murfreesboro, Tenn.: 1941), p. 65.
50. Franson, "Prophesying Daughters," p. 24.
51. In Philip Ennis, ed., *Seven Questions About the Profession of Librarianship* (Chicago: University of Chicago Press, 1961), p. 83, as quoted in Dee Garrison, "The Tender Technicians: The Feminization of Public Librarianship, 1876–1905," Mary Hartman and Lois W. Banner, eds., *Clio's Consciousness Raised* (New York: Harper & Row, 1974), p. 167.
52. "Women Preachers," *The Christian Century* 40 (August 16, 1923): p. 1031.
53. Carl W. Wilson, s.v.,"Women, Ordination of," *Baker's Dictionary of Theology* (Grand Rapids, Mich.: Baker Book House, 1960), p. 557.
54. Faith Coxe Bailey, "Meet Ruth Graham," Part II, *Moody Monthly* (December 1954): p. 67.
55. James Barr, *Fundamentalism* (Philadelphia: Westminster Press, 1977), pp. 45, 191. On the dispensational movement, see also Marsden, *Fundamentalism and American Culture*.
56. *The Scofield Reference Bible*, C. I. Scofield, ed. (New York: Oxford University Press, 1917 edition).
57. Letha Dawson Scanzoni, "The Great Chain of Being and the Chain of Command," *The Reformed Journal* 26, no. 8 (October 1976): 14–18, and in a revised version in Janet Kalven and Mary I. Buckley, eds., *Women's Spirit Bonding* (New York: Pilgrim Press, 1984).
58. See Jack B. Rogers and Donald K. McKim, *The Authority and Interpretation of the Bible: An Historical Approach* (San Francisco: Harper & Row, 1979); Marsden, *Fundamentalism and American Culture;* Gerald T. Sheppard, "Biblical Hermeneutics: The Academic Language of Evangelical Identity," *Union Seminary Quarterly Review* 32, no. 2 (Winter 1977): pp. 81–94; and Donald W. Dayton, "The Social and Political Conservatism of Modern American Evangelicalism: A Preliminary Search for the Reasons," in *Ibid.*, pp. 71–80.
59. Russell C. Prohl, *Woman in the Church* (Grand Rapids, Mich.: Wm.B. Eerdmans, 1957).
60. Katharine C. Bushnell, *God's Word to Women* (Privately published, 1912/1923). Quotation from introductory "Author's Note," no page numbers.
61. See note 15.
62. Mary Lee Cagle, "My Call to the Ministry," in Hunter, *Women Preachers*, pp. 70–74.
63. Hunter, *Women Preachers*, p. 95.
64. *Ibid.*, pp. 99–100.
65. Mrs. J. Ellen Foster, "Work for Women," *The Institute Tie* IX (February 1909): p. 483.
66. Jamie Buckingham, *Daughter of Destiny* (Plainfield, N.J.: Logos International, 1976).

67. "Healing in the Spirit," an exclusive interview with Kathryn Kuhlman, *Christianity Today* XVII, no. 21 (July 20, 1973): pp. 4–10.

68. Aimee Semple McPherson, *This is That: Personal Experiences, Sermons and Writings of Aimee Semple McPherson* (Los Angeles: Echo Park Evangelistic Association, Inc., 1923), pp. 74–79; 81–86.

69. Raymond L. Cox, *Aimee: Life Story of Aimee Semple McPherson* (Los Angeles: Foursquare Publications, 1979), p. 232.

70. Stanley, "Alma White and the Pillar of Fire Church," pp. 9–16.

71. Alma White, "Woman's Place," in *Radio Sermons and Lectures* (Denver: Pillar of Fire, 1936), pp. 204–211.

72. "Dr. Katherine [sic] Bushnell," *Oakland (California) Tribune,* Knave Section, February 10, 1946. (An expanded follow-up summary of her life, written to complement obituary accounts published upon her death two and a half weeks earlier.) Also, see "Introduction" in Jessie Penn-Lewis, *The Magna Charta of Woman* (Minneapolis: Bethany Fellowship, Inc., 1975). Penn-Lewis's work was originally published in England in 1919.

73. Katharine C. Bushnell, *God's Word to Women,* n.p. This excerpt is from the 1923 edition, reprinted by Ray B. Munson, Box 52, North Collins, NY, 14111. Reprint also available from God's Word to Women Publishers, Box 315 Mossville, IL 61552.

74. P. W. Wilson, *General Evangeline Booth of the Salvation Army,* (New York: Charles Scribners' Sons, 1948).

75. Catherine Booth, *Female Ministry: Woman's Right to Preach the Gospel* [1859] reprint (New York: Salvation Army Supplies Printing and Publishing Dept., 1975).

76. Evangeline Booth, *Woman* (New York: Fleming H. Revell, 1930), pp. 7, 16, 27–29.

77. Lee Anna Starr, *The Bible Status of Woman* (New York: Fleming H. Revell, 1926), pp. 387–389.

78. John R. Rice, *Prayer—Asking and Receiving,* (Wheaton, Ill.:Sword of the Lord Publishers, 1942), pp. 278–81.

79. John R. Rice, *Bobbed Hair,* pp. 18, 82; John R. Rice, "Men and Their Sins," sermon delivered to men only at the First Methodist Church, Lewistown, Pennsylvania, December 7, 1947, during a citywide revival campaign. Printed in *Sword of the Lord* XLI (August 1, 1975): pp. 11–12.

80. Donald Grey Barnhouse, "The Wife with Two Heads," *Eternity,* as reprinted in the July, 1963 issue, p. 3.

81. Yvonne K. Woods, "The Wife God Uses," *His* (February 1960).

82. Catherine Marshall, *A Man Called Peter* (New York: McGraw Hill, 1951), pp. 55–56; Catherine Marshall, *To Live Again* (Carmel, N.Y.: Guideposts Associates, 1957), p. 21.

83. Victoria Booth Demarest, privately printed by the author, 1963.

Patterns of Laywomen's Leadership in Twentieth-Century Protestantism

1. Louise A. Cattan, *Lamps Are for Lighting: The Story of Helen Barrett Montgomery and Lucy Waterbury Peabody* (Grand Rapids, Mich.: Wm. B. Eerdmans, 1972), p. 11.

2. *Ibid.,* pp. 18–21; Lucy W. Peabody, "Message to the Woman's American Baptist Foreign Mission Society on its 70th Birthday," Peabody Biographical File, Woman's American Baptist Foreign Missionary Society Library, Valley Forge, Pa. Also see Edward T. James, ed., *Notable American Women,* vol. III (Cambridge, Mass.: Belknap Press 1971), pp 36–38; and for her first marriage: *Annual Reports of American Baptist Telugu Mission,* 1882–1888.

3. Lucy W. Peabody, *Henry Wayland Peabody, Merchant* (1909); Cattan, *Lamps are for Lighting,* pp. 43–44.

4. Cattan, *Lamps Are for Lighting,* pp. 32–35, 49–51.

5. *Ibid.,* Ch. 7. Also see James, *Notable American Women,* vol. II, pp. 566–568; among the books written by Montgomery regarding the world missionary movement and her involvement in it are *Western Women in Eastern Lands: Fifty Years of Woman's Work in Foreign Missions* (New York: Macmillan Co., 1910) and *From Jerusalem to Jerusalem* (Cambridge, Mass.: Central Committee on the United Study of Foreign Missions, 1929).

6. I am particularly indebted to the work of Virginia Shadron, "The Laity Rights Movement, 1906–1918: Woman's Suffrage in the Methodist Episcopal Church, South," in Hilah Thomas and Rosemary Keller, eds., *Women in New Worlds,* vol. I (Nashville:

Abingdon, 1981), pp, 261–275. Also see Carolyn Stapleton, "Belle Harris Bennett: Model of Holistic Christianity," *Methodist History* XXI, no. 3 (April 1983): 131–142; Virginia Brereton, "Preparing Women for the Lord's Work: The Story of Three Methodist Training Schools, 1880–1940," in Thomas and Keller, *Women in New Worlds*, vol. I, pp. 178–199 and James, *Notable American Women*, vol. I, pp. 132–133.

7. Shadron, "The Laity Rights Movement," p. 264.
8. *Ibid.*
9. *Ibid.*, p. 266.
10. *Daily Christian Advocate*, Methodist Episcopal Church, South, General Conference, May 20, 1910, p. 118.
11. *Ibid.*, p. 117.
12. *Ibid.*, p. 118.
13. I am especially appreciative for the work of Martha Scott, her unpublished Ph.D. dissertation on the life and theology of Georgia Harkness, and her article "Georgia Harkness: Social Activist and/or Mystic," in Thomas and Keller, *Women in New Worlds*, vol. I, pp. 117–140. Here see "Days of My Years,';' unpublished autobiography of Dr. Georgia Harkness, written for the Pacific Coast Theologial Group, in Harkness Papers, Garrett-Evangelical Theological Seminary, p. 18.
14. Scott, "Georgia harkness: Social Activist and/or Mystic," in Thomas and Keller, *Women in New Worlds*, vol. I. Also see Joan Engelsman, "The Legacy of Georgia Harkness," in Rosemary Keller, Louise Queen, Hilah Thomas, eds., *Women in New Worlds*, vol. II (Nashville: Abingdon, 1982), pp 338–358.
15. Harkness, "Days of My Years," p. 21.
16. Scott, "A Goodly Heritage: The Making of a Woman Theologian," in unpublished Ph.D. dissertation.
17. Harkness, "Days of My Years," p. 28.
18. Scott, "A Goodly Heritage."
19. R. Pierce Beaver, *All Loves Excelling* (Grand Rapids, Mich., Wm. B. Eerdmans, 1968), pp. 131–132.
20. Margaret Seebach, "Indian Goddess: Anna S. Kugler, M.D.," in Mable H. Erdman, ed., *Answering Distant Calls* (New York: Association Press, 1942), p. 130.
21. *Ibid.*, pp. 131–135.
22. Anna Kugler, *Guntur Mission Hospital* (Philadelphia: United Lutheran Church in America, 1928), p. 64.
23. *Ibid.*, p. 63.
24. *Ibid.*, Ch. IV, "The Patients."
25. Seebach, "Indian Goddess," in Eerdman, *Answering Distant Calls*, pp. 132, 133.
26. Barbara Sicherman and Carol Green, eds., *Notable American Women*, vol. IV (Cambridge, Mass.: Belknap Press, 1980), pp. 634–636; Dorothy Wilson, *Dr. Ida: The Story of Dr. Ida Scudder of Vellore* (New York: McGraw Hill, 1959).
27. Ruth Fries, "A Women for Other Women," unpublished paper, pp. 12, 13.
28. *Ibid.*
29. Abby Gunn Baker, *The Watchman Examiner*, November 30, 1922, pp. 1526, 1527.
30. Helen Barrett Montgomery, "Presidential Address," Northern Baptist Convention, *Missions Magazine* 13, no. 7 (July 1922): pp. 410, 411.
31. "A Post-Convention Message from Mrs. Montgomery," *Missions Magazine* 13, no. 7 (July 1922): p. 407.
32. *Daily Christian Advocate*, Methodist Episcopal Church, South, General Conference, (May 20, 1910): pp. 117–118.
33. *Ibid.* (May 6, 1914): pp. 106–107.
34. "Germany's Place in the Shadow," *The Christian Advocate* (Jan. 22, 1925): 111; "Germany and the War-Peace," *Zion's Herald* (Jan. 7, 1925): pp. 11–12.
35. "The One and the Many," *Zion's Herald* (Feb. 25, 1925): pp. 239–240.
36. "The Ministry as a Vocation for Women," *The Christian Advocate* (April 10, 1924): pp. 454–455.
37. Kugler, *Guntur Mission Hospital*, pp. 116–119.
38. *Ibid.*, pp. 126–127.
39. Quoted in Fries, "A Woman for Other Women," pp. 13–14.
40. *Missionary Medical College for Women, Vellore, Incorporated.* (Vellore: American Section of the Governing Board of the Women's Missionary Medical College, 1936), p. 32.

Women in Religious Education: Pioneers for Women in Professional Ministry

1. Sophia Lyon Fahs, *The Old Story of Salvation,* (Boston: Beacon Press, 1955), p. xiii.
2. Letter to O. B. Fanning from Dr. John Q. Schisler, executive secretary of the Division of the Local Church, Board of Education, Methodist Church, Dec. 21, 1950.
3. B. S. Winchester, "The Annual Survey of the Progress of Sunday-School Work," *Religious Education* V (April 1910): p. 65.
4. Ethel May Baldwin and David V. Benson, *Henrietta Mears and How She Did It!* (Ventura, Ca: Regal Books, 1966), pp. 55–56, 62–63.
5. Barbara Hudson Powers, *The Henrietta Mears Story* (Westwood, N.J.: Fleming H. Revell, 1957), pp. 58–59.
6. Edith Hunter, *Sophia Lyon Fahs* (Boston: Beacon Press, 1966.), pp. 42; 129–130; 198; 207–208.
7. From a mimeographed copy of sermon. An adaptation of the sermon was published in *The Unitarian Register* (May 1959): pp. 9–10.
8. "Preliminary Program, Seventh General Convention," *Religious Education* (10 February 1910): 14; and B. S. Winchester, "The Annual Survey of the Progress of Sunday-School Work," *Religious Education* (April 1910): p. 65.
9. "Directors of Religious Education [minutes]," *Religious Education* (August 1912): pp. 279–280; "The Association of Church Directors of Religious Education," *Religious Education* (February 1917): 50–52; *Religious Education as a Vocation. Occasional Papers* XX, no. 1 (January 2, 1920): pp. 21–23.
10. Personal correspondence with Dorothy Jean Furnish, February 12, 1968.
11. Aubrey N. Brown, Jr., "What DCEs Have Done—Are Doing—For Us," *The Presbyterian Outlook* (November 1, 1982).
12. Advance release by General News Service of the Methodist Church of address excerpts, "Standing On Top Of Today," January 7, 1964, Dr. Mary Alice Jones, at Sheraton-Dallas Hotel in Dallas, Texas.
13. Arlo Ayres Brown, *Religious Education in Recent Times* (New York: Abingdon, 1923), pp. 102–103, 105–110.
14. From conversation with Dorothy Jean Furnish, July 20, 1984, Hartford, Conn.; and Edna M. Baxter, *Ventures in Serving Mankind: An Autobiography* (Allison Park, Pa.: Pickwick Publications, 1984), pp. 105; 106; 110–111.

Winning Ordination for Women in Mainstream Protestant Churches

1. For an analysis of the pro and con arguments used in this effort by these denominations, see Barbara Brown Zikmund, "The Struggle for the Right to Preach" in Rosemary Radford Ruether and Rosemary Skinner Keller, eds., *Women and Religion in America; Volume 1; The Nineteenth Century* (San Francisco: Harper & Row, 1981), pp. 193–241.
2. A detailed listing of most major denominations in America and the dates when each first ordained women is found in Constant H. Jacquet, Jr., *Women Ministers in 1977,* a mimeographed report printed by the Office of Research, Evaluation and Planning, National Council of Churches, New York, New York, March 1978. See also Jackson W. Carroll, Barbara Hargrove, and Adair T. Lummis, *Women of the Cloth: A New Opportunity for the Churches* (San Francisco: Harper & Row, 1983); and Virginia Lieson Brereton and Christa Ressmeyer Klein, "American Women in Ministry: A History of Protestant Beginning Points" in Rosemary Ruether and Eleanor Mclaughlin, eds., *Women of Spirit: Female Leadership in the Jewish and Christian Traditions* (New York: Simon and Schuster, 1979), pp. 301–332.
3. Anna Howard Shaw, *The Story of a Pioneer* (New York and London: Harper and Brothers, 1915), pp. 122–125.
4. Brereton and Klein, "American Women in Ministry," p. 312.
5. "Report of the Commission on Licensing and Ordaining Women," from the *Journal of the Twenty-ninth Delegated General Conference of the Methodist Episcopal Church held at Springfield, Massachusetts, May 21 to May 29, 1924,* Raymond J. Wade, ed. (New York and Cincinnati: Methodist Book Concern, 1924), pp. 1697–1698. A description of these events was written by Madeline Southard, "Methodist Conference," *The Woman's Pulpit* XIV (May-June 1936): p. 3.

6. Madeline Southard, "M. E. General Conference," *The Woman's Pulpit* I (March-April 1924): pp. 3–4.
7. Florence Resor Jardine, "The Methodist Uniting Conference and the Ministry of Women," *The Woman's Pulpit,* XVII (May-June 1939): pp. 1–4.
8. Lud H. Estes, ed., *Journal of the General Conference of the Methodist Church, held at Minneapolis, Minnesota* (Nashville: Methodist Publishing House, 1956), pp. 683–721. See also "When Women are Ministers" and "Lady Ministers Win Full Status in Church," *Christian Advocate* 131 (May 24, 1956): pp. 13, 15.
9. James E. Will, "Ordination of Women: The Issue in the Church of the United Brethren in Christ," in Rosemary Skinner Keller, Louise L. Queen, and Hilah F. Thomas, eds., *Women in New Worlds: Historical Prespectives on the Wesleyan Tradition,* vol. II (Nashville: Abingdon, 1982), pp. 290–297.
10. J. Bruce Behney and Paul H. Eller, *The History of the Evangelical United Brethren Church* (Nashville: Abingdon, 1979), p. 160.
11. Will, "Ordination of Women," p. 296.
12. Behney and Eller, *History,* p. 361.
13. Lois A. Boyd and R. Douglas Brackenridge, *Presbyterian Women in America: Two Centuries of a Quest for Status* (Westport, Conn.: Greenwood Press, 1983), p. 112.
14. Elizabeth Howell Verdesi, *In But Still Out: Women in the Church* (Philadelphia: Westminster, 1976).
15. Katharine Bennett and Margaret Hodge, *Causes of Unrest Among Women of the Church, Report of a Special Committee to the General Council of the Presbyterian Church in the U.S.A.* (Philadelphia, Presbyterian Church in the U.S.A., 1927) and *Findings of the Conference on Women's Status and Service in the Church* (Philadelphia: Presbyterian Church in the U.S.A., 1929).
16. Letter from Katherine Bennett to Robert K. Speer, January 29, 1929.
17. Boyd and Brackenridge, *Presbyterian Women,* p. 137.
18. *Ibid.,* pp. 179–180.
19. *Ibid.,* pp. 144–146.
20. Lyman Richard Hartley, "Women as Ministers: The Pros and Cons," *New York Times Magazine* (April 10, 1947): pp. 19, 59.
21. Helen C. Woolson, "Shall Women Be Ordained?" *Outreach* (August-September 1955): pp. 199–200.
22. Boyd and Brackenridge, *Presbyterian Women,* p. 149–152.
23. Arthur B. Cooper, "Women Pastors," *Monday Morning* (September 24, 1956): pp. 3–5.
24. Boyd and Brackenridge, *Presbyterian Women,* pp. 153–155.
25. Hazel E. Foster, "Ecclesiastical Status of Women," *The Woman's Pulpit,* XL (July-December, 1964): p. 8.
26. Boyd and Brackenridge, *Presbyterian Women,* pp. 113–118. See also Ben M. Barrus, Milton L. Baugh and Thomas H. Campbell, *A People Called Cumberland Presbyterians: A History of the Cumberland Church* (Memphis: Frontier Press, 1972).
27. Raymond Tiemeyer, [A condensation of] *The Ordination of Women: A Report Distributed by Authorization of the Church Body Presidents as a Contribution to Further Study, based on Materials Produced through the Division of Theological Studies of the Lutheran Council in the U.S.A.* (Minneapolis: Augsburg, 1970), pp. 34–37.
28. Foster "Ecclesiastical Status of Women," *The Woman's Pulpit* XXXII (January–March 1954): p. 4.
29. Russell C. Prohl, *Women in the Church: A Restudy of Woman's Place in Building the Kingdom* (Grand Rapids, Mich.: Wm. B. Eerdmans, 1957).
30. Fritz Zerbst, *The Office of Woman in the Church: A Study in Practical Theology,* Albert G. Merkens, trans. (St. Louis: Concordia, 1955), p. 121.
31. Tiemeyer, *The Ordination of Women,* p. 8.
32. Emily C. Hewitt and Suzanne R. Hiatt, *Women Priests: Yes or No?* (New York: Seabury, 1973), p. 102.
33. Charles E. Raven, *Women and the Ministry,* with an American introduction by Elizabeth Wilson (Garden City, N.Y.: Doubleday, Doran and Co., 1929), p. 125
34. Hewitt and Hiatt, *Women Priests,* p. 103. See also Kathleen Bliss, *The Service and Status of Women in the Churches* (London: SCM, 1952); *Men and Women in Church and Society* (Geneva: World Council of Churches, 1956); and M. E. Thrall, *The Ordination of Women to the Priesthood: A Study of the Biblical Evidence* (London: SCM, 1958).

35. Hewitt and Hiatt, *Women Priests,* p. 103.

36. "Progress Report to the House of Bishops from The Committee to Study the Proper Place of Women in the Ministry of the Church, October, 1966," *Journal of the General Convention of the Protestant Episcopal Church in the United States of America* (1967). Reprinted in Hewitt and Hiatt, *Women Priests,* pp. 109–116 (quotation found on p. 111).

37. See a special issue "Daughters of Prophecy: Episcopal Women Priests 10th Anniversary 1974–1984," *The Witness* (Summer 1984). A powerful personal story of this process is found in Carter Heyward, *A Priest Forever: The Formation of a Woman Priest* (New York: Harper & Row, 1976).

38. See Carroll, Hargrove, and Lummis, *Women of the Cloth;* and Georgia Harkness, *Women in Church and Society: A Historical and Theological Inquiry* (Nashville: Abingdon, 1972).

39. See George M. Marsden, *Fundamentalism and American Culture: The Shaping of Twentieth Century Evangelicalism 1870–1925* (New York and London: Oxford University Press, 1980). Changing attitudes about women's ordination among conservative evangelicals is seen in Charles Caldwell Ryrie, *The Place of Women in the Church* (New York: Macmillan, 1958) and Paul K. Jewett, *The Ordination of Women* (Grand Rapids, Mich.: Wm. B. Eerdmans, 1980).

40. John R. Rice, *Bobbed Hair, Bossy Wives and Women Preachers: Significant Questions for Honest Christian Women Settled by the Word of God* (Wheaton, Ill.: Sword of the Lord, 1941).

41. *New York Times* (June 15, 1984): p. 7.

42. The most important materials on this issue are the *Revised Interim Report of a Study on the Life and Work of Women in the Church* (Geneva: World Council of Churches, 1948); Inez M. Cavert, *Women in American Church Life: A Study Prepared for the Federal Council of Churches* (New York: Friendship Press, 1948); Kathleen Bliss, *The Service and Status of Women in the Churches* (London: SCM, 1952); *Men and Women in Church and Society* (Geneva: World Council of Churches, 1956); *Concerning the Ordination of Women* (Geneva: World Council of Churches, 1964); *The Deaconess: A Service of Women in the World Today,* WCC Studies No. 4 (Geneva: World Council of Churches, 1966); Francine Dumas, *Man and Woman: Similarity and Difference* (Geneva: World Council of Churches, 1966); Constance F. Parvey, ed., *Ordination of Women in Ecumenical Perspective: Workbook for the Church's Future,* Faith and Order Paper 105 (Geneva: World Council of Churches, 1980).

43. Florence Resor Jardine, "Why I Became a Minister," *The Woman's Pulpit* XXII (September-October 1944): p. 2.

44. Beatrice M. Weaver, "The Role of the Ordained Woman in the Church," *Bulletin of the Theological Seminary of the Evangelical and Reformed Church,* Lancaster, Pennsylvania, XXV (October 1954), pp. 21–34.

45. Louise S. Eby, "Can Women Make Their Way into the Ministry?" *Christian Education* IX (June 1929): pp. 534–539.

46. See note 5 (for Document 1).

47. Madeline Southard, *The Woman's Pulpit* I (1924): 3; Madeline Southard, *The Woman's Pulpit* IV (1928): p. 6; Florence Resor Jardine, "The Case for Women in the Methodist Ministry," *The Woman's Pulpit* XXVIII (April-June 1950): p. 2; *Ibid.,* pp. 2–3; *Ibid.,* p. 3.

48. *Journal of the 1956 Annual Conference,* pp. 688–689.

49. *Ibid.,* pp. 705–706; *Ibid.,* pp. 707–708.

50. See note 16 (for Document 4).

51. See note 20 (for Document 5).

52. See note 21 (for Document 6).

53. Cooper, "Women Pastors," pp. 4–5.

54. Prohl, *Women in the Church,* pp. 79–80.

55. Zerbst, *Office of Women,* pp. 119–121.

56. Elizabeth Wilson, in Raven, *Women and the Ministry,* pp. 33–36.

57. "Progress Report" as reprinted in Hewitt and Hiatt, *Women Priests,* pp. 111–116.

58. *Interim Report,* pp. 39–49; *Concerning the Ordination of Women,* pp. 5–6.

59. See note 43 (for Document 13).

60. Weaver, "The Role of the Ordained Woman," pp. 32–34.

61. Eby, "Can Women Make Their Way," pp. 538–539.

Index